The Cockatoos

The Cockatoos

A Complete Guide to the 21 Species

EDWARD JOHN MULAWKA

McFarland & Company, Inc., Publishers

Jefferson, North Carolina

LIBRARY OF CONGRESS CATALOGUING-IN-PUBLICATION DATA

Mulawka, Edward J. (Edward John), 1936–
The cockatoos : a complete guide to the
21 species / Edward John Mulawka.
p.   cm
Includes bibliographical references and index.

ISBN 978-0-7864-7925-2 (softcover : acid free paper) ∞
ISBN 978-1-4766-1471-7 (ebook)

1. Cockatoos—Classification.   2. Cockatoos—Identification.   I. Title.
QL696.P7M85 2014   598.7′1—dc23   2014023700

BRITISH LIBRARY CATALOGUING DATA ARE AVAILABLE

On the cover: Cockatoo (iStockphoto/Thinkstock)

Printed in the United States of America

McFarland & Company, Inc., Publishers
Box 611, Jefferson, North Carolina 28640
www.mcfarlandpub.com

Dedicated to my children,
Astra, Nadi, Katie and John,
and to Ginny,
their mother.

What is more glorious than a mob of Rose Breasted Cockatoos ... , airing their beauties and graces as they take a constitutional before retiring for the night? Probably no other kind of bird shows better company flying than Galahs; now one sheet of grey lavender, and the next instant a flash of brilliant salmon pink, as the whole company turns and wheels, obedient to some command or signal unperceived by us; again, the sun lights up the pale pink crests and grey backs, as they turn once more and wheel, screeching, to continue their evolutions further.

—Dr. J. A. Leach, Australian ornithologist and teacher (1870–1929)

Table of Contents

PART THREE. THE BLACK COCKATOOS
Genus: *Callocephalon, Probosciger* and *Calyptorhynchus*
Subgenus: *Calyptorhynchus* (Zanda)

PART FOUR. SMALL COCKATOOS
Genus: *Nymphicus*

Preface

There are currently an estimated 10,000 different bird species extant in the world, but it is estimated that at least one-eighth of them will become extinct before the year 2025. Of those diverse bird species, there are only twenty-one recognized species of cockatoos, and some of them are now considered endangered.

My involvement with parrots began during the early Seventies when I became a junior partner with an importer in California who imported exotic avifauna, principally Amazon parrots and macaws. We purchased parrots in large numbers from a wide variety of Latin American sources, quarantined them as required by the United States Department of Agriculture (USDA), and upon their release from quarantine, sold them wholesale to pet shops across the country. While the American public was already familiar with the colorful Central and South American parrots, there began to develop at the time a growing interest in cockatoos, generated in part by a Sulphur-crested Cockatoo named Fred who starred in the popular detective television series Baretta, which ran for several years. The cockatoo performed remarkable feats, almost unbelievable for a bird. We began receiving serious inquiries from pet shops regarding the availability of cockatoos.

At the time, we knew virtually little about cockatoos except that they were endemic to the Australasian part of the South Pacific, notably Australia, and that they were rarely encountered in North America. On the basis of the frequency of pet shop inquiries we were receiving, my partner flew to Indonesia to arrange for a shipment of approximately 500 cockatoos of diverse species. After clearing the quarantine period, we sold those birds in short time, profitably.

Over the intervening years there were several more shipments of cockatoos following that initial trial importation. Because we knew very little about the various species we were importing, and there was little information about them easily available, much of our involvement with the birds and our husbandry of them was initially *ad hoc*, but we spent considerable time in libraries learning as much as we could about the species we were importing.

After several successful trips to the South Pacific, on returning to Los Angeles from his latest Australasian buying trip, my partner informed me that he had paid a substantial premium for several birds in the shipment that was to arrive later that month; he told me that those cockatoos had been harvested from the nest as nestlings and had been hand fed via eyedroppers and specially designed small spoons until they could feed themselves—time-consuming foster parenting. We were already familiar with the hand feeding of Central American Amazon parrots, but the Amazons and macaws were taken from the nest when they were already almost fully quilled, and they were soon ready to fledge. The cockatoo nestlings were taken from the nest long before their first quill feathers emerged.

When the shipment arrived, the hand fed young birds were clearly behaviorally distinct from the rest of the shipment of field-captured adult cockatoos: the hand fed juveniles welcomed our approach to their cages, whereas the wild-caught cockatoos shrieked, hissed and swayed, their crests erect from fear. The daily routine of cleaning their cages and providing them food and water caused a continuous raucous bedlam from the wild-caught Cockatoos. The hand fed juvenile birds were simply undisturbed by our presence.

We retailed those hand fed young juveniles at twice the going price of the wild-captured birds. They were simply too irresistible when they were perched on one's shoulder, cuddled against one's neck, bending their heads downward, eagerly awaiting a head scratching. It was always love at first sight.

We soon recognized that there was much more profit to be made by selling adorable hand fed young birds. There was even more money to be made by breeding the cockatoos and hand feeding them, thus eliminating the overseas supplier, the costly overseas trips, and the paperwork demanded by the USDA. We rented a farm property outside of Los Angeles where we constructed several large aviaries with the intent to breed cockatoos and hand feed their young. Our venture appeared promising, but after three years it failed for a wide variety of reasons, most of them resulting from my partner's marital difficulties.

Shortly following our failed venture, I returned to Canada, built several aviaries in an enclosed large greenhouse that was heated in the winter with gas furnaces, and bred various species of parrots until I retired two decades later. Because of the difficulties we had encountered getting information on cockatoos, I decided to write a book on cockatoos that would be informative and useful to pet owners, naturalists, and aviculturalists. I had already published other books on parrots and felt I understood the kinds of information that would be most appealing to readers interested in the cockatoo family.

Specifically, my original intent was to provide the reader information on the breeding of the cockatoo and its qualities as a pet. In researching library sources, I soon realized that there was a wealth of interesting historical information on the cockatoos, and large amounts of taxonomical information that could be also included in my book. But there was very little on breeding or other information pertaining to their life requirements.

Altogether, there was simply too much information to compile into one useful reference book. I hence decided on focusing on providing the reader with information about each cockatoo species: its rarity, description, distribution, habitat, propagation in both the wild and captivity, and its qualities as a pet companion. For many of the cockatoo species, there was little or no information available about one aspect of their life cycle or another, but that absence of information was in itself useful insofar as it indicated the work that still needed to be done.

It was with considerable reluctance that I decided against including in this book an exploration of the various taxonomical controversies about the various species. Some of those controversies will continue into the future as new scientific methods provide evidence challenging previously held views regarding speciation, subspeciation, and biological relationships. As well, while the various controversies have persisted in one form or another for over 150 years, it was simply not possible to explore them in depth.

In researching the various species, a wealth of historical information emerged about the exploration of the Australasian world and the discoveries of myriads of diverse life forms, particularly avifauna, and specifically the cockatoos. The experiences of those early adventurers, ornithologists, naturalists, and colonists provide volumes of insights into cockatoo life.

There is a wide variety of tidbits of information published regarding all of the twenty-one cockatoo species. But no one current reference book provides both a historical and contemporary perspective on all the various cockatoo species. Based on what is currently known about the cockatoos, this reference book attempts to provide the reader with a portrait of each species, its past, its current status, and its future prospects.

Introduction

There are numerous historical accounts of birds kept in captivity. The earliest are found in ancient Egyptian hieroglyphics, some of which appear to depict pet birds. In Europe, in 397 BC, Ctesia's work *Indica* described an exotic species of a bird that is a reasonably accurate match for the Plum Headed Parakeet, a parrot, *Psittacula cyanocephola* (McMillan 1997). Other references to parrots are encountered in the writings of Aristotle (385–322 BC); much later, circa 50 BC, in the writings of Diodorus Siculus, a Greek; and then again approximately a century later in 50 AD, when Pliny wrote of a parrot similar to that described by Siculus.

While assorted parrots were mentioned in various personal written accounts during the intervening centuries, there was no mention of a cockatoo-type bird until an Umbrella Cockatoo was presented to Frederick II, the powerful Holy Roman Emperor (1194–1250 AD), by the sultan of Babylon (Alderton 2002); the cockatoo reportedly became the most popular of all the many different exotic birds Frederick reputedly owned. The fact that this cockatoo was common to the south Pacific, specifically the Australasian Pacific, and had been transported thousands of kilometers to the Northern Hemisphere, is indicative of the symbolic value and prestige that these rare exotic birds bestowed on the politically and economically privileged ruling classes.

While the discovery of the New World by Columbus in 1492 brought a wide variety of wonders to Europe, including a pair of Cuban Amazons that were presented to Columbus' patron, Queen Isabella of Spain, it was not until 1699 that William Dampier, a British buccaneer, landed on a small island off the northwestern coast of Australia, where he saw a flock of Little Corella cockatoos *Cacatua sanguinea* (Alderton 2002), and wrote the first written record of Australia's avifauna. However, Portuguese mariners had already been exploring the South Pacific, and their maps from that period clearly outlined an area they named *Psitacarum Regio* (region of parrots), a region some historians believe is the land mass now known as Australia. However, this reference to "region of parrots" could be just as easily be applied to the entire region where cockatoos, and other parrot forms, could be encountered, the region including not only Australia but the entire eastern Indonesia area land masses including the islands of Wallacea, New Guinea, the Solomon Islands, and as far northwest as the Philippines. Those early maps indicate that the region was already familiar to European mariners at least two centuries before the first European settlers set foot on Botany Bay in Australia (MacMillan 2012). While there has always been substantive trade in parrots and other exotic birds for Europe's privileged classes over the centuries, since the time of ancient Rome, it was with the discovery of the New World that trade in live parrots expanded, a trade that continues today despite efforts to constrain it. And Australia, with its uniquely exotic life forms, attracted adventurers and naturalists of every persuasion to its shores, and its varied colorful birds fuelled European demand for Australasian birds, particularly the cockatoos.

Australia's history, beginning with the arrival of Europeans on its shores, is in itself a fascinating story. For naturalists, and the early ornithologists, the identification and classification of the 54 or so diverse species of parrots, and their subspecies, on the island continent provided opportunities to attain almost instant fame. Additionally, for bird watchers with other avian interests, there were hundreds of species to discover, name, and classify. To have discovered a bird, to classify it taxonomically, to write about it and have the discovery published, could give a field worker not only scientific stature, but international repute as an expert, a naturalist, an explorer who had earned his reputation of expertise, and an individual following in Darwin's footsteps who will similarly also make his mark on scientific history.

The more information was gathered, and the more biological specifics were quantified to support a given taxonomical decision, the more frequent were the debates, some of them heated, regarding the classification of a given population of birds. For example, there are always variances in size, or color, or some other specifically unique biological differentiations in a given population that may consist of several hundred thousand individuals. (Think of people in your own community, for a moment. Some people are tall, others short. Some are overweight. Some are thin. Some are blond whereas others are black haired, and so on.) If, therefore, the females and males at the eastern edge of a species' distribution are slightly larger than those at its western edge, does that signify that there are actually two subspecies? Because of their size difference? And if so, how much difference must there be before one can say with confidence that the eastern and western distributions are distinctly different? And if they are different, how does one determine the demarcation line in their distribution where one population is actually different from the other? Or is there in fact only one species, the obvious variance in size being nothing more than the variance expected in interpreting the figures on a normal distribution curve?

In researching and preparing this manuscript, there were encountered countless problematic scientific disagreements and contradictions pertaining to the various cockatoo species classifications, and to the exact numbers of cockatoo species. It is not realistically possible in this short work to explore the extensive and often convoluted history of the differences in ornithological interpretations that resulted in one classification as opposed to another, resulting in counts of eighteen species of cockatoos, nineteen, twenty-two and so on. Those differences in opinion will persist, and they will complicate any and all attempts to classify taxonomically with universal agreement regarding all species long into the future.

The taxonomy utilized within this work is generally accepted by most ornithological taxonomists, despite some considerable differences in professional opinion. The Cockatiel (*Nymphicus hollandicus*) is a case in point. While there appears to be sufficient biological evidence to conclude that the Cockatiel, despite its diminutive size as compared to all the other cockatoo species, is in fact biologically related to the cockatoo family, there is still some opposition against including the bird with the other cockatoos in the *Cacatua familia*. For the purposes of this book, despite these differences in opinion, the Cockatiel is considered a cockatoo, and the cockatoos are treated as being composed of twenty-one species. While there are a number of subspecies (regarding which there is also some disagreement), those subspecies are considered in the specific exposition of the species they are considered to be a member of.

In preparing this manuscript, every effort was made to avoid scientific jargon. Each chapter pertains to a specific one of the twenty-one species. The format of the chapters is similar. Each chapter provides the cockatoo's scientific name and common name(s), the species' life expectancy, its general description, its behavior in the wild, its habitat and distribution, its propagation in the wild, its breeding history while in captivity, and its qualities as a household pet and companion. In many instances, despite the popularity and endearing notoriety of the various cockatoo species, legions of details are unavailable: reliable informative questions can often be asked for which there is no experiential, anecdotal, or observational answers available. Since there are an estimated 10,000 different bird species and subspecies worldwide, and the cockatoo species only number 21, it should not be at all surprising that there is still much to learn about the various cockatoo species. There is the one exception in the cockatoo family, of course, again, and that is the Cockatiel, the second most popular household avian pet following the budgie. There are reams of information written about this popular, delightful household pet, and the aviculturalism associated with it, perhaps more than that written about the farm fowl upon which we depend on for food.

Each of the 21 species discussed herein are identified as to their level of vulnerability to extinction. Most of the cockatoo species are considered threatened with possible extinction; some are more immediately threatened than others.

In 1963, the International Union for Conservation of Nature (IUCN) was founded upon the principle of monitoring the world's various wildlife forms and rating each form in terms of its possible extinction on a scale ranging from a species being of "least concern" to one that has already gone extinct. Population assessments are regularly taken of various species considered to be at risk in any given political unit, that is country: a species may be common in a particular country but be extinct in an adjacent nation that is similar in climate, terrain, and food availability. A country where a species is common may nevertheless have regions in which the species has become extinct. Of the 397+ known species of parrots, at least twenty-five of them that have already become extinct. An additional fifteen other species are currently considered "critically endangered."

While a few cockatoo species are actually expanding their geographical distribution, and some are even modestly increasing in numbers, others are so few in number in the wild that their extinction is probable. It is not a question of *if* but of when. Many zoos and private bird collectors try to breed threatened species in captivity so the species will not be lost forever, despite their extinction in the wild. In addition, there are various governmental programs throughout much of the world to rehabilitate forested areas where threatened species can be re-introduced into the wild. There are also other programs expending considerable financial and human resources to ensure a species' survival: good examples of successful programs are the efforts made to reintroduce the American Condor (*Gymnogyps californiapus*) into the wilds, and the U.S./Canadian effort to preserve the Whooping Crane (*Grus americana*). In regards to the condor, in the late 1980s the last remaining 22 wild condors were captured in California, and every effort was made to encourage captive breeding. Today, there are over 120 condors now soaring American Western skies, still under severe protection. As for the Whooping Crane, in 1941, there were only 21 wild cranes plus two in captivity. As of 2011, almost 70 years later, there are now 437 cranes in the wild and 165 in captivity. These preservation efforts are costly and resource-consuming, but they can be fruitful.

In regards to extinction, a species may be extinct locally in that the species is no longer found in areas where it was once considered common; extinction can also mean that there are no longer any living individuals of the species anywhere in the world. Think of the Dodo (*Raphus cucullatus*), as an example of an extinct species. Or the North American Passenger Pigeon (*Ectopistes migratorius*). Or the American Caroline Parakeet (*Conurospsis carolinensis*)—the only American parrot species.

The IUCN regularly quantifies and analyses field data on a host of different life forms to determine their degree of vulnerability, regardless of threat cause or lack of it. The degree of a species' jeopardy is assessed, and it is classified accordingly. The classification code is as follows:

Least Concern	Near Threatened	Vulnerable	Endangered	Critically Endangered	Extinct in Wild	Extinct
LC	NT	VU	EN	CR	EW	EX

Of the twenty-one species of cockatoos and their subspecies discussed in this work, twelve are classified somewhere on the scale from Vulnerable to Critically Endangered. This is not good news. In taking into account the degree to which a species is threatened, a host of variables are considered: the reproductive rate of the species, the availability of habitat for both feeding and nesting, the number of mature birds of breeding age, human persecution, harvesting for the pet trade, other diversified threats, and other comparable, sometimes subtle, critical issues of unknown cause. Think for a moment about our experience with the insecticide DDT. The chemical was a godsend, for it saved countless people from death by malaria and other insect-caused diseases. It was only after its use for several years that we discovered our eagle and hawk populations dropping rapidly. Everywhere. The chemical, entering the food chain, played serious havoc with nesting birds: the shells of their eggs were soft and broke easily. It was only after the chemical was banned throughout most of the world that the birds on top of the food chain began to slowly recover in number.

So it is with the cockatoos. There are undoubtedly some variables regarding their declining numbers that we may simply not be aware of.

At the time the IUCN was founded internationally, the preliminary planning was already underway to establish what was later to become the Convention on the International Trade in Endangered Species of Wild Fauna and Flora (CITES). This organization, comprising over 176 United Nations member states, was given the responsibility of monitoring and controlling all cross-border trade in designated wild-captured species: in essence, all trafficking in field-captured wild livestock, be it Siberian Tigers, Costa Rican tree frogs, cockatoos, and even rare exotic plants, is illegal without a CITES license.

To obtain the necessary documentation, the exporter from the country of origin must first acquire permissive documentation from his own government to export the wild-caught species in question, and the recipient nation (also a CITES signatory) provides their importer the licence permitting the importer to legally import the species of CITES concern.

So, for example, assume that the Greater Vancouver Zoo in British Columbia wishes to embark upon a cooperative breeding program with Philippine conservation agencies to breed the Red-vented Cockatoo (*Cacatua haemapygia*), a species in very serious trouble; if the Vancouver Zoo already has two mature males, it will be necessary to acquire at least two sexually mature females in order for the breeding program to be initiated. The Red-vented Cockatoo is cited in the Appendix II listing, which means that wild-captured birds cannot be exported or imported without CITES approval. If the birds are captive bred, CITES accepts documentation that the birds were not captured illegally and taken from the wilds, and thus the birds can be freely exported or imported without encumbrance. If a species is given a CITES II rating, it means the species in the wild is threatened. Thus, there can be no trade in the species without CITES approval.

In essence, CITES II is a legal manoeuver to prevent individuals or organizations from capturing specimens from the wild and exporting or importing species that are scientifically considered threatened. Exceptions are made when the exporting or importing agencies are involved in conservation, such as a zoo whose primary intent with a threatened species would be to increase its population. The conservation work focused on China's adorable Panda Bear, considered Endangered, is an excellent international example of efforts made to preserve fascinating species, to even breed them, and to also introduce the species to people in various countries.

CITES fauna can also be labelled Appendix I: this rating designates the species as being so threatened in the wild, and even in captivity, that the normal protocols governing cross-border trade in wild species are no longer applicable. It is illegal for the exporting country to issue an exporting licence, and it is equally illegal for the importing country to permit the importation of a CITES I designated species. Currently (2013), CITES has on record 34,000 species listed in Appendix II. In Appendix I, however, CITES has listed 600 animal forms and 300 plant species that are so critically threatened that all trade is prohibited, everywhere.

While not all cockatoos are considered endangered, all cockatoos species are in trouble, regardless of their numbers, because of the international demand for pet companion cockatoos. The international illegal trade to satisfy the demand for cockatoos is a lucrative enterprise. Fortunately, because of Australia's stringent and heavily enforced conservation laws, the international demand for Australian cockatoos (and other scarce Australian wild fauna) is for the most part unsatisfied, creating in turn a vacuum encouraging the black market trade in cockatoos to flourish.

Of the 21 cockatoo species, the only one not in CITES Appendix II is the diminutive Cockatiel—and that only because it is a prolific breeder and can be found in all corners of the globe.

The question is, why are the cockatoos in trouble?

First and foremost of course is the demand for cockatoos as pet companions. But the threat to cockatoos is due to a variety of other major, significant causes. Almost all of the cockatoo species nest in the hollows of towering trees, trees that are usually over two centuries old and that are normally the first to be harvested for their lumber because of their size and value. Deforestation for agricultural production also reduces nesting opportunities. It should be noted that other species of birds compete for the same nesting hollows that the cockatoos require; feral European bees also compete for those same nesting hollows to construct their hives. The fact that a swarm of bees will conscript a tree hollow at the expense of a pair of cockatoos who might now be unable to locate a hollow in which to raise a (usually) sole nestling is an important fact contributing to the cockatoo's population deficit. This is especially true since deforestation is rampant in all areas inhabited by cockatoos.

With deforestation, there is a concurrent loss of native foods that the diverse species have relied upon. More frequently than not, dense forests are reduced to patches of forest, mere isolated fragments in some instances, and there are invariably almost no forested corridors connecting these forest patches: it becomes difficult if not impossible for a pair of cockatoos interested in nesting to find refuge, food, or nesting opportunities in their habitual terrain without having to fly considerable distances.

While deforestation results in the loss of traditional native food foraging areas, some species have adapted to the loss of native foods and have learned to forage cereal grains, rice, and diverse agricultural produce, and even to feed on pine cones of introduced pine trees, in the process often damaging or killing those trees. But this adaptation is usually at the expense of being shot, poisoned (a practice now illegal in Australia) or maltreated in a variety of other ways to protect the agricultural industry.

Because of the damage the cockatoos inflict on crops, farmers in some regions of Australian states can obtain a license to kill cockatoos that are raiding their crops, even though those same states issuing the licences have contradictorily enacted laws preventing the harvesting of the cockatoos for the pet trade, or obtaining one for a personal pet, with severe penalties for anyone convicted of taking most cockatoo species from the wild, and despite the fact that the Australian federal government has in place strict conservation practices to protect the nation's wildlife. Thus, while one can obtain a licence to kill a specific species, one cannot obtain a licence to take a nestling of that same species as a pet. Or, bluntly, while it is perfectly acceptable to kill the birds, it is illegal to take one home as a pet. (There are some exceptions: a few cockatoo species, such as the Sulphur-crested Cockatoo [Cacatua sulpurea] or the Galah Cockatoo [Eolophus roseicapilla] are so numerous that there are no prohibitions against taking one from the wild.) Additionally, some cockatoos are illegally and covertly shot by irate farmers, despite the heavy fines imposed upon conviction of non-sanctioned "pest" control. The number of cockatoos illegally shot, or the number of persons convicted, if caught, is not known.

Besides being considered a pest that damages agricultural crops in its search for food, some cockatoos species can be now found in suburban areas, where they also cause considerable damage in that they chew ornamental trees and shrubbery, woodwork, and benches, and can often be found digging for corms or grubs in parks or in golf courses. These birds forage on whatever food is available, which includes the food provided by the public to the birds—a practice common to urban centers throughout the world, where people feed feral pigeons, or in American and Canadian cities, where feral Canada Geese are frequently fed by the public, for example—and despite the damage the cockatoos cause, they are welcomed, or at least tolerated, albeit perhaps grudgingly, by those suburbanites negatively affected by cockatoos in their immediate vicinity. The cockatoos are in part what helps make Australia unique. They are an exotic environmental asset that is good for tourism, like it or not.

In addition to these concerns impinging on the cockatoo's population viability, many of the cockatoo species do not become sexually mature until their fourth or fifth year of life. The normal successful nest of most cockatoo species will rarely have more than one juvenile fledging. Although the average sized egg clutch for most species is two eggs, with rare exception, only one nestling survives, regardless of species—the Cockatiel, Galah, Red-vented and Leadbeater cockatoos being the exceptions because they have clutches of eggs containing more than one or two. Aside from those four species, it is generally believed that over half of a given year's cockatoo fledglings do not survive their first year of life, although there is no hard data substantiating that conclusion.

In Australia, as noted earlier, there are stringent laws protecting birds from illegal harvesting, this harvesting often fuelling the lucrative black market trade in wild life: however, the financial rewards for collecting rare birds from the wild and successfully exporting them to markets where such birds command a high price is a major incentive to violate the laws. While Australia has the resources to control illicit harvesting of nestlings and/or cockatoo eggs, other countries such as Indonesia or the Philippines lack the necessary resources to protect their endemic wildlife species. In the Philippines, for example, where a laborer's wage is approximately a dollar an hour, plundering a nest of its Red-vented Cockatoo (*Cacatua haemapygia*) nestling(s) can earn that laborer $500 per nestling. And that is if it is sold locally; more can be earned if it is smuggled abroad. The Red-vented Cockatoo is now listed in CITES Appendix I. It is believed that the illegal trafficking in wild species of exotic birds, mammals and reptiles is a worldwide multi-billion-dollar illicit enterprise responding to the worldwide public's demand for exotic and unique pets.

Birds are smuggled out of Australia by sedating them, as is done elsewhere where governments abide by CITES exportation regulations. In Australia, the sedated birds are normally wrapped in nylon stockings and are then stuffed into PVC tubing and shipped out of the country as unaccompanied luggage on international flights. Given the extensive Australian coastline, birds and other CITES-protected species are also undoubtedly smuggled out of the country by boats, both pleasure and commercial.

Similarly, birds (and other exotic life forms) are smuggled out of Indonesia, the Philippines, and the countless islands throughout that region by boat, the birds encased in crates or in bamboo tubes. Additionally, throughout the Australasian region exotic birds' eggs, which are much easier to smuggle than actual livestock, are carried aboard international aircraft by smugglers wearing specially fabricated vests with secure pouches that will hold several eggs. Upon passing customs officials, and arriving at a safe destination, the eggs can be immediately placed into artificial incubators (Cameron 2007). While Australia makes every effort to prevent illegal export of its wildlife, the illegal trade continues. To what degree is unknown; but it is a lucrative industry.

There is also the major concern that illegally captured wild birds are "laundered": the wild-captured birds are illegally smuggled out of their country of origin to another country where the same species are legally bred in captivity by professional aviculturalists, although not always successfully. It is alleged by some that these "professional aviculturalists" actually operate their aviaries as a front to cover their illicit activities. While the recipient country may be a signatory to CITES, the wildlife is surreptitiously delivered to the recipient breeder, who in turn signs documents that the birds (illegally in his possession) were in fact bred in his aviaries, and hence were therefore legally exportable under a CITES II Appendix. In essence, the illegally captured wild livestock enters the legal pet trade as a laundered product. It is believed by some that many of the various cockatoo species, especially popular rare cockatoo species, and various mammals and reptiles of the Australasian region that are CITES II designated, are illicitly routed to Singapore breeders who immediately provide the illegally captured fauna the legitimacy for legal commercial transfer to other nations who abide by CITES restrictions. There is no evidence or documentation to substantiate these widely held beliefs. Also, while there are 176 nations who are on paper committed to enforcing the CITES mandate to protect endangered species, not all of those nations are stringent in their enforcement of importation and exportation bans. As well, there is the question of corruption, wherein customs officials are bribed to permit the trafficking of particular fauna.

Many of the nestling cockatoos and/or their eggs taken from nests are destined for local domestic sale. And while the income from the sale of these poached young birds to urban dwellers can be an important supplement to a poacher's otherwise meagre daily income, the successful sale of smuggled birds to international black market avian traders can mean the difference between poverty and relative prosperity. This is not to suggest that poaching is acceptable. The problem does not lie with the poacher attempting to improve his family's standard of living: the problem centers on the consumer who desires to fulfill his or her fantasy, regardless of cost.

A concluding note regarding the organization of this reference book: Each chapter deals with one species of cockatoo only. In organizing this work, each chapter was treated as a book in itself. Hence, there is a separate bibliography for each chapter. Hopefully, those resources will motivate the reader to search out additional information.

Common Cockatoo Names Index

While there are only twenty-one species of cockatoos, there are a wide variety of names by which they are called. In fact, as the list of names below clearly indicates, there are at least a total of 120 popular names used locally, nationally (in Australia), and/or internationally in reference to different species. This text refers mostly to the English names accorded the birds. Although our search for different names was comparatively exhaustive, undoubtedly there are some locations, mainly Australian, but also internationally, where the birds are accorded different names from those listed below, and hence remained unidentified here.

When searching for information on a specific species, this index can be used to search by the popular name, and the formal ornithological name of the bird and the chapter covering it will be immediately identified. For example, the name Goliah Aratoos will direct the reader to the appropriate chapter, the Palm Cockatoo, Chapter 15. As well, the same name may be used to refer to two completely unrelated species. For example, Blue-eyed Cockatoo is the name of an Australian cockatoo as well as the name given to a completely different species endemic to two islands (New Ireland and New Britain) hundreds of miles from Australia.

Common Characteristics

- While there are over 397 parrot species known to science, there are only twenty-one species of cockatoos, and all these cockatoo species are endemic to the Australasian region of the world, and nowhere else.
- Fourteen species of cockatoos, and their fourteen subspecies, are endemic to Australia. Seven other species and their four subspecies are endemic to the countries and islands in the South Pacific north of Australia.
- All cockatoos are known to be gregarious. They are found in flocks numbering from just a few birds, to thousands. Because of their gregariousness and sociability, they can often be found preening each other.
- All cockatoos have a crest that normally lies recumbent on their crown from front to back; if the bird becomes distressed, alarmed, afraid, curious, or otherwise emotionally aroused, the crest is erected. The erected crest serves as a communicative device to other cockatoos. No other parrot species has a crest.
- When threatened or frightened, cockatoos often emit hissing sounds, and/or often sway side to side, particularly if escape seems impossible to the bird.
- Most cockatoos secrete a white powder that is used by the bird in its grooming and preening; while cockatoos live in variety of different terrains, from semi-arid to tropical rain forests, in wet climates the powder is invaluable in preventing the bird's feathers from becoming waterlogged during torrential rains, which would render the bird unable to escape danger by flight. (Some people with breathing problems may find this powder detrimental to their health.)
- Some cockatoos have been known to live into their eighties and nineties, and even longer.
- Cockatoos are quite adaptable: depending on the species, they can be found inhabiting tropical forests, dry savannah (providing there is available water), and grassy plains.
- While many parrot types are considered more intelligent than the common garden sparrow, cockatoos are considered extremely intelligent and are considered by some parrot experts to have the inherent intelligence of a one- to two-year-old human child.
- All cockatoos eggs are white and are believed to be laid in the late afternoon or early evening.
- Some male cockatoos, use a self-constructed tool as a communication device by beating a peeled stick against a tree trunk to convey to interested females the suitable nesting opportunities they have to offer.

- Most cockatoos like to bathe, some by flying in the rain and some by fluttering through wet foliage during or after a rainfall. And still others hang upside down during a rainfall to allow the rain to penetrate the feathers to their skin.
- Cockatoos are notorious for being "velcro birds": because of their intelligence, and their propensity to bond with their owners, they demand affection and interaction between themselves and their owner; they are happiest when they are with their owner. They often become morose when they are deprived of reasonable interaction with the owner. Emotionally deprived cockatoos are notorious for becoming "feather pluckers," plucking feather after feather from their bodies until they are fundamentally naked. They also can become obnoxious shriekers. Consider the cockatoo as being like a small lap dog that needs to be with its mistress, preferably on her lap, most of the time.
- Because of a cockatoo's intelligence, it needs activities to occupy it, such as chewing wooden or leather toys. Keeping a cockatoo caged without anything to occupy its time is akin to putting a person in a solitary cell without recourse to stimulation and forgetting about him there.
- Most cockatoos average two eggs per clutch, but except for the Galah, Leadbeater and the Cockatiel, it is rare for a nesting pair to fledge more than one nestling.
- All cockatoos but the Cockatiel use their right foot to balance themselves on a branch while they are feeding themselves with their left foot.
- Cockatoos are unusual among parrot species in that of all twenty-one species, and their subspecies, completely lack blue or green in their feathers, colors that are common to most other parrot species.
- Most cockatoos mate for life and are not known to philander. After losing a mate, the surviving cockatoo often becomes depressed. The "divorce" rate for cockatoo pairs is virtually zero.
- Most cockatoos eat a wide variety of foods ranging from seeds and nuts to diverse fruits and vegetables.
- Cockatoos are reputedly noisier and more raucous than other parrot species, and certainly more than most cats and dogs. While a dog's bark may be annoying, a simple command normally ends the annoying noise. But ordering a shrieking cockatoo to sit and be quiet is akin to telling the skies to stop a drenching and freezing downpour. This indictment about cockatoos being more raucous is functionally a matter of opinion. However, if unexpected ear-piercing shrieks could be a major issue of concern for a potential bird owner, perhaps a cockatiel or even goldfish might prove to be a more suitable household pet.

ENDEMIC TERRITORY OF AUSTRALIAN COCKATOO SPECIES

Gulf of Carpentaria

NORTHERN TERRITORY

QUEENSLAND

Alice Springs

WESTERN AUSTRALIA

Geraldton

Perth

Esperance

SOUTH AUSTRALIA

Brisbane

NEW SOUTH WALES

Adelaide

Sydney

VICTORIA
Melbourne

Bairnsdale

TASMANIA

Hobart

Endemic Territory of Australian Cockatoo Species (Bruce Jones Design).

PART ONE

THE WHITE COCKATOOS

Genus *Cacatua*
Subgenus *Cacatua*

1

Umbrella Cockatoo
Cacatua alba (Müller, 1776)

COMMON NAMES: White Cockatoo, Great White Cockatoo, Great White Crested Cockatoo (Britain), Umbrella-crested Cockatoo, U2, Kakatua Putih (Indonesia).
SUBSPECIES: None
LIFESPAN: 70 years[1]
IUCN RED LIST OF THREATENED SPECIES: Vulnerable
CITES: II

Description

The outstanding color feature of the Umbrella Cockatoo is its nearly uniform snow white body plumage, excepting a faint yellow wash on both the under tail and under wing, which lightly flash and when the cockatoo is airborne. The lower and upper surfaces of the inner half of the trailing edge of the flight feathers are faintly yellow. The yellow portion of wing undersides is noticeable because the yellow portion of the upper surface of the feather is covered by the white of the feather closest to the body and immediately above. Similarly, larger tail feathers are covered by other feathers that are yellowish tinted. The cockatoo is medium sized with blunt ended feathers, is approximately 46 cm (18") long, and weighs from 400 grams (14 ounces), for the smaller females, up to 800 grams (28 ounces) for some of the larger males. The wing span is generally 25–31 cm (9"–12") (Arndt and Pittman 2003).

Its crest, when recumbent, is barely discernible. The crest is somewhat backward recurving, to the extent that the crest plumage does not totally follow the bird's contour of the head when in a rested state. Indeed, as the crest is extremely long considering the size of the bird, when the crest lies flat its tips sometimes extend past the occiput, but not as dramatically as in the case of the Sulphur-crested Cockatoo (*Cacatua galerita*). When surprised or distressed, the cockatoo extends its crest into a large and striking semicircular shape, somewhat like an umbrella or the traditional ceremonial headdresses of North American indigenous people.

The crest is different from other species within the family *Cacatuinea*. The feathers are broader, totally white, forming a periphery around the forefront of the forehead and crown, and do not, as in the case of the other "White Cockatoos," stand in a row more or less one feather behind the other. Another distinctive difference is that each of the other "White

Cockatoos are internationally known for being "velcro birds" because they hunger for affection and reciprocate it. They are intelligent and through trial and error often devise ways to escape locked cages. They can be taught a wide variety of complex tasks. Because they are also loving and gentle, they make excellent pets (photograph by Eunice [last name unknown]).

Cockatoos" have either yellow, orange, or pink crest feathers in their crests in sharp contrast to the Umbrella's lack of color (World Parrot Trust 2012).

The feet of the cockatoo are mealy black and the thighs are a slightly bluish-grey color; the upper legs are closely covered by short white feathers. The bare periophthalmic eye ring is an off-white color, exhibiting a faint hint of blue-grey.

The Umbrella is sexually dimorphic. While the whiteness is characteristic of both males and females, the males are distinctly larger than the females. The male has a broader head and a much larger beak than the female. The beak is an ebony black, but since the species relies heavily on its powder glands for the powder secretions it uses during its grooming, the beak may convey a greyish black appearance. The female's head and beak are smaller than the male's. The irises of the male are darkish brown, almost black, whereas the female's are reddish brown with maturity. Because the differences between the sexes are not outstanding, their sex should be determined through DNA testing or surgical procedure.

Juvenile Umbrella Cockatoos closely resemble the adults except for the eye coloration, which is a milky brown. During puberty, however, the juvenile female begins to develop her reddish brown iris color much earlier date than the male juvenile's eye color changes to the brownish black of the adult.

Behavior

There is an astounding scarcity of information available on the Umbrella Cockatoo as compared to other cockatoo species. This paucity of information applies both to the species in the wilds and in captivity.

While the cockatoo favors heavily forested areas for feeding, nesting, and communal roosting, it can also be found in diverse terrains ranging from mangroves to the edges of clearings. The species may make minor migratory forays (Bird Life Species Factsheet 2012). Their vocalizations are loud enough to be heard almost five kilometers (three miles) away. Avianweb (2012) describes their calls as a "very loud, and a very loud screeching noise" while BirdLife Species Factsheet describes their calls as "loud, short, a nasal high pitched screech, and [sometimes during flight] ... a rapid series of lower pitched notes." When alarmed, the voice often becomes a grating screech accompanied by loud hissing.

The Umbrella Cockatoo is gregarious and social, often found in pairs or small groups, and occasionally in small flocks consisting of fifteen or so individuals. Generally, however, it occurs singly. Although the species is characterized as social, unlike some other species of avifauna, the Umbrella Cockatoo does not appear to form close bonds with others, the exception being nesting pairs. Lane (2004) argues that there is no clearly defined order of dominance in the Umbrella Cockatoo community because of this consistent lack of social bonding. The species is diurnal, and although it tends to be generally sedentary, it may become modestly nomadic in its wanderings for food.

The Umbrella Cockatoo is primarily an arboreal feeder, feeding mainly on fruits. It is known for eating papayas, durian, langsat, rambutan, and various nuts, and is known to forage in corn fields causing considerable damage to crops (Birdlife International 2012). They are also known to feed on crickets (order *Orthoptera*) and skinks (family *Scincidae*).

Besides loud vocalizations, the Umbrella Cockatoo uses its crest to communicate with its mate and others. The crest, when lying recumbent on the head of the cockatoo and barely visible, indicates the bird's general approachability, friendliness, and calmness. But the raising of the crest can communicate a variety of other emotions: surprise, excitement, curiosity, frustration or fear. When a cockatoo raises its crest, at times accompanying it with hissing, the cockatoo is issuing a warning of an impending bite if there's an attempt to touch it (Avianweb 2012). The raised crest can also be a message to its flock, or a warning in defense of its territory. Of course, the raising of the crest can also represent a courtship display for its mate or potential mate.

In respect to warnings, Lantermann et al. (2000) reported seeing Umbrella Cockatoos using pieces of wood to bang on trees or logs as a warning to other cockatoos that the territory belonged to them.

There have been some reports that the bird also uses sticks to scratch its back. These reports are poorly documented and unconfirmed, however.

Habitat and Distribution

The Umbrella Cockatoo is endemic to several islands and groups of islands in Indonesia. In specific, the species is endemic to the islands of Halmahera, Ternate, Tidore, Kasiruta, and Central and Northern Moluccas (aka Maluka islands) in Indonesia (Birdlife International 2006). Avianweb 2012 includes the islands of Bacan and Mandioli as part of its distribution. They are also reported on the island of Bisa and its neighboring island of Obi, but it is suspected that the birds in the wild there are escaped pets brought to the islands (Juniper and Parr 1998; Birdlife International 2006). The cockatoos that are there now are well established and are considered common (BirdsLife Species Fact Sheet 2012).

The Umbrella Cockatoo inhabits a wide range of habitats. It can be found in forests, mangroves, swamps, open woodlands, and even those cleared areas where agriculture is a primary industry and where fruit and grain productions have attracted the cockatoo. It occurs in plantations (including coconut), and is considered a pest in these agricultural areas. Its presence in habitat-modified regions suggests the species not only tolerates habitat changes but accommodates its foraging practices to those changes. However, despite its general distribution throughout most of its range, its highest population densities can be found in the forests where the large trees needed for nesting can be found. Additionally, it can be found in elevated areas, as much as 900 meters (1100') above sea level (Indonesia Parrot Protection for Life 2006), and particularly along the edges of natural clearings, and by streams and rivers. Much of its time is spent in the tree canopies.

Propagation

As is typical of most cockatoo species, the Umbrella Cockatoo breeds in the hollows or cavities of towering trees, preferably in thickly forested areas, generally nesting anywhere from 5 to 30 or so meters (15'–100') above ground level (Avianweb 2012). The breeding season is dependent on the weather, for although the species is endemic to the tropics, the breeding season does not reach its peak until vegetative growth is lush and food is readily and abundantly available (generally from December to March). The cockatoo develops strong bonds with its mate, and is known to be monogamous and to mate for life. It has been observed that in captivity, the separation or death of one will leave the other in a state of depression, and while in captivity, the loss of its mate will encourage the surviving bird to substitute its caretaker for its departed mate (Lantermann et al. 2000).

The Umbrella Cockatoo only breeds once a year. According to Forshaw (1977), the egg size is 40.5–41.1 mm × 30.0–31.6 mm (approximately 1.5"–1.2"), the egg measurements of two eggs in the Berlin Museum Collection; the two eggs, incidentally, were from captive birds. The eggs are white. While there is no reported average clutch size based on studies of numerous wild breeding pairs nests, data from captive breedings as reported in the literature indicate that the normal sized clutch has two eggs, or sometimes three eggs. (Much of the information on the breeding of the species in the wild has been hypothesized from the data gathered by scientific observation or word-of-mouth anecdotal observations of the breeding activities of captive-bred pairs.)

Both males and females reach sexual maturity in their fifth to sixth year of life, although as in other species of cockatoos, younger birds have been known to breed before completely reaching adult maturity. Usually, prior to breeding season, individual unpaired or young cockatoos are found in small, loosely knit flocks. With maturity and interest in breeding, in courtship the male erects his crest, spreads his wings, and ruffles his feathers. He may strut a bit, bowing now and then. Should the female accept the courtship display, the pair may allopreen and/or scratch each other in the head and tail regions. Allopreening strengthens the developing bond between the pair. Ultimately, the pair will copulate (Avianweb 2012). It has been noted that for bonded pairs the courtship ritual display may not be prolonged, and in fact the female may initiate the copulatory rituals. Once the pair have committed themselves, they will leave the local social groups to search for a suitable nest site.

Pairs that have previously raised a clutch return to the nest site used the season before. A newly bonded, mated pair, however, need to seek out a suitable nesting site. Because of the territorial limits each pair lays claim to, and because Umbrella Cockatoo social norms prevent the pair from nesting within a kilometer (approximately one quarter of a mile) of another nesting pair, and since the species nests communally, it may take some time before the new pair can find a suitable nest site: this is particularly true if there is considerable logging in the area, or many trees have been cleared for agricultural purposes. Additionally, the pair requires a mature, towering tree—the higher the better. Finding a tall tree is always problematic because of both deforestation and the territorial limits that pairs establish for themselves.

The incubation of the clutch of two or three eggs is approximately 28–30 days. Both adults participate in the incubation of the eggs, and once the eggs have hatched, both adults care for the young, although the female plays a larger role in the raising of the young. The newly hatched are born altricial. It is rare for more than one nestling being reared to fledgling age.

When more than one egg is hatched, it is believed by some that the first hatched nestling will be larger by the time its sibling(s) hatch, and hence will be more successful in obtaining food from its parents (Alderton 2003); following this line of logic, size and dominance ensures that the first hatched nestling will be the first fed and will be fed the most (Indonesia Parrot Protection 2006). In effect, the underfed second or (or third) nestling is assured to perish from malnutrition. There are others who argue that the adults are genetically programmed to only care for and raise one healthy chick (Lane 2004). Avianweb (2012) argues, as have others, that should the first nestling be malformed or weak, the parents will tend to the second, younger nestling at the expense of the first. If in fact the parents cater to a younger nestling because the first hatched is weak and/or malformed, then again the adults have been genetically programmed to ensure that the healthy younger sibling receives most, if not all, of the food. Reliable field and aviary study is needed to clear up this question.

The juveniles leave the nest at approximately 84 days (Alderton 2003, 204), but Lantermann et al. (2000) claim the young learn to fly on average at three months of age. The newly fledged young will continue to remain dependent on the adult pair for an additional period of twenty-one or so days (Juniper and Parr 1998).

Aviary Notes

An exhaustive search of the literature regarding the Umbrella Cockatoo proves disappointing. In North America the species is reportedly commonly bred in captivity, but there is little verifiable material on its breeding. Much of the descriptive, anecdotal, and research data is in many instances simply repeating data from other sources, often not only word for word, but full paragraphs without properly referencing the source of the information. Nevertheless, the first reported breeding of the Umbrella Cockatoo in captivity was reported by Dr. Greene (1979)[2] over a century ago when he wrote his three volumes of *Parrots in Captivity*.

Given the good doctor's propensity to innocently pass on rumor, hearsay, and second or third person understandings as fact, the authenticity of the purported breeding should be considered with a smidgen of caution. He wrote, "One of these birds [an Umbrella Cockatoo], flying at liberty in the woods near Northrepps Hall, mated with a hen Leadbeater (*Lophochroa leadbeaeri*) ... and the pair produced a couple of fine hybrids, partaking of the characteristics of both parents ... which were ... subsequently shot by a stupid farmer."

A search of Prestwick's various publications half a century ago on the first breedings of parrots finds him mentioning the Greene reference. But, since a host of later aviculturalists/collectors, including the Marquess of Tavistock, assumed the purported Greene breeding to be fact, and were constantly referring to it, Preswick investigated further and concluded that Dr. Greene was in error: the purported Leadbeater-Umbrella breeding was actually a mating between the Greater Sulphur-crested Cockatoo (*Cacatua sulphurea*) and the Leadbeater Cockatoo (*Lophochroa leadbeateri*) (Prestwick 1951).

While early references to the successful breeding of the Umbrella Cockatoo are rare, the cockatoo does breed relatively easy in captivity, enough so that the captive cockatoo breeding program in the United States can meet part of the domestic demand for the cockatoo, although the birds are expensive. The first successful breeding in the United States was in southern California in 1960 (Schneider 1960), followed by a confirmed first breeding at Rode in Great Britain (Risdon 1968) which earned the gardens a certificate of merit from the Aviculturalist Society. Another notable captive breeding, was in Indiana, a state with abysmal winter conditions, where a pair successfully hatched and reared two clutches in two consecutive years (Guinn 1970).

Based on the literature, it appears that the species was not successfully bred much prior to 1960 because it was relatively rare in captivity. Dr. Greene, for example, while devoting six pages to the Umbrella Cockatoo, did not once mention having personally encountered the species. A search of the earliest editions of *Aviculture Magazine*, one of the first magazines to devote its pages to avicultural and avian concerns, reveals almost no mention of the species. A search in sister magazines produces similar results. While the cockatoo was certainly not rare during Dr. Greene's lifetime, and in the first fifty or so years of the twentieth century, it may very well be that the Umbrella Cockatoo was never captured for resale in either Europe or North America because it was simply a plain-looking bird when compared with all the other excitingly colorful bird species available for purchase.

That there is little information on the Umbrella Cockatoo, its life habits, reproduction and personality is therefore not surprising. It was a species that did not enter Europe or North America in significant enough numbers to capture widespread avicultural interest. Plath and Davis, as late as 1971, wrote, "Recently this shy bird has been offered in pet shops, which is an indication that we may have the opportunity to obtain the bird in numbers." By the late seventies, in southern California the species was no longer considered a rare, exotic species.

The aviary for the Umbrella Cockatoo needs to be spacious, given the bird is a larger species. Flights provided the species initially were 15 × 2.5 × 2.8 meters (16' × 8' × 9.1') (Risdon 1968), whereas Scheider in 1960, almost a decade earlier, had his pair in an aviary measuring 9 × 2 × 2.5 meters (29' × 7.5' × 8'). Currently, contemporary breeders provide their pairs a sheltered and spacious flight at least 5 × 2 × 2 meters (16' × 7.5' × 7.5'), with an adjoining shelter. Several natural wooden perches of different lengths and thicknesses hung at different heights will complete the basics for the caged environment. A heavy gauge welded mesh wire fencing enclosing the aviary is necessary because of the birds' strong beaks.

The species is not finicky regarding nest box accommodations. The cockatoo pair will accept grandfather-style nests, or upright logs at least two meters high (6'), with a cavity. Metal barrels, garbage cans, and plastic pickle barrels can be used, although a wooden nesting structure may be preferable in that it encourages chewing, thereby stimulating reproductive behavior (Clubb 2012). In 1960 Schneider provided his pair with an enclosed box with an entrance hole cut into it, whereas Guinn in 1970 simply hung a nest box from the ceiling with the open end facing south. Whatever the nesting arrangement, the bottom should be filled with humus and rotting wood. Once the birds begin showing an interest in mating, they will begin rearranging the nesting materials and adding to them from materials left outside the nest box.

Because the birds are vigorous chewers, there should be ample nontoxic fresh branches available on which these intelligent creatures can chew, and with which they can amuse themselves. As they are avid chewers, expect to have to replace the branches, and perches, regularly. Boredom leads to neurotic behavior, specifically self mutilization via feather plucking, and excessive shrieking.

In the United States, eggs are generally laid from the middle of May to early July. Incubation takes 28–30 days, both parents dutifully attending to the incubating, and both later tending to the nestlings' needs. The young are never left without at least one parent in attendance, until about their seventh week.

The diet provided captive birds is primarily composed of fruits, particularly peeled oranges, which the young nestlings relish. Other foods, such as sunflower seeds and canary seeds, corn, bread, beats and diverse greens are accepted. Nuts and seeds should be provided sparingly, however, because they provide considerable fat but little nutrition; Clubb (2012) recommends nuts and similar treats only as rewards for good behavior and to provide the cockatoos with psychological enrichment—part of the conditioning process. She cautions that the Umbrella Cockatoo can easily become obese, especially if being hand fed, and so a balanced diet is essential. Juveniles are notoriously picky eaters: their diet should be calibrated to provide a nutritious balance of suitable foods.

The growth and development of the young is poorly documented. By the time the young are almost four weeks old they are already quilled, and the crest feathering is more advanced than body plumage. At approximately the fifth week the young are almost completely feathered and by the eighth week the full plumage characteristic of the adult has been acquired. Upon fledging, the juveniles are for all intents and purposes identical to adults, except for the eye color.

The Umbrella Cockatoo is an ideal aviary candidate for breeding: it accepts captivity readily, as well as human presence, is not finicky concerning foods, and does not have behavioral tendencies that can be troublesome. Finally, Schneider (1960), who had reported that the Tropical Bird Garden pair were shy cockatoos, also noted they raised their surviving youngster in an aviary that was on public display and that was exposed to a "stream of hundreds of visitors passing it daily throughout the summer!"

Pet Companion

The Umbrella Cockatoo makes an excellent companion bird, a delightful household pet. Like other cockatoos it is fondly called the "Velcro Cockatoo" because it faithfully attaches itself to its owner as if they were partners in life, unlike some other species of parrots. A loving hug from a visitor is just as welcome as the hug from its master. The species is easy to take care of, is not overly demanding in its needs, and is imaginative and intelligent; and while its mimicry abilities are poor, what it lacks in mimicry it makes up for its strong, loving emotional bond which it develops with its owner(s).

This writer has never had the ill fortune of owning or having to tame an individual Umbrella Cockatoo that had an obnoxious disposition. The species is somewhat shy, absolutely non-aggressive, and may at first glance appear somewhat retiring or intimidated by people (dignified seems a more appropriate adjective), but it quickly responds to affection. Most Umbrella Cockatoos sold in North America, Europe and elsewhere have been hand fed and raised, and are completely "domesticated." Given the various restrictions on importing wild caught Umbrella Cockatoos, there are few fully wild cockatoos offered for sale, legally that is. Thirty years ago most Umbrella Cockatoos offered for sale (in California, at the time) were wild-caught, imported birds.

I recollect one individual Umbrella Cockatoo, while I was living in southern California, which I acquired for taming and as a possible gift for a friend. Without abusing the bird whatever, within half an hour the cockatoo could be trusted not to bite, and within three days or so, the bird could be trusted with young children, allowing them to pick it up for cuddling. The cockatoo was simply marvelously adaptable.

There was another similar Umbrella cockatoo, completely clever, adaptable, imaginative, and intelligent, but wild when he was brought to me for taming. Because of his size, the charming couple who brought him to me saw him as a huge bird with a ferociously dangerous beak. They were intimidated by this beautiful cockatoo that impulse alone had compelled them to purchase. During his second or so taming session he discovered that the rewards (almonds, raisins, or hazel nuts) he was receiving were coming from my shirt pocket. He quickly seized on every occasion from that insight to exploit me by immediately flying to my shoulder to bend down to search my shirt pocket for a treat. He soon generalized that insight to land on the shoulder of any visiting guest to search for any treats that might have been hidden in the guest's pocket. Of course, this behavior soon endeared him to all visitors in my household so that it was totally impossible not to conspire with household guests thereby allowing him to indulge his vice, much to everyone's delight. We were indeed heartbroken to have to return him to his owners, despite all our efforts to purchase him outright—regardless of cost!

There was another Umbrella Cockatoo who comes to mind and who displayed a remarkable individualism: Whitey. This particular bird, friendly, cuddling from time to time, never really acted like a velcro bird, perhaps feeling that such behavior was somehow undignified. He was tolerant of caresses, however, on his head and under his wing pits, and would indulge my coaxing caresses from time to time, as the mood struck him. When he tired of the attention I loved lavishing on him, he would gently grab my offending finger between his mandibles and just as gently push my finger and hand out of the way. There was no bite. No squawk. No shriek. No raised crest. Simply a gentle push of the finger and hand.

There was no point to deceiving Whitey by trying to sneak my hand behind his head. Whitey would simply about-face on his perch and, just as gently as before, push my hand away. Lest my interpretation of his behavior be misconstrued, Whitey was not cantankerous. He might have been a bit eccentric for an Umbrella Cockatoo, but he did not have one malicious feather, beak, shriek, or intent. His refusal to submit to intimacies, except when it suited him, was a constant source of amusement for me and visiting friends alike. But, he was, nevertheless, a loving bird and a great companion.

The Umbrella Cockatoo is easy to care for. It is loyal and loving, and will treat you as if you are *its* pet! It needs considerable attention, and deserves it. As already noted, it is intelligent, clever, loving, and learns quickly; it can master a variety of tricks (Mulawka 1981), and does so in a dignified manner. The cockatoo's cleverness was recognized well over a century ago when Dr. Green wrote, "They may be readily taught to throw up their wings, dance on their perch, hold out a foot to shake hands, and bow their head in salutation to a visitor." It is not surprising that Umbrella Cockatoos are often star performers in circus performances.

The Umbrella Cockatoo is a marvelous bird to have as a pet companion. Thirty years ago the cockatoo sold in southern California in the $400–$500 range, depending on the pet vendor. Today (2012) a healthy hand fed specimen will cost in the vicinity of $2,000. It is a cockatoo that requires quality time with humans: "They love to snuggle, kiss, and be petted all the time.... They require this attention or problems will result in the form of screeching or feather plucking. This is a highly intelligent bird" (Avian Companions 2012).

The cockatoo enjoys bathing. Routine misting is healthy not only for the plumage but also for the skin. After it has been misted with lukewarm water, it can be placed on a perch in the sun or gently dried with a hair dryer. The cockatoo should have its primary wing feathers clipped, but not so much so that should the bird fall off its perch it will fall straight down as would a rock: the flighty feathers should be clipped just enough to permit the cockatoo to glide to the floor, hence avoiding injury.

For individuals suffering from asthma or other breathing ailments, the Umbrella Cockatoo, despite its many favorable personal attributes, is not a good choice for a pet companion. Like many of the other cockatoo species, it exudes a white powder that is essential to the grooming of its feathers. That white powder does not limit itself to the bird, and within a short time it will be found forming a light powdering throughout the household. In favorable climates, the bird can be kept outdoors, but reciprocal intimacy with the cockatoo would be ill advised if your breathing would be adversely affected.

2

Moluccan Cockatoo

Cacatua moluccensis (Gmelin, 1788)

COMMON NAMES: Salmon-crested Cockatoo, Moluccan Cockatoo, Pink-crested Cock-
    atoo, Rose-crested Cockatoo (Great Britain)
SUBSPECIES: None
LIFESPAN: 80 years (London Zoo); 85 years (San Diego Zoo)[1]
IUCN RED LIST OF THREATENED SPECIES: Vulnerable
CITES: II

Description

Endemic to eastern Indonesia, the Moluccan Cockatoo is the largest species of the
loosely generalized group of cockatoos called the White Cockatoos, in contrast to the other
principal group of cockatoos, the Black Cockatoos. The species' average weight is almost a
kilo (2.2 lbs), and it ranges in size from 47 to 52 cm (18" to 20"). Unlike most other species
of birds, where males are usually larger than females, the Moluccan female is generally larger
than the male, but the size differential is not large. The cockatoos are basically white on
both top and bottom, suffused with a blush of pinkish peach that changes to a pinkish
salmon color with increasing age; almost a rose tinge, but quite delicate. In both juveniles
and adults, the feathers of the lower throat, breast, and abdominal feathers are faintly tinged
with pink.

I have owned several Moluccan Cockatoos over the years. Some of the individual birds
had only slight blushes of rose pink on the upper throat, breast and abdominal areas, while
others had a deeper pinkish salmon flush. Differences in color intensity, while not outstanding, could be attributed to local genetic pools, but there is some reason to suggest that color
intensity may be more an attribute of age than of other variables; while the cockatoo is easy
to tame, and train, those individuals with a deeper pink flush were more difficult to socialize
than those whose color was less intense—i.e., they were older.

The outstanding physical feature of the species, aside from its size, is the cockatoo's
crest. It is a large, abundant crest, retractable and recumbent, white on top, with an occasional
salmon pink color struggling to poke its color into the open. Because of its copiousness, the
crest gives the cockatoo the appearance of having a much larger head than it actually does
have. Additionally, the crest does not lie perfectly flat, following the curve of the crown to

the hind neck, but instead, because of its fullness, lies very loose and feathery on the crown. When erected, the crest fans in the center much in the manner of the Umbrella Cockatoo (*Cacatua alba*) rather than in a linear fashion from front to back as is common to most other White Cockatoos such as the Sulphur-crested Cockatoo (*Cacatua sulphurea*).

When the cockatoo's crest is erected it is always due to an emotional response such as fear or curiosity; when erected, the crest reveals bright orangish-red plumes that prior to the flashing of the crest were concealed; this bright crest is striking, to say the least.

The curved beak is large, black, and usually finely covered with grooming powder, which gives the cockatoo the appearance of having a greyish beak.[2] The periophthalmic ring is bare and slightly tinged with bluish-white.

The undersides of both wings and tail are washed in a yellowish orange hue. The feet and legs are greyish black.

The Moluccan Cockatoo is for all intents and purposes sexually monomorphic, although the male's eyes are black and the female's have a reddish brown iris, a difference at times difficult to distinguish. Additionally, while females are slightly larger than males, the size differential is not an accurate diagnostic for differentiating between sexes.

Nestlings, when still covered with pin quills, already have salmon colored crest feathers in evidence. At approximately three months of age juveniles appear for all intents and purposes identical to adult Moluccan Cockatoos.

Behavior

There is a shocking scarcity of published materials concerning the Moluccan Cockatoo in the wild state: because of the cockatoo's beauty and intelligence, it was collected by Pierre Poivre for the exotic bird trade as early as the 1751–1756 period (Stressman 1952). Yet during that entire period into the next century and a half, while naturalists were feverishly documenting Australian avifauna in detail, this Indonesian cockatoo somehow remained outside their scientific curiosity, despite its attractiveness. Today circumstances are not much different: scientific research is meagre. Indeed, a search of both the Internet and avian literature produces very little information on the species based on field studies. Almost all information concerning the cockatoo is derived from observations made of its behavior while in captivity; such data can be held suspect because the species' behavior in captivity may be different from its natural behavior in the wilds.

The Moluccan Cockatoo is considered to be a social being, quite gregarious, and hence is usually found in small, loose flocks of twelve to fifteen individuals outside of the breeding season, although it is generally assumed that the flocks would have been considerably larger prior to its heavy exploitation by the pet trade. During the mating period, it is found either singly or in pairs. It is considered a shy species (World Parrot Trust 2012). It has a loud voice, though, one of the loudest in the parrot world, a harsh shrill screeching that labels it unmistakably as a Moluccan Cockatoo. There is virtually no data based on actual field observation of the species in the wild. However, data from observations of the species in captivity reveals that the cockatoo uses its crest communicatively. A crest that lies flat on the head indicates the cockatoo is approachable, friendly and calm. The crest is raised in response to different emotional states: curiosity, surprise, frustration, and fear, among others. It could be assumed

The Moluccan Cockatoo is an extremely intelligent bird and certainly one of the most attractive of the so-called White Cockatoos. They are avian escape artists, however, known as real feathered Houdinis, because of their ability though trial and error to find the means to open their cage door (photograph by Marie Hale).

that in the wild a raised crest might also be part of a courtship ritual, a defence of territory, or a call to flock members (Avian Web 2011).

The Moluccan Cockatoo is considered extremely intelligent.

The cockatoo has a flight pattern best described as a few shallow wing beats followed by gliding, a relatively slow flight. It prefers perching in towering trees where pairs allopreen, and is best seen during early morning or late in the evening on its way to or from roosting places.

The Moluccan's diet consists of various seeds, nuts, berries, grains, and fruits such as papaya, durian, langsat, and rambutan, as well as both insects and their larvae. They are considered pests by some plantation owners because they also forage in palm plantations, where they can quickly shred the green husk off a young coconut to get at its flesh and milk. The cockatoos also causes considerable damage to corn fields (Avian Web 2011).

Like other cockatoo species, they are quite adept at holding food with one foot while using the other to break off a piece.

Habitat and Distribution

The Moluccan Cockatoo is endemic to several central Moluccan Islands in eastern Indonesia. Initially it was common on the islands of Seram, Ambon, Saparua and Haruku in South Maluku. But there have been no recent sightings of the species from Saparua or Haruku, where it is now considered extinct and, it is believed that it might still be found in small numbers on Ambon, but at only one locality. On the island of Seram, where it was once considered abundant, exploitation by the pet trade has deeply diminished its population so much so that it remains common only in the Manusela National Park, and speculatively perhaps in eastern Seram (BirdLife International 2012). By the 1950s the cockatoo was already rarely encountered in the central regions of Seram, and Streseman reported that it was common only along coastal areas. It is estimated that with the continued forest loss, forest fragmentation, human settlement and hydroelectric development, the existing population of cockatoos on Seram may be lost within twenty-five years (International Association 2012). Despite being protected both by Indonesian conservation legislation and CITES, while trapping for the international black market bird trade has declined significantly, birds are still being openly offered for sale in Indonesian marketplaces—the birds for sale are apparently without consequence to bird poachers and/or sellers. This internal open capture and sale of the species is a threat to the one major population at the Mansuela National Park. The total land area of the territories previously and now currently inhabited by the Moluccan Cockatoo, including those islands where it is now extinct, is only approximately 7,000 square miles (approximately 11,000 square kilometers).

There have been few studies of populations, although as noted above, it is clear that the species is already extinct in much of its former regions of habitation. The available, albeit limited, statistical data is at best confusing. Although the Kinnaird et al. (2003) study in 1998 reported an estimated population of 62,416–195,242 individuals, Persulessy (2007) reported a significantly lower estimated population size of only 9,640 birds in 2007. The difference between the two estimates is striking. The IUCN used both studies to estimate a total population of 10,000–99,999 individuals, of which approximately 6,700 to 67,000 are considered mature birds (ICUN Red List). The real number of individuals still surviving in the wild is unknown.

According to the World Parrot Trust (2012), the species inhabits lowland forests at altitudes up to approximately 1,200 meters (approximately 4,000'), particularly along rivers where there can be found mature, open canopy forests with low vegetation. Studies have found that population densities are higher in primary and secondary forests, and significantly lower in recently logged forests. The highest densities of populations can be found in primary lowland coastal forests below 180 meters (550'). In 2003, Kinnaird et al. found that the species population density was closely correlated to the availability of trees with suitable nesting sites and to the presence of strangler figs.

Propagation

There is little information available regarding the Moluccan Cockatoo's breeding in the wild. It is believed the species' breeding season begins in July–August (World Parrot Trust 2012) at a time when vegetative growth is at its peak and food supplies are abundant. In courtship, as is typical of many other cockatoo species, the Moluccan Cockatoo cock spreads his wings, ruffles his feathers, erects his crest, and struts about. And, as is also typical, the female generally ignores the initial courtship overtures, appearing indifferent, until at some point she finally accepts his courtship. The pair soon allopreen each other's heads and tail feathers, the allopreening strengthening the newly developing pair bonding. Similar to the Umbrella Cockatoo (*Cacatua alba*), the annual pre-copulative courting ritual is shorter for long-term bonded pairs, and it has been noted that with the onset of the breeding season at times the female may even encourage the male by approaching him. In the event one of the bonded pairs dies or disappears, the remaining cockatoo will display signs of a deep depression. It is unknown how long a mateless cockatoo remains in that breeding limbo. In captivity, often, the captive bird will act as if its caretaker is its mate.

The Moluccan Cockatoo prefers nesting in towering trees, in cavities or rotted hollows as high as thirty meters (100') above the ground level. Little is known of the nest preparations that the pair makes in the hollow. Little is also known about whether or not a pair will use the same nest site during the following year's breeding season. The pair breeds only once annually, the average clutch being two eggs, occasionally one or three. The eggs are white and elliptical. In his 1964 field studies, Schonwetter measured the eggs of seven clutches (all clutches had two eggs but one, which had only one egg), reporting that the eggs measured 50.0 mm × 33.4 mm (2" × 1.6").

Depending on the source reporting the information, the incubation period varies from 25 to 30 days. Both parents participate in the incubating, leaving the nest only to drink or feed. At night, the male leaves the nest and roosts outside, nearby. When hatched the nestlings have a yellow primary down, which disappears within a few days due to abrasion. The nestlings are also hatched altricial. The juveniles fledge in twelve to fourteen weeks after hatching and are normally fully independent within a month of fledging. It is believed by some the cockatoo generally reaches sexual maturity when five to six years old, but it is believed by others that some birds as young as three years of age are already sexually mature. The lack of data results in obscurity regarding the age of maturation.

Aviary Notes

Although the Moluccan Cockatoo has been bred in captivity, the successful breedings are far fewer than some avicultural folklore would have us believe. Experience suggests that captive breeding is fraught with difficulties. Historical as well as current avicultural publications are rife with interesting developments, experiences, experiments, successes and failures, regarding virtually every species of birds imaginable, captive or otherwise. It is difficult to imagine that although a wide variety of parrots, and other exotic diverse species, have been collected and bred in captivity since at least 1750, there is virtually no historical published information on the breeding of captive Moluccan Cockatoos. Despite the vast amounts of information instantly accessible on the Internet, there is virtually no information on the particulars of breeding this species in captivity, except for some generalizations, none of which appear to be derived from hands-on experience. There is little fundamental information available in the print literature, either. (Yet on Internet "Cockatoos for sale" Web sites, one finds an abundance of advertisements of Moluccan Cockatoos [domestically bred] for sale both in the United States and Europe, particularly in Great Britain, adult birds from persons wishing to divest themselves of a Moloccan Cockatoo, and aviaries with recently hatched fledglings, both hand and parent fed, and adult cockatoos.)

As noted earlier, the Moluccan Cockatoo was already being harvested for collectors as early as 1752, and has been in avian collections since that early date. But it had been bred so rarely in captivity that it was widely believed that this beautiful cockatoo was basically unbreedable in captivity; as recently as 1974 a brief note published by an anonymous correspondent in the *Avicultural Bulletin* informed the bulletin's readership, "They have never been bred in confinement. "

The first purported breeding of the Moluccan was mentioned by Dr. Greene (1979), quoting from a letter published in 1887 in *Bazaar* that makes mention of a Moluccan Cockatoo hen that laid eggs on several occasions. And this was the first mention of a purported breeding, over a century after the first cockatoos entered Europe's aviaries and collections. (Dr. Greene did not report whether the eggs were fertile and incubated, if the eggs hatched, or what was the outcome of the hatchlings.)

Dr. Greene also referred to a certain Mr. Dusek of Vienna, Austria, who had a pair that produced a clutch of one solitary egg. A search of the late 19th century avicultural literature produced no confirmation of either of these purported two breeding pairs, and although Dr. Greene had earned for himself a solid reputation as a major authority on birds because of his exotic bird collections, ornithological expeditions, and countless published articles, at times he had a tendency to pass off as established fact hearsay, rumors, and beliefs, without verifying their accuracy or veracity, which may very well be the case in his reference to these two instances that he reported.

For example, concerning the Moluccan Cockatoo hen that had laid several eggs, he quoted the correspondent: "Then it did not sit as ordinary birds do on their eggs, but laid sideways and rolled about." Dr. Greene did not question this (directly quoted) assertion, or even comment on it with raised eyebrows. Despite such shortcomings, Dr. Greene's volumes provide interesting reading on the evolution of ornithology and aviculture in general during his times.

While there might have been successful breedings of the species between Dr. Greene's era and the middle of the twentieth century, there were no published breedings, factual or hearsay, until the mid-twentieth century, when Stott in 1951 took it upon himself to itemize the numerous breeding successes of exotic birds in the San Diego Zoo (in California); in his research he found and wrote about a pair that in 1941 hatched two nestlings, both of which died shortly after hatching, cause unspecified. The zoo, however, did finally realize success: in 1951 Lint wrote that a pair had successfully hatched one of two eggs, and the nestling at the time of his reporting was almost at fledgling age, but that event came only after "fifteen years of continuous effort to induce the species to breed."

Ten years later, in 1961, Jones reported that he had a pair that started a second clutch and hatching one nestling. The parents soon abandoned it, and it subsequently died. Similarly, in 1972, O'Connor of Surrey in Great Britain wrote that he had a pair that reared a youngster—from all appearances both healthy and normal in all respects—until in its 82nd day, at which point it died for reasons unknown. Another breeding was reported in southern California four years later, by Cliff Wright whose pair had previously produced clutches, but which at the time of his account had only incubated one egg and successfully hatched it—at 104 days it was still healthy and doing well.

There are common themes through all of these early accounts: infertile eggs and the death of nestlings shortly after hatching. Of the seven clutches, there were only two surviving juveniles, and those two were each less than four months old. This is the reported history of over a century. The fact is, the bird does not breed well in captivity, but it does breed.

Despite the apparently dismal breeding history of this beautiful species in captivity, and the virtual absence of breeding literature, which would suggest to the average aviculturalist that the species is difficult at best to breed in captivity, there are in fact numerous Moluccan Cockatoos available for purchase: *but these birds for the pet trade commerce are not sourced from illegal importations, which strongly suggests that while common knowledge has us believe the bird breeds poorly in captivity, there are numerous successful breedings that never get reported.* Because of the cockatoo's vulnerable status, the United States, as well as Great Britain and other European nations, are signatories to CITES, and hence they prohibit both trade and importation of wild-caught Moluccan Cockatoos. It is obvious that the species is being bred in captivity, in large enough numbers that it is not an expensive personal investment, although the number being produced annually for the pet trade both in Europe and the United States is not clear. (In Australia, there is little interest in breeding the species because the bird is expensive for Australians, Australian breeders, professional specialists or hobbyists, prefer to breed their own endemic species, particularly those threatened with extinction.)

A cursory search for Moluccan Cockatoos for sale on the Internet finds a large number are available for purchase immediately. A sampling from that cursory search during the autumn of 2012: one Web site (of several that were identified) had nine different classified advertisements of the cockatoo being offered for sale, prices averaging from $650 to $1,200. Some of the classifieds were from individuals wishing to dispose of a bird companion, while others were from professional breeders. In another listing of several classifieds, a New Jersey breeder was offering hand fed babies for $1,600, the price including the cost of shipping. In fact, there were numerous American breeders located in both the warm southern states and the colder northern states, almost all offering the more expensive hand fed juveniles, as well as nest reared juveniles at a reduced price, for immediate delivery; and there were a large number of individual cockatoos being offered for sale by their owners. (In the U.K., hand fed babies were offered for sale at approximately £1750.) Anyone desirous of a Moluccan Cockatoo has available an abundant number of choices, male or female, old or young, hand fed or bird parent fed, all at competitive, reasonable prices vis-à-vis the price of other cockatoos and parrots.

For those who wish to meet the challenge and breed this outstandingly beautiful, intelligent cockatoo, however, several concerns need to be addressed: the bird is known for its screeching vocalizations, a screaming quite natural for the species, but neighbors, in a suburb, for example, will not appreciate its jungle naturalness, particularly in the middle of the night when the moon is full, the moon a stimulus for Moluccan Cockatoo lung exercising. Indeed, the owner may himself find the screaming intolerable. Breeding the Moluccan Cockatoo in a suburban environment can therefore become quite problematic. Further, the Moluccan Cockatoo is not a small bird like a Cockatiel, which will breed and raise a clutch in a cage measuring one meter by one meter (3' × 3' × 3') or less; the cockatoo requires aviary space of quite some size, and that aviary cannot be crammed amidst a variety of other aviaries cheek to jowl. If the breeder wants to successfully have young cockatoos, the mated pair require some semblance of ordered privacy in order to conduct their family responsibilities—having another pair, or other species, within that same aviary can be counterproductive.

Because the Moluccan Cockatoo is such a large bird, its aviary accommodations should be as large as possible, the dimensions being at minimum at least 5 × 2 × 2 meters (16' × 6' × 6'), the length providing the birds the opportunity for some limited flying. The aviary should be enclosed with a 12-gauge welded wire mesh, and located away from other aviaries and possible disturbances. Several natural wooden perches should be provided as well as fresh nontoxic tree branches; the chewing of these branches provides these intelligent cockatoos with entertainment, occupation, and a means to control beak growth. Because of the species' propensity to vigorously chew all chewables, expect to regularly replace both chewing branches and perches as a routine maintenance chore. Additionally, anyone in the southern United States, where opossums are common, needs to provide outdoor caging to protect the birds from this mammal to prevent the Moluccan Cockatoo pair from being exposed to the parasite *Sarcocytis falcatula,* which can cause a fatal lung infection in the birds.

Although the species has been known to nest in garbage cans, metal barrels and even plastic pickle barrels, a wooden nesting structure is preferable because it provides the birds an opportunity to chew, hence stimulating reproductive behavior. A log or tree stump ranging approximately 40 cm by 1.5 meters high (16" × 5') with a large enough hollow can be provided, or a grandfather-styled wooden nesting box. For both log and grandfather-styled nesting arrangements, a climbing structure inside the nesting chamber needs to be provided below the entrance hole for easy exit from the nesting site.

Some other potential nesting arrangements should be scattered about the aviary, and once the pair have shown an interest in a particular nesting box or log, the other arrangements should be gradually removed. The nesting box should have an escape route for the female, especially since some males have been known to be aggressive with their mates, severely biting legs, wings, or head. One way to minimize and even prevent the male's aggression is to cut short the leading three flight feathers from each of his wings prior to the onset of the breeding season, but leave enough to permit the bird to glide to the floor should it fall from its perch.

The usual clutch is two eggs, and both parents remain in the nest, except to feed. But the eggs/nestlings are never left unattended without at least one of the pair remaining in the nest (O'Connor 1972); and, notably, the female, which may have been perfectly tame prior to brooding her clutch, often becomes defensive, threatening and aggressive when the aviary is approached. Because nesting parents are nervous birds, prone to be startled easily at the slightest unusual sound, it is best that interferences near or at the aviary be minimized. If the eggs have hatched, nestlings and juveniles will regurgitate their food when distressed.

The incubation period is 28–30 days (BirdCare 2012), although Wright (1948) claimed it as 36 days; he also reported that the young could be heard two or three days after hatching. Both parents participate in the feeding of the young, but at dusk the male usually leaves the nest to roost elsewhere in the aviary.

The food provided breeding pairs varies considerably, which is not so much a matter of the breeder's lack of knowledge as it is that the Moluccan Cockatoo is not finicky about food choices and accepts a wide range of greens, fruits, nuts and seeds. O'Connor in 1972 reported that his pair consumed large quantities of peanuts, carrots, and spinach; but soaked sunflower and oats, as well as hard boiled eggs, were rejected. Wright's pair that bred successfully in 1976, on the other hand, were fed peanuts, cheese, bread, honey, maggots, apples, spray millet, sunflower, budgie mix, chickweed, and sunflower. At the San Diego Zoo, the birds were fed corn on the cob, sunflower, piñon nuts, oranges, bananas, oats, peanuts, and dried bread.

While the Moluccan Cockatoo is a dutiful and consistent parent regarding the feeding of its young, it is also a nervous bird, easily disturbed or distressed, so much so that at times it will ignore the hungry cries of its nestlings. At such times the breeder has to intervene to save the young birds from starvation. Wright hand fed his nestling with strained baby food via syringe. The San Diego Zoo fed its nestling every four hours via spoon, the food a standardized but complex psittacine formula. It was not until their nestling was 56 days old that it was given its first piece of fruit, an orange.

To date, the young Moluccan Cockatoo's stages of development are not fully documented in detail. They are born altricial, their eyes are barely open by ten days, and they sport a light yellow down when hatched. Their legs and feet are so large that they appear out of proportion to the rest of the nestling's body. Color is already visible when the nestling is still encased in pin feathers. By the eleventh week the primary feathers are already well grown, and by the fifteenth week the fledgling is capable of flying. It is reported that hand feeding young birds, while demanding in terms of time, is not difficult. For those breeders who are either forced to hand feed the nestling, or choose to, there are a variety of hand rearing formulas available. Kaytee Exact is a popular formula, particularly because it is not high in fat, but there are other suitable formulas.

It should be noted that hand fed Moluccan Cockatoos, especially the males, become imprinted and may consequently not breed until they are eight to ten years old, if they breed at all.

Pet Companion

The Moluccan Cockatoo is an outstandingly beautiful and intelligent bird, adaptive, and noted for its trainability, as evidenced by the fact that the cockatoo is a common participant in circuses and trained bird shows. Of all the cockatoos, and all of them are known to be intelligent, the Moluccan Cockatoo is probably the most intelligent of them all, and while not well known for its mimicry, it is undoubtedly clever, being known to even independently figure out through trial and error how to unlatch locks on its cages, compelling owners to devise cage closing devices to thwart cockatoo freedom excursions. They are avian escape artists.

Because the bird is a highly social being, it quickly develops bonds with its owner. It likes to cuddle, to be affectionate, and is generally an extremely gentle bird. All of these positive dispositions are what makes the Moluccan Cockatoo an ideal bird companion for those persons *who have the time, patience, and willingness to reciprocate demands for affection from* an intelligent being.

Despite these positive personal attributes of this beautiful bird, the Moluccan Cockatoo is not the ideal pet candidate for most people who dream of owning a loving parrot, a clever one, a constant source of pleasant entertaining companionship, like the Sulphur-crested Cockatoo that co-starred in the *Barrata* detective television series several years ago—there is no similarity between a Moluccan Cockatoo and a cat that will sleep on its owner's lap until it is put on the floor, a pet that makes no demands except to meow when the refrigerator door is opened, that will purr contentedly after being fed a treat, and that will leap onto the couch or someone's bed to sleep, with or without someone's lap.

There are worlds of difference between pet companion Moluccan Cockatoos and pet companion Persian felines. The differences between fur and feathers is the least of the differences; it is the difference in personality and psychological dispositions. For example, Moluccan Cockatoos are known to develop severe emotional problems when separated from their owner with whom it bonds itself, or separated from its mate. Cats couldn't care less, as long as there is someone to open the refrigerator door. The cockatoo, however, may become excessively aggressive, destructive, and noisy—very noisy.

Moluccan Cockatoos are demanding. They are possessive. And imprinted individuals are extremely possessive. Once they have bonded with their owner, they often do so at the total exclusion of relating with anyone else in the family, and may even attack them out of jealousy. Ignoring the cockatoo's emotional needs or failing to provide them an appropriately stimulating environment can result in feather plucking and other forms of self-mutilation, aggression, destructiveness of diverse items in the household or bird room, or outrageous, incessant screeching for minutes on end. A half hour's screeching by the cockatoo perched nearby in the same room can not only get an owner to question his sanity for going Moluccan, but the screeching is guaranteed to alienate one's immediate neighbors, regardless of previous reciprocal friendliness and bar-b-ques. As Avian Companions (2012) observes: "You have not lived until you are in the same room with a Moluccan and it screams!!"

An intelligent Moluccan Cockatoo requires a dedicated, loving, patient owner. Because the species is so intelligent and so emotionally demanding, it requires a great deal of attention and activity if it is to remain emotionally healthy and be a loved asset in the household. The cockatoo requires constant involvement and attention, particularly training to socialize it and thereby discourage unacceptable behaviors, and training to amuse itself when you or another family member is unavailable: toys to play with, to chew upon, and foraging toys that force the bird to work for its food.

Many people simply do not have the time, or the patience, to provide their Moluccan Cockatoo with the attention it craves and deserves. After a while, for any number of reasons, the owner decides to sell the bird. The bird could have become too aggressive, too noisy, or too demanding. To socialize the bird requires daily work. And many people simply do not have enough spare time to do what has to be done. Regrettably, many perfectly wonderful Moluccan Cockatoos go through serial owners. Perhaps that is why there are significant numbers of domestically bred cockatoos available for sale in the classifieds by owners at more than reasonable prices, given their general rarity.

Despite all of the above, anyone desirous of a Moluccan Cockatoo should not be dissuaded from acquiring one. It would be advisable, however, to reconsider such an acquisition if time is a major concern, if one lives in an apartment or suburb, and/or if one's general patience level is sometimes in short supply. And for those individuals who suffer respiratory problems, the powder the cockatoo exudes for its grooming can be problematic, seriously aggravating an existing health problem.

For those individuals who wish to own a Moluccan Cockatoo and who will take the time needed to socialize them and provide them with the affection that they will without question reciprocate, this cockatoo can provide hours of delight and fascination. As noted earlier, they are not difficult to feed, and they are trainable.

Their cage should be large, at least a macaw-sized cage, with ample wooden toys to chew upon. During the day, they should be let out of their cage for a while, permitting them to interact with the owner.

Cockatoos enjoy bathing, and routine showering is essential for the bird to maintain healthy skin and good plumage condition. It is also good for its emotional well-being. Misting the cockatoo is always appreciated by the bird, and if there is no bird room per se for the cockatoo to dry in, it can be gently blow-dried with a hair dryer.

Amongst other good maintenance and socialization practices is to teach the bird that there is a usual time when it has to return to its cage for sleep. My favorite Moluccan Cockatoo named Augie was trained to recognize the tattered blanket with which his cage was covered each night: when he saw me approach him with his blanket, he would hop off his perch, jump into his cage, and stretch his head out to be given a final loving scratch. Then the cage door was shut (locked) and the cage was covered with the blanket. We always found it amusing to see his eye peeping through one of the blanket tatters to keep abreast with events still ongoing outside his cage before the lights were shut off. The blanket also helped him learn to curtail his usual brief but still horrendous evening screech. But his eye peeping through the tatter—delightful, unforgettable, an emotional experience to remember a lifetime.

3

Yellow-crested Cockatoo
Cacatua sulphurea (Gmelin, 1788)

COMMON NAMES: Lesser Sulphur, Lesser-Sulphur-crested Cockatoo, Dwarf Sulphur-crested, Yellow-crested, Timor Sulphur-crested (in Great Britain), Citrin-crested Cockatoo (AKA Orange-crested in North America)

SUBSPECIES:

1. *Cacatua sulphurea sulphurea* (Gmelin, 1788)—Nominate Race
2. *Cacatua sulphurea abbotti* (Oberholser, 1917)
3. *Cacatua sulphurea citrinocristata* (Fraser, 1844)
4. *Cacatua sulfurea parvula* (Bonaparte, 1850)

NOTE: Until several years ago, the species was considered to comprise six races: in addition to the above four subspecies there were also the *C.s. occidentis* and the *C.s. djampeana*, which had been classified as subspecies based on bill size differences, until it was discovered that the bill size varied considerably within any island's aggregate population.

LIFESPAN: (estimated) 49.7 years[1]

IUCN RED LIST OF THREATENED SPECIES: All four subspecies are considered Critically Endangered[2]

CITES: I[3]

Description

The Yellow-crested Cockatoo is a medium sized bird approximately 33 cm (13") in length, and the 2012 World Parrot Trust profile report on the species notes that it averages 308–380 grams (11–13.5 ounces), the variance related to subspecies differences and sex differentials. Forshaw had in 1977 concluded that their wing span ranged in size from 211 mm to 257 mm (8.5"–10"), the span depending again on the race.

Both adults are almost completely white on both upper and lower parts. Underpart plumage bases are flushed with a pale yellow, the yellow hue non detectable beneath the white terminal ends of the feathers unless they are ruffled. There is a strong yellow component to both primary flight and tail feather under coverts.

But, conspicuously, it is the long, recursive, forward curling crest of the cockatoo consisting of bold lemon colored feathers that captures the eye. The length of the crest, when laid back, points towards the tail, but the crest feather ends themselves are both slightly curved up and pointed forward towards the beak. The feathers lie back one on top of the

The Yellow-crested Cockatoo comprises four subspecies, all of them endemic to Indonesia. Poaching of the species has been so rampant to feed the illicit trade in wildlife that in 2009 it was estimated that fewer than 7,000 birds still existed in the wild. This poaching still continues today even though a convicted poacher may receive up to five years' imprisonment and a $21,000 fine (photograph by Jeff Chau).

other, a scant few white feathers on the front preceding the yellow curved feathers. The magnificent recursive feather ends are narrow and totally unlike the recumbent crest feathers of some other cockatoo species such as the Umbrella Cockatoo (*Cacatua alba*) or the Little Corella (*Cacatua sanguinea*). Of the four subspecies it is only the *C.s. citrinocristata* whose crest differs in color from the striking yellow of the other three: it is a bright warm orange.

Excluding the *C.s. citrinocristata*, the other three subspecies also have bright yellow ear coverts, but the yellow is marginally subdued in tone compared to the bright crest coloration. The Citrin-crested Cockatoo's ear coverts are colored orange, the same shade as its crest. Common to all four subspecies, all other head feathers are white at the terminal ends but are a light yellow hue at their base.

Its beak is slate grey. All subspecies have a featherless, soft white, slightly blue tinged periophthalmic ring. The male's eyes are deep brown whereas the female's are reddish brown. Their feet are mealy black and zygodactyl. Often, the Yellow-crested Cockatoo is understandably mistaken for the Sulphur-crested Cockatoo (*Cacatua sulphurea*), which it closely resembles, and concurrently, the Sulphur-crested Cockatoo is just as understandably mistaken for the Yellow-crested Cockatoo. The Sulphur-crested Cockatoo (*Cacatua galerita*), however, is considerably larger, and has a periophthalmic ring that is white skinned as opposed to a bluish tinged white. Yellow-crested Cockatoos have a beak that is heavier and wider than that of the Sulphur-crested Cockatoo (*C.s. galerita*), but the beak is less protruding. Additionally, their crest is usually narrower (Animal World 2012). That there is some confusion really rests on the fact that the birds are so similar that it takes a trained, discriminating, and knowledgeable eye to differentiate one from the other. They are, however, geographically separated from each other by quite some distance.

Aside from the distinctive crest and cheek patch color difference between the Citrin-crested Cockatoo and the other three races, there are no other physiological differences that can be employed with confidence in distinguishing one race from the other. All four subspecies, aside from that one major color difference, are more or less alike.

But there are minor differences, though they are not always readily obvious. The *C.s. parvula* is similar to the Nominate race *C.s. sulphurea,* except that the bases to the underpart feathers and yellow ear coverts are somewhat paler. The *C.s. abbotti* is the same as the *C.s. parvula* except that it is marginally a smaller bird (World Parrot Trust 2012). Size is an unreliable method for determining subspeciation, except, of course, for the *C.s. citrinocristata,* which is noticeably slightly larger than the other races (but then again it also sports a different colored crest and cheek patch, which immediately identifies it as being uniquely different without chance of error). Succinctly, the minor differentials catalogued above problematic at best are as a means of determining the race of a specific specimen.

Finally, the species is sexually monomorphic. While there is the minor color difference between male and female eyes, this one feature is not a totally reliable method for sex determination. And although males tend to be larger than females, there is a significant variation in sizes in any given population: i.e., some males may be smaller than others, and some females may be as large as a small male from that same population. The sex of a given bird, however, can be reliably ascertained through either DNA testing or a surgical procedure.

Behavior

It is not uncommon to search the literature regarding a particular species and discover that there is very little, if any, field-gathered information on the species' behavior, either in the wild or in captivity. This is especially disturbing if the species is considered rare.

That there is sparse field study reporting of the Yellow-crested Cockatoo's behavior and history from the heyday of exploration over a century ago is not really surprising. At a time when much of the world's fauna was yet to be discovered and catalogued, a scientific endeavor that is still ongoing,[4] the newly discovered lands provided considerable opportunities for the post–Darwinian scientific world to identify and classify a host of new life forms, hitherto unknown to the scientific world. That the Yellow-crested Cockatoo is meagerly represented in early ornithological documentation is not surprising given the haste to discover and document as many as possible of the countless diverse new world species.[5]

The ornithological literature published between approximately 1870 and the 1920s reveals that there were a handful of ornithological giants who dominated the scientific literature with their discoveries of new species, their systematics, their publications, their theories and their interpretations of the data gathered. One is left with the impression, right or wrong, that there was considerable professional and personal rivalry between those giants vis-à-vis who would discover the most species, classify them, publish findings, and so on. The literature of the time is abundant with polemical debates, rebuttals, subtle insults in some instances, and adamant and sometimes extravagant claims regarding the identification of new species, while concurrently discounting arguments to the contrary.

Assuming such an interpretation of that historical period of history is accurate, it would not be surprising therefore to conclude that many of the professionally motivated scientists and naturalists preferred to explore vast virgin terrains such as Australia, or the Amazonian rain forests, where there were endless numbers of unknown species still remaining to be discovered, and classified, as opposed to a few minor islands where such fame acquiring opportunities were limited. Succinctly, it was much easier to assure oneself an international reputation and a permanent niche in scientific and ornithological history when such a reputation was contingent on the number of species one discovered, and races identified, classified, and systematized. Australian field work provided far more opportunities for discoveries than comparable field work pursued on small islands with limited numbers of diverse life forms.[6]

The Yellow-crested Cockatoo is primarily arboreal in most of its life habits, feeding in fruiting trees, although it is known to feed on the ground when various berries and seeds are in season. Depending on the island environmental terrain, the species prefers to roost in heavy montane forests. Field observations on Masakabing Island suggest that the species has a variety of favorite foods: berries, flowers and bulbs, diverse seeds and fruits. Previously, when they were in greater numbers, they were persecuted as pests because of their feeding in cultivated areas, maize being one of their popular foods, and the resulting damage to the crops. Decades ago, they were commonly found in large flocks feeding in fruiting orchards and coconut plantations. Field observations have shown that the species' favorite foods included the Coconut Palm (*Cocos nuofera*), flowers and fruits, mangos, the flowers and young leaves of the *Ceiba petandia*, among a variety of other forest fruits, in addition to the fruit of the *gassampinus,* another fruit popular with the cockatoo. With sharply declined numbers in population, and the fragmentation of the forest terrains, the birds are now rarely seen, and then only in pairs or in small flocks of up to ten or so birds. Occasionally, the Red-sided Eclectus Parrot (*Eclectus roratus*) can be observed in their company (Arndt-Verlag 2012). But the Red-sided Eclectus is also a target for poachers catering to the pet trade.

Usually, if the island is not too heavily deforested where there are still some small remaining populations, the cockatoos can be found occupying the forest's canopy, and while not always visible, they are conspicuous because they are noisy. In more mountainous areas, although they generally roost at lower altitudes, they can sometimes be seen flying to lower elevations in order to feed during the early morning.

When flying, their flight has been described as noisy, "fairly swift with shallow wing movements and accompanied by cries; [the] call harsh, repeated screech" (Arndt-Verlag 2012).

Depending on the source reporting, while some describe the bird as noisy, others consider the species to be a relatively quiet cockatoo. Their call is described as a harsh shriek, but not as raucous as that of the Sulphur-crested Cockatoo (*Cacatua galerita*). At times it whistles and even makes low-toned squeaks. The Yellow-crested Cockatoo's crest, like that of other cockatoos, can be erected. When it is, the erection is in response to an emotive state: curiosity, fear, danger, anger, courtship, or any other emotional state, as well as a communication to other cockatoos.

Habitat and Distribution

The Yellow-crested Cockatoo was endemic to Timore-Leste (formerly known as East Timor) and Indonesia, where it was common from Bali to Timor, the region known as Nusa Tangarra. The species occupied a wide range of diverse environments, depending on the particular island. While the Yellow-crested Cockatoo preferred heavily closed-canopied primary forest, it adapted remarkably well to heavy deforestation.

The species could be found resident in subtropical/tropical dry terrains, subtropical/tropical mangrove areas above high tide level, moist tropical and subtropical environments, and, of course, agricultural lands; while the cockatoo could be found near human communities with their agricultural activities, it did not generally breed in those vicinities.

In 1937 Mayre reported on the *C.s. sulphurea*'s distribution throughout the island of Sulawesi, over which he travelled extensively. His field report shows that the Sulawesi race had a somewhat scattered distribution, in that while there were coastal populations at various points of interest, there did not appear to be a continuity of distribution between these diversely scattered coastal populations. Moreover, Mayre also visited several of Sulawesi's satellite islands and found that on some islands the indigenous inhabitants had never heard of the species. He concluded that this pattern of infrequent and random distribution might be seasonal, but was ultimately forced to reject this hypothesis when it became clear that the species was not known in areas where it should have been known if it was following seasonal movements. He hence declared, "*Cacatua sulphurea* must be declared a rare bird, in this sense, that its distribution is a very interrupted one in Celebes Sulawesi."

Mayre's field observations were quite correct concerning the species' coastal habituation: he noted that when deHaan (in Van Bemma and Voous 1951) collected specimens, or obtained them through barter, they were always obtained near seashore villages bordered by teak forests.

The Yellow-crested Cockatoo still prefers tall trees, both primary and secondary growth, for nesting and roosting, but can also be found in dry coastal woodlands and thorn scrub, terrains that are common, for example, to the Komodo National Park (Butchart et al. 1996). Although it can be occasionally found at altitudes as high as 1,200 meters (approximately three-quarters of a mile high), the species throughout its entire distribution was always more frequent in terrains at much lower altitudes. For example, while on a field expedition in Flores and Busawa, Rensch (1931) collected all of his specimens at altitudes well below 800 meters (2,600').

As noted earlier, the species has thrived in a host of environments. On Sumbawa, for example, the birds were often observed in semi-evergreen forests and roosting on tall riverine trees (Johnstone and Jepson 1996; Butchart et al. 1996). It could also be found in wooded areas adjacent to cleared regions where the species would normally be foraging food from agricultural crops. But deforestation has had a direct negative impact on the species' population viability; for example, on Masakambing, where most of the original habitat has been cleared leaving only mangroves, the species has been left with limited availability of suitable nesting sites. Similarly, the Citrin-crested Cockatoo, which depends on closed canopy forests at low altitudes, particularly valley bottoms (Jones et al. 1995), it is now either extinct or rare in forested areas less than ten square kilometers (.6 square miles) (Convention 2004). The cumulative effect of rampant harvesting of the species and the deforestation of old growth forests on existing population numbers is disheartening, especially when these activities are not anticipated to decrease.

The total range of its distribution, originally, reached from Sulawesi and its satellite islands to the Lesser Sundra Islands. However, most of the islands the species historically inhabited are small. Aside from Sulawesi and its immediate neighbors, the other islands are for the most part geographically separated from each other by considerable distances, providing therefore an insular regionalism for each of the species' races. Despite these considerable distances, early studies a century ago and even until the 1950s documented the cockatoos as common throughout "Wallacea," the central archipelago of Indonesia.

The birds are no longer common on the numerous islands they once occupied, indeed, the harvesting of the species particularly during the last quarter of the 20th century has resulted in a dramatic decline in the races' numbers to where they are not only extinct on most of the islands they once inhabited, but their remaining scattered pocket population numbers are so small that they are also threatened with total extinction in the wild throughout all of what remains of their previously inhabited range of distribution.

The rapid degradation of forests critical for nesting and roosting opportunities, loss of native foods, a low reproductive rate, and illegal harvesting of the species for the black market pet trade accelerates even further the decline in the races' populations.

Regarding the different races of the Yellow-crested Cockatoo, they are distributed as follows[7]:

C.s. sulphurea: This race originally inhabited the islands of Buton, Muna (Van Bemma and Voous 1951), Tukangbesi in the north Flores Sea, Djampea, Kajuadi, Kaloatoa, and Sulawesi, all in Indonesia (Behrens 1995; MacKinnon and Phillips 1993; Innskipp et al. 1992), plus several smaller islands (also Indonesian). It is now considered extinct throughout most of all its former range, and close to extinction on the other islands (Bird Life) 2012 where a quarter of a century ago it was still considered common. There are a few small, fragmented populations in the Tukangbesi Islands, on Oroho Island, and on Roti Island (Johnstone and Jepson 1996; Trainor 2007). At the time of this writing, several years after these reports, it is unclear whether there are any populations left on the islands noted above. On Sulawesi, where historically it was always absent in the wetter northern parts and in the island's central region, but very common elsewhere, though it is now no longer distributed over much of that large island, there remain a few isolated small pockets of populations of the birds; how many birds, no one knows.

They are small scattered population remnants of approximately 200–300 individuals (IUCN Red List 2012); and throughout most of its former satellite islands, the bird is rare and for the most part considered extinct. In Rawa Aopa Waturnohai National Park, the population in 2001 was estimated at only about 100 individuals, and on Pasoso Island the population was believed to be 7–15 individuals (Agista and Rubyanto 2001; Agista et. al. 2001).

All four races of the Lesser-crested Cockatoo are fully protected in Indonesia.[8] Because the numbers of birds still remaining in the wilds are so few, and the penalties upon conviction of poaching are so heavy, there are fewer birds being illegally captured for the pet trade. However, ironically, it is reported that since the birds are so rare, they are still being illegally poached, but now for sale to government officials because owning such a rare bird bestows upon its owner considerable prestige (Indonesian Parrot Project 2012).

C.s parvula: This race was common to the islands of Lombok, Moyo, Komodo (the Komodo Islands are one of Indonesia's national parks), Sumbawa, Penida, Sernau, and Alor plus several smaller islets (Behrens 1995). The species is now considered extinct, or nearing so, on almost all islands excepting Komodo, where a small population still persists. Although Komodo is a national park, and all wildlife there is protected, it is believed that some poaching still continues: between 2000 and 2005 the population was estimated to have declined 60 percent (Imansyah et al. 2005). At the last report there was a population of only c. 500 on Komodo, and a few tiny isolated populations of a few individuals on the other islands in the Komodo Islands grouping (Walker et al. 2005). As part of its conservation efforts, the Indonesian government has established what are known as East Timor Important Bird Areas (IBAs); despite these conservation efforts in Timor-Leste, *C.s. parvula* was recorded in only six of the nine established IBAs (Trainor 2002).

C.s. abbotti: This race occurs now only at Masakambing in the Masalembo Islands group. The 2008 intensive surveys of Masakambing Island resulted in finding only ten birds remaining (Nandika 2006). In 2009, the following year, there were only eight recorded sightings. According to Nandika, local residents informed him that the species was extirpated from Masalembo in 1987, following the capture and killing of the species that accompanied the exploration of the archipelago in the 1980s. The few remaining birds were seen nesting and feeding in coconut trees because there was no natural forest left (Convention 2004).

C.s. citrinocristata is endemic to the island of Sumba (Collar et al. 1994), due east of Timor-Leste. Numerous decades earlier, it was observed in large flocks feeding in trees, occasionally associated with Eclectus Parrots (*Electus oratus*). In 1992 Sumba had the largest regional population still remaining, tentatively estimated at c 3,200 individuals at the time, but believed declining by as much as 500 individuals a year; currently (2012), the island has barely 10 percent of its original forests still remaining, and what remains is severely fragmented into 34 parcels scattered about the island—a scarcely favorable opportunity to find suitable nesting sites (Walker et al. 2005).

All population figures post–2004 are estimates derived from data provided by various governmental agencies, conservation authorities, naturalists, field workers, and ornithologists. The population data pertaining to the current wild status of the four races should be considered outdated estimates at best, for a number of reasons. Firstly, while some data were compiled through actual observation and count, other data were purely estimated. Secondly, while all races are protected by law, illegal harvesting assuredly continues given its profitability; the removal of nestlings dramatically negates the introduction of future reproductive members essential to replace the current aging adult population. The harvesting of wild nestlings not only reduces expected population stability and/or population number increase, but has assuredly reduced the numbers in the wild. Thirdly, despite conservation efforts, deforestation ultimately reduces nesting opportunities. In short, all data as presented above suggesting current population estimates must be viewed with some caution. The estimates above, are based on the latest documented information available at the time of this writing.

There is a population of an estimated several hundred feral Lesser Sulphur-crested Cockatoos in Hong Kong where, legendary history has it, Sir Mark Aitchison Young, the Governor of Hong Kong at the time during WWII, ordered the entire Government House exotic bird collection released just hours before he surrendered the city to the invading Japanese army in December 1941 (*HK Magazine* 2005). The birds released included Yellow-crested Cockatoos, and the particular race was reportedly the *C.s. parvula* from Lombok. There are also reputed to be some small feral populations of the species in Singapore, a matter over which there is considerable debate (Behrens 1995; MacKinnon and Phillips 1993); their numbers are unquantified and their distribution is equally unknown.

While the numbers of birds in Hong Kong and Singapore are not quantified, it is generally believed that in the Hong Kong wild environs there are several hundreds.

The current quantification of cockatoo numbers in their original habitats is at best a distressing situation. All field study reports make it obvious that the various races occur in very small numbers, and on only a fraction of their former ranges; and on those islands where there are still some isolated populations found, their numbers are few. In 2012, World Parrot Trust Wild Status gave the world population at less than 3,000 individuals, the estimate applicable to two years earlier, the 2010 year.

Bird Life International (2012) quantifies the species (based on data in the literature published prior to 2009) as an (optimistically) estimated global population of fewer than 7,000: 3200–5000 on Sumba, 500 on Komodo (and adjacent islets), 200–300 on Timor Leste, 200–300 on Sulawesi, 20–50 on West Timor, 40–70 on Flores, 100 on Rinca, and 700 other birds on various tiny islet locations in total (Trainer 2007; Bird Life 2012; IUCN 2012). The low numbers are abysmally disturbing, for while the species breeds relatively well in captivity, at the current rate of illegal harvesting the Lesser-crested Cockatoo's future in the wild is a forgone conclusion. The estimated population figures reported above by both the World Parrot Trust (2012) and Trainer (2007), while as accurate as can be expected at the time of reporting, depend on the reporting source and its quantification methodology. Because of ongoing covert harvesting of the species, those figures should be considered unreliable; the population numbers in the wild are probably now significantly diminished.

Propagation

There is little material in the ornithological literature regarding the Yellow-crested Cockatoo's reproductive behavior in the wild. While there are some reports from field naturalists, most of them pertains to the quantification of the species, its taxonomy, and its general distribution (regardless of the species' particular habitat), or matters pertaining to its reproductivity. Much of what is known about the species and its reproduction has been garnered from aviculturalists, and even that information is at times sparse.

There are a few field observations that are of value. Throughout the species' distribution, its breeding cycle generally takes place from September to May on some of the islands (Walker et al. 2005). But those dates vary. World Parrot Trust (2012) notes that the species' breeding season on Buton, for example, begins in September–October but in the Nusa Tenggara regions begins in April–May.

Because of the rapid deforestation and degradation of previously densely forested lands, critically important trees essential for nesting opportunities are either burned down in a slash-and-burn economy or chain-sawed for lumber, leaving the few remaining birds even fewer nesting opportunities. The Yellow-crested Cockatoo nests in tree trunk cavities, preferably in the hollow of a Gossampinus tree; often it occupies nesting sites previously prepared and used by other avian species, and usually, the nesting sites can be found in dead or rotting trees (Nandika 2006). The cockatoos not only are in competition with other cockatoos for what few nesting sites are available, but also are in competition with other bird species.

Young nestlings are highly desirable as pets, especially if they have been hand fed; when a nesting pair only produces on average fewer than two surviving nestlings, the harvesting of nestlings results in a population of cockatoos that becomes increasingly geriatric, a population without sufficient numbers of healthy, young adult birds replacing the older birds, a replacement essential to ensure a stable population (Jones et al. 1995). Furthermore, because of poaching, the few birds that still exist in the wild are in isolated, tiny population pockets whose genetic pool is continually shrinking without the addition of new breeding-aged birds.

Although every effort is being made to protect the few remaining birds in wild, and there are severe punishments for poaching, poaching still continues: wild captured birds are smuggled to Singapore where the birds are allegedly issued a CITES II certificate (which means they are captive bred, a "laundering" of illegal-status birds into legal-status ones), and can therefore be legally sold internationally. Despite the ban on capture, in the period 2001–2003 there were 100–300 wild-captured birds for sale at local markets in Bali and Java (Convention on International Trade 2004), in addition to those illegally exported whose numbers are unknown.

Aviary Notes

There is a voluminous amount of published materials pertaining to the breeding of the Yellow-crested Cockatoo in captivity. This is particularly true of the Orange-crested Cockatoo, undoubtedly because it is distinctive when compared to the other three races, and it is not a subspecies that is frequently encountered in captivity as are the other three.

The aviary size varies considerably from breeder to breeder. Breeding successes are reported by aviculturalists employing smaller aviary accommodations just as frequently as by those breeders providing their breeding pairs larger, over-sized aviaries. Kendall (1955, 1956, 1960) employed three different-sized flights ranging from as small as twelve feet in length to thirty-five feet (approximately 4 meters to 12 meters), all with equal success. In 1976, McPeek reported having successfully bred his bonded pair, which reared six fledglings from four separate clutches, in an aviary approximately 7.5 meters long × 1.5 meters wide × 1.5 meters high (24' × 5' × 5').

Upright grandfather-clock-type nest boxes and hollow logs were equally acceptable to breeding pairs, the actual nests in all cases being a meter to a meter and a half (3' to 5') above the ground. In the United States the cockatoos are introduced to the nest boxes from approximately the first week of April to the last week of May. Usually, the birds show an interest in the nest site almost immediately after its introduction. It is important to take into account that the males are known to be aggressive and have been known to injure the females, and also sometimes the offspring. Good husbandry includes clipping the three foremost flight feathers off one wing, just enough so that should the cock fall off its perch, it will be able to glide to the floor without injuring itself; by clipping the male's flight feathers, the male's flight will be hampered enough to permit the hen to escape his aggression if need be. Additionally, the nest box should be so constructed that should the male becomes dangerously aggressive, the female can easily flee the nest box without being harmed. World Parrot Trust (2012) recommends a nest box approximately 30.5 mm × 30.5 mm × 36.0 mm (12" × 12" × 14").

Compared to other species of cockatoo, the Yellow-crested Cockatoo is not as particular about the adequacy of the nest box provided it. Current cockatoo breeding husbandry recommends providing the cockatoo pair three to four assorted nesting site arrangements situated at different locations in the aviary. Once the birds have shown an interest favoring one of the nesting sites, it is recommended that the others be gradually removed. The Yellow-crested Cockatoo appears to be more accepting of whatever it is provided, based on the information provided by professional breeders, and the three to four different nesting boxes is reported usually not to be necessary.

The mating itself involves a considerable amount of courtship display before the first copulation. Kendal (1955) informs us that the male usually commenced with hopping movements towards the female, raising and lowering its wings, the male often covering the female with his wings. This was followed by a complicated bowing and head-to-tail display combined with beak clicking. Mutual preening was never reported being seen. Preening of any description does not seem to be associated with sexual display.

Mutual preening does often occur, however, just after a pair have been initially introduced to each other (McPeek 1976), and quite frequently there is also a considerable amount of beak clicking on such first introductions (Kendall; Rudkin 1942).

While the species has been known to breed as early as two years of age, the Yellow-crested Cockatoo is believed to normally reach sexual maturity from three to four years of age. The first egg is usually laid within two weeks of the first introduction to the nest box.

In this connection, as an amusing historical anecdote, it might be of interest to quote from Dr. Greene (reprint 1979) who, the reader will recollect, was a self-professed avian authority during the latter part of the 1800s. Green quoted from a correspondent referred to only as Jardin:

> In captivity, the female [i.e., Lesser Sulphur, race unidentified] sometimes produces eggs, and we now have specimens which are laid but one at peculiar periods; namely, the 21st of June, 21st of September, and 21st of December; but whether this resulted from the peculiar economy of the bird, as acted upon by the seasons, or was the effect of confinement, we are unable to determine.

Concerning this rather extremely strange anomaly, Greene later wrote, "The fact of the bird laying every three months on the same day of the month, is certainly very singular, and we are of the opinion it was simply a matter of coincidence and nothing more."

The average clutch is two elliptical eggs, occasionally three, the eggs measuring on average 41.0–27.0 mm (1.6" × 1") (World Parrot Trust 2012). In his *Handbuch der Oologie,*

Schonwetter (1964) reported the egg sizes as 38.1–44.0 mm and 25.7–28.4 mm (1.5″ × 1.2″). The second egg is normally laid five days after the first, and the second nestling fledges five to six days after the first. While there is at least one published account of a nesting pair being unperturbed by intrusion into the aviary (Wright 1948), the great majority of nesting pairs become aggressive and defensive when intruded upon (Rudkin 1942); indeed, Rudkin would only enter his aviary during his pair's brooding when he was armed with a bird net with which he could protect himself.

Incubation begins immediately after the first egg is laid, with the female doing most of the incubation. But during her sojourn on the nest, the male frequently enters the nest site at various intervals, presumably to feed her. During the entire incubation period the cock roosts outside, but once the eggs have hatched, the male begins spending the nights in the nest box.

Most breeders are reluctant to daily inspect the nest box, given the species' hostile temperament and response to intrusions on their rearing, and hence there is some confusion concerning the exact incubation time. Historically, a variety of time frames were suggested. McPeek (1976) confessed his incubation periods records were not exact because he had been reluctant to intrude on his nesting pairs; his notes reported a 28 day period, but a second nesting pair took 32 days. In 1955, Kendall, on the other hand, while he surmised his Orange-crested Cockatoo required 28 days, observed that his *C.s. parvula* had an incubation period that took three weeks.

Both adults share in parental responsibilities. Frequently, both adults are in the nest at the same time to feed the young. Kendall (1955) described the vocalizations of the young as an "eek-eek-eek," a sound accompanied by various "grumbles" and "querulous whines."

Kendall was usually quite methodological in his note keeping, noting important issues related to cockatoo husbandry. He informs us that at approximately one month of age the young birds were fully covered with quills and already had "quite well developed crests." At approximately six weeks the *C.s. parvula* juveniles were fully feathered. McPeek (1976) reported that one of his juvenile Orange-crested Cockatoos (age unspecified) had a yellow coloration to its breast area and that its cheeks were a deeper orange than that found on adults.

On fledging, there is little difference in appearance between the adults and the juveniles, except that the eye coloration is greyish in the young birds. Within a short time (period not specified), juvenile males and females acquire the eye color of their respective adult sexes: male iris color brown-black, and female eye color reddish-brown.

Just as there is ambiguity regarding the incubation period, so too is there confusion regarding the species' age of total independence after fledging.[9] Depending on the source, that age varies from ten to thirteen weeks. There may be some variance related to subspecies, but such a hypotheses is purely conjectural at this point without systematic scientific observation. It would appear, however, that the fledging age is between ten and twelve weeks. Smith (1970), for example, gives his *C.s. sulphurea* a ten-week period, whereas Kendall's *C.s. parvula* juveniles (according to the estimated dates Kendall provided) fledged in their twelfth or thirteenth week, and his Orange-crested Cockatoo juveniles fledged at eleven weeks.

The types of food provided the incubating and brooding pairs was reportedly a somewhat simple diet. Foods accepted by the various subspecies during this period appears to be contingent on what they had been accustomed to prior to breeding. Depending on the aviculturalist, professional or otherwise, there is some variance in the specific foods proffered the parenting birds. Staples in the birds' diets, however, appeared to be consistent from breeder to breeder. Seeds, sunflower, budgie mixes, and various cereals (barley, wheat, cracked maize) were basic. Dandelions were apparently the only greens that were consistently provided and just as consistently accepted, regardless of race. Sometimes, again depending on breeder, sweet corn or apples were provided to the brooding pairs.

Contemporary breeders provide their cockatoos with a greater variety of fruits and green foods, and limit the amount of seeds, particularly sunflower, peanuts, and safflower, because of their fat content, which tends to make captive birds obese. Vegetables such as celery, carrots, zucchini, butter beans, lentils, boiled maize, various green leaf produce consisting of chard, dandelions or chickweed, fruits such as oranges, apples, and bananas, and various nuts such as walnuts, pecans, hazelnuts are welcomed by even the birds with the most conservative of feeding habits (Arndt-verlag 2012; World Parrot Trust 2012).

Finally, the Yellow-crested Cockatoo likes to chew anything that is chewable. In the wild state, it chews on tree branches and strips bark from both trees and branches; such activities keep it physically and emotionally healthy. Captive birds should be provided comparable opportunities for maintaining their well-being. Several wooden perches of varying sizes and diameters should be installed throughout the aviary. Wooden and (vegetable oil cured) leather toys not only provoke the birds' interest but also keep the birds safe from boredom. In the wild the birds have many challenges. They have very few in captivity, unless provided some. Wild birds do not become neurotic because there is no stimulation. Caged birds do.

Nontoxic live branches complete with buds, leaves and/or fruit offer the birds not only things to chew upon, but food to eat. Be prepared to accept the necessity of ensuring the birds' well-being by replacing from time to time not only the totally devastated, and no longer interesting, toys, but also the very perches upon which they sit, and on which they frequently chew while perched upon them. The provision of some dangling ropes, not as easily destroyed and hence not necessarily requiring frequent replacement, can provide these intelligent birds with opportunities for exploration and diversion.

These captive, darling, intelligent birds deserve every opportunity to remain healthy, both emotionally and physically.

Pet Companion

A word or two of caution. The cockatoo exudes a white powder, which the bird uses in its feather grooming. Over a period of time, enough of the powder is exuded that it will be visible on nearby darker household objects. Anyone suffering breathing difficulties, such as asthmatic attacks, would be well advised to obtain another type of pet companion, because the powder could be detrimental to the health.

While the Yellow-crested Cockatoo has always been a popular pet in Indonesia and neighboring countries, it gained considerable popularity during the 1970s in the United States due to a weekly detective show called *Baretta* concerning a maverick New York detective (played by actor Robert Blake). The series had a considerable loyal following partly due to the "co-star" in the series, a Sulphur-crested Cockatoo named Fred who delighted his television audience with his various antics. (The cockatoo was actually a Triton Cockatoo *Cacatua galerita triton,* a species endemic to Australia, and not a Yellow-crested Cockatoo.) For the most part, North Americans' familiarity with parrots was limited to Central or South American parrot species, and in the public's mind cockatoos with a yellow crest were all the same—they were all cockatoos. From 1980 to 1984 the United States became the largest importer of the bird, importing 14,656 individuals in those four years, shortly after the television series' demise, and in the next eight years the U.S. imported an additional 24,000 birds (Convention 2004). The next biggest importer of the Yellow-crested Cockatoo was Singapore with 17,714 birds, most of which allegedly were subsequently exported elsewhere under the guise of being captive-bred birds, hence satisfying nations concerned with potentially violating CITES' embargo against capture of wild parrots for sale in the pet trade.

The species' popularity is due to a variety of factors. It can be taught tricks, say a few words and/or phrases, sing, and sit contentedly on one's shoulder, from time to time proffering kisses. Primary of them all, the Yellow-crested Cockatoo can develop strong bonds with its owner, with whom it identifies, as is true of most cockatoos; because they are so intelligent, they emotionally interact with their owners—a reciprocal emotional interaction that is mutually beneficial and mutually rewarding. This person-bird interaction is essential in order to ensure the bird's emotional health. By its very nature, the bird has to be outside of its cage if it is going to interact with anyone.

When the bird is freed from its caged confines, it should not be left alone. Aside from damaging furniture or other items in the room, it can cause injury, or even death to itself, because every room in every household has various dangerous circumstances and objects that the bird companion should be protected from, such as electrical wires.

There is some disagreement regarding the emotional demands that the cockatoo makes on its owner: there are some who argue that the species is too "clingy," a "velcro" bird, an unfavorable personality trait if an owner does not have the time to devote to his pet's demands. Others argue that the species is no less demanding, and hence clinging, than other cockatoo species: anyone desirous of a cockatoo companion needs to have three or four free hours daily for interaction with her pet. Otherwise, the bird can develop neurotic behaviors such as feather plucking or excessive shrieking.

While the species is endearing to just about everyone except to avian-phobic individuals, the Yellow-crested Cockatoo has a loud voice, one that can soon alienate neighbors, particularly in a condominium or apartment building, even those neighbors who initially found the cockatoo delightful and endearing.

The cockatoo is known for its loving personality, and while it can acquire a limited vocabulary if its trainer is persistent, its vocabulary will be limited as compared to other psittacidines. The Triton Cockatoo, in the *Baretta* television series, had an extensive vocabulary, was capable of riding a bike or scooter, ran on a treadmill, and performed other delightful antics. The Yellow-crested Cockatoo can also be trained to perform various tricks such as dancing or lying on its back, or more complicated feats. Patience and perseverance are required, but the daily interaction between owner and the pet can be a catalyst and be put to good use in training the bird.

While the species and its various races are sharply declining in numbers in the wild, they are bred in captivity and are therefore available for purchase from time to time in limited numbers. In some countries, such as Great Britain, the Yellow-crested Cockatoo cannot be sold or purchased unless it is accompanied by a CITES Article 10 Certificate. Wild-caught birds are no longer available for purchase in most countries, even though some birds are still poached from the wild and surreptitiously smuggled into countries where CITES prohibitions are ignored. And while Indonesia has stringent laws to protect the species, they are still being poached in the wild and sold locally.

Birds now bred in captivity are often implanted with a microchip identifying the bird, its source, history, and so on. A search on the Internet (2012) for Yellow-crested Cockatoos for sale in the United States and Canada (Winter 2013) resulted in six classified ads, the prices ranging from $850 to $1,500, depending on the seller and the age of the cockatoo. In Great Britain a comparable bird accompanied by a CITES certificate was comparably priced. (There were no ads for the *C.s. citrinocristata*.)

Besides an adequate and nutritious diet, the cockatoo requires suitable housing, preferably in a room where there are considerable family activities and opportunities for ample interaction between the bird and family members. A bird cage, if a bird room is not possible, should be at least a meter cubed (3' × 3' × 3'): the bigger the better. Being intelligent, cockatoos are notorious for being escape artists: the cage should be outfitted with a locking system to prevent escapes when there is no one available to chaperone the bird to prevent mischief.

In the cage, provide at least two wooden perches of different lengths and diameters, several leather and wooden toys to chew, a dangling rope to swing on from time to time, and whenever possible, a live branch from a nontoxic tree. If it should also have some fruit, so much the better. Because these toys, branches, and wooden perches are essential to keeping the pet occupied, as opposed to bored by its limited environment, be prepared to periodically replace all those items from time to time as they are routinely demolished.

The Yellow-crested Cockatoo loves to bathe. Spray it occasionally with a spray misting bottle. If need be, the bird can be gently blown dry with a hair blower. The mist spraying is fun for everyone.

Finally, it cannot be overemphasized: unless you have at least three or so hours a day in which you and your pet can interact emotively, it is best not to acquire a cockatoo.

4

Sulphur-crested Cockatoo
Cacatua galerita (Latham, 1790)

COMMON NAMES: Greater Sulphur-crested Cockatoo (USA usage), Yellow-crested
      Cockatoo, Mathews Cockatoo (Fitzroy Cockatoo), White Cockatoo
      (Australia, now obsolete), Cocky (Australian usage)

SUBSPECIES:
1. Greater Sulphur-crested Cockatoo, *Cacatua galerita galerita* (Latham, 1790)—Nominate Race
2. Triton Cockatoo, *Cacatua galerita triton* (Temminck, 1849)
3. Eleanora Cockatoo, *Cacatua galerita eleanora* (Finsch, 1863)
4. Fitzroy Cockatoo, *Cacatua galerita fitzroy* (Mathews, 1912)

LIFESPAN: (authenticated 82+ years[1]); authenticated 80, 81, and 120 years[2] (in all
    instances the particular race of the *C. galerita* was not disclosed).

IUCN RED LIST OF THREATENED SPECIES: Least Concern

CITES: Appendix II

Description

All four races of *Cacatua galerita* are completely white except for the crest, iris color, feet, and some minor yellow colorations of the underparts of the wing and tail. They are the largest of white cockatoos, on average weighing 700–950 grams (24.7–31.75 ounces) with a body length of 45–50 cm (17.7"–19.6"); the two Australian races *(C.s. galerita* and *C.s. fitzroyi)* are larger than the two *C. Galerita* forms from nearby New Guinea and various satellite islands (Forshaw 1977).

The entire head is white except for the long, recurvent crest, whose bright yellow feather tips curve slightly upwards and forward towards the beak when the crest is lying flat. The ear coverts have a yellow tinge, but such coloration is neither outstanding in brightness nor consistently distributed in all individuals throughout any given regional population. All other neck and head feathers are white at the terminal ends and faint yellow at the base.

All four races have a naked periophthalmic ring, and depending on the subspecies, the ring may be either bluish tinted or bare white. The bill is black, curved, and downward pointing, with the upper mandible slightly longer than the lower mandible. Although the beak is genetically black, it appears greyish given the large amount of white powder that the species generates through the disintegration of its down and uses in grooming its feathers.

The inner webs of the flight feathers are yellow with some yellow also washed lightly through the under coverts. Similarly, the under tail coverts are also yellow-washed.

The feet are mealy black, the four toes are zygodactyl, and the inner thighs are grey. For all intents and purposes, the species can be considered sexually monomorphic despite the fact that there is a slight eye coloration difference between the males and females, and males have a marginally larger head; the male's eye color is a dark blackish brown whereas the female's is a reddish brown. The difference in color of the irises is so slight that unless the light of the day is just right, providing optimal light conditions, differentiating sex by eye color is difficult and hence unreliable. Often a flashlight is necessary, and that in itself is not an assured guarantee of being able to accurately determine an individual's sex.

Upon fledging, the juvenile birds closely resemble the overall appearance of the adult. However, the juvenile's eye color is that of an adult female, and the eye color may remain on juvenile males for some time after fledging, making it virtually impossible to differentiate juvenile females from males without DNA testing or surgical procedures.

The basic differences between the various races lie primarily in size differentials, although there are some slight color differences in respect to the brightness of the yellow parts, in periophthalmic ring color, and in some other minor physiological characteristics.

The two Australian races—*C.s. galerita* and *C.s. fitzroyi*—are similar in size; on average the *C.s. galerita* is the larger of the two races, with a wing span ranging from as little as 311 mm to 391 mm (approximately 12"–15"), whereas the *C.s. fitzroyi* has a wing span ranging from 316 mm to 354 mm (approximately 12.5"–14"). The *C.s. galerita* has a somewhat narrower beak and a stronger, brighter yellow coloration to its ear coverts, in addition to having a slightly bluish tinge to its periophthalmic ring. A separation can be made, however, by a simple comparison of the two forms by their periophthalmic rings: the Fitzroy Cockatoo has the bluish ring whereas the Sulphur-crested Cockatoo's ring is white. In addition, although it is a totally unreliable method of differentiating the two forms, the Fitzroy Cockatoo has less yellow than the Nominate Race.

In regards to the two extralimital races, the *C.s. eleanora* (Avian Web 2012a) and the *C.s. triton* are considerably smaller than the Australian forms. The Triton Cockatoo also differs from the mainland races in that its crest feathers are more rounded and broad, and there is almost no yellow to its ear coverts. Like the Fitzroy Cockatoo, its periophthalmic ring is bluish tinged. Forshaw notes that the Eleanora Cockatoo,[3] the smallest of the four races with a wing span ranging 267 mm–292 mm (10.5"–11.5"), while closely resembling the Triton Cockatoo with somewhat more yellow to the ear coverts and underlying bases to throat feathers, has a much smaller bill. The distinctive feature unique to all four races is their yellow-tipped recumbent crest feathers; their crests are also similar to three of the races of the slightly smaller Yellow-crested Cockatoo forms, whose crests are also yellow-tinged at the end of their recumbent crest feathers.

The Greater Sulphur-crested Cockatoos are frequently and easily confused with the smaller Yellow-crested Cockatoos. Although only two of the four Sulphur-crested Cockatoos are endemic to Australia, all four Yellow-crested Cockatoos are endemic to Indonesia and Timor-leste, and none to Australia. The Yellow-crested Cockatoos are smaller, their beaks are wider and heavier, and their upper mandible is less protruding. Additionally, their crests are somewhat narrower than those of the Sulphur-crested Cockatoos. Finally, while two of the four Sulphur- crested Cockatoos are extralimital to Australia, their distribu-

The Sulphur-crested Cockatoo is probably the most readily recognized of all the parrot species. It is intelligent and affectionate, and it can be taught a variety of complicated tasks such as riding a bicycle. It also is a raucous bird whose screeching can alienate neighbors and often family members, frequently leading to it being sold or given to a zoo or bird park (photograph by Charles Lam).

tion in the myriad of land masses and island archipelagos north of that continent is limited and does not overlap with any of the distributions of the Yellow-crested Cockatoo's populations.

As is true of other cockatoo species, the Sulphur-crested Cockatoo's crests usually lie flat on the top of the head, but can be erected at will. When the cockatoo erects its crest it is in response to any number of emotive states: defense of territory, fear, curiosity, anger, danger, as a warning, or part of a courtship display, or any one of a number of other diverse emotional responses to an environmental situation or provocation. A lowered crest indicates a general approachability, friendliness, or a state of well-being, calmness.

Behavior

The Sulphur-crested Cockatoo is a gregarious species; in Australia both races often gather in flocks numbering in the thousands, although in general, most flocks number fewer than three hundred or so individuals. While flocking behavior always excites the viewer's attention, it is the large immense flocks that are most impressive. As early as the turn of the nineteenth century the flocking phenomenon captured naturalists' attention. White in 1913, for example, recounted his experience seeing one such flock: "During several mornings ... the pointed top of the hill has been covered by thousands of Cockatoos, crowded so closely together that from a distance the mass represents the exact appearance of snow—*in fact, several people who witnessed the sight for the first time declared the hill was covered with snow!*" (emphasis added).

In some areas, however, flocks are rarely encountered. In areas where human intrusion has dramatically altered the environment so that native feeding and nesting grounds have virtually vanished, or where the birds have been ruthlessly persecuted because they are considered pests, the Sulphur-crested Cockatoo is generally found only in small groups (Roberts 1957). Regardless of environmental conditions or human persecution, however, the Triton Cockatoo is rarely encountered in groups larger than three or four individuals (Rand and Gilliard 1968).

The two subspecies' normal food choices include the seed pods of the caussarina, various palm berries, leaf buds, ant eggs, hawthorn berries, beetle larvae, various tuberous roots, and even sea weed, but with the advent of wide scale grain production, grain has become a basic staple in the species' diet.

The Sulphur-crested Cockatoo shows a high degree of adaptability in responding to wide spread agribusiness, which places hundreds of thousands of hectares under grain production. The species has learned to raid planted fields with apparent immunity despite a host of attempts to protect crops from extensive damage.

The Australian races have developed a sentinel system in response to farmers' efforts to protect their grain crops. At most times, when flocks arrive at a grain field to feed, various sentries will post themselves high on nearby trees to warn the feeding flock of any impending danger. Periodically, each sentinel is replaced by an already-fed individual from the flock, who then assumes sentinel duty while the replaced sentinel rejoins the feeding flock. Given the sentinel system, it is virtually impossible to approach the feeding—and crop-devastating—birds: at the slightest alarm call from a sentinel, the entire flock immediately flees with immunity.

Such was not always the case earlier in the relationship between the species and the grain producers. As early as 1907, Batey argued that as agricultural practices concentrated on grain production, there concurrently developed a proliferation of variegated thistles. This type of underbrush is preferred by Sulphur-crested Cockatoos as a natural environmental cover. Since the thistles are closely associated with agricultural practices, the cockatoos were subsequently and inadvertently attracted to grain fields. Since that analysis over a century ago, the grain fields have remained a major food destination, regardless of all efforts to protect the crops.

The early reports of grain damage by the species about the turn of the last century were almost always accompanied by observations that in some localities combined gunfire and poisons[4] had been so lethally effective that the Sulphur-crested Cockatoo had become rare in some areas where it had been common. During the intervening sixty years or so, however, the species has become exceedingly wary; its sentinel system negates the value of gunfire to control its numbers and grain-foraging damage.

The birds are always wary, regardless of whether or not they are feeding and regardless of the particular situation the species may encounter at any given moment. In 1916 Hill observed, for example, that a bird would silently fly away even though Hill was at least 300 yards distant. He wrote, "Although I walked as silently as possible, against the wind, it made no difference, the bird always flew away." Interestingly, in his field experiments, he found that when he approached a particular bird it would fly away even though at times it was impossible for the bird to have seen him.

Many species of wildlife adapt well with diverse strategies to cope with the dangers emanating from humans. The sentinel strategy of the Sulphur-crested Cockatoo reminds me of a comparable avian intelligence. When I was a young man in southern Ontario in Canada, I annually hunted pheasants during the autumn hunting season. Prior to the pheasant season opening, my hunting cronies and I would walk through open pastures and unharvested agricultural fields, particularly unharvested corn fields, to determine whether or not there were any small flocks of pheasants in that region so that on the opening day of the pheasant season, we had some idea where we could find birds. Regardless of where we went in our pre-hunt explorations, we saw numerous crows who paid us little attention, going about their daily business of feeding, resting, or assessing us as potential threats. On opening day, after sunrise when the season officially opened, when we arrived the crows ignored our vehicle, as usual. They ignored us as we disembarked. They ignored us when we went to the trunk to get our shotguns. But when the shotguns came into view, every crow, young and old, immediately fled, crying out discordantly their warning calls. I am pleased to say I have not hunted for almost fifty years, and have come to admire the species for its cleverness.

So too, the Sulphur-crested Cockatoo is now apparently able to differentiate between armed and unarmed men, so that the matter of even attempting to approach crop-feeding flocks with a shotgun in hand becomes a useless exercise in the constant war against the species. Scarecrows are just as ineffective. In 1973 Cayley ironically noted that sentinels are often posted on the scarecrows themselves, a behavior also characteristic of crows, regardless of the region of the world.

Interestingly, the Sulphur-crested Cockatoos' sentinel system is not characteristic behavior of the two non–Australian subspecies, as it is with the two continental Australian forms. The difference between the Australian forms and the extralimital races may be a matter of evolutionary function directly related to flocking tendencies and to local agricultural food production practices, which consist primarily of small family garden plots. The Triton Cockatoo, for example, is almost exclusively arboreal and is rarely found in groups numbering more than half a dozen individuals. Since this particular race is a minor threat to agricultural production at best, and its damages to crops are minor, it is not vigorously persecuted, and indeed, as has been noted earlier, this subspecies' adaptation to the encroachment by humans has been simply to move into heavily forested areas at higher altitudes. Given its arboreal habits, its more solitary in nature, and its general avoidance of cultivated areas, there has been no need for the evolution of a sophisticated sentinel system.

While the non–Australian forms are benign towards agriculture, the Australian races are responsible for a considerable degree of destruction to grain crops. The species will not only raid fields that have yet to be harvested, but will also raid grain fields where the grain has just been recently sown. The birds are attracted to the seeds still unsprouted and to seeds already revealing young, green sprouts. The birds will later plunder that same field just when the crop is mature and ready for harvesting.

When fields are ripening, a few "prospectors" or "scouts" will generally arrive at the farmer's fields, remaining in the vicinity a few days and then disappearing. A few days later, as Batey a century ago observed in 1907, the main flock will appear at the ripening crop fields. Grain that had already been harvested is no less immune to the cockatoos' depredations. Grain bagged in the field and remaining there for removal is plundered with equal effectiveness. As early as 1916 Mellor (in Mathews 1916) wrote, "Where the farmers stack their wheat in the open ... they [the Greater Sulphur-crested Cockatoos] will soon find it out, and rip open the bags, let the golden grain out, and then eat it at their leisure."

These feeding practices, at the risk of appearing anthromorphic, suggest several characteristics pertaining to the Greater Sulphur-crested Cockatoo's behavior. The species is not only capable of devising a successful protective sentinel system to warn flock members of danger, but also appears to have developed the wherewithal to scout new foraging opportunities, especially large scale grain production areas, and convey that information to other members of a much larger flock community. Prior to the advent of human agricultural practices that altered the traditional feed resource opportunities, and in fact expanded them, the species historically fed at different areas during different seasons as various native food stuffs became seasonably available. Now, this cockatoo has generalized its communal knowledge of seasonal food availability to include the introduced human crops of grain, and the periods when it is available.

Despite the relentless war waged against the species, the Sulphur-crested Cockatoo maintains its population numbers as if it were totally immune to gunfire and to the various other methods devised against them to protect the grain fields. The failure of the onslaught against the species can be attributed to nothing more than the species' uncanny wariness, in addition to its intelligence. This wariness is so effective a protective strategy that a flock will continue using the same roosting site for years on end, despite constant, successive, and persistent efforts to decimate the community's numbers there. In 1916, Mathews wrote of one such flock numbering in the thousands that used the same nesting site for thirty-five years without any appreciable effect on its population, despite the consistent yearly onslaught against it.

Each resident flocks is not only a permanent resident in its own particular locality, but is distinctly a population unit in itself, quite separate from other local flocks in the same area. In the Goulbourne District, for example, Bedgegood wrote in 1958 of his amazement when he realized that after almost a century of unsuccessful persecution of local flocks in efforts to prevent or at least to minimize crop predation, he was still able to identify seven such original flocks that were permanent residents in the area, and had been so for at least a century, each flock numbering at least 200 individuals.

Even capture for the pet trade had little effect on flocks. In 1914, MacGillivray wrote that extremely large numbers of cockatoos were annually captured for the pet trade without noticeable reduction in population numbers. He wrote, "A family of bird catchers ... sent over 300 young birds ... away to market in 1899 ... and have been doing so for the past fifteen years without appreciably diminishing their numbers." The bird catchers were capturing their birds from the same flock, year after year.

However, in some localities, flocks may suddenly appear as if from nowhere, as visitors, tourists in a manner of speaking. Baldwin in 1975 reported that the flocks appearing in the New South Wales region of Inverell were "irregular, nomadic in fluctuating numbers." It is speculated that this irregularity may in fact be related to uncertain food supplies, and that perhaps the species is more nomadic than currently understood.

When going to roost, these large flocks make a most impressive sight. For those accustomed to the harsh shrieking vocalizations of the Sulphur-crested Cockatoo, one can just imagine the overwhelming din emanating from hundreds, if not thousands, of these cockatoos, their vocal din deafening, assaulting the ear with wave after wave of discordant, harsh cries. The panorama of flock behavior during these shrieking orchestrations is no less impressive: countless individuals rising above the tree tops, settling down again, only to rise once, twice, or more times, while countless other birds also rise and settle, over and over. The birds call constantly to each other until gradually one by one the birds settle down for the night and the pre-roosting ballet gradually concludes.

These roosting sites, as noted above, may be occupied continuously by the same flock for years, despite consistent and unrelenting harassment and persecution from farmers, hunters, and livestock dealers, and despite the fact that often, depending on the availability of food supplies, the cockatoos may have to fly considerable distances to their feeding grounds. Moreover, since the birds are so wary, making it virtually impossible to approach them during the day, the species is sometimes shot at night when it is roosting. But night hunting has some distinct disadvantages vis-à-vis the numbers of birds that can be located in thick forests during poor lighting, and then subsequently shot. Additionally, a farmer who is confronted with a wide number of daily chores would be hard pressed to find several nights a week to find and shoot the grain foragers. However, while night hunting may be problematic when a farmer is burdened with chores, shooting the cockatoos can help reduce the grocery bill. It has long been noted that the Sulphur-crested Cockatoo makes an excellent meal.

Even many field expeditionists have shot them for supper (see, for example, Bennet 1935). Given that the bird is considered a palatable meal, it would not be unreasonable to assume that farmers who killed several while protecting their crops would add them to their freezers, similar to bagging pheasants in Great Britain or southern Ontario.

Departure from the roosting site in the morning is not expedited by the rising sun. With sunrise, the shrieking and squabbling begin anew. The flock eventually moves on to its favorite watering hole.

The best that can be said about the species, gift of vocalization is that it is a most unpleasant screeching, and that it is so unpleasant to the ear that few aviculturalists or avian companion bird enthusiasts are prepared to tolerate it from a pet bird for any length of time. Indeed, while the species is considerable a desirable pet companion, most owners are ultimately forced to sell their screeching bird, or donate it to a zoo or other such agency.

Individual birds and their vocal propensities have been described in a host of ways, none of them complimentary. Tavistock and Delacour (1926), both noted aviculturalists, wrote, "If it gets excited it screams horribly." Frith described their vocalizations as "a disyllabic, metallic screech ... even when squabbling a series of sharp, grating shrieks." While some wildlife observers and/or environmental tourists may be awed at the spectacle of a throng of cockatoos and described their awesome behaviors and discordant eardrum-threatening vocalizations as a "thrill of a life time," a differing point of view was best described by a Mr. Elsey, who wrote to Mathews (in Mathews 1916), "The presence of a flock ... is certain to be indicated by their screaming notes, the discordance of which may be easily conceived by those who have heard the peculiarly loud, piercing grating scream of the bird in captivity, always remembering the immense increase of the din occasioned by the large number of birds emitting their harsh notes at the same moment."

While the birds' vocalizations can be considered at best horrendous, their flight can be described as nature's artistry: the birds' brief periods of gentle gliding interspersed by shallow wing beats is "candy" to the eye. The flight path is usually at considerable altitudes, and when landing, the cockatoos gradually glide down in long sweeping circles, an impressive, tranquil spectacle in itself.

After watering, the birds fly to their feeding grounds, which vary between seasons depending on which food sources are currently available, and which might be still sustainable despite several days of feeding at the given site. A popular feeding area will be exploited day after day until the food supply is exhausted. This daily persistence to continue to feed at a given resource until there is insufficient food left to sustain the flock can have an obvious grave implication for a grain field's productivity, and the economic consequences for the farmer. In order to protect the grain fields' economic viability, considerable pest control efforts are essential, even though they may prove for the most part ineffective.

In some instances, because the flocks are so multitudinous, this food exhaustion occurs within a few days and thereafter the flock must rely on a large number of other available foods, some of them at considerable distances from each other and from the roosting site. While the food sources vary in their distances one from the other, the roosting site remains the same, usually year after year.

Once the birds have left their roosting areas, their feeding activities begin after they have watered, and will continue so well into midmorning.

The behavior of the extralimital non–Australian races follows a considerably different daily pattern. While on rare occasions a flock consisting of 100–200 individuals may be encountered, such flocks for the most part are rare, and the usual number of birds per group generally varies between two or three to half a dozen birds. And, unlike mainland Australian races, where large flocks are common, larger non–Australian flocks of several individuals normally break up into smaller groups of two to four birds for feeding purposes. As adaptable and clever as the species is, this variance in feeding behavior may be the direct result of the particular agricultural practices employed in island agricultural economies; large-acreage grain farms in Australia favor species congregations and can more readily support large numbers of foraging birds, whereas agricultural practices for indigenous island farmers involve small garden plots that not only are unable to sustain large flocks of birds, but are not grain-oriented.

During mid-day, when the day is hottest, the Sulphur-crested Cockatoo rests in the trees. Resting may be punctuated by mutual preening behavior, but in general, the birds occupy themselves by stripping off the bark from the branches and by nipping off both leaves and buds. Later in the afternoon, after the day's heat has abated, the cockatoos return to their feeding grounds, where they remain until the early evening hours. Then they return to their roosting areas and the rituals that will accompany their pre-roosting behavior there.

Habitat and Distribution

The species has two distinct populations insofar as two of the four races are endemic to the continent of Australia, and the other two are extraterritorial. The two Australian races are themselves separate from each other geographically; the other two non–Australian Sulphur-crested Cockatoo subspecies similarly occupy various island groups geographically separate from each other.

In Australia, the Greater Sulphur-crested Cockatoo (*C.s. galerita*) is common along the eastern coast, where it can be found as far south Victoria, southwards to Tasmania, and as far north as Cape York in Queensland. The race is also endemic to South Australia westwards up to the Spence Bay area. Kangeroo Island and Tasmania are included in this distribution, as is King Island, situated between Tasmania (Rowley) and the southern coast of Victoria. The species was introduced to New Zealand as early as 1955 and is now considered well established at several locations, but poorly documented. It has also been successfully introduced to Singapore, where it is now estimated to number between 500 and 2,000 individuals (Avian Web 2012b); the species has been also introduced to Taiwan, Brazil and reportedly to Hong Kong (Oiseaux 2012).

The Fitzroy Cockatoo (*C.s. fitzsroyi*) can be found occupying northern Australia from the Gulf of Carpentaria to as far west as Kimberley in Western Australia. The two subspecies meet around the Gulf of Carpenteria, where their ranges overlap. It is also common to Melville Island and some of the larger islands off the northern coast. During the 1930s several individuals were either released and/or were escaped pets in the Perth region, and their descendants have now multiplied into a considerable population that is thriving in the Perth area.

Both races are relatively rare in extremely arid terrains, or in regions where there are few trees. There does not appear to be a line of integration between the two Australian forms. Both races exhibit specific characteristics in size, beak shape, and minor color differentials that are unique to their respective populations, but the genetic traits common to either of the two races cannot be considered either exclusive or restrictive. There are wide variances from genetic norms within the given populations, and such deviations have been so consistently encountered throughout each population that there has been considerable controversy concerning the degree of subspeciation that has taken place.

The species reveals a remarkable adaptability to humans despite its wariness and long history of persecution. It is now abundant and commonly found in the suburbs of several cities: Brisbane, Adelaide, Sydney, Melbourne, and Canberra. In these cities and their suburbs, while many citizens welcome their presence, the cockatoos are known to cause damage to wooden structures such as benches, verandas, and fences. Some urban residents enjoy feeding the birds, which encourages the birds to return habitually, and often when there are no feedings available, the birds damage wooden structures.

The extralimital species, the Eleanor and Triton cockatoos, both occupy islands in the Indonesia area: the Eleanora Cockatoo is native to the Aru Islands in the province of Maluku in eastern Indonesia, the islands situated approximately 200 kilometers west of West Iran and 500 kilometers north of Arnhem Land, Australia. Their natural habitat includes woodlands, mallees and scrubs. It has also been introduced to mainland Indonesia as well.

The Triton Cockatoo (*C.s. triton*) occupies a wide geographical area including most of New Guinea and its diverse island groups such as those found off the west coast of Papua, in the Serera Bay Islands in West Irian, the D'Entrecasteaux Islands off eastern Japua, and the more southern Louisiade Archipelago. Indeed, this race is commonly encountered throughout most of the island groups in the western area of the Solomon Sea.

The Sulphur-crested Cockatoo is a remarkable species. Quite intelligent, it is adaptable to diverse environments. Because two of the four races occupy totally different terrains from the other two forms, the range of the Australian form's distribution based on its environmental amenability and adaptability is remarkable: in Australia, it can be found occupying both humid and semi-humid areas, and if water is available, it can be found even in semi-arid terrains, although not in large, awe-inspiring flocks. The species is commonly encountered throughout much of its range in mallees, pine grove regions, open areas, and red gum lake localities (Jones 1954). In other regions, the species may show a distinctive preference for one terrain over another ostensibly comparable terrain, the preference may be based on a number of different variables such as water accessibility, distance from traditional roosting areas, nesting opportunities, and frequency of persecution.

Both the Australian and non–Australian races show considerable differences in their daily lives and behaviors, but the differences are determined in a large part by environmental constraints or opportunities rather than race differences.

In New Guinea, for example, a vast island (complete with a host of satellite islands), the species prefers the thick jungles found on hillsides (Tubb 1945), and while the Sulphur-crested Cockatoo is more commonly found in lower and more moderate elevations, it is by no means uncommon in the forests often associated with higher elevations (Mosey 1956)—in some instances it can be found as high as 6000 feet (approximately 1850 meters) above sea level (Diamond 1972).

Ripley in 1964 argued that the forest destruction at the lower altitudes was in response to increased demand for agricultural products; as forests were felled to expand plantations, the cockatoos were driven to new altitudes, an excellent adaptative response to man's alteration of the environment.

It has also been found that there is a direct correlation between the size of the birds and the altitude of the terrains they occupy, at least in the Triton Cockatoo. Rand (1942) found that birds collected at higher altitudes were significantly larger than individuals collected at lower altitudes.

Propagation

The species' breeding season varies, depending on where the cockatoos are located. In southern Australia the season stretches from August to January, whereas in Northern Australia the breeding begins in May and ends in September; there is a similar breeding period for the extralimital forms in Indonesia and the diverse islands north of Australia.

The species generally reaches sexual maturity at four to five years of age, at which time the first breeding usually occurs. However, while the four- to five-year period appears to be the norm for sexual maturity, there are records of some individuals that did not breed until their sixth or even seventh year, and there have been some instances of the species breeding as young as two years of age. These variances relate to food availability and various other environmental circumstances, some too subtle to identify.

The Sulphur-crested Cockatoo has a courtship display similar to that of the Leadbeater Cockatoo (*Lophochroa leadbeateri*). It is simple and brief: the male struts along the tree limb towards the female, his crest erect, his tail feathers spread wide, his head moving in a figure-eight, his courtship seduction accompanied by a serenade consisting of a low keyed but continuous chatter. After the display, and if the seduction is successful, the cock and hen mutually preen each other and indulge in considerable beak touching. Pairs mate for life. Once the hen has accepted the cock, their construction of their nest begins. During the entire nest construction process there are periodic courtship displays, and many similar displays prior to actual copulation. These constant displays undoubtedly reinforce the bonding of the pair, a bonding that culminates in the lifelong pairing.

The Sulphur-crested Cockatoo appears to be adaptable and diversified in its choice of tree so long as it has an appropriate nest hollow, and the hollow is at least ten meters (35') above ground level. The cockatoo, however, does prefer the eucalyptus tree, and prefers a tree located near a waterway. Because it is a gregarious bird, it will be found communally nesting with countless other pairs in its immediate vicinity. In various regions where the species is commonly found and trees are scarce, they are known to nest in colonies in cliffs high above a waterway. Captain White (in Mathews 1916) described one of the cliff breeding communal colonies: "They congregate in great numbers at nesting time and take possession of the holes worn by the weather into the high cliffs rising several hundreds of feet out of the water; here they lay their eggs upon the bare sand.... It is a very interesting sight to see many hundreds of these birds half out of their nesting holes or sitting upon the ledges of rock near their nests." They have even been known to nest on top of haystacks (IAATE 2012).

For pairs nesting in trees, the appropriate site is usually located in the hollow of the trunk or the stump of a limb, the nest itself being as much as six feet (two meters) down from the entrance. Such nesting hollows are at a premium, and the Sulphur-crested Cockatoo is in competition with other breeding pairs, including those of other avian species. When preparing the nest, both adults chew at the entrance; the chips falling to the bottom add to whatever nesting materials are already there. Besides the chipped wood and rotted core-wood dust in the hollow, the pair will often snip off buds from branches adjacent to the nest site entrance and use them to complement the nesting materials already there. Sometimes, trees will be stripped in their entirety of all buds, and if the tree is used year after year, it will ultimately die due to the continual defoliating. Such trees will be eventually overlooked in preference for live trees during later breeding seasons, but if live options are unavailable, a nest-oriented pair will claim a hollow in a dead tree so long as the hollow meets their requirements.

In the wild, little is known of the growth cycle of the young, the foods they are fed, their appearance, and other particulars concerning their development. The lack of information is in part due to the fact that nests are often located in difficult-to-access sites such as in towering trees or cliffs; even when there is some scaling opportunity permitting access to a nest, if sensing danger the female will quietly slip away from the nest thereby concealing its presence.

On fledging, the juveniles remain with the adults as a family unit, a bond that is believed to last several years, although there is not systematic data supporting that belief.

Aviary Notes

While the Sulphur-crested Cockatoo is recognized internationally for the beautiful and intelligent bird that it is, the species is not commonly bred in captivity for a number of practical reasons, particularly in Australia. In the first place, in Australia, where there are a wide variety of parrot and cockatoos species available for both hobbyists and professional breeders, an aviary-bred Sulphur-crested Cockatoo is difficult to sell given that without a licence, nestlings can be legally taken from the wilds and hand trained. Why pay for a bird when one can be obtained without cost? But with a wild bird, there is always the possibility that it may be harboring the virus of the Psittaccine Beak and Feather Disease (PBFD), a disease that can be easily spread to other birds in one's aviaries. There is no known cure for this disease: an infected bird has to be destroyed. For an Australian, the solution to this difficulty is to purchase a bird from a professional aviculturalist. But there is a Catch–22 for all concerned. Despite being intelligent and a strikingly beautiful bird, it is a species difficult to live with: it is an extremely emotionally demanding bird, a bird capable of considerable damage to personal property, a cockatoo whose shrieking and screaming becomes intolerable for most owners, causing the bird to finally be removed from the home. Given the bird's negative reputation as a pet, an Australian professional aviculturalist breeding them for sale in order to meet operating expenses and still earn enough money upon which to live is facing an unsound business venture. And the Sulphur-crested Cockatoo is, when compared with other birds, including aviary bred cockatoos, quite inexpensive. Today (January 2013) birds were available in New South Wales for AU$110, and AU$250 for a proven pair. Hand fed juveniles were available for only AU$400. Additionally, the cockatoo is considered difficult to breed and its breeding is recommended for specialist breeders only (Bird Care 2012).

In addition to having to acquire some expertise in aviary husbandry of the Sulphur-crested Cockatoo, it is important to obtain two birds that are compatible with each other. The bird does not always breed well in captivity, and to have a pair of incompatible cockatoos who are interested neither in each other nor in raising a family, and probably might never be, dooms the venture to failure regardless of the degree of expertise and knowledge of the breeder. Additionally, if the pair is incompatible there is always the risk that the male will become aggressive and injure the female.

In Europe or North America where there are far fewer Sulphur-crested Cockatoos available for sale, breeding the species does not entail the difficulties associated with breeding a species that few people want. The few hand fed babies that are annually available for sale are exceeded by the number of willing purchasers. In the southern United States the species nests between August and January.

Since the Sulphur-crested Cockatoo is a large bird, an appropriately large aviary is necessitated. Bird Care (2012) recommends an aviary of minimally four to five meters long, preferably up to 7 meters long, and at minimum 1.2 to 1.5 meters wide and about 2.1 meters high (about 16' × 5' × 7'). The aviary should be sheathed in a heavy-gauge wire mesh, preferably one that is galvanized and welded. The added length of the aviary provides the birds opportunities to maintain good health and obtain adequate exercise.

Several perches of varying lengths and thickness should be interspersed throughout the aviary. Given sufficient space within the aviary, the pair should be provided with a choice of potential nesting sites: four or five hollow, upright logs and/or grandfather-clock-style nest boxes. Once the pair have shown an interest in a particular one, the other nest boxes or logs should be gradually removed. Should that particular year's nesting prove successful, that same nest box or log should be retained for that pair for the following year.

The log or nesting box is recommended by Bird Care to have a length of at least 1000 mm (3.5') and to have an internal hollow diameter of approximately 350 mm (1.3'). The bottom should be lined with wood chips, decomposed nontoxic sawdust, or other suitable but nontoxic materials.

The Sulphur-crested Cockatoo enjoys chewing and should be provided ample opportunities to do so. Live, nontoxic tree branches should be provided the birds, preferably branches with leaves and or buds still on them; the birds enjoy shredding and demolishing the branches. Because the cockatoos are intelligent and inquisitive, simple wooden toys can be purchased or home manufactured and provided to the birds for both amusement and exercise. Because the species are active chewers, all wooden additions to the aviary, including all toys, branches and perches, will periodically have to be replaced as they are routinely demolished and reduced to toothpicks. The availability of ample chewing opportunities is essential because it prevents boredom by providing intelligent, inquisitive birds with sources for engagement and entertainment.

The average clutch is two oviate white colored eggs, occasionally three, measuring 43.2–48.0 mm × 30.0–34.0 mm (1.7–1.9" × 1.1–1.3"). Both parents equally share in the incubation, which lasts approximately 28–30 days. The young birds fledge 8–12 weeks after hatching and become totally independent approximately three months thereafter.

The Sulphur-crested Cockatoo is not a finicky eater and will accept a wide range of foods, although the species is not fond of bananas. Various fruits such as apples are welcome, as are various green vegetables such as broccoli, peas, and beans. While the birds enjoy lettuce, and will devour all that is provided them, lettuce has little nutritional value and should be sparingly provided, as should be sunflower or safflower seeds in any quantity because they have an opposite effect: the birds tend to become obese when eating too many of these seeds. Other seeds such as corn, millet, grass seeds, and hulled oats are welcome, as are various nuts—walnuts, almonds, peanuts, hazelnuts and the like.

Pet Companion

A description of the Sulphur-crested Cockatoo and the pros and cons of owning one evokes a story. The good news/bad news story dichotomy. It is reminiscent of ubiquitous stories regarding ownership of a pleasure boat. There are two good days associated with boat ownership: the first "good" day is when you beam proudly after purchasing the vessel of your dreams, the vessel to fulfill fantasies since childhood of cruising along the Great Barrier Reef, exploring the wonders of the ocean, champagne and all; and the second "good" day is some time later when you hugs your spouse in sheer joy for finally having been able to finally sell it, give it away, or even sink what has become an albatross about your neck.

So it is with having a Sulphur-crested Cockatoo as a pet companion, regardless of the particular race.

Every prospective owner of a pet companion Sulphur-crested Cockatoo envisions a pet that will bring companionship, joy, and entertainment into the home. The bird is purchased. It is proudly brought home. Friends are invited. They adore the bird. Everyone loves it. It mimics, does tricks, bonds well, reciprocates affection, gives and receives kisses, and so on. But this darling bird has a terrible habit of screeching, often at the most awkward moments. It is soon a serious obstacle obstructing normal familial harmony. Plus, it may have a propensity to hate your wife, the mother of your children, despite the fact that she feeds it daily; and perhaps it is also not overly fond of your children, either.

For many owners there are two good days related to owning a Sulphur-crested Cockatoo: the first being the day when this remarkably intelligent bird becomes a member of the household, and everyone is completely enamoured by it, and argues over who next can have the bird sit on his or her shoulder—and laughs when the bird initiates its first blood-curdling scream for no observable reason. The second being some days, weeks, months, or even years down the road, when the bird is sold or given to a zoo or to anyone willing to take it.

The tragedy, of course, is that many pet Sulphur-crested Cockatoos become rolling stones, going from one owner to another.

Aside from its outstanding attractiveness, the Sulphur-crested Cockatoo is a remarkable, magnificent avian species. It has been estimated that the bird has the intelligence capability of a one- to two-year-old child. In addition to appearing as a co-star in the detective television series *Baretta*, Fred, as the cockatoo was called, was a frequent performer in a variety of capacities in circuses, bird shows, zoos, educational institutions, and so on. Since its demise, other specimens carry on the traditions of the *Baretta* cockatoo. They can be taught to whistle, imitate various everyday sounds, mimic human expressions, and do so quite well; they can even be trained to ride bicycles and motor scooters, and to do a variety of other amazing stunts, too many to itemize herein.

It has also been long noted that this species dances when music is played. What was unknown until recently is that the species actually dances in response to the particular tempo being played at the moment: for example, while the music is a samba beat, the cockatoo dances to that particular tempo, but as soon as the music is changed to a meringue tempo, the bird's foot movements change accordingly (Patel et al. 2008). It is believed the cockatoo responds to as many as seventeen different tempos.

And that is not all. This species is probably more loyal to its owner than some married couples are to each other. The cockatoo develops a strong bond with its owner, whether male or female, and is totally responsive to that owner, and is mutually interactive with that owner. Being interactive necessitates emotional reciprocity. The Sulphur-crested Cockatoo thrives on emotive interaction: it thrives on being with its owner, on being cuddled by its owner.

These are the kinds of character attributes that most would-be parrot owners fantasize the bird they will eventually possess will have: a striking bird on their shoulder, kissing them, and engaging everyone with verbal pleasantries such as "Hello," "How are you," "Would you like a drink," and so on. Greeting specific guests with "Hi, Karen" when it is actually Karen who walks in, whether by accident or by recognition, is what most folks desire in a parrot.

Regrettably, however, as with purchasing a boat, there is some bad news associated with owning a Sulphur-crested Cockatoo.

The Sulphur-crested Cockatoo counters its positive attributes with its negative ones. This species, regardless of race, as clever and intelligent as it is, is without question unsuitable not only for most households but also for the neighborhood. It has horrendous shrieking, a shrieking that is not only usually unprovoked, but also is part and parcel of the bird's psychological make-up, a shrieking that is not only guaranteed to alienate neighbors, permanently, but will undoubtedly alienate family members, equally permanently.

Additionally, the cockatoo is emotionally demanding, and failure to respond to the bird's demands is a provocation. The bird will shriek when ignored, and if ignored further, can become destructive if let loose from its cage. Because it is emotionally demanding, the owner needs to spend several hours a day with his pet companion. Failure to supervise the bird (i.e., control what it does, and where it goes when free of the cage's constraints, so that it causes no injury to itself, or to the household contents) can result in considerable shrieking. The Sulphur-crested Cockatoo requires at least three hours daily to remain emotionally healthy, but that may be more than the average pet owner can afford to expend interacting with a demanding pet, particularly if there are household and family matters that demand attention.

It is common knowledge that most pet Sulphur-crested Cockatoos ultimately become wards of zoos or circuses, or are given or sold to another family or organization.

For those persons who have the facilities appropriate for a Sulphur-crested Cockatoo and are immune to cockatoo emotional demands and shrieking, and who by virtue of location are immune to a neighbor's possible umbrage at the cockatoo's shrieking, the Sulphur-crested Cockatoo can prove to be an ideal pet companion. It can provide hours of loving entertainment.

In respect to housing, since the species is a large bird, the cage needs to be at least a meter cubed (three to four feet cubed), larger if the size of the household accommodations permit it. Two or three wooden perches, preferably tree branches, with lengths and diameters differing, should be placed at various positions in the cage. Hanging a rope from the top of the cage provides the bird opportunity for entertainment. Depending on the available space, fresh, nontoxic branches should be provided that the bird can strip and chew. Given the bird's intelligence, various toys, wooden or leather, provide the bird with opportunities to avoid boredom. Since it is highly advisable to allow the pet companion some freedom from its confinement, a stand near its cage on which the bird can perch when allowed out is salubrious, especially if the stand's location provides the bird and its owner opportunities for interaction.

As indicated earlier, the Sulphur-crested Cockatoo is not a finicky eater. Avoid overindulging the pet companion with lettuce (it has little nutritional value) or safflower or sunflower seeds (their fat content makes the cockatoo obese). Aside from bananas, the Sulphur-crested Cockatoo enjoys most fruits and berries and will eat most vegetables such as peas, beans, corn and broccoli, various nuts such as almonds or peanuts or walnuts, and a variety of seeds such as wheat, grass, corn milo, and canary seeds, among others.

5

Blue-eyed Cockatoo
Cacatua ophthalmica (Sclater, 1864)

COMMON NAMES: White Cockatoo
SUBSPECIES: None
LIFESPAN: 40 years in captivity[1] (estimated 50 to 60 years in the wild[2]).
IUCN RED LIST OF THREATENED SPECIES: Vulnerable[3]
CITES II: ENDANGERED

Description

The Blue-eyed Cockatoo is a beautiful, medium/large sized cockatoo, on average 45–50 cm (17.5–19.5") in length, and weighing 500–570 grams (17.6–20.1 oz.).

It is similar in size and superficial appearance to the Sulphur-crested Cockatoo (*Cacatua galerita*), and had previously been considered the same, but unlike the Sulphur-crested Cockatoo, the Blue-eyed Cockatoo has a backward-curving crest that is similar in appearance and structure to the crests of the Moluccan Cockatoo (*Cacatua moluccensis*) and the Umbrella Cockatoo (*Cacatua alba*). Additionally, its eye ring is much bluer, its skull is shaped differently, and it has less yellow in its crest than the Sulphur-crested Cockatoo.

As with other species in the White Cockatoo grouping, the Blue-eyed Cockatoo is white on both top and bottom; the bases of the breast, neck and under wing and under tail feathers, however, are sometimes lightly tinged in yellow. There is a slight yellow suffusion to the ear coverts. The crest's feathers are white and yellow, the white feathers dominating at the front of the crest. The yellow feathers are only visible when the crest is erected. The crest is erected whenever the bird is stressed, curious, or in any other emotive state.

The bird's periophthalmic ring is sky blue in color,[4] and its skin is wattled and featherless. The beak is curved, black, and medium sized, and has a moderately over-projecting upper mandible. The legs and feet are dark grey. As is common to all cockatoo species, the Blue-eyed Cockatoo has zygodactyl feet: the first and fourth toes reach backwards while the second and third project forward, a feature permitting the bird to hold onto a branch and onto food with the same foot, and thus allowing it to rip off pieces of food with its other foot. Although common to most parrots, this feature is unusual for many bird species.

One of the most interesting anatomical features of the species in relation to others in the genus *Cacatua* is its backward-curving crest. The crest differs from the other species in

The Blue-eyed Cockatoo is rarely encountered in either Europe or North America. It is frequently mistaken for or considered a subspecies of the Sulphur-crested Cockatoo. The blue ring surrounding the eye is unique, giving the bird its name, but the eye's pupil is actually brown (photograph by Lee Hunter).

the group not only in the direction the terminal ends of the feathers lie, but also in that the crest has a much fuller appearance.

Another distinctive crest feature of the Blue-eyed Cockatoo is the manifestation of the crest when it is erected: the Blue-eyed Cockatoo's crest opens in a cluster without apparent or seeming pattern, whereas the crests of most other cockatoos have a geometrical linearity in that each crest feather is directly behind the feather preceding it.[5]

The males and females are so similar in appearance that from a short distance away the species can appear monomorphic; but upon close examination of the birds there is a minor, but fundamental sexual difference: the female's eye is reddish brown while the male's is a brownish black. The eye color differences are not always easily obvious, however, and hence are not totally dependable as a gender indicator; and if a bird is intended for a breeding program, DNA analysis or surgical determination is advised.

Immature birds closely resemble the adults except that their eyes are greyish (Juniper and Parr 1998). The sex-differentiating eye coloration may not be noticeable for some time after the young have fledged. Again, medical sexing is also essential for anyone purchasing the birds while young with the intent to breed them in the future.

Behavior

The Blue-eyed Cockatoo has been rarely studied in the wild, so there is little published material on the species based on actual field observation and research. The problem is that few trained experts have visited either New Britain or New Ireland islands (the cockatoo is not endemic to New Ireland, but is believed a transplant from New Britain) with the intent of documenting the species' life habits, or even determining the number and distribution of the species. As well, the species keeps mainly to the rain forest canopy. There were two recent studies conducted from December 1998 to April 1999 along New Britain's east coast, however (Forshaw 2012): those studies provide a better understanding of the cockatoo's population density and habitat preferences. But research on the species' life parameters and day-to-day behavior and activities is still severely limited. In short, the species remains a mystery. As noted by Forshaw (2012), "Restricted to New Britain, the blue-eyed cockatoo (*Cacatua ophthalmica*) is one of the least-known cockatoos, both in the wild and in captivity."

The Blue-eyed Cockatoo is especially conspicuous because of its discordant calls and screeching (Marsden et al. 2001), the calling loud and distinctive enough that it can be heard long before the bird comes into view.

The cockatoo can be encountered either singly, in pairs, or in small, loose flocks (Juniper and Parr 1998). Occasionally, a flock may number up to forty or so individuals, but such larger flocks are the exception. A flock may consist of just a few individuals, but because the cockatoos sometimes form larger flocks when feeding, some observers are led to conclude that the species has a relatively high population. But there is concern that the actual numbers of Blue-eyed Cockatoos are in fact much smaller than what such appearances suggest, for the feeding-flocking behavior attracts individuals, young and old, from a wide area, temporarily inflating the population density in a given area, precisely the region under study by field researchers. Given the terrain the cockatoo inhabits, quantifying its numbers is difficult at best. Like all other cockatoos, the Blue-eyed Cockatoo is aware of what native foods are seasonably available, and seeks that food source, as do other cockatoos in that region. The fact that large groups of cockatoos are foraging a food source is an unreliable measure of both population density and regional numbers.

Regarding pairs in the wild, field studies have not determined whether observed pairs are mated, bonded pairs, or whether a twosome is simply a social event, although in captivity the cockatoo is known to mate for life. It is assumed the pair mate for life, despite an absence of concrete observational data. The limited field notes observe that the cockatoos—like most other birds—are most active in the early morning hours and during the late afternoon. They are known to fly aerobatics prior to roosting (Planet of Birds 2012), the aerobatics accompanied by considerable screeching. During the rest of the day the birds remain in the dense forest canopy, usually singly.

The loud vocalizations of the cockatoo are a means of communication. Their calls are described as nasal and loud, and during flight are repeated, each note ending "in a downward fashion; call notes are high pitched and sad-sounding" (Tumblr 2012). The Blue-eyed Cockatoo also communicates, similarly to other cockatoo species, diverse emotional states via the erection of its crest: fear, curiosity, courtship, warnings about impending danger, and other cockatoo emotive issues.

An interesting description of the birds in flight was provided by E.T. Gilliard and M. Lecroy based on their 1958 and 1959 field expedition to New Britain. They wrote that the species was

> abundant in the tropical rain forest; usually observed in pairs flying above the forest, and screaming all the while. Rare above an altitude of 3000 feet, the senior author watched a white cockatoo as it descended a steep mountain slope nearly a thousand feet ... the flight as a long fluttering glide, with the wings moving but slightly. Towards the end of this flight, the bird began turning and twisting as though to reduce speed. It then doubled back and disappeared into a forested canyon.

Rutger (1970) in his book *Birds of New Guinea* states, "They are nearly always seen in large flocks in trees," a statement inconsistent with Gilliard and Leroy's observation that the species was usually seen in pairs. A search of the research literature shows no evidence of the inferred commonality of large flocks by different researchers or naturalists, but then there is a marked absence of field notes and research. It is not clear where Rutgers obtained his information, and just as unclear is whether Gilroy and Leroy's observations were made during the species' breeding season.

On a final but sombre historical note regarding the Blue-eyed Cockatoo, Layard in 1880 commented that the species was "very common in New Britain and makes capital soup. The natives keep many tame ones; name Tui Tui."

The cockatoo's diet in the wild has been observationally generalized to include "fruits, flowers, and the seeds of a variety of tree species, including figs and coconut palms" (Juniper and Parr 1998; World Parrot Trust 2012; Wilkinson et al. 2000). The specific seeds, flowers, and other foods were not identified. The Blue-eyed Cockatoo is also known to feed on insects and their larvae (Parrot Link 2012). Forshaw (2012) reports that they feed on Melanolepis fruits, blossoms of Eucalyptus deglupta, and wild figs. The cockatoo is also reported to forage cocoa bean crops, and is considered a pest by some indigenous growers whose crops are affected, although it is not clear what foods the birds forage from cultivated garden plots, aside from cocoa beans.

Habitat and Distribution

The Blue-eyed Cockatoo is endemic to the Island of New Britain in the Bismarck Archipelago, off the northeast coast of Papua New Guinea,[6] the island being approximately 40,500 square kilometers (approximately 25,500 square miles). Although the species is now also found on the Island of New Ireland (Juniper and Parr 1998; World Parrot Trust 2012; Cameron 2007), its presence there is generally believed to be the result of either escaped caged birds, or cockatoos deliberately caught on the former island and released in New Ireland (New Ireland is 7,404 square kilometers, or approximately 4,600 square miles). Despite its presence there, the species is not considered to be endemic to New Ireland although there is no historical evidence supporting this belief. The numbers of cockatoos on New Ireland is speculative at best, but Forshaw found that the cockatoos were commonly kept there as pets, and that they were regularly offered for sale in the markets in Rabaul for approximately $8 (Marsden et al. 2001) in the early 2000s or thereabouts. Whether these captive birds were transported from New Britain in the course of normal commerce between the two islands, or whether the birds were captured locally, is unknown. While the number of feral Blue-eyed Cockatoos in the wild now on New Ireland is unquantified and suspected to be small, their long-term status in respect to possible population stability and/or growth is questionable, given that deforestation and the consequential loss of suitable nesting trees and native food resources are critical negative elements shaping and limiting the species' prospects of viability.

In New Britain, the species can be found in terrains up to 950 meters (approximately 2,700'). While they may be found in disturbed rain forests, the cockatoo prefers virgin forested terrains, presumably because it is there that the species can readily find nesting sites in suitably large trees (Dutson 2011); it can also be found occasionally in partly cleared areas, and when not in breeding season, can be described as common in lowlands. The species is largely absent from non-forested areas. Although the species has been recorded near settlements early in the morning, for the most part it avoids human settlements, and if approaching them when there is usual human activity, it does so stealthfully (Marsden et al. 2001).

In the field study conducted by Marsden et al. from December 1998 to April 1999, it was found that in selectively logged primary forests the estimated cockatoo population was 54 individuals per square kilometer (roughly half a square mile), similar as the estimate for undisturbed primary rain forests. However, where there were forest gardens tended by indigenous people, there were only six individuals in one of the square kilometers studied, and only 27 in a second square kilometer. The study concluded tentatively that the species ranges over much of New Britain's land area, excepting the higher altitude terrains, but its population density in a region is closely related to the degree and intensity of deforestation, and most probably also to the presence of human activity.

Although the species seems numerous, and its population appears both stable and healthy, there is some reason to believe that its population numbers may be seriously declining. While New Britain still retains much of its pristine rain forest and while the very few field expeditions there have not observed a noticeable decline in population density, the initial impression that the Blue-eyed Cockatoo has a healthy population may be in fact be deceiving: the species is long-lived, but its reproductive output may be in actual decline, as the large trees upon which the species relies upon for nesting fall to the loggers' chain saws. Fewer nesting sites translates into fewer nests, fewer matings, and hence fewer young entering the population—an important concern when the species typically only fledge one youngster per year. In essence, if in fact there are fewer young adults entering the breeding aged population, then in fact the population is aging. It is not a healthy scenario.

Recent remote sensing technology has shown that the lowland forests are being rapidly harvested—at issue, of course, is the loss of suitable towering trees with nesting potentialities (Tumblr 2012). Birdlife in 2012 reports that there has been a significant loss of breeding habitat due to the rapid conversion of lowland rain forests to palm tree oil plantations. The rate of deforestation is calculated at 35 percent over three generations. Bromerley in 2012 also notes that because of this rapid deforestation and the loss of suitable nesting trees, the species has been uplisted to Vulnerable; they have been considered Vulnerable by IUCN since 2008 (World Parrot Trust 2012).

In contrast, over a quarter century earlier, in 1967, Gilliard and LeCroy described the species as abundant, as did Orenstein in 1976: the trapping of the cockatoos for the pet trade was non-threatening to the species at the time, the cockatoo appeared to be numerous, and the healthy forest upon which the cockatoo relied upon for nesting sites were all variables favorable to the cockatoo's population stability; therefore the taxon was at that time judged to be of "Least Concern" in the wider context. Just a quarter century later, Marsden et al. in 2001 surmised that the cockatoo population was probably already declining. By 2012 World Parrot Trust warned that the deforestation of the lowland forest upon which the bird depends for breeding purposes "in all probability is causing the population to decline *precipitously*."[7] While the Marsden field researchers in 2011 hesitated to extrapolate a population estimate for the island, despite the fact that the researchers had concluded that the species appeared to be well distributed over its range, a conservative estimate of mature birds places their numbers at approximately 15,000 individuals (BirdLife 2012). In 2012 Forshaw provided a "cautious extrapolation of population figures from the study sites [Marsden et al. 2001] ... applied to New Britain ... [and] produced an estimate of 115,000 total birds."

Forshaw's conclusion is in sharp contrast to the original conclusion drawn by the researchers who did the actual field work.

Propagation

As noted above, there is little data concerning the Blue-eyed Cockatoo in the wild state. Much of the information regarding the cockatoo's reproduction is based on the limited numbers of breedings of the species in captivity. And what information there is sparse at best. The cockatoo is rare in captivity.

The Blue-eyed Cockatoo breeds from May to October on New Britain Island in the Bismarck Archipelago. The pair is believed to mate for life, and if so, the pair bonding suggests a tight family bond. It is reported that display behaviors are generally absent, except when the pair are first introduced to each other (Wilkinson et al. 2000). It has been noted in other cockatoo species who pair for life that the death or departure of one of the pair leaves the other in what in human terms we describe as a depression. While there is no evidence to support this phenomenon in the Blue-eyed Cockatoo, the cockatoo probably responds with a depression-like state similar to the other cockatoo species when confronted with the loss or death of its mate, given its taxonomical similarity.

As is typical of the species within the White Cockatoo group, the Blue-eyed Cockatoo prefers tall trees, trees that are mature, and trees that have hollows in either the trunk or a broken branch (Juniper et al. 1998) high off the ground. Nests are situated as high as 13 to 50 meters (or 40' to 160') (Birdchannel 2012). The nest entrances measure up to 52 centimeters in length and 38 centimeters in width (20" × 15"). The 2001 Marsden et al. field study reported several nests but provided few details concerning them.

Based on field research, there is virtually no information on the Blue-eyed Cockatoo's breeding in the wild. After mating, the female typically lays two elliptical eggs, sometimes three, the second following three to six days after the first, the eggs generally laid early in the morning. World Parrot Trust (2012) notes that egg sizes average 52.0 × 31.5 mm (2" × 1.2"). Although there are usually two (or more) eggs, commonly only one nestling is reared to fledgling age (Wilkinson 1999). Although there may be more than one egg constituting the clutch, the fact that there is a several-day interval between the laying of the first and second egg (and at times the third egg) has significant implications regarding the number of nestlings that will reach fledgling age: the first laid egg, and therefore the first hatched, will have several days of constant feeding and consequential growth. By the time the second egg hatches, the first hatched nestling will have acquired a size and weight advantage over the second (and third, if there is one) nestling, which ensures in the competition for food that the older nestling will be the first to be fed. Hence only one fledgling per nest survives to fledgling age because subsequent nestlings starve to death or die from malnutrition.

The female does most of the incubating. The eggs hatch at 28 and 30 days and the nestlings are blind until they are about ten days old. They are born with a thin wisp of yellow down on their thighs, crown and back. Both parents feed and care for the chicks until they are weaned at about 14 to 16 weeks (Avian Web 2012). The young reach breeding age between three and five years of age (Wilkinson 1999).

Observations in the wild suggest that once the young fledge, the juveniles continue to depend on their parents for feeding for one month or so; when several individual cockatoos gather to form a small, loosely knit flock during feeding periods, the young participate in the flocking.

Aviary Notes

Succinctly, and regrettably, because this cockatoo is not only beautiful but is a diamond in personality and intelligence, it is rare and there are no legal means by which the bird can be imported from New Britain Island for European or North American private breeders, or bird fanciers longing for an exceptional bird pet companion. While the pet trade in the species is severely limited (because of New Guinea legislation and CITES), the financial incentive that its rarity can stimulate undoubtedly encourages trapping the species not only for local sales at village markets but for animal traders involved with the international black market in wildlife.

As noted earlier, there is little known about this rare cockatoo. It is extremely rare in captivity, and is rarely seen outside of New Britain or New Ireland. There is some good news though: it is established from breeding experience that the species breeds consistently and successfully until its third decade of life (Wilkinson et al. 2000). Due to its rarity and ultimate possible extinction in the wild, the Cooperative Breeding Program in the United States in 2005 legally imported nine pairs of young Blue-eyed Cockatoos just reaching breeding age with the intention of breeding enough of the species in captivity to some day have a sustainable population (The Website of Everything 2010),[8] and perhaps reintroduce it into the wild. As of the date of this writing (2013) two pairs have already laid eggs.

Prior to the 1950s, there were no published reports of the species' breeding in captivity. The first captive breeding was reported to the avicultural community in 1951 by Dr. A. Lendon, who, after a trip to Australia, wrote to *Aviculture Magazine*, "Mr. E.J.L. Hallstrom has bred the Blue-eyed Cockatoo (*K. ophthalmica*) of New Britain. I think this is a first record?"

The second successful captive breeding took place in 1964 at Llandyssyl, Cards, in Wales, by A.V. Griffiths. He reported that prior to the successful hatching, his pair had on several previous occasions laid eggs but in each instance the nesting efforts were failures. (The number of clutches, eggs, and suspected reasons for failure were not reported.)

After these successive failures, the Griffiths' pair were introduced in 1963 to a flight measuring 36' × 4' × 7' (approximately 10 meters × 1.5 × 2 meters). The hen laid one egg in October, and became bound with the second egg, eventually passing it. The next spring the pair were again introduced to the flight outside; the flight this time had been reduced to half its previous length. The hen became egg bound again, eventually passing a soft-shelled egg, whereupon she was returned to the aviary. Later, on July 19, Griffith found a clutch of two eggs during his periodic inspections. By August 11 one egg hatched; the other egg contained a dead embryo.

Concerning the surviving chick's growth and development, Griffiths wrote that it "could stand up quite strongly and was sporting quills" and that by the sixth week "it was fully feathered, even to the yellow on the underside of the crest." The juvenile fledged November 10, approximately three months after hatching.

It is interesting to note that the Blue-eyed Cockatoo pair may have been sexually immature when Griffiths purchased them (source undisclosed); it may be that the hen was in fact sexually immature, and hence the cause of the egg failures. The following year in 1966 an unidentified correspondent to *Aviculture Magazine* informed the readers that the Griffiths' pair successfully raised a second youngster, which fledged on New Year's Day.

In reporting on his success Griffiths found his pair were "unenthusiastic" about sunflower seeds, preferring almost exclusively Paddy Rice and canary seed. Since this diet was low in protein, he confessed he "was at a loss what to do." However, since his Triton (*Cacatua galerita triton*) accepted maggots, Griffiths began feeding his Blue-eyed Cockatoos a diet of two handfuls of maggots both morning and night, in addition to apples cut into small pieces. He found that his pair rejected everything else, including greens, even though he offered a variety of different types.

The aviary flight should be as large as possible: the Chester Zoo in the UK provided their pairs with an indoor shelter measuring 3.7 m × 3.7 m × 3.7 m (approximately 12' x12' × 12'), and that shelter was connected to an outdoor aviary of the same size (Wilkinson et al. 2000). The flight should be covered with a 12-gauge mesh. Three or four different nesting arrangements dispersed about the caged area should be provided for the birds to choose from—logs with hollows, grandfather-styled nesting boxes. The World Parrot Trust (2012) recommends that the nesting box should be at least 40 cm × 40 cm × 100 cm (approximately 16" × 16" × 40"). Once the pair begin showing a distinct interest in one of the proffered nesting sites, the others should be removed, leaving the chosen nesting box. Rotted sawdust, wood shavings and other suitable nesting materials should be placed in the nest to the depth of approximately 10 cm (3–4").

Several wooden perches should be provided, as well as branches with leaves from non-toxic trees for the birds to chew upon. Not only is the chewing physically healthy, but it is emotionally stimulating for the birds, keeping these intelligent cockatoos from becoming bored. Hanging ropes also provide behavioral stimulations to enrich the birds' daily living. The provision of the wooden perches and chewing materials necessitates replacing them periodically as they soon become destroyed, a minor inconvenience to ensure good health to this marvellous cockatoo.

The cockatoo may lay its eggs as early as March or as late as November, but the eggs normally hatch (in Great Britain) in July and August. The incubation period is approximately 28–30 days. The nestlings' eyes open 10 to 20 days after they have hatched, and their feathers begin showing at approximately 15 to 20 days. In approximately 140 days the juveniles are fully feathered, and for all intents and purposes resemble their parents.

While Griffiths reported his mated pair were finicky eaters, the World Parrot Trust (2012) recommends a wide variety of different foods that the cockatoo will readily accept: a mixture of diverse seeds, either dry, soaked or sprouted; cooked butterbeans and lentils; boiled maize; various green leaves ranging from dandelions to chard; vegetables such as carrots and peas; complete kibble; diverse fruits as wide ranging as apples to cactus fruits; and various nuts, including peanuts. Understandably, captive birds will develop preferences, and the breeder can tailor the feeding regime accordingly to provide a balanced diet based on those indicated preferences.

Pet Companion

The Blue-eyed Cockatoo is extremely rare in captivity. *It is a species which should be considered **too rare** to be a pet* (Avian Companions 2012). Of all the cockatoos, it is considered one of the best personalities—a bird that can mimic just about everything, that likes to play, that shows affection and reciprocates it, and that can be taught numerous feats, such as lying on its back. It is a species that is loved and admired throughout the world because of its overall friendliness, its beauty and intelligence, its enjoyment of being handled, and its playfulness (Avian Web 2012).

While the species is considered rare and is protected by international conventions as well as New Guinea legislation, it has to date not yet been blatantly exploited for the pet trade as have other species of exotic birds, particularly various parrot species (World Parrot Trust 2012; Marsden et al. 2001; Wilkinson et al. 2000). Yet, as noted earlier, the species is found available for sale (despite New Guinea contraventions) in Rabaul, New Ireland, and there is evidence that the species is being traded in increasing numbers (Marsden et al. 2001). In view of the decreasing habitat available to breeding pairs of Blue-eyed Cockatoos, even limited trapping is detrimental to the species' overall population, and does not bode well regarding its future prospects.

This exotic diamond of a cockatoo, regrettably, is relatively inexpensive, vis-à-vis other cockatoo species, even though it is rare and is loved and admired: a search of the Internet (January 2013) found several Blue-eyed Cockatoos for sale internationally. A female was offered for sale on Ebay in September in Texas for $1,000, another in March located in Topeka, Texas, for $1,000 (described as "talks, kisses, whistles, prefers men"), and still another for $1,800. In Britain there were two separate birds for sale at £3,000. As well, there was a bird for sale in Johannesburg, another on Facebook, and still another in Sri Lanka.

For those very few individuals fortunate enough to acquire a Blue-eyed Cockatoo, special care should be taken to ensure the bird's emotional health. They should be provided ample wooden toys to chew upon so that they do not become bored. Boredom for an intelligent species results in neurotic behavior, and the cockatoo no longer remains a loving pet or even a suitable breeding candidate.

The species is reported to enjoy being handled, so regular interaction and playing with the cockatoo provides it with mental stimulation, an essential component for the overall well-being of an intelligent bird. If housed in a bird cage, the cage should be at least as large as a macaw cage. The species is not difficult to feed (see above, Aviary Notes, regarding dietary provisions).

Simply caging the cockatoo and tending to its physical needs will do little to keep this intelligent bird mentally healthy. It needs some degree of relative freedom from the cage during the day, and it thrives best when it has stimulating interaction with people and its environment.

That said, because of the rarity of the Blue-eyed Cockatoo and the embargos severely limiting illegal harvesting of the species for the pet trade, and because the species has not yet been sufficiently bred in sufficient numbers to ensure a sustainable domestic population, the opportunity to purchase this desirable, outstanding, rare cockatoo is fortunately currently highly uncommon.

European Captive-Breeding Program

In full compliance with CITES, in the United States the Cooperative Breeding Program was initiated, a program in which species considered endangered can be legally imported by established aviculturalists on application to comply with CITES regulations, and whose intended purpose is to ensure the breeding of sustainable populations of diverse species considered at risk. Among other species of concern, in 2005 the Blue-eyed Cockatoo was added to the list of chosen species, and it is now beginning to breed successfully in captivity in the American breeding program.

Several decades earlier the British began to successfully breed the species at the Chester Zoo; that breeding program has evolved into a cooperative multinational breeding regimen with a comparable goal: species survival.

The Chester Zoo in England has successfully bred the Blue-eyed Cockatoo on numerous occasions since 1966, and until October 1997 the zoo reared 38 young juveniles to independence, 27 of them hand reared. Because of the biological dangers inherent with inbreeding, and the legal difficulties in obtaining wild stock, the Chester Zoo has made arrangements with a substantial number of European zoos, coordinating a multinational breeding program for the cockatoo. The zoo has loaned birds bred in the Chester Zoo aviaries to other institutions that have Blue-eyed Cockatoos, including the Rotterdam Zoo, Paignton Zoo, Hayle Paradise Park, Belfast Zoo, and other similar established institutions known for their own breeding successes. Additional captive-bred birds have been obtained from North America, Switzerland, and Malaysia; in addition, birds that were initially wild-caught and sold in the pet trade, and that became pets, were volunteered to the cooperative breeding program to broaden the genetic base. Some of the former pets added to the breeding stock went to the Newquay Zoo in Cornwall. The introduction of new birds to the eight cooperating institutions with their own Blue-eyed Cockatoos ensures that the inbreeding problem will be dramatically diminished by new blood lines. Previously, much of the captive breeding population had been previously dominated by Chester Zoo stock. As of December 1998 the Chester Zoo studbook listed 72 Blue-eyed Cockatoos, with 28 of the original Chester stock being distributed among the other cooperating institutions (Wilkinson 1999).

6

Slender-billed Cockatoo

Cacatua tenuirostris (Kuhl, 1820)

COMMON NAMES: Slender-billed Cockatoo, Eastern Long-billed Corella, Long-billed Corella, *Licmetis nasica* (now archaic and obsolete).
SUBSPECIES: None[1]
LIFESPAN: estimated 50 years (poorly documented).
IUCN RED LIST OF THREATENED SPECIES: Least Concern
CITES II: Endangered

Description

The Slender-billed Cockatoo is endemic to southeastern Australia. Males and females are generally similar in size: they are approximately 370 mm (14.5") in length (Bird Care 2012), and average 600 to 650 grams (21–23 ounces) (Avian Companions 2012), but may reach as much as much as 900 grams (31 ounces). They have a wingspan of 80–90 cm (26–29") on average (Birds in Backyards 2012; Info Barrel 2012).

The Slender-billed Cockatoo is a medium sized, basically white bird, but with some orangish-red coloration on the head, breast, and undersides of the wing and tail. Feathers on the cheek, upper throat, neck, and hind neck are rosy colored at the base and white at the terminal ends. Feathering on the head and lores is an orange-scarlet. A small patch of the same color stretches across the upper breast area. Because of the bird's feeding habits, its breast feathers are frequently soiled from the excavations it makes in the earth in its search for tubers. The inner webs of the flight and tail feathers are a sulphur yellow. The two central tail feathers are white.

In contrast to other species of cockatoos, most of which have prominent crests, this cockatoo's crest is short (not always readily visible), recumbent, and normally folded out of sight. Depending on the cockatoo's emotional state at any given time, the crest can be erected, and when erected it is helmet shaped.

The beak is horn white and long, and is quite unusual for a cockatoo because it is long and slender, particularly the upper mandible, which is considerably elongated beyond the lower mandible, an adaptation to the species' practice of digging up *drosera* tubers, of which it is particularly fond. The periophthalmic ring is somewhat elliptical, more prominent beneath the eye than above, similar to the Bare-eyed Cockatoo (*Cacatua sanguinea*), other-

While unpopular because of its general unattractiveness compared to other parrot species, this cockatoo has many loyal advocates because it is noted for its playfulness, emotional reciprocity, and docility. It is considered to be the best mimic of all the cockatoo species (photograph by Steve Wilson).

wise also known as the Little Corella. This ring is featherless and bluish. Eye color for males is a brownish black and for the females may be tinged reddish; but the iris colors are not always consistent with descriptions because of their variability. Note that the eye color is hence not a reliable determination of sex, and the cockatoo's sex should be confirmed by DNA sexing or by surgical sexing, if the sex of the bird is important.

The legs are greyish and the feet are mealy colored, as is true of most of the other cockatoo species.

The Slender-billed Cockatoo is monomorphic. However, males are generally a bit larger than females, and tend to have larger beaks and heads.

The Slender-billed Cockatoo is often confused with the Little Corella (*C. Sanguinea*), but on close inspection it is readily evident that the Slender-billed Cockatoo has a longer, slim upper mandible, has bright red-orange head patches, and is slightly larger and heavier. It also has a shorter tail than the Little Corella.

Juveniles are similar to their parents except that their bills, particularly the upper mandible, are shorter.

Behavior

The Slender-billed Cockatoo is gregarious and social, and can often be found in flocks numbering fifty or more individuals. Early field studies at about the turn of the twentieth century or before frequently reported flock sizes comprising hundreds of individuals, but

The Slender-billed Corella is believed to be maintaining a healthy population in the wild, and unlike some other Cockatoo species, both Australian and extralimital, it is believed to be actually expanding its territorial distribution despite being persecuted as an agricultural "pest" (photograph by Ralph Green).

this was long before the species began to radically decline in numbers because of efforts to eradicate it, the cockatoo being considered an agricultural pest. There were numerous reports of these huge flocks. For example, Bennet (in Mathews 1916) wrote, "I have seen immense flocks feeding on the plains," and Bernard (in Mathews 1916) also wrote that as late as 1914 he saw them in "flocks of hundreds." Indeed, even though the species was already considered by some field workers a rarity as early as the turn of the nineteenth century, as late as 1949 Binns was still able to report that he saw a flock during that year which was a "flock of several hundreds, flying in a boomerang-shaped formation." Such reports today are an extreme rarity; while occasional larger flocks can be seen, they must be painstakingly searched out.

The feeding behavior of the species in the wild is unique. While it is primarily an arboreal bird in most respects, it feeds on tubers, which it digs out of the ground, sometimes as much as several centimeters (inches) down, and on the seeds of various ground-level plants. Often, long before the sun has risen, the cockatoos leave their communal roosting trees for nearby water holes. Their flight is erratic in both beat and glide. After drinking, the Slender-billed Cockatoo departs for open plains areas, where it spends the rest of the day foraging along the ground for various seeds, fruits, leaf and flower buds, insects, fruiting bodies from native shrubs and bushes, and tubers. The species is known to feed on native plants such as Murnong and *Microseris lanceolata* (Birds in Back Yards 2012). But the chief source of food for the species is the bulbs of the *drosera*, which it digs from the ground with its bill. It is when it is feeding on these tubers that its breast feathers become markedly soiled. Increasingly, though, a substantial portion of its daily diet now includes introduced seeds, and grains.

With the advent of agribusiness and economic emphasis on grain production, the Slender-billed Cockatoo has concurrently developed a fondness for grains. Freshly sown fields are favorite feeding grounds for the Long-billed Cockatoo, as are fields where crops are ripening.

Like the Sulphur-crested Cockatoo (*Cacatua galerita*), the Slender-billed Cockatoo has developed a sentinel system in which individual birds are posted on the highest trees, prepared to warn the feeding flock of impending danger; it is a similar warning system to that practiced by the wiley North American crow. The cockatoos employ the sentinel system regardless of where they are feeding, whether in planted fields or uncultivated lands.

At times the Slender-billed Cockatoo can be found in the company of the Sulphur-crested Cockatoo (*Cacatua galerita*) during feeding, the two flocks mixed together. Usually, however, the Sulphur-crested Cockatoos far outnumber the Slender-billed Cockatoos in such mixed company.

For the Slender-billed Cockatoo, unlike most other species within the cockatoo family, feeding is a full-time, day-long activity. The feeding flock, often accompanied by other species besides the Sulphur-crested Cockatoo, may cover several hundred square meters (yards) during foraging over the course of the day. Towards evening, the entire flock departs for its usual roosting sites, localities in which towering trees are often clustered around a waterway.

The voice of the cockatoo has been variously described. In general, it is a harsh shriek. Forshaw describes the cockatoo's call as "very similar as that of the Little Corella" but Lendon (1973) wrote that "Forshaw's statement ... is quite incorrect." The call has been described by Slater as being "a peculiar, disyllabic, chuckling cry; also a series of sharp shrieks when alarmed." Pizzey and Knight describe the call as a quick and quavering falsetto *currup* while Birds in Backyards (2012) describes the call as "*wulluk-wulluk*, or *cadillac-cadillac*" combined with harsh shrieks.

Their behavior of the species in the roosting trees is quite animated. Bennet (in Mathews 1916) recorded one such scene:

> Hundreds of birds dash here and there with rapid flight through the trees, their white plumage contrasting sharply with heavy green foliage of the towering Eucalyptus, and thrown into stronger relief by the rays of the setting sun. In some of the trees, the birds might be observed clinging in all kinds of altitudes, or jumping nimbly from branch to branch. Whilst in other places numbers were clinging head downwards at the extreme ends of the branches, the whole flock meanwhile keeping up an incessant and almost deafening noise.

Habitat and Distribution

The exact distribution of the Slender-billed Cockatoo is difficult to define, as are its population numbers. In fact, in 2012, the cockatoo's population numbers had still not been quantified (IUCN Red List). In the past, the species suffered a marked population decline and a proportional loss of habitable terrain. The species was primarily restricted to relatively small populations in the extreme southeast of Australia: along the coastal region between the town of Terang and Cape Otway in Victoria. In the Port Phillip Bay it was already considered rare by the mid-seventies. A small population was identified in the Lachan and Hurrimidgee River Districts in southeastern New South Wales. In 1950 Lendon reported a small population in the immediate vicinity of the towns of Narcotta and Penola in southeastern South Australia, a short distance from the border with Victoria, but in 1970 he expressed his concern that the species was now extinct in that region. What is notable in reading the histories of the period is the fact that the species' population had become quite fragmented. While it is now obvious that the species has not become extinct in the above-mentioned areas, and that in fact its territory has increased with the commercialization of agricultural production, it is uncertain whether there is in fact a contiguous population between these known populations.

The Slender-billed Cockatoo frequents eucalyptus forests and riverine woodlands near grasslands and now agricultural lands. Unlike the Little Corella (*Cacatua sanguinea*), which inhabits more arid terrains, a bird with which it is often confused, the Slender-billed Cockatoo prefers humid areas where it is equally at home in both forests, forest perimeters, and open plain, and is seldom far from permanent waterways or ponds. Along riverways, the species is commonly found on gum trees, particularly towering Red Gum trees (*Eucalyptus camacdulensis*). Because of agricultural expansion providing the species with an assured food supply, the range of the species has actually been extended so that now it is occasionally seen in urban areas (Bird Care 2012). Because of the original habitat degradation, these new areas of agricultural land developments provide the species opportunities to expand its range, and it is generally suspected that this range expansion is instrumental in an increase in the birds' population (Bird Life 2012). The documentation supporting this suspicion is vague at best.

The cockatoo is normally found in southern New South Wales, western Victoria, and the extreme southeastern South Australia. There are now also isolated feral populations in areas it has not inhabited in recent memory, or had ever inhabited: for example, Sydney, Hobart in Tasmania, and South East Queensland. In southeastern Australia its range was considerably larger in the past, prior to grain cultivation on a commercial scale—but the emphasis on increased grain production proved an invaluable new food source for the cockatoo, which resulted in its persecution as a pest because of its damage to crops. The current distribution of the species is supplemented by formerly caged birds that have escaped or have been released and that now form flocks in various regions, including in the Brisbane environs. Despite the loss of nesting habitat to agriculture and persecution for foraging on agricultural crops, the species is considered to have a global population of 100,000 to 499,999 individuals (Bird Life 2012).

Its range has expanded over the past fifteen years so that it is now common throughout most of central Victoria, including the populated areas surrounding Melbourne.

But now, as a matter of concern, there are also scattered feral populations of the Slender-billed Cockatoo in the Perth area on the opposite side of the continent, a region thousands of kilometers distant. Those distant feral populations are believed to be both deliberately released cockatoos and aviary escapees that are now breeding in the Perth area (Government of Australia 2012). The presence of breeding-age Slender-billed Cockatoos in western Australia raises concerns that the cockatoo may hybridize with the endangered southern race of the Western Corella (*Cacatua pastinator pastinator*).

Propagation

There is sparse information regarding the species' propagation in the wild, primarily because this cockatoo has not been a popular species either in the aviary or as a pet companion; consequently, there has been little field research done on the species, and much of the information available regarding the birds' propagation is that derived from observations of captive bird breedings, and those in themselves are few and far between. Again, the lack of data pertains to the historic unpopularity of this species, even though the cockatoo is both clever and intelligent.

Breeding takes place in Australia from July to November, with most clutches being laid in September (Pizzey and Knight 1997). Several pairs may nest in the immediate area, and it is not uncommon to find two or three pairs using the same tree. The Slender-billed Cockatoo is completely monogamous and mates for life. Although there is no published report regarding the pair bonding between a pair of Slender-billed Cockatoos, if they are at all similar in emotional disposition to other cockatoo species, the death or loss of one of the pair thrusts the surviving other into an emotional state akin to depression.

The mated pair exclusively choose a large, old eucalyptus tree with a hollow for their nest—the tallest tree available. All other trees are ignored, regardless of height, and only live trees are chosen; the clutch is laid on the decayed wood already present in the hollow. Surprisingly, they have been reported to also occasionally nest in cavities of loosely gravelled cliffs (Birds in Backyards 2012), but no details regarding nesting materials has been reported (Info Barrel 2012).

Both the male and female prepare the nesting site, and both share in the incubation of the young. They only raise one brood a year.

The typical clutch consists of two or three eggs, two being the norm. The second egg is laid shortly after the first, which generally assures that both nestlings will fledge, because if there is a significant time differential between the laying of the eggs, on hatching the first nestling will get most of the food during feeding, ultimately starving its sibling to death. If there is a third egg, it usually follows three or four days after the second. The cock sits during a good portion of the daylight, and the female replaces him mid-afternoon to remain brooding until the early morning hours (Lendon 1950). The dull, white, oval egg averages 37.0 × 28–31.7 mm (1.5"–1.1"). Incubation time is 24 days[2] and the nesting period is 56 days (Birds in Back Yards 2012). Both parents raise the young. At approximately six weeks the juveniles fledge. The juveniles will continue to remain dependent on the adult parents for approximately a month after fledging (Bird Care 2012). On fledging the juveniles resemble their parents, except that there is less breast coloration and an appreciably shorter bill.

The young birds prove to be excellent flyers immediately upon fledging. As a matter of fact, newly fledged juveniles are such capable flyers that many a bird hunter, anxious to obtain a fledgling for a pet, has found that "just as the tree was falling they ... had emerged and flown strongly away" (Carter, in Mathews 1916).

Aviary Notes

Because the Slender-billed Cockatoo has historically never been a popular bird as a companion pet, or as part of an aviary collection, the cockatoo is rarely bred in captivity in Australia (Bird Care 2012), although there are some people who do have the cockatoo as a companion pet. Its unpopularity, is due to its general unattractiveness when compared with other cockatoo species or parrot types. But to quote a hackneyed expression, "Beauty is in the eyes of the beholder"; the species has many dedicated advocates!

Despite its general unpopularity, there have been some limited efforts to breed the species in captivity. But because of the Slender-billed Cockatoo's general unpopularity, and its consequential inexpensiveness, commercial professional breeders are not inclined to breed the species as a source of income. Plus, the cockatoo does not breed well in captivity, despite efforts to encourage the birds to do so. The first reported successful breeding took place at the San Diego, California, zoo during 1959; Lint that year wrote, "Every trick in the book was used to induce this pair of birds to nest in captivity—different nesting facilities, nutrition, care and management were all important factors leading to the event." Lint did not specify the reasons for the species' lack of breeding interest, because the reasons were not obvious. The cockatoo is known to be quite finicky concerning its nest, whether boxes or logs, whether they are presented horizontally, vertically, inclined, etc. (North West Bird Club 2012). The San Diego success was followed a few years later by a breeding in Dorothy Speed's aviaries (*Aviculture Magazine* 1966) near Fresno, California, and then again finally in 1969 at the Adelaide Zoo in Australia.

Bird Care suggests, however, that the species is not difficult to breed in captivity because the "Level of Knowledge Required" to breed the bird is "Intermediate." While Bird Care is a reliable source for breeding and species information on a host of diverse avian fauna, it fails to provide detailed information on the breeding of this cockatoo.

While the Slender-billed Cockatoo is extremely rare in captivity outside Australia, it is readily available to Australians and can be purchased for as little as AU$200 a pair (Bird Care 2012). The aviculturalist may be encouraged to know that the species has been successfully crossed with the Galah Cockatoo (*Cacatua roseicapilla*) both in Tasmania and at the Adelaide Zoo; and it has been successfully mated with the Little Corella (*Ducorps san-guinea*) in New South Wales (*Aviculture Magazine* 1966); in 1954 Prestwick reported that it had also been successfully mated with the "Greater" Sulphur-crested Cockatoo (*Cacatua galerita* [?]) in New Zealand.

For anyone considering breeding the species, an aviary four to five meters (13'–16') long will provide the birds with sufficient freedom to fly about and obtain exercise. The aviary should be about 1.5 meters (4.5') wide and about two meters (6.5') high. It should be enclosed with a galvanized, heavy-gauge mesh. Several wooden perches situated at various heights dispersed through the aviary confines provide simulation of a tree environment. Suitable nontoxic branches with leaves should be also provided the birds for chewing. The chewing provides both exercise and entertainment, elements essential to a bird's emotional well-being. Boredom is not only detrimental to the bird's mental well-being, but it also encourages the development of neurotic behaviors, such as feather plucking and/or abysmal shrieking.

The nest box should be suitable to the pair. If there is sufficient space in the aviary, two or three different nesting boxes should be provided and placed at different locations about the aviary, and once the birds begin to favor one or another of the other nesting boxes, the others should be gradually removed. Since the pair mate for life, the nest box favored by the pair should be kept exclusively for them, for later nestings.

The cockatoos can also be housed and bred within a suspended cage. The cage should be about 3 meters (10') long, about a meter (3') wide, and a meter (3') high. For best results, it is best to transfer the pair to an aviary after the breeding season is finished. The cockatoo is generally intolerant of other birds in its aviary, and have been known to attack or kill other birds confined in the same space.

Bird Care advises that the nest box should be a log with a hollow to a depth of 600–800 mm (23"–32") with the internal diameter of the hollow approximately 200–250 mm (8"–10"). The nest box should be situated as close to the ceiling of the cage as possible, but not so close that the heat from the roof can negatively impact on the nestlings and the brooding adults. The nesting box should have a climbing structure within the hollow providing the birds easy access out.

The cockatoos are easily fed, as they readily accept most foods ranging from seeds to nuts to fruits: apples, wheat, corn on the cob, sweet potatoes, carrots, sunflower seeds, peanuts, lettuce, pinion nuts, various greens, meal worms and garden snails, dry dog food, or any of the commercially prepared parrot food pellets. The amount of sunflower and safflower seeds should be limited (Bird Care 2012) because they have a tendency to make the cockatoos obese.

The cockatoo likes to bath. Besides providing them a container from which they can drink fresh water, a larger container filled with shallow water should be available for them to bath in.

Pet Companion

Because the Slender-billed Cockatoo lacks the attractiveness characteristic of much of Australian's avian fauna, the cockatoo was historically only occasionally kept as a companion pet. Yet its versatility and amenability to mimicry were recognized over a century ago. For example, in a letter written to Dr. Greene well over a hundred years ago a certain Mr. Gedney, after grossly exaggerating the species' overall qualities of mimicry (and pantomime), informed Dr. Greene, "When first I had him, he knew, I should think, about twenty sentences, and never misapplied them." While Mr. Gedney may have had some hyperbolic views concerning the "super bird's" intellectual ability to apply just the right sentence to the appropriate circumstance, he was by no means exaggerating the cockatoo's ability to mimic.

The cockatoo is an intelligent, inquisitive, and docile bird that is grossly underrated. Those who own one have found them to be affectionate, gentle and playful—an outstanding pet despite its generally unattractive appearance. Additionally, the Slender-billed Cockatoo is not as demanding or as loud as other cockatoos. Because of these qualities, the bird is becoming increasingly popular in Australia. Because of its outstanding mimicry ability, it has been labelled the best "talker" of the Australian cockatoos. It has consistently proven itself to be able to mimic not only words but whole long sentences to near perfection. Plus, this remarkable cockatoo is inexpensive.

Regrettably, the Slender-billed Cockatoo is virtually impossible to purchase outside of Australia, and few non–Australians will ever have the opportunity to see or hear one.

While the cockatoo is not quite as demanding emotionally as other cockatoo species, the bird does require some human interaction. In addition to receiving affection, the cockatoo should have available a number of interesting toys to chew upon and entertain itself. By providing it with loving attention and toys with which it can occupy itself , the owner will be rewarded with a loyal, loving, and entertaining companion.

Feeding the companion cockatoo is not difficult. It will eat just about everything that grows (see above, Aviary Notes). Once it is determined which of the foods the cockatoo views as treats, the bird can be trained not only to mimic certain sounds or sentences but to do various tricks.

A cage for the cockatoo should be at least large enough for it to stretch out its wings. Depending on one's household circumstances, the larger the cage, the better. It should be at least 1.5 × 1.5 × 2 meters (approximately 5' × 5' × 6') with a couple of perches placed within at different heights. Because of the cockatoo's intelligence, it may learn through trial and error how to unlatch its door. An escape-proof locking system will have to be devised. Otherwise, you may arrive home from work and discover your pet perched on top of your favorite household plants, amusing itself by shredding it to pieces. In consolation, you can devise a fail-proof, unlatchable locking system, and train the cockatoo to return to the confines of its cage.

Note

While the Slender-billed Cockatoo is not considered a threatened species, it is considered a pest in the agricultural community, particularly in western Victoria, because the species is using farmland crops as an alternative food source. It is known to cause damage to sunflower and cereal crops. Sometimes permits are issued permitting farmers to shoot the cockatoos, particularly at harvest time. There has been some concern that the population may be in a slow decline because of the loss of nesting sites as the chainsaws fell suitable old trees with hollows. In effect, while the species' population at the present time appears to be remaining stable, its habitat is actually decreasing.

7

Western Long-billed Corella
Cacatua pastinator (Gould, 1841)

COMMON NAMES: Corella, Western Long-billed Corella, Western Long-billed Cocka-
too, Dampier's Cockatoo, Muir's Cockatoo, Lake Muir's Cockatoo,
White Cockatoo, Butler's Cockatoo, Butler's Corella, Derebyi
Corella

SUBSPECIES:
1. Muir's Corella (*Cacatua pastinator pastinator*) (Gould, 1841) Nominate
Race
2. Butler's Corella (*Cacatua pastinator derbyi*) (Mathews, 1916)[1]

LIFESPAN: (Both subspecies)[2]
1. Muir's Corella (estimated) 50+ years
2. Butler's Corella (estimated) 50+ years

IUCN RED LIST OF ENDANGERED SPECIES:
1. Muir's Corella: Least Concern[3]
Endangered[4]
Vulnerable[5]
2. Butler's Corella: Least Concern

Description

Endemic to the state of Western Australia in Australia, the Western Long-billed Corella
is comparable in size to the Sulphur-crested Cockatoo (*Cacatua galerita*). It is approximately
40–48 cm (16"–19") in length and weighs on average 700–800 grams (25–32 ounces). The
Australian government records its wing span at generally 90 cm (25-plus inches). In overall
appearance it is a white bird that is sometimes mistaken for a Little Corella (*Ducorps sanguinea*).

The Western Long-billed Corella is comprised of two subspecies, Muir's Corella (the
nominate race) and Butler's Corella, both races being similar in overall description.

The species is sexually monomorphic for all intents and purposes, except that the male
is marginally larger than the female.

Both male and female adults are predominately white, but with prominent orangish
red lories. The feathers between the elongated beak and the eyes are a deep salmon color.
There are small traces of the salmon color in a parallel bar of feathers on the throat. The
bases of the feathers on the head and breast are also salmon colored; this color is normally
concealed beneath the white terminal ends of the feathers. The color becomes obvious during

94

Because the species learned to forage in wheat fields, causing much damage, these birds were extensively poisoned and shot until the Muir's Corella subspecies' population plummeted to approximately 100 individuals in the 1940s. Every effort was made to prevent its extinction. Finally, more than 70 years later, the government announced on November 12, 2012, that the species was no longer in danger of extinction (photograph by Joe Pennock).

preening or during high winds, and when wet, the under-down of the cockatoo appears as an intense pinkish hue through the white outer feathers until the feathers are once again dry. Usually, the white breast feathers are stained from the soil in which the cockatoos forage for various tubers and corms.

The bluish grey periophthalmic ring is broad, bare of feathers, and elongated more extensively below the eye, somewhat akin to a teardrop shape, similarly shaped to that of the Bare-eyed Cockatoo (*Cacatua sanguinea*), also known as the Little Corella. The bird's eyes are brown.

Since eye color and general appearance of individual cockatoos of the Western Long-billed Corella can provide no reliable indication of the birds' sex, when a bird's sex is important for breeding purposes it should be determined either by DNA analysis or surgical procedure.

As is common in other cockatoos, the Western Long-billed Corella has a distinct erectile crest, white and somewhat larger than that of the Slender-billed Cockatoo. The erection of the bird's crest indicates an emotional state: fear, curiosity, wariness, courtship display, or any one of a number of emotional convolutions. The cockatoo's bill is horn colored and slender, and the upper mandible is hooked, an adaptation facilitating digging in the ground for food. The upper mandible is also longer than the lower mandible (but slightly smaller than that of the Slender-billed Cockatoo, *Cacatua tenuirostris*).

Both feet and legs are mealy grey. The undersides of both the tail and the wings are washed in a light shade of yellow.

Juvenile birds initially appear to be exact copies of their parents, but upon close inspection differences between the mature and immature birds become obvious. The juvenile's lores color of orange-red is minimal, the pale yellow on the rump and underparts is barely visible (World Parrot Trust 2012), and the yellow to the underbelly is quite faint (Higgins 1999).

The periophthalmic ring is considerably paler and the ring itself is less obvious on the juveniles (Higgins 1999). Sometimes there is a hint of pink to the underpart of the ring. The juvenile's beak has a smoother texture, on closed inspection, and is shorter, with a correspondingly shorter upper mandible.

While both the Butler's and Muir's Corellas are quite similar in appearance, and initially difficult to distinguish, there are some minor variations between them.

The Butler's Corella is similar in all respects to the Muir's Corella except that it is generally smaller. The weight of the Butler's Corella averages 600–750 grams (approximately 21–26.5 ounces), and the bird is 40–47.5 cm (15.7"–18.7") in length, whereas the Muir's Corella averages 560–815 grams (19.75–28.7 ounces) (Johnstone and Storr 1998; Higgins 1999), and is 43–48 cm (16.8"–18.9") in length. Additionally, the Butler's Corella has a slightly larger red "cut throat" feathering than the other race. Overall, in general appearance the Muir's Corella appears both larger and stockier, and its upper mandible is longer.

Behavior

The Western Long-billed Corella is an active bird, energetic. Its recent and current history in the state of Western Australia is a distinctly twofold development, determined more by the geographical separation of the two subspecies than by physiological differences between them or differences in behavior resulting from environmental conditions and influences. Their behavior is fundamentally the same.

The species is gregarious, commonly found in flocks, often in the company of Galahs (World Parrot Trust 2012), especially along watercourses and where seeding grasses are in abundance. It is commonly found near farmlands in lightly wooded country with tall trees and where there is available water and food, particularly the seeds of the Doublegee weed (*Emex australis*), an obnoxious weed. The cockatoos forage on the ground for a wide variety of other seeds of both introduced and native plants, as well as corms and tubers, which they dig from the ground using their upper mandible. It is this digging for tubers that soils their otherwise white breast feathers. During the winter and spring, the birds feed on corms of grass. With the introduction of grain agriculture, however, the species quickly adapted to this new food source. Carter (1916) described this adaptation a century ago:

> Owing to their destructive habits to the grain crops—which comprised eating the newly sown seed, pulling out the young plants to eat the grain at their roots, pulling down and trampling flat the ripening crops. And eating the ripe grain from the tops of stocks—the struggling settlers and pioneers systematically poisoned them wholesale with poisoned corn, and shot them to such an extent that one may now travel hundreds of miles through districts where they previously occurred in countless numbers and never see a specimen.

The extent of damage done to crops can best be judged when one considers that when Carter was finally able in 1912 to locate a flock of "hundreds of birds" feeding on stock tops (a rare event even in his day), he found a field "about two hundred yards in length and thirty in width" (approximating a planted field 185 meters × 27 meters) that had been completely ruined because the grain had been pulled down, trampled and the grain devoured. The farmers' retaliation was not only swift, but thorough. At Perth, for example, where the Western Long-billed Corella was common when settlers founded the colony in 1829, the persecution of the cockatoo was so complete that almost a century later in 1924 inhabitants in the Perth region could only recollect the species from their childhood, and live individuals in the wild had not been seen in living memory (Serventy and Whittell 1962). The species' adaptation to modern grain production as a source of food is still problematic, and despite the fact that the species is few in number, and hence protected, shooting licences are still sometimes issued.

The species has at times also become a nuisance in more highly populated areas. The birds have adapted to humans and their alteration of the natural habitat: the birds dig up the grass on race tracks and lawns, eating the roots, for example. At times they are also known to damage grain storage facilities by their penetration of tarpaulins protecting the harvested grain (Department of Environment and Conservation 2007, "Note No. 19").While the species' foraging on cereal crops is damaging, the Butler's Corella is also considered a pest because of the damage it also does to native trees, ornamental trees, lawns, power lines and television aerials. It is a declared pest under the provisions of the *Agriculture and Related Resources Protection Act of 1976* (Johnstone 2011).

In the wild, the species prefers towering trees, particularly eucalyptus trees, both for nesting and roosting. In the grain belts of Western Australia, however, much of the original forest has been cleared to provide more acreage for grain production, cattle, and sheep grazing. Because of this deforestation, the species flies increasingly long distances for food and water. Their wing beats are considered shallow, and when in flight there is considerable screeching and raucous calling.

In addition to feeding on barley, oats, wheat and other seed crops, and various introduced plants, both races can be found in flocks of varying sizes, foraging on the ground for seeds from native plants. As is typical with birds' calls, the call of the Western Long-billed Corella has been described variously: "harsh" and "shriek" being the most common descriptions. Similarly, cage bird enthusiasts differ in their opinion concerning the overall noisiness of the species: some consider the bird relatively quiet, while others consider it obnoxiously noisy. Forshaw describes the call as "very similar to that of the Little Corella," whereas in 2012 the World Parrot Trust likened the call to "chuckling with three notes, similar to the Little Corella, also a shorter disyllabic call, with the second note being more high pitched." The trust concludes their description by noting that when agitated the species shrieks and screeches.

Habitat and Distribution

Muir's Corella is currently primarily confined to areas south of Perth, in the extreme southwest of Western Australia (Schodde and Mason 1997), in the general Muir's Lake region. It is commonly found in eucalyptus woodlands dominated by Marri, Wandoo, Eucalyptus Wandoo, and Jarrah patches. Butler's Corella, on the other hand, is commonly found east of Perth, and several hundred kilometers (miles) north and northeast of Muir's Cockatoo. It chooses similar trees for perching, roosting, nesting.

The Muir's Corella's actual territory covers an area of approximately 3,000 square kilometers (circa 1,875 square miles), but the cockatoo is only common on about 500 square kilometers (circa 315 square miles) of that extended range (Garnet and Crowley 2000). During colonial times its range of distribution extended up to the Swan and Avon rivers (Storr 1991), but the species disappeared from those ranges by 1900 (Masters and Milninch 1974). Up to about 1900 its territorial range was still considerably larger than today, but its persecution as an agricultural pest during the late nineteenth and early twentieth centuries continued and almost resulted in its extinction. By the 1920s its distribution had shrunk to the areas adjacent to Lake Muir. There has been considerable concern over this Corella population and its survival, particularly the nominate Muir's Corella race, whose population fell to an abysmally dangerous level of c. 100 mature individuals during the 1940s (IUCN 2012; Bird Life Fact Sheet 2012).[6] Every effort was expended to save the species from extinction.

Because of its precarious circumstance, the Western Australian Department of Conservation and Management captured specimens and distributed them to licensed aviculturalists as part of a captive breeding program, as well as providing the Perth Zoo and other zoos and institutions, both Australian and worldwide, with birds for breeding (Chapman and Cale 2006; ISIS 2006). It is uncertain what percentage of these captive breeding birds are the southern species *C.p. pastinator,* if any. The World Parrot Trust (2012) now estimates the population of the Muir's Corella to be approximately 3,000 individuals; after considerable efforts to preserve the species, the government of Western Australia recently proudly announced on November 12, 2012, that the species was no longer in imminent danger of going extinct—a pronouncement that actually made international news.

A year earlier in 2011, however, Johnstone estimated the current population at 12,000 to 15,000, and increasing: the stark discrepancy between the two estimates leads to questions of the reliability of the data and the manner in which it was derived.

Shooting and poisoning the species had been prohibited, allowing the Muir's Corella population numbers to gradually increase from the brink of extinction. The expansion of acreage put into cereal and wheat production actually proved beneficial to the species once it was protected: the loss of native food sources was concurrently accompanied by the establishment of permanent water reserves, and a variety of grain cereals upon which to forage. While the forested terrain that the species occupied a century ago had been transformed by the plough to increase agricultural production, that same habitat transformation provided suitable habitat for the species, particularly new reliable sources of food on which to forage. The transformation of the habitat to agricultural production is undoubtedly instrumental in facilitating the cockatoo's population growth, despite its persecution as a pest.

Muir's Corella can now be found in small populations from Boyup Brook and Qualcup to the Perup River and Cambellup, generally now as far north as the Swan and Avon rivers, and as far as Broome in the East and August to the west (Bird Life 2012). While the cockatoo has been recorded in various nature reserves and the Stoate State Forest, most of its population and breeding habitat are actually found on private property (Chapman and Cale 2006), where it is commonly seen on the farmlands. It has been able to persist in what remains of its former habitat because agriculture provides permanent water and ample supplies of cereal crops, and isolated trees and forested patches provide nesting and roosting opportunities. The fragmenting of the forests and general habitat has not been as overly detrimental to the species as has been its persecution and the dimunization and/or loss of nesting and roosting habitat.

The fragmenting of the population is consistent with the breakup of the forest remnants. As early as 1912, Carter observed that patches of forest remnants occurring along road sides and watercourses, and a few isolated shade trees in otherwise cleared paddocks, favor the cockatoos' ability to survive, an observation still maintained by contemporary naturalists (Higgins 1999; Garnet and Crowley 2000; Smith and Moore 1991). These fragmented terrains of natural habitat, however, are not conducive to population growth.

Muir's Corella occurs frequently on crop lands and pastures where there are ample trees available for roosting and nesting, particularly where there are also reliable water sources nearby. Carter during his 1912 fieldwork observed that the species will perch on the tops of dead trees, but Smith (in Higgins 1999) almost a century later observed that during hot days Muir's Corella will only perch on trees with full foliage. As noted earlier, grain agriculture has benefited the species so that it is often found foraging cereal crops close to its preferred roosting habitat (Carter 1924; Massam and Long 1992; Chapman and Cale 2006).

The cockatoo can be encountered in pairs or small flocks. While a century ago both in 1912 and 1924 Carter reported occasionally seeing the birds in flocks numbering approximately 1,000 individuals, more contemporary field workers have also reported flocks numbering up to a thousand (see Massam and Long 1992; Storr 1991; or Chapman and Cale 2006, for example), which is questionable given that their numbers are few, and not fully or reliably quantified. While the Muir's Corella does not appear to migrate seasonally, even in short movements to other nearby local regions, and is generally disbursed through its territorial distribution, the other subspecies, the Butler's Corella in the northeastern section of the Wheat Belt, migrates westwards with its offspring at the conclusion of the breeding season, and during those migrations flocks of this race numbering up to 7,000 birds have been seen (Department of Environment and Conservation 2007, "Note No. 19"): but such large flock numbers of 1,000 birds for the Muir's Corella are estimates whose accuracy is questionable given the species' small overall population numbers.

While there had been some speculation that the Muir's race migrates northwards at the end of the breeding season, Massam (in Higgins 1999) found that such population movements were not confirmed by field workers studying the birds during the 1991 to 1997 period. In 1992, Smith and Moore did note, however, that while breeding pairs remain within the general area of their nesting sites, non-breeding birds possibly roamed about over an area of 250 or so square kilometers (approximately 175 square miles). Their whereabouts is poorly documented at best, and is not actually known.

The northern subspecies, Butler's Corella, is endemic to the central and northern wheat belts of Western Australia, a considerable distance north of the Muir's habitat range. Its geographical distribution is significantly larger than the territorial regions inhabited by Muir's Corella, and is more clearly defined. Its historical range, however, was significantly reduced when early settlers began converting virgin forests into agricultural cereal production.

Over a century ago this subspecies enjoyed a confirmed territorial distribution that extended along the western coast to a point considerably north of Perth. Indeed, there has been some belief that that distribution may have extended as far north as the Geraldton region, where the first settlers arrived in the area. But by 1916, Mathews reported the species was already considered rare at the Swan River District, which is approximately 300 kilometers south of Geraldton.

The rapid decline of the northern subspecies population was undoubtedly a consequence of poisoning and shooting because it was also considered a pest due to the damage it caused in wheat and cereal crop fields. Similarly to the Muir's Corella, the Butler race proved itself highly adaptable to the settlers' deforestation and the rapid conversion of the deforested lands to cereal production. Agriculture was accompanied not only by new food sources but also by reliable water resources. Additionally, legislation prohibiting the poisoning and unfettered shooting of the Butler's Corella helped prevent any further decline in the subspecies population. (A limited number of licences to shoot the subspecies are still available today in some agricultural districts.)

The subspecies in fact has extended its territory eastwards. As with Muir's Corella, quantifying the Butler is nevertheless difficult because it is somewhat nomadic and it is at times difficult to locate individual birds or flocks: from time to time certain flocks are known to frequent identifiable general localities during specific seasons. But the uncertainty about subspecies numbers is compounded because of its nomadic tendencies, in that its presence at a particular locality that it had been known to frequent in the past cannot be depended upon as a source for a reliable assessment of current population numbers: the birds may simply not return for several years to an area they inhabited in the past.

While the Butler's Corella numbers have not been quantified, the subspecies was never considered to be threatened with extinction. Its current population is now estimated to number 20,000 to 30,000 individuals (Department of Environment and Conservation 2007, "Note No. 19"). As is true of most other cockatoo species, the Butler's Corella remains a protected species.

Like the Muir's Corella, the Butler's race prefers lightly wooded country, particularly with high trees for nesting and roosting, woodlands along rivers, and farmlands with ample large trees and permanent water resources. They have been seen in mallee and mulga areas, and are now known around gardens and in the suburbs of towns (World Parrot Trust 2012) where they prosper; this adaptation is favorable to the species because killing them in populated urban areas would be difficult to justify, particularly if urban inhabitants develop a fondness for the species. And due to the establishment of farm dams to conserve water for the cultivation of cereal crops, the subspecies has simply extended its territory to these new, ample food and water resources, and trees for roosting and nesting.

Outside the breeding season the Butler's Corella is often seen gathered in large flocks at water holes, or while foraging, often accompanied by Galahs (*Eolophus roseicapilla*) (World Parrot Trust 2012). Presently, the bulk of its population is considered to be distributed between Dongara, Mingenew, Morawa and Three Springs. Originally, a large population inhabited the area between Moora and Dongra in the 1920s, but the population shifted both east and southeast as agriculture provided the subspecies more opportunities for food and permanent water (Department of Environment and Conservation 2007, "Note No. 19"). The distribution of Butler's Corella southwards towards terrain inhabited by Muir's Cockatoo raises the possibility that the two subspecies may someday cross-breed.

Propagation

The breeding characteristics of the species have been studied extensively in the wild, particularly Butler's Corella. It is assumed there are few if any differences between the two subspecies regarding their reproductive data. Both subspecies choose similar species trees with hollows containing at their bottoms rotted wood on which to nest, especially Marri, Jarrah, Flood Gum, and Salmon Gum (Johnstone 2011). Dead trees are chosen if live trees with suitable nesting hollows are unavailable. In the northern regions the Corella begins breeding in August (World Parrot Trust 2012), and in the southern regions eggs are laid in September and as late as November (Johnstone and Storr 1998). Clutches range in size from one to four eggs, the mode being three (Feral).

In a six-year study of the species it was found that the mean clutch size was 2.7 eggs, the mean brood size was 1.9 nestlings, and the mean number of young that fledged was 1.6 juveniles (Feral 2012). The field researchers found no significant annual differences in those data during their six years of field work. The incubation period is 24–29 days (Department of Environment and Conservation 2007, "Note No. 19"), although several sources have reported that the incubation period for the Muir's Corella is actually 26 to 29 days (Chapman and Cale 2006; Higgins 1999; North 1912; Johnstone and Storr 1998). Both parents incubate and feed the nestlings. The researchers found that hatching was asynchronous and the youngest nestlings did not survive in nests where the first hatched were considerably larger (Smith and Moore 1991). At about the sixtieth day the juveniles fledge, after which they remain dependent on their parents for approximately six months, but begin foraging for themselves two to three weeks after fledging (Department of Environment and Conservation 2007, "Note No. 19").

Once fledged the juveniles move with their parents to roosting sites and feeding areas, where they join other families that disperse to other regions for summer feeding. The young remain with the parents until the next breeding season, whereupon the immature birds join other young birds while the adults return to their breeding nest sites (Department of Environment and Conservation 2007, "Note No. 19"). It is believed that the corella reaches breeding age from three to five years of age, but based on the species' low population growth, it is also generally believed that most young birds do not live long enough to reach breeding age (Department of Environment and Conservation 2007, "Note No. 19"); given the species' low reproductivity, and the low percentage of young birds reaching reproductive age, it is estimated that a pair needs to be at least ten years old to replace themselves (Department of Environment and Conservation 2007, "Note No. 19"). The long-term study of the species found that in general pair-bonds tended to be long lasting, but the researchers also found that the divorce rate for first time breeders was 25 percent (Feral 2012). Smith and Moore in 1992 observed that breeding adults rarely separated from each other except when incubating or feeding.

Aviary Notes

The Western Long-billed Corella has been known to be difficult to breed in captivity. The species is quite intolerant of most other birds, and if housed with other species, as aviculturalists are prone to do with different but sometimes community compatible species, the Western Long-billed Corella is liable to injure or even kill the other birds occupying the same cage space. The male is also known to be aggressive from time to time both to the hen and their offspring. Where there is more than one aviary side by side, double mesh is recommended to prevent injuries or even avicide. Bird Care observes that the species is "rarely bred," and recommends that the breeding of the species necessitates an aviculturalist with the qualifications at the Specialist Breeder level.

Obtaining a pair of Western Long-billed Corellas (either race) for breeding is not difficult, if one is an Australian. A search of the Internet resulted in several advertisements in which the corella was offered for sale at various prices ranging from AU$300 to AU$450 per pair. A comparable search in both Europe and North America produced no advertisements offering the birds for sale.

The cockatoos require a large aviary: Bird Care (2012) recommends a minimum size of 4.5 meters long × 1.2 to 1.5 meters wide, and approximately 2.1 meters high (14.5' × 5' × 6'). The larger the aviary the more opportunity there is for the birds to adequately exercise, an important consideration when confinement restricts movement and encourages obesity.

The aviary should house several prospective nesting opportunities for the birds. Logs with hollows, or nesting boxes, should be large enough to have the nest as deep as 800 mm (3') from the entrance. The prospective nest box or logs can be vertical or on a slight angle. Once the pair have shown interest in one of the potential nest sites, the alternative logs or nest boxes should be gradually removed from the aviary. Rotted sawdust or wood shavings or comparable nontoxic materials, such as leaves, should compose the nesting materials in the nest box.

Although the species spends a considerable amount of time on the ground, where it feeds, several branches of different lengths and thicknesses should be provided to serve as perches, hung at different heights throughout the aviary. The Western Long-billed Corella is a curious, intelligent bird, known to be playful. Wooden toys can be strewn about to occupy the birds, toys that they can chew and throw about, and that will keep their beaks in trim. Live (nontoxic) tree branches with buds and/or leaves can also provide chewing opportunities. Additionally, chains or ropes can be hung from the ceiling, on which the birds can swing and climb. All of these measures are essential to provide the bird with opportunities for active involvement with its environment, an involvement essential to the birds' well-being and the prevention of boredom. From time to time, all of the aviary's wooden supplements such as perches and toys will have to be replaced as bit by bit the corellas destroy them in their daily search for diversion.

The birds should be fed with much of the native foods with which they are familiar, such as hawthorn bushes with ripening fruit, seeds of the Eucalypt, and acacia seeds, as well as the pine cones of introduced pine species, wheat and oats, or other grain types. But the corella will also eat a wide variety of foods with which it has no experience: walnuts, dry dog kibble, almonds, oranges, apples, other fruits, and various vegetables such as peas or broccoli or corn, to provide some notion of the bird's palate flexibility. Specially formulated parrot pellets can be purchased as a supplement to provide the birds a more nutritious variety.

If the pair is compatible with each other, expect two to three eggs, which the hen alone will incubate for 23–24 days (World Parrot Trust 2012). Approximately six to eight weeks after hatching the nestlings will fledge. They will become independent approximately four weeks afterwards, but will still rely on their parents to be occasionally fed. Based on experience, BirdCare (2012) advises that while the parent birds are generally responsible in their caring for their young, should they show any aggression towards their offspring, the young should be immediately removed to safety in another aviary.

Pet Companion

Despite its relative unattractiveness as compared to other parrots or cockatoos, and despite the fact that the Western Long-billed Corella has a general reputation as a pest in the farming community, it has nevertheless been a popular pet companion because of its excellence in talking, playfulness, intelligence, affectionate qualities, and bonding to its owner. The species has an aptitude to mimic, to dance, and to learn tricks without much training (Mulawka 1981). These qualities have been recognized for well over a century.

BirdCare writes that the bird may voluntarily roll over on its back while on the ground in its aviary or elsewhere and play with a toy, its feet up. While there is little anecdotal literature regarding the specie's antics, the reader is urged to go to the household computer and log onto the Internet: Google "Western Long-billed Cockatoo YouTube." There are at least twenty short videos of this species as pet companions (and a few of wild birds in trees in urban back yards). The videos will delight and astound you.

One video demonstrating the bird's remarkable intelligence comes immediately to mind: the woman (name undisclosed) was sitting on a couch in Australia (community unidentified) with her pet companion corella on the couch an arm's length away. The woman had a number of colored plastic drinking tumblers, the type that one provides toddlers—the child inserts a smaller tumbler into a larger one, and continues so with the remaining tumblers until all are fitted together in one neat little stack.

The woman would pick up a tumbler, the next size smaller than the biggest one sitting on the couch between herself and the bird, put that tumbler on the couch, and instruct the corella to pick it up and put it into the larger tumbler already in place in front of it, which the bird would do. Tumbler by tumbler, the corella fitted each new (smaller) tumbler into the stack until there were no more tumblers left, and all that remained was one small stack of tightly fitting tumblers sitting in front of the corella. The lady and her pet companion repeated the exercise. Again, the corella responded by stacking the tumblers together without hesitation or fumbling. Not once did the corella drop a tumbler. There were approximately ten tumblers. Try to get your cat to accomplish that insightful trick ... or your dog...

The lady then emptied a box of poker chips onto the couch and placed the now empty box in front of the corella. One by one, she picked a poker chip from the pile and laid it in front of the bird, and instructed the corella to pick it up and put it into the box. The bird did so for all twenty or thirty chips, one at a time as instructed, not hesitating whatever. Then she inverted the box, dumping the chips out again, but this time left the box inverted (i.e., box bottom facing towards the ceiling). On the bottom of the box was a slot, the kind of slot a child would find on her piggy bank allowing her to deposit coins. One by one the plastic chips were held out for the bird to take, and when instructed to do so, and only when told to do so, the corella would insert the chip into the slot, until one by one all twenty or thirty chips were thus disposed of.

There are other home videos, all of them worth viewing. As the ancient Chinese proverb has it, "A picture is worth a thousand words." The reader is encouraged to venture into that delightful You Tube world of the Western Long-billed Corella.

Regrettably, those of us living abroad will never have the opportunity to acquire this remarkable Australian bird, even though we can receive a smattering of delight by vicariously watching Australians interact with this marvellous and totally delightful avifauna.

8

Ducorps Cockatoo

Cacatua ducorpsii (Pucheran, 1853)

COMMON NAMES: Solomon's Cockatoo, *Cacatua ducorpsii,* Ducorps Cockatoo, Solomon Island Cockatoo, Solomonenkakadul, Solomon's Corella, Broad-crested Corella.
SUBSPECIES: None
LIFESPAN: (Estimated) 40 to 60 years.
IUCN RED LIST OF THREATENED SPECIES: Least Concern[1]
CITES RATING: Appendix II

Description

Endemic to several islands north of Australia, the Ducorps Cockatoo is somewhat larger than the Goffins Cockatoo, AKA the Tanimbar Cockatoo (*Cacatua goffini*), a cockatoo species for which it is often mistaken. And, it is smaller than the Umbrella Cockatoo (*Cacatua alba*), another white species for which it is also often mistaken. The cockatoo is approximately 30 cm (approximately 12") from beak to tail, weighing on average 300–450 grams (11–16 oz.), and is predominately white. Forshaw reports the wing span as 235–274 mm (9.2"–10.8") for males and 232–262 mm (9.1"–10.3") for females.

While the Ducorps Cockatoo closely resembles the Tanimbar Cockatoo (*Cacatua goffini*), it is completely white except that both the flight and tail underside feathers are lightly suffused with yellow. Additionally, the bases of both the chest and head feathers are a light carnation pink which is concealed by the white terminal ends of the feathers. But there are instances where some specimens have been known to have a few pinkish breast feathers that are pink from base to terminal ends. Often there is a faint pink wash to the head, brighter on the cheeks.

Like all other cockatoo species, the Ducorps Corella has a crest that it can erect at will. The crest is barely notable in the recumbent state, but when erected, it resembles a sail. The crest lacks any color except a faint pinkish hue to the feather bases, in contrast, for example, to the Leadbeater, Sulphur-crested, or Galah Cockatoos, whose crests are distinctly colorful. The Ducorps crest is short, abrupt, round and very broad, much like that of the Goffins Cockatoo, but larger. As is true of the other cockatoo species, the crest can be erected at will when the cockatoo is distressed, frightened, wary or in any other emotive state. By erecting the crest, the bird is communicating to fellow cockatoos, and to the cause of its distress: e.g., a predator, or another cockatoo attempting to usurp a nesting site.

The Ducorps Cockatoo is endemic to New Guinea and to many of the islands in the Solomon Islands area, but it is rarely seen in Europe or North America. The cockatoo has a reputation of being an ideal pet companion. Despite its healthy population of approximately 100,000 birds, every effort is made to prevent both legal and illegal trade in the species (photograph by Charles Lamb).

The Ducorps' periophthalmic ring is bare, but tinged in blue. The male's eye is deep brown while the female's has a reddish tinge to the brown. For all intents and purposes the species can be described as sexually monomorphic, because the eye color differential between the two sexes is so slight that the coloration can be easily mistaken. If the sex of a specific bird is important, then it is best to obtain a DNA test for the bird, or have its sex surgically ascertained. The eye color of juvenile birds is darker than an adult's, but in all other respects juveniles resemble their parents (World Parrot Trust 2012).

The beak is medium sized and horn colored, and the upper mandible is short and hooked. The legs and feet are greyish.

Differences in wing span, weight, and overall size between the sexes are insufficient to determine the sex by either appearance or measurement, even though males are often slightly larger.

Behavior

The Ducorps Cockatoo communicates in numerous ways. One way, of course, is through its vocalizations. The bird's crest, however, is also an important communicative device. When erected its crest is an emotional response to some condition in its environment: fear, aggression, frustration, excitement, curiosity, surprise, and any other of a variety of emotional issues.

Unlike other species of cockatoos, the Ducorps Cockatoo has been considered by some field workers and observers to be a relatively non-social cockatoo (Malaysia Bird Forum 2012).[2] But most field observations suggest otherwise. For example, Forshaw (1977) observed that the cockatoo could be frequently found in pairs (presumably mated pairs), and in his field studies during the 1940s, Mayr occasionally observed them in small flocks numbering up to six or eight individuals. Contemporary reports note observations of small flocks often seen flying above the tree canopy.

The species is, nevertheless, wary, cautious, and often nervous, and can generally be found perching only in the highest trees in a given region (Mayr 1945), where they are conspicuously visible and noisy. Whenever disturbed, they fly off with considerable shrieking. When the birds are on the ground feeding or watering, a sentinel cockatoo will remain perched on a nearby towering tree, and in the event of any suspicious or threatening activity, its distress call will send the others into the air, screeching.

Small flocks of Ducorps Cockatoo will often forage in cultivated garden plots, where they cause some damage. In his field studies during 1977 Forshaw observed that small flocks occasionally raided the plots for "pawpaws and ... sweet potatoes." But at other times, the Ducorps Cockatoo is known to descend in large flocks on plantations, causing considerable damage to crops of bananas, papaya, and sweet potatoes (Malaysia Bird Forum 2012); discussion on the Malaysian Bird Forum claims the damage is tolerated by the islanders who are reported never to harm the birds, an assertion that raises eyebrows.

Almost a century earlier, during 1880, Lanyard observed the Ducorps feeding on mangroves along sea arms, but it is not clear whether such mangroves were in cultivated areas or whether they were growing in the wild. The birds are known to feed on seeds, nuts, native fruits and berries, and insects and their larvae, and also some epiphytes (World Parrot Trust 2012). In fact, gizzard and stomach contents of dissected birds confirms that their diet is composed primarily of fruits and greens, and some soft bodied insects such as caterpillars (Cain and Gailbraith 1956).

The cockatoo's voice has been variously described. Cain and Gailbraith in 1956 described the call as a harsh "erek ... errk," the call often ending in a prolonged screech. World Parrot Trust (2012) describes the vocalization as "harsh and somewhat screechy; [the] screech can be continuous and resemble [the] Little Corella."

Habitat and Distribution

The Ducorps Cockatoo is endemic to the Bougainville and Baka islands in East Papua New Guinea, and the Solomon Islands east to Malaita Island, and as far south as Makira, but does not occur in the San Cristobal group of islands, not far distant. It is common throughout most of its range.

The species' choice of habitat includes a variety of environs, ranging from mountains as high as cloud level at 1,700 meters (just over a mile high), as Cain and Galbraith observed, to coastal regions as low as sea level, as Mayre found. The species is prone to prefer terrains under 700 meters (approximately 2,000'); however, where the birds were common, Layard in 1880 regularly observed them along water edges in inland sea arms. They can also be found in rain forests, along their edges, and woodlands and townships, and while they prefer the tropical forests they can also be found in secondary growths and even open areas (World Parrot Trust 2012). Mayre found that the Ducorps often frequented settlement areas, where it was attracted by small garden plots planted by the islanders.

While the population of the species is spread over several islands and its territorial habitat is limited in size, the Ducorps Cockatoo population is not fragmented in those areas. To date its population has not been quantified, but it is reported as being stable throughout its territorial range; its current population worldwide is estimated to be above 100,000 (IUCN Red List 2012).

Propagation

Until relatively recently, the early 1990s, the Ducorps Cockatoo was rarely encountered in captivity. It was not only rare in respect to its availability for the pet trade; there was and still is virtually little field research regarding this species and its life cycle. Because the species is a CITES II listing, there are virtually no Ducorps in North American or European aviaries, either as breeding stock or as companion pets. As a CITES signatory, Australia prohibits the importation of the species.

The cockatoo normally breeds from July to September in its natural habitat, and has been reported to breed as late as December (Malaysia Bird Forum 2012)—whether the late December breedings applied to captive birds or pairs in the wild was not specified. As is typical of cockatoos, the Ducorp's Cockatoo chooses the tallest available tree with a hollow either in the trunk or the stump of a broken branch. Rotten wood at the bottom of the hollow normally forms the nest bedding upon which two to three elliptical, white eggs are laid. There are no recent reports of egg sizes, but in the British Museum in 1977 Forshaw found several eggs whose dimensions are 37.5 (35.5–36.50) mm × 26.7 (25.4–27.9) mm (1.4" [1.44"–1.3"] × 1" [1"–1.1"]).

The ideal location of the chosen nest site is close to both food and water resources. Since the cockatoo is relatively asocial, and is known to be aggressive to other breeding pairs, its nest is typically some distance away from any other nesting pairs. Both parents take part in the incubation and the feeding of the young. The incubation period is 26 to 28 days (World Parrot Trust 2012) and the juveniles fledge approximately 62 days after hatching (Alderton 2003). The young are believed to reach sexual maturity from three to five years of age.

The Ducorp's Cockatoo is reported to consistently return to the same nesting site each year (Malaysia Bird Forum 2012). Given the sparse fieldwork studies regarding this species, it is unclear how that conclusion was reached. While it is true that some cockatoo species mate for life, and some do return yearly to a preferred nest site, it is not necessarily true that the Ducorps Cockatoo follows the same pattern.

Aviary Notes

The data on the Ducorps Cockatoo's breeding in captivity is sparse at best. While the Ducorps Cockatoo is considered an exceptional cockatoo because of its aesthetic attractiveness and its delightful personality, it is extremely rare in captivity. It is currently not considered a threatened species, but it is listed as CITES Appendix II, which means that few members of this cockatoo are exported, legally or otherwise, to meet the pet trade demand for exotic birds. In the United States, a very few Ducorps Cockatoos were imported prior to 1993, at which time the United States prohibited all further commercial importations of bird fauna, except under special circumstances. Since then, the United States has prohibited the commercial importation of any birds listed by CITES, regardless of its origin or the purpose for which it is being imported (by zoos, for example, for exhibition), which in fact includes most parrots (Sea World 2012). The Ducorps Cockatoo falls in the prohibited importation class.

Obtaining specimens for breeding purposes will be difficult at best. In view of the limited amount of information available for the successful breeding of the species, and the difficulty in obtaining a breeding pair, it is advised that such a project should be embarked upon by specialist breeders only, and only after a compatible bonded pair of legally acquired birds have been identified and acquired.

Because of the size of the bird, the aviary should be at least four to five meters (13'–16') long, approximately 1.2 to 1.5 meters wide (4'–4.5'), and approximately 2 meters (6') high (World Parrot Trust 2012). It should be partially covered to provide the cockatoos shelter from the sun and rain. In northern climates, frost and cold, wintery conditions are major concerns if the birds are to be kept outdoors. Because the species shows an intolerance for other birds, including its own peers, not only should the pair be placed in an aviary by themselves, but the aviary should be isolated from others.

The pair should be provided three to four different possible nesting sites in the aviary, scattered at different locations: logs with hollows in them, and grandfather-clock-type nesting boxes. If the birds have been obtained from a breeder, it would be advisable to find out the nesting arrangements in which the birds were hatched and reared at the aviculturalist's aviary. The nesting sites offered the birds should emulate those of the breeders. Once the birds have shown a definite interest in a specific nesting site, the other nesting alternatives should be gradually removed.

The male Ducorps Cockatoo is known to be an excessively aggressive bird during the breeding period, and can injure the hen. In addition, it is generally believed that if disturbed the male may harm the eggs (Malaysia Bird Forum 2012). The nesting site should be constructed in such a manner as to provide the female an opportunity to escape the male's aggression. It is also advisable to clip short two or three of the male's flight feathers on one of its wings; they should be clipped just short enough to prevent the cock from pursuing the fleeing female should he become aggressive, but not so short that he would be unable to glide safely to the floor should he fall off a perch, or so short as to cut into the blood vein.

The Ducorps Cockatoo is an intelligent bird requiring a stimulating environment. Ropes can be hung from the ceiling; chewable, disposable wooden or leather toys should be provided to interest the birds; and several wooden perches of different diameters and lengths at various heights and locations should be also provided. Because the cockatoo enjoys chewing, be prepared to replace demolished toys and perches on a regular basis as needed. Additionally, nontoxic, live branches with buds, leaves and/or fruit will keep the cockatoos busy and partly fed. The chewing not only entertains the birds but keeps them from becoming bored; and, of course, the activity also provides excellent beak exercise and trim.

The diet for the cockatoos can consist in a wide range of foods: mixtures of small seeds, beans (dry or sprouted), butter beans and lentils, various green leaves such a dandelions, lettuce or shard, and various fruits ranging from those commonly grown in northern climates such as apples and pears to those grown in the Southern Hemisphere such as bananas and papaya. Of course, nuts are also relished by the birds (World Parrot Trust 2012). A word of caution: while most birds relish seeds and nuts, an over-reliance on them as a main part of their daily diet is not advisable because the fat content in some of the seeds tends to make the birds obese, sunflower seeds being a good example. The bird's water and food bowls should be secured, for otherwise the birds will either overturn them in their play or simply empty them by turning them upside down—just for something to do that's different.

As noted earlier, the Ducorps Cockatoo is a nervous bird, and unnecessary intrusions in the aviary area should be avoided.

Pet Companion

It is a rare individual living in either Europe or North America who has been able to acquire a Ducorps Cockatoo. A thorough search of the Internet in November 2012 produced only one American advertisement for a Ducorps Cockatoo for sale: the asking price was $895. Given its rarity in the United States, the asking price was more than reasonable. In addition to that one American advertisement, there were four or five in Great Britain, the asking prices there ranging from £350 ($550) for a bird that was described as "unfriendly" to four or five hand-weaned nestlings starting at £895 ($1,400) per specimen.

Although the Ducorps Cockatoo is a rare bird in captivity, there are a few scattered about Europe and North America. The Ducorps Cockatoo are particularly popular cockatoos because of their elegance, intelligence, mimicry, inquisitiveness, and gentle and loving nature. They are beautiful, particularly with their bluish-tinged periophthalmic ring. They are generally quite affectionate with humans and appear quite comfortable with large numbers of people (Sea World 2012). Compared with other cockatoos, the Ducorps Cockatoo is considered quieter, but be forewarned that a trauma from the bird's perspective can set it screeching at a volume that could easily alienate nearby neighbors.

The cockatoo should be housed in as large a cage as possible given the size of one's living accommodations. If it is impossible to keep the bird in its own separate room, the cockatoo will do quite well in a cage in a common room in the home where there is frequent traffic, and where there is some regular interaction possible with the companion pet. The larger its cage the better; a cage should at least approach a meter square (3' × 3' × 3') to provide the bird ample room to stretch its wings.

The bird should be provided several wooden toys upon which to chew. Its food and water bowls should be secured to the cage to prevent them from being upturned in the bird's quest for activity. Additionally, the cockatoo demonstrates its cleverness by devising means to escape the confines of its cage when boredom strikes it. Some cockatoo owners devise complex locking devices to keep the avian escape artist confined, while others simply padlock the cage with a small lock. While an escaped, inquisitive bird could cause some damage to household items, more critically it could also injure itself by its natural exploration of the contents of the room: exploration such as chewing on electrical wires could prove lethal, for example. A chewed knickknack is much easier to replace than a living, loved creature, considered a family member, that has been electrocuted

The Ducorps Cockatoo's personality requires constant stimulation, attention, and interaction from its owner. Much of the stimulation can be provided the bird through the various toys placed in its cage, and regular replacements with novel wooden or leather objects. But because the cockatoo requires attention, the owner needs to be both extremely dedicated to his pet and willing to provide the attention it deserves. This means spending some high quality, interactive time with it. Consistent training is needed to ensure that the pet does not acquire annoying and destructive habits. Cockatoos constantly left to their own devices do not emotionally thrive, and they tend to develop behaviors that are difficult to reverse. Like other living beings, farm animals, for example, the Ducorps Cockatoo thrives better when there is a definite routine in the home, and the routine involves the pet companion.

The species can become a good mimic, acquiring reasonable vocabularies of words and various sounds common in a typical household, and can display various behaviors of attachment and endearment.[3] It can be taught diverse tricks (Mulawka 1981; Muth 2012), and are known to sometimes even dance to music.

The Ducorps Cockatoo is easy to feed: as noted earlier, it appears to eat just about anything.

Finally, it is advisable to identify a veterinarian who *specializes* in birds and their ailments. Most veterinarians, while knowledgeable about health issues pertaining to mammals, know little about birds. A good rule of thumb to remember: if your bird does not eat anything today, be concerned. If it eats nothing the following day, get it to a vet immediately.

Taking care of a pet companion Ducorps Cockatoo is the smallest worry a prospective owner will have to contend with. The real problem rests in being able to locate one that is for sale and getting the opportunity to buy it before someone else does.

9

Goffin's Cockatoo

Cacatua goffiniana (Finsch, 1863)

COMMON NAMES: Tanimbar Cockatoo, Goffin's Corella, Tanimbar Corella
SUBSPECIES: None
LIFESPAN: (estimated) up to 40 years in captivity
IUCN RED LIST OF THREATENED SPECIES: Near Threatened
CITES: Appendix II[1]

Description

The Goffin's Cockatoo is the smallest of all the cockatoo forms, aside from the Cockatiel (*Nymphicus hollandicus*), which is uniquely different from all the other cockatoo types. The Goffin's Cockatoo weighs on average 350 grams (12 oz.) and is on average approximately 32 cm (11") in length from the tip of the beak to the tip of the tail.

In overall appearance the cockatoo is white feathered with some minor head coloration. The lores are a salmon-pink color, and the ear covers are tinged faintly in yellow. The periophthalmic ring is both bare and white/blue, and the curved beak is greyish-bone colored. Both the undersides of the undertail coverts and the flight feathers are tinged in light yellow.

As with other cockatoo species, the Goffin's Cockatoo has a crest: its crest is white, short, and recumbent backwards. But unlike the other cockatoo species, this cockatoo's crest feathers do not extend past the rear of the crown. Depending on the emotional state of the cockatoo, the crest can be raised and lowered at will. When raised, the crest is round, broad, and helmet shaped. The proximal, deeper parts of the crest feathers are also faintly tinged salmon-pink. When the crest is recumbent, this color is hidden by the upper white crest plumage, it does not come into view unless the crest is raised. The deeper proximal feathers are also faintly salmon colored, the color hidden by the superficial distal areas of these feathers.

All other plumage is stark white.

The lower parts of the legs are greyish, particularly the inner thighs (due to a sparsity of feathers and down), and the feet are mealy colored. As with other cockatoos, the Goffin's foot is zygodactyl: two toes face forward and the other two toes face backward.

The species can be best described as monomorphic in appearance, although upon close examination there is a difference in eye color: the female's eyes are reddish brown, whereas the male's eye coloration is distinctly brown. This color differential is not always readily obvious, however. When the sex of the Goffin's Cockatoo is important, a DNA test or surgical procedure is advised. Males are distinctly larger than females, both in weight, wing, and tail dimensions, but again these differences are not reliable sex predicators.

The Goffin's Cockatoo is often confused with the Bare-eyed Cockatoo (*Cacatua sanguinea*), also known as the Little Corella, because of their similar general appearance. Although related, the two cockatoo types are separated by hundreds of kilometers (miles).

Behavior

As is typical of most of the cockatoos common to the Indonesian islands, there is little documented study of the species in the wild. Information on their life activities and behavior is sparse at best, despite the fact that the species has been collected for many decades for the pet trade, both legally in the past and now illegally in the present.

The Goffin's Cockatoo, AKA Timimbar Corella, is endemic to Indonesia and is the second smallest of all the cockatoos. It is an intelligent bird, cuddly and playful, and reciprocates emotional relations. It is estimated there are approximately 400,000–500,000 Goffin's worldwide (photograph by Lip Kee).

The Goffin's Cockatoo is a social bird, having been seen in flocks numbering as many as 300 individuals when not in the breeding season. The species is also a communal roosting bird, which makes it extremely vulnerable to trapping for the pet trade. Despite the limited land mass on which the species is endemic and despite heavy trapping for the pet trade, the cockatoo appears to have maintained a stable population (BirdLife International 2012b). During the breeding season, however, these birds are often only seen in pairs or small flocks. They are conspicuous not only because of their whiteness and flocking behavior, but because they are quite noisy.

Being omnivorous, the cockatoos feed primarily in the tree tops on diverse fruits, blossoms and seeds and nuts. They are believed to also feed on insects and their larvae. Specifics on exactly what foods are eaten is generalized because little is known of their exact diet in the wild (World Parrot Trust 2012). The cockatoo is known to forage on crops, however, particularly maize, which causes much damage to agriculture; it is considered a pest by indigenous farmers.

World Parrot Trust (an organization dedicated to collecting data on the species and educating the public on its protection) has no available information on the species' behavior in the wild, except to say it "may be vocal at night. In display birds strut, crest raised." Parrot Link (2012) reports that the strutting is accompanied by shrieking. Avian Web (2012) describes the cockatoo's flight as graceful (with no other details provided).

Habitat and Distribution

The Goffin's Cockatoo is endemic to Indonesia, specifically to all forested areas of all islands in the Tanimbar Islands archipelago—Maluku Province (Juniper and Parr 1998). The species has also been introduced to Puerto Rico and Singapore (BirdLife Species Fact Sheet 2012), and to the Kai Islands, Indonesia (Juniper and Parr 1998). In fact, in Singapore, feral populations of the Goffin's Cockatoo are reported as being common in urban gardens and parklands (World Parrot Trust 2012). Over a century ago, Hartert (1901) reported the birds common on Kai Kecil, where it is believed to have been introduced. The species is relatively common to the forests of Selaru, Yamdena, and Larat, but the deforestation taking place on the islands is a major threat to population density, particularly in view of the pet trade trapping.

The species is typically found in the moist, lowland coastal forests, deciduous forests, and other regions thick with vegetation. The species' total territory over the various islands, most of them small, is less than 5,000 square kilometers (approximately less than 3,200 square miles). While there has been considerable logging of tropical forests, the cockatoos' population has not been severely fragmented or restricted to a few isolated locations (BirdLife International 2012). While the cockatoo prefers lowland primary forests, it can also be readily found in both secondary forest growth and in cultivated areas. The species has not been quantified in any of its endemic habitats, and there is no information available about its numbers in regions where it has been introduced.

Propagation

There are very few field notes concerning the Goffin in the wild except for a few hand lists of birds either collected or sighted during field expeditions, and those expeditions were few and far apart, indeed. What little is known of the species' breeding has been almost exclusively drawn from observational experiences of the Goffin in captivity.

Aviary Notes

The Goffin's Cockatoo breeds in captivity more frequently and successfully than some correspondents would have the avicultural world believe. The published materials on the species' breedability in captivity falls into two main camps: there are some reports that claim that the cockatoo is difficult to breed in captivity, without providing evidence for that conclusion; then there are various published accounts that claim that the species is easily bred. The evidence provided that they do breed well in captivity is the oft-quoted estimate of there being approximately 400,000–500,000 goffins in the world (BirdLife International 2012b), most of them believed to have been bred in captivity. How this figure was arrived at is unclear, for even during the pre-commercial harvesting of the birds for the pet trade, it is difficult to imagine those numbers of birds inhabiting a few small islands. Early field notes never report the species in numbers larger than 200–400 birds per flock, and based on breeding reports, while the species breeds easily in captivity, it does not breed as prolifically as the Cockatiel, for example, which may have five or sex nestlings per clutch, and two or three clutches per year. Hence the purported 400,000–500,000 population is questionable.

Despite its reported easy breeding, published particulars regarding the technical aspects associated with captive breeding are unavailable. A search of the Internet at the time of this writing found at least 100 Goffin's Cockatoos for sale in the United States, at prices ranging as low as $450 to $850 (hand-reared and weaned). The relatively low price of the birds would suggest one of two probabilities: first, that there are more birds being hatched and reared to fledgling age than there are customers clamoring to obtain one, or second, that the cockatoo is so unfavorably perceived that there is a very limited market. But in 1985, Mrs. Low included the Goffin in her book *Endangered Parrots*, noting that it is the most common parrot in captivity as well as being the least expensive and "least appreciated."

In Australia, which has stringent laws regarding both the import and export of fauna, the species is an expensive investment. In Great Britain, proof that the Goffin's Cockatoo is domestically bred is required before a licence will be issued providing the bird fancier permission to purchase and/or possess the cockatoo. These types of governmental demands are not made when in fact a species breeds easily in captivity and there is no overt concern of illegally acquired birds threatening the species' viability.

Historically, the Goffin's Cockatoo in captivity was considered difficult to breed. In fact, there are no published records prior to 1970 of the bird having been bred in captivity, although Alderton in 1982 reported that the bird had been bred in small numbers both in Europe and Great Britain. In writing about the species over a century ago Dr. Greene boldly conveyed the impression that the species was readily bred in a captive environment, for he briefly advised his contemporary aviculturalists on the appropriate care of the young and the various precautions essential to ensure their survival. However, despite the fact that the British meticulously kept records of the "first breeding" of all the myriad of avian species that flooded into Britain after their discoveries in the South Pacific and South America, plus all the other newly discovered lands in the 18th and 19th centuries, the distinguished recognition of "first breeding" for the Goffin Cockatoo was never awarded to a British or European aviculturalist for the successful breeding of the species during those two centuries. In fact, it was not until 1977 that the cockatoo was officially recognized as having been successfully bred in Great Britain, an event that resulted in the breeder's nomination for the "first breeder" award.

The first reported successful breeding of the Goffin Cockatoo was by E.G.B. Schulte in 1975 in California, whose pair had three clutches within two years. All three clutches hatched, but only the four nestlings from the last two clutches were successfully raised past the fledgling stage.

The second published successful breeding—Britain's first—was an event in Neil O'Connor's aviaries at Coulsdon, Surrey, in 1977. O'Connor's pair produced a clutch of three, but the parents only raised one to maturity.

The aviary sizes reported by both aviculturalists were surprisingly small, given the common practice of providing cockatoos with larger living accommodations. O'Connor's pair were housed in an aviary measuring 9 × 3 × 6 feet high (approximately 3 meters × 1 meter × 2 meters) with a nest box 22" × 15" × 11" (564 cm × 38 cm × 28 cm), whereas Schulte's Goffins were housed in a box cage measuring 87 cm × 44 cm × 70 cm high (33" × 17" × 27", with a nest box 25 cm × 25 cm × 40 cm (10" × 10" × 16").

In both cases the birds showed immediate interest in the nesting facilities. In 1977 O'Connor described the Goffin's copulation as "versatile." He described the behavior as follows:

> Both birds remain on the perch facing opposite directions and back on to each other with tails raised and appear to perform the function in this manner. Another variation involves the cock gripping the perch with one foot and the wire side of the aviary with the other adopting an upside down posture with the vent on the same level as the perch; the hen remains on the perch and positions herself in a suitable manner.

Schulte did not report any similar variances to the normal copulatory behavior of his birds.

Copulation was frequent, continuing well after the clutches had been successfully incubated (even as late as mid-winter, when frost covered the perches). Mutual preening of the vent areas proceeded and followed copulation. There was no other mating or courtship behavior observed.

Clutches were laid in late spring, with the eggs hatching before July. Both adults in both pairs attended their nests, and each pair remained in the nest box from the time the first egg was laid until about a month after hatching, according to Schulte. O'Connor reported that his pair displayed considerable nervousness whenever there were any intrusions in the immediate aviary area, a behavior that was not reported by Schulte.

A pair usually mates for life. The average clutch consists of two or three white eggs, occasionally four. A pair normally have one clutch a year. Schulte (1975) reported his three eggs' sizes as 40–38 mm × 36–27 mm (1.6"–1.5" × 1.4"–1.1"). These figures are in conflict with sizes provided by the World Parrot Trust, which were 38.5 × 28.5 mm (1.5" × 1.1"), sizes almost identical to those provided by Forshaw (1977), whose sizes were obtained from both the British Museum and Berlin Museum collections.

The incubation period is approximately 28 days, with both parents participating in the incubation. Newly hatched nestlings have no colored down. By the third week feather sheaths begin appearing on both the wings and the head. The young fledge from ten to twelve weeks after hatching. The young resemble their parents except for the irises which are black. For approximately three weeks afterwards the hen continues to feed her fledged young. After that the newly fledged appear quite independent.

As noted earlier, the Shulte and O'Connor aviaries were relatively small, as compared to most aviaries for other cockatoo species. But then, the Goffin's Cockatoo is a small bird. Most cockatoo housing arrangements are approximately 5 meters long × 1.5 meters wide × 2.1 meters high (16' × 4.5' × 6.5'). While a larger housing arrangement is preferable to a smaller one, the Goffin's Cockatoo is quite content with smaller enclosures. Regarding nesting provisions, either a log with a hollow or a normal nesting box 25 cm × 25 cm × 40 cm (10" × 10" × 16") is quite suitable for nesting. Three or four nesting boxes or logs should be scattered about the aviary, preferably in secluded, darker areas, providing the pair with a choice. Once the cockatoos begin favoring one of the potential nesting sites, the others should be gradually removed. Nesting materials such as sawdust, wood shavings and even paper should be provided. What the birds do not want, or consider surplus, they will dispose of.

The nest box itself should be constructed in such a way as to provide the hen an easy escape should the male become aggressive, which at times they are apt to become during the breeding season. Extremely aggressive males should have their flight feathers clipped just enough so that the cock cannot fly and pursue the fleeing hen. The feather clipping, however, should not prevent the male from gliding gently to the floor in the event it should fall off a perch, and in cutting the feathers one needs to be careful not to cut into the vein. (Indeed, males that reveal a tendency to be aggressive should have their wings clipped before introducing them to a female.)

Because the cockatoo tends to be a shy bird, preferring some privacy, inspections and interference with the birds' daily life should be minimized (Bird Care 2012).

Since the Goffin's Cockatoo likes to chew, fresh branches from nontoxic trees or bushes should be provided, as well as sturdy wooden toys. Rope curled and hanging from the ceiling provides the birds with some stimulating resemblance of tropical forest vegetation. Wooden perches should be provided. Because of the cockatoo's propensity to chew and destroy perches, toys, branches, and wooden cage paraphernalia, all will have to be routinely replaced.

As noted in the following section, the Goffin's Cockatoo is not a finicky eater and will accept a diverse foods including leafy vegetable greens, dandelions, fruits such as oranges and apples, seeds such as buckwheat, oats, maize, diverse nuts, and commercially produced, nutritionally balanced pellets.

On a final note, the Goffin's defecation is more watery than dry. To prevent disease and sickness, the living space should be cleaned regularly.

Pet Companion

Anyone suffering from a respiratory ailment, or asthma, would be well advised not to purchase a Goffin's Cockatoo: the bird exudes a white powder that it uses to groom its feathers. Since the powder is not confined to the feathers, it could be hazardous to the health and aggravate breathing difficulties.

The Goffin's Cockatoo has unfortunately not been as popular a companion cockatoo as have some other species of the cockatoo family, for example the Sulphur-crested species (*Cacatua sulphurea*), despite its captive commonality. The Goffin's Cockatoo is not quite as flamboyant or colorful a cockatoo as some of the other cockatoo species that are available to potential pet owners; not as eye catching, and not an accomplished mimic. Yet, for the right owner, the Goffin's Cockatoo is a desirable pet that can provide hours of enjoyment for the family. There are more advantages to the ownership of this cockatoo than there are disadvantages. Besides, this cockatoo is one of the world's most elegant birds, and it is not expensive.

The cockatoo is considerably smaller than the other cockatoo species, an ideal size for persons without the home space that is normally required for larger species. While a large sized cage such as a macaw cage would be preferable, a smaller cage—32" × 23" × 36" (800 cm × 600 cm × 900 cm) with the metal bars spaced no further than one inch apart—will be quite adequate. A couple of wooden perches of varying size and diameters should be provided.

Because the cockatoo is smaller, it is easier to handle, to carry about on one's shoulder, for example. If provided a stimulating caged environment, the cockatoo is often quite content to spend its time without humans, chewing on the diverse toys provided it, and/or climbing on ropes or other jungle-type climbing obstacles. Chewing toys should be changed routinely to provide the cockatoo with variety. The toys are physically beneficial to the birds because they provide some beak exercise.

But the cockatoo requires some freedom from its cage during some of its regular daily regimen. The freedom from constant confinement provides the cockatoo opportunity to escape imprisonment-imposed boredom and all the negative consequences of that boredom. Bored cockatoos can develop severe behavioral problems when constantly caged and without a stimulating environment and without interaction with family members.

Although Goffin's Cockatoos are generally shy, they are affectionate and will reciprocate affection; they appear to relish social interaction with their owners, and they are known for their cuddliness, all incentives for the owner to engage with the pet. The cockatoos enjoy being stroked and handled. They have a reputation for being playful, and are equally renowned for their high intelligence. It is not at all uncommon for a Goffin's Cockatoo to learn by watching and through trial and error eventually determine how to open the latch to its cage with its beak, and hence escape, only to have its owner arrive home later and be totally astounded to find the Goffin perched on the top of its cage.

Because they are intelligent and socially oriented, they are easy to train, and can be taught tricks, such as lying on their backs in the palm of the hand, and being gently tossed into the air (Mulawka 1981).

While the Goffin's Cockatoo is quieter than most other cockatoo species, it can be a noisy bird from time to time, particularly if it does not have an enriching or stimulating environment, or at least some minimal social interaction with the owner. While the occasional individual cockatoo can imitate some human speech, particularly if hand-reared from hatching, in general the species is not known for being good talkers, or imitators of other interesting sounds.

The Goffin's Cockatoo is easy to maintain regarding its diet. While there are a variety of commercially produced formulated cockatoo diets, seed-based mixtures should be sparingly provided the cockatoo, because the seed-only diet has a high fat content, detrimental to good health. There are also available specially formulated, balanced, feed pellets with all the necessary nutrients. But cockatoos require a varied diet and will readily accept most of what is provided them. They enjoy fruits such as slices of apples, oranges and bananas, for example. Various vegetables such as broccoli and leafy greens provide calcium and are excellent supplements. Providing the Goffin with chopped hard-boiled eggs or bits of cooked meat adds protein to their diet. The list is endless.

Hand feeding the cockatoo a treat once or twice a day will help bond the bird to its owner. It is a rare Goffin that cannot be seduced by a raisin.

Despite what may appear above to be a glowing account of this charming cockatoo, there are some concerns the Goffin owner should be aware of. While it is not necessarily a noisy bird, an individual cockatoo that has acquired shrieking tendencies can be problematic for nearby neighbors. This is particularly a common problem with young Goffins that have been hand reared by a breeder but were poorly weaned (Goffin's Cockatoo 2012). Their screeching can be controlled through the provision of various activities, affection, and lots of attention. Constant attention and interaction with the cockatoo is essential not only to discourage and hence diminish shrieking, but also to prevent the bird from acquiring this unpleasant behavior. A Goffin proves to be a delightful pet. Try one, if you can acquire one, and you will be a rare individual if you do not fall in love with it, almost instantaneously.

Scientific Naming History

In 1863 Otto Finsch discovered the Goffin's Cockatoo. He named the species after his friend Andreas Goffin. In the year 2000 it became obvious that Finsch's description of the species was based upon two specimens of an entirely different species, the Ducorps Cockatoo, *Cacatua ducorpsi* (Roselaar and Prins 2000). In effect, the Goffin's Cockatoo was left without a proper description or scientific name. In 2004, the species was formally named *Cacatua goffiniana* (Roselaar and Michels 2004).

While the species is now formally known as the Tanimbar Cockatoo as its common name, the cockatoo is still more often than not referred to as the Goffin's Cockatoo, as we have done herein.

10

Little Corella

Cacatua sanguinea (Gould, 1843)

COMMON NAMES: Blood-stained Cockatoo, Bare-eyed Cockatoo, Short-billed Cockatoo, Blue-eyed Cockatoo, Corella, Dampier's Corella, Little Corella
Cockatoo, Little Cockatoo, Sclater's Bare-eyed Cockatoo, Mathew's
Little Corella, New Guinea Little Corella, *Cacatua pastinator pastinator*, a Latin nomenclenture mistakenly applied to the Little Corella
when in fact it is the Latin name for the Western Long-billed Corella.

SUBSPECIES:
1. *Cacatua sanguinea saguinea* (Gould, 1843)—Nominate Race
2. *Cacatua sanguinea normantoni* (Mathews, 1871)
3. *Cacatua sanguinea transfreta* (Mees, 1982)
4. *Cacatua sanguinea gymnopis* (Sclater, 1871)
5. *Cacatua sanguinea westralensis* (Gould, 1843)

LIFESPAN: Estimated from as low as twenty-plus years to eighty.

IUCN RED LIST OF THREATENED SPECIES: Least Concern

Description

The Little Corella is a medium sized bird ranging from 36 to 39 cm (14"–15.2") long and weighing anywhere from 350 grams (12.3 oz.) to as much as 630 grams (22 oz.), depending upon subspecies. Forshaw provides the wing lengths as ranging from 238 to 280 mm (approximately 9"–11"), the differences again reflecting the particular subspecies differentials. The bird is primarily white on both upper and lower parts, and can be described at best as a homely bird and at worst as a blatantly unattractive bird; because of its feeding habits, the breast often has a dirty reddish color that results from the soils in which it forages. Additionally, despite its remarkably delightful, playful personality, its positive qualities are contaminated by the generally held opinion that they are (agriculturally) pests, and hence undesirable.

Nevertheless, the species is unique in many ways. In terms of color, the basal portions of its cheek, throat and hind neck feathers are rose colored, whereas lores feathers are orangish pink from basal to terminal ends. The ear coverts are a dusky yellow. All other head feathers, however, are white, as is the rest of the bird's plumage. The Little Corella can be easily distinguished from the Western Long-billed Corella (*C.p. pastinator*), for which it is often mistaken, by the absence of an orange throat bar (Pizzey and Knight 1997).

The Little Corella has earned itself the reputation of being an agricultural "pest." It is believed that there are well over a million of these cockatoos. While their agricultural damage is cause for considerable concern, individuals who have them as pets have nothing but praise for their talents in mimicry, and even dancing (photograph by Melanie C. Underwood).

The bird's crest is short, almost blunt, and recumbent, and when compared to the rest of the various cockatoo species, can be best described as non-distinctive, and without of colorful flamboyancy as compared to, for example, a Moluccan Cockatoo's (*Cacatua moluccensis*). Like other cockatoos, the Little Corella will erect its crest when it is alarmed, curious, distressed, angry, or in any other emotional state. Usually, however, the crest lies recumbent and is not conspicuous.

The cockatoo's bill is a horn white, with both mandibles being of equal length. The tail is short and blunt.

The most unusual feature of the species is the periophthalmic eye ring, which, unlike the rings of other cockatoos, which are more or less round in contour, is elongated and extends well below the eye, almost teardrop shaped. The entire ring is bare of feathers and is colored a slate blue. The iris for both males and females is a rich brown. There is a faint wash of yellow to the bases of all flight feathers and to the inner webs of both primary and tail feathers, excepting the middle two, which are sulphur yellow in coloration. The feet are bluish grey, and are zygodactyl.

Upon fledging, juvenile birds closely resemble the adults in appearance, the exception being that the lower part of the periophthalmic ring elongation is not quite fully developed; the ring is more symmetrically circular in shape than on mature adults. The juvenile Little Corella Nominate subspecies *C.s. sanguinea* has a much paler blue periophthalmic ring than the other Lesser Corella juvenile subspecies.

The Little Corella is sexually monomorphic, and the only way to reliably determine the bird's sex with any degree of assured accuracy is either through surgical means or through DNA analysis. Males tend to be slightly larger, but the size difference is not always easily obvious and is therefore an unreliable means of sex determination.

In respect to the various subspecies, there are some coloration and size differentials. The *C.s. normantoni* is similar to the Nominate race, the *C.s. sanguinea,* except that it is slightly smaller. The *C.s. transfreta* is similar in size to the *normantoni* but the undertail and underwing feathers are yellowish brown as compared to the *C.s. normantoni.* The *C.s. gymnopsis* has a brighter rosy pink to its lores and head feathers, as well as to its upper breast, back of neck, and foreneck feathers, and it has a darker blue periophthalmic ring. The colors of the *C.s. westralensis* are brighter and more intense than the colors on the *gymnopsis,* the colors actually reaching down to both thighs and underparts, and the tail is washed in a light tinge of yellow (World Parrot Trust 2012). For the average observer, however, it would be difficult to tell one race from another.

Behavior

The Little Corella is a diurnal, exceptionally gregarious cockatoo that is almost always found in flocks, some flocks numbering many thousands. Over a century ago Kilgour in 1904 noted seeing flocks that he estimated to have as many as fifty to sixty thousand individuals.

Flocking behavior is quite noticeable both before and after the breeding season, and most particularly during the winter months. While flocking behavior is directly correlated to breeding seasons, the availability of particular food supplies undoubtedly also played an important role in flocking behavior a century ago, long before large, modern cultivation of cereal crops became a major food source for the corella and made food supplies constantly available. For example, in a note written to Mathews, a Mr. J.P. Rogers (in Mathews 1916) wrote, "Last month (January 20) these Little Corellas were in small flocks of from 10 to 30 birds, and were feeding on the fruits of a small bush.... The fruit is finished and the birds are now feeding on the seeds of the Mitchell grass, acres which have been beaten down by the birds, which are now in a large flock of thousands." The Rogers note was dated February 23, barely a month after his first observation that the species was feeding in small flocks.

Flocking behavior appears to be related to other variables affecting the life cycle of the species. Its flocking behavior is conditioned in part by seasonal rains, particularly in those regions that are more arid and where rainfall is unpredictable. Traditional native food sources were then, as is still true today, undoubtedly affected by droughts, an environmental disaster precipitating flocking behavior and encouraging nomadicism in the birds' search for water and food. Widespread grain production, however, accompanied by the establishment of permanent, easily accessed agricultural water resources, has undoubtedly reduced the corella's need to search distances for water.

Yet, in the past, some localized populations of the species developed flocking and nomadic behavior tendencies that are distinctive from other Little Corella populations, in other areas, and that are not necessarily related to adverse environmental conditions. In the Meraukla district of West Irian, in New Guinea, in those areas where rice production is extensive, the Little Corella begins flocking just before the rice is sown in January and just again before harvesting begins. Damage to rice paddies is extensive (Hougerwerf 1964). Similarly, in the Darwin area in Australia, the flocks begin foraging from June to August in order to feed on the rice fields (Crawford 1972). But, at times, the flocking behavior of the species cannot be attributed to any discernible cause related to food or breeding, but rather to the general gregariousness of the species.

In 1911 Hill wrote that small flocks would gather on Augustus Island during August, joining many other small groups that staggered onto the island over the course of a few weeks. Carter (in Mathews 1916) observed interesting flocking behavior for which there appeared to be no specific purpose. He wrote, "About Point Coats and Maud's Landing ... where there is no timber growing within thirty miles, large flocks of these cockatoos used to come down to the coast sand hills almost every year in May. The birds did it for only a few days and flew about in a restless, aimless sort of way." In his same note to Mathews, Carter also commented that he frequently encountered the Little Corellas in flocks that roosted on the beach sand itself on the Exmouth Gulf.

The behavior associated with a large flock feeding is a phenomenon that can only be termed unique and breathtaking. Rogers (in Mathews 1916) in a personal communication to Mathews wrote of one massive flock he observed feeding:

> The birds all travel in one direction [i.e., when feeding on the ground] and the last birds of the flock are continuously rising and flying ahead of the leaders. They fly very low and from a distance there appears to be a wall of white which is stationary (by a distance I mean about three quarters of a mile, the individual birds cannot be seen at this distance) over the flock of feeding birds, which cannot be seen as they are hidden by the grass.

Among the Little Corella's favorite foods are the diverse roots that grow in swamp areas. When the bird has been digging through the moist swamp earth for a while, its plumage becomes quite soiled, and because of the color of the soil, which is red, its entire breast plumage becomes reddened, the stain given rise to the name Blood-stained Cockatoo, a popular Australian name for the species. Even when not foraging in moist earth, the red dust from the soil contaminates its otherwise white breast with redness. In addition to domestically grown grain crops such as wheat and barley, which it has learned to plunder, the species consumes various native flowers and buds, corms, grass seeds, berries and fruits, insects, and wood-boring larvae.

While the Little Corella primarily feeds while on the ground, it also feeds arboreally, its feeding practices resembling those of the Yellow-tailed Black Cockatoo (*Calyptorhyncgus funereus*). The Little Corella neatly cuts off flowering twigs or branches bearing specific fruits, and after devouring the tidbits, drops the severed twig to the ground (Hill 1916). Within a short time, the entire area beneath a tree is simply littered with debris. It has been speculated that the Little Corella, like the Yellow-tailed Black Cockatoo, has evolved this particular pattern of behavior as a means of avoiding going over branches in search of food when those branches have already been picked over.

After hydrating themselves in the morning at a waterway, the birds usually fly to a food source, and after feeding repair to shade trees for the day, especially during the hot afternoon. In the late afternoon the flock will leave its afternoon roosting area for another feed until the evening, at which times it returns to the trees to roost. It is common for the birds to share the trees with Galahs (*Eolophus roseicapilla*), but whenever the two species are found sharing the same tree, the Little Corella is invariably perched in the highest branches.

When resting, the Little Corella is rarely sedate and silent. The noise is profuse when the birds settle in a flock, regardless of how small. As would be expected, even though the Little Corella is considered by some pet owners to be a relatively quiet bird, the clamor of their vast numbers has been described by numerous other observers as deafening and annoying (Carter 1904). Depending on the size of the flock, more than one tree may be used, with the result that from a distance the trees appear to be in full bloom. While perched in the trees during the hot afternoon hours, the birds amuse themselves by screeching and quarrelling, and by stripping away all vestiges of bark, twigs, and leaves (see Macgillivray in North 1911). They also indulge in remarkable acrobatics such as hanging upside down with one foot while reaching for a twig or leaf.

Depending on the size of the flock, a tree can be stripped bare, skeletonized, within a relatively short period of time, at which point the entire congregation abandons the denuded tree for another, and the denuding process begins anew at another hapless tree. This type of activity is accompanied by loud shrieking, continuing throughout the day until the next feeding period. When flocks are immense, several trees are stripped bare during the course of their visit. Such behavior towards planted ornamental trees is considered deserving of lethal "pest" control.

Water is of course an important element shaping the bird's behavior, as noted above, especially in the more arid regions of Australia. While the species may pursue many of its daytime activities in open terrains, particularly during food foraging, most of its other habits are intimately connected with trees bordering water bodies, including marine estuaries. Interestingly, along such saltwater bodies the Little Corella often maintains flock integrity for months at a time, such flocks even remaining as permanent residents along the saltwater shores. Generally, the species prefers various gum trees such as the white or red gum trees that border many waterways, but it can also be found in mangroves, palms, and tall paper barks quite readily (White 1913) when gum trees are scarce or unavailable.

Regarding their flight, Goodfellow in 1935 described it as consisting of very rapid wing beats interspersed with long periods of gliding. After analyzing their flight habits, he discovered that "their flight is slightly different ... twelve rapid flaps, followed by a long glide. By this alone, I could always distinguish them."

While diverse other cockatoo species were common during the early periods of Australian settlement, they were never as numerous as the Little Corellas. The Little Corella's large flocks are still commonly encountered. World Parrot Trust (2012), for example, reports flocks commonly numbering as many as 70,000 individuals, even today; and Galahs (*Eolophus roseicapilla*) are still in the company of those flocks, be they large or small. Because of their large numbers, Little Corellas can be found throughout most of Australia. But because of their widespread distribution and their foraging in grain fields, their presence is not always considered an environmental blessing: they are considered pests in most farming communities; because they are considered agricultural liabilities, they can be legally shot on private land, at any time. Yet despite their persecution to prevent them from damaging cereal crops, their numbers appear to be increasing even as the traditional habitat of the country is being transformed. Ironically, in Western Australia and elsewhere where the Double Gees *(Amex australis)* can be found growing, a noxious creeping weed that is alleged to lame sheep, the birds feed on the plant's seeds, hence controlling the spread of the plant; the birds are considered pests nevertheless, and are persecuted accordingly.

The corella has proven itself adept in dealing both with the transformation of its environment and the loss of much of its previous food and nesting resources, but it appears to have adapted remarkably well to the emerging opportunities for food and water resources that these human-made transformations provide. Indeed, despite its persecution, the corella shows a remarkable tameness when in areas heavily populated by humans. In some western communities it is frequently found in the company of doves and pigeons. Storr (in Cayley 1973) wrote that the corella was so tame that when foraging for roots in a heavily populated township familiar to him, they took "little notice of towns' people crossing the rail tracks. When flushed, they flew up into nearby gimlets uttering quavering cries."

Mention has earlier been made of the Little Corella's raucous vocalizations when in flocks. Some consider the Little Corella to be a trifle "less noisy" than other cockatoos. Nevertheless, its call is loud enough to be disconcerting. The bird's call is described by some field workers as a series of high pitched screeches and notes that resemble those of the Sulphur-crested Cockatoo.

Finally, a small matter of historical interest regarding the species' contribution to the exploration and settlement of the Australian continent: early travellers and settlers, when crossing any one of the many arid and desert regions in the country, were often aided in locating safe water sources by simply following flocks of Little Corellas during their routine morning and evening flights to and from water holes and roosting sites.

Habitat and Distribution

The Little Corella is endemic to most of Australia and southern New Guinea. Four subspecies inhabit Australia, and the fifth subspecies, *C.s. transfreta*, populates the region between the village of Kumbe on the shores of the Aratura Sea and the lower Fly River (Parr and Juniper 2010) in southern New Guinea. There is scant field information on the distribution of the New Guinea population, and their numbers have never been quantified by either scientific methodology or estimation. In fact, it was not until 1982 that the New Guinea birds were recognized as being different from the Australian races and were therefore treated as a different race. In Australia, the population of all four races has been estimated at 1,000,000-plus birds (World Parrot Trust 2012), but in this figure there is no quantification by race: the figure is an aggregate guess. It is unclear whether World Parrot Trust includes in their estimate the New Guinea population.

In respect to Australia, the Little Corella is a remarkable species that can be found in almost every conceivable environment on the continent, excepting a few coastal regions.

While it is few in numbers in some of the extremely arid desert terrains, the birds that are there are known to fly great distances to obtain water.

The Little Corella appears to be an adaptable opportunist that makes its living wherever a living can be made. It is common to mangrove swamps, open or lightly treed grasslands, shrub lands, acacia/eucalyptus scrub lands, tropical forests, woodlands, roadsides, deserts, plains, monsoon woodlands, mountainous areas, and now even suburban areas. It has adapted itself well to human activities. As noted earlier, large-scale cereal agriculture has simply provided the species with more opportunities for food and water, and human agricultural activities offer the species new and different sources of foods, such as olives. There are even feral populations in many urban suburbs now.

While some of these urban populations may be escaped aviary or cage bird pets is irrelevant; the probability is that the birds find that cities can also provide sustenance for which they do not have to work hard. Like the common pigeon, which inhabits virtually every urban community across the globe, the urbanized Little Corellas are not shot at or persecuted as they might be in agricultural farmlands. In fact, urban dwellers everywhere across the globe enjoy feeding the common pigeon while sitting on a bench in a city park. As for the Little Corella, despite its large numbers, and the persecution that must have some impact on its overall population, it is still a protected species in every state except South Australia, and is still nevertheless widely believed to be increasing in numbers.

The *C.s. sanguinea* can be found in North Australia, Northern Territory, and the Kimberley in Western Australia, including many of the larger islands off shore. The *C.s. gymnopsis* populates the eastern half of the interior throughout North Queensland, as far north as the town of Weipa, near the tip of E. Cape York Peninsula. At times the race can be found along the east coast (Mdahlem 2012). It populates areas as far south and westwards as northwest South Australia, and has been introduced to Tasmania. The *C.s. normantoni* is found in northern Queensland to the W. Cape York Peninsula and as far south as the Gulf of Carpentaria. *C.s. westralensis* populates coastal and inland central and western Australia, from Great Sandy Desert to Moora District and eastwards to longitude 123 degrees (World Parrot Trust 2012). There are now feral populations of *C.s. gymnopsis* in the Perth region. As noted earlier above, the *C.s. transfreta* race populates southern New Guinea.

Propagation

The Little Corella is as variable in its choice of a breeding site as it is in its feeding behavior and preferences for diverse foods and nomadic wanderings. Since the species is totally reliant on stable water supplies, nest sites are always chosen near reliable water sources. When trees are available with suitable hollows for nesting, the corella will choose the most towering in which to nest, preferring to nest when possible in gum trees. But small trees will do equally well. Additionally, given that the species is extremely gregarious, it is not at all uncommon to find several nesting pairs in the same tree, the nesting birds part of a much larger colony in the immediate region of similarly occupied Little Corellas.

Since the Little Corella populates a wide diversity of differing terrains, preferred desirable nesting sites are not always available in some of the species' localities of distribution. In some regions that are exceptionally arid, there are often few trees, and those that somehow cling to life are scarcely towering pillars of housing opportunities in which to raise a family. In such arid areas, the corella is known to lay its clutch in hollows on top of large termite hills (Carter 1904). It is unknown whether the nesting pairs actually excavate hollows into the termite hills or whether the hollows are the result of the construction practices of the insects' community development. In other areas, such as the Point Coates region, the Little Corella is just as content to nest in the cavities found in the high cliffs of the various ranges (Carter, in Mathews 1916).

Whatever the case, the Little Corella will choose the most accessible site (Whitlock 1910). If the pair choose to nest in a tree, the cavity chosen will be a hollow in the trunk of a tree, or a broken branch, with the actual nest as much as a meter (3') down into the hollow.

When preparing a nest in a tree, the birds will gnaw away at the entrance to the nesting site. The resulting wood chips supplement the rotting wood normally found in the hollow, and thus form the basis of the nesting materials upon which the clutch is laid. Bonded pairs are known to use the same nesting site for several years in a row.

In the northern regions of Australia, the breeding season may begin as early as May, but usually it is more common to August and as late as October (Pizzey and Knight 1997); in Queensland the breeding season is December and April, July and October, and February to May, depending where the corellas are living at the time; in the more southerly stretches of the species' distribution, the season stretches from May to October (Pizzey and Knight 1997). The exact period of nesting, however, especially in those areas that tend to be arid, may differ depending on the availability of dependable water supplies.

As a rule of thumb the breeding season begins after the end of the rainy season in the north. Moreover, in those regions where water supplies are known to be both reliable and constant, the breeding season itself may vary from year to year for unfathomable reasons. For example, MacGillivray in 1914 reported examining the eggs and the young of the *C. normantoni* in northern Queensland as early as February and March.

As can be expected, because of the scarcity of permanent water supplies at times, regions suffering periods of severe drought dramatically affect the success of breeding pairs. Often, during such droughts, not only do fewer pairs of Little Corellas attempt nesting, but as well, of those clutches that are laid, only a minority of nestlings survive long enough to fledge.

In some regions where nesting sites are at a premium, there is considerable competition between the Little Corellas and Galah Cockatoos (*Eolophus roseicapilla*) for the few available sites that may be available given the particular terrain. The Little Corellas have been known to drive the Galahs from the nests that they had already prepared, nests in which there are already clutches of Galah eggs, and then lay their own eggs in it; eventually, the Little Corella pair raises the Galah nestlings with their own offspring, foster parenting *au naturel*. As early as 1916 Macgillvary wrote a note to Mathews (in Mathews 1916) telling him of the brooding Little Corellas raising nestling Galahs. In such instances, he added, the nesting materials consisted of leaves and various other vegetative materials, kinds not commonly employed by Little Corellas. He correctly deduced that after Galah nesting pairs had already laid their clutch they were driven away by Little Corella nest usurpers desperate for a suitable nesting site.

As is common with most cockatoos, the Little Corella is monogamous. Both sexes incubate the eggs. Many authorities report the number of eggs per clutch as averaging three. This figure is high, however. As early as 1914 Macgillivary examined several nests and reported that "the nests contained either two eggs or young." The fact is there are normally only two ovate white eggs in a clutch, rarely more, but occasionally three; according to World Parrot Trust (2012) the eggs average 39.0 × 28.5 mm (1.5" × 1.1"), whereas Forshaw (1977) similarly reports that the eggs in the H.L. White collection measure 38.8 (32.8–42.2) × 28.5 (25.5–31.1) mm. (1.5" [1.3"–1.7"] × 1.1" [1"–1.2"]).

The nestlings are hatched naked.

The eggs are incubated for 26 days. Both parents responsibly incubate them and raise the nestlings to fledgling age, which is between six and eight weeks. Upon fledging the juveniles are dependent on their parents for three to four weeks, and after fledging, the family joins the other corellas in the region in flocking. There is no documentation regarding fledged Galah juveniles that had been raised by Little Corella foster parents: i.e., whether the young Galahs were fed by foster parents after they fledged, when or if the young Galahs joined flocks of their own species, and so on.

The corella is also known to use the same nest site year after year, which strongly suggests that the species, regardless of race, despite its nomadic tendencies, is territorially localized.

Aviary Notes

Any person wishing to breed the Little Corella faces several obstacles before even releasing a pair into an aviary. For an Australian who breeds birds as a livelihood, successfully breeding the Little Corella results in young birds that few people wish to purchase because wild nestlings can be legally harvested without licence or cost. Unlike other cockatoos and parrots, there are no prohibitions or restrictions on trapping in the wild Little Corellas, or on owning, trading, selling, or breeding them. An individual desiring a Little Corella for a pet can simply find a nest and remove a nestling. It is as simple as that. While the cost of a pair of the birds in Australia is approximately AU$80 a pair (World Parrot Trust 2012), there are few individuals harvesting the species for sale. CITES curtails the export of the species to service the international black-market pet demand, and the Australian domestic pet trade market for Little Corellas is virtually nonexistent given the large numbers of the species in the wild that can be obtained without cost.

Additionally, the species is not only considered unattractive when compared to other parrot species endemic to Australia, but also universally condemned as a confirmed pest.

For an Australian avicultural hobbyist breeding diverse species for any one of a variety of laudable reasons, there is little reason to breed the Little Corella, which numbers in the hundreds of thousands in the wild—so many of them that farmers and others with land can shoot and kill them with impunity—when there are numerous other species of avian wildlife that are threatened with extinction. And even if the Little Corella is bred by a dedicated hobbyist because of the challenge that the breeding might represent, this amateur breeder cannot sell the young birds as a means of offsetting the cost of the aviary, its maintenance, and the cost of food when, again, his neighbor can take a Sunday drive during breeding season and snatch a nestling, assuming they had a ladder, if one was necessary. Worse still, the neighbor may shoot one of the hand-fed Little Corella darlings that the avicultural hobbyist had dedicated many painstaking hours to, should it somehow escape its aviary, because the corella's singing was not too pleasant to the neighbor's ear.

As for persons not resident in Australia who wish to breed the species, obtaining breeding stock is a major obstacle. Australia prohibits the exportation of its wildlife. There are a few New Guinea Little Corellas (*C.s. transfreta*) being exported from New Guinea (number of birds, and destinations, unknown). But, since most nations subscribe to CITES, the pet trade in the species is prohibited and hence specimens will be not be allowed to cross subscribing countries' borders. In short, the availability of the Little Corella to international breeders, hobbyists or professional, is virtually zero.

There is also a remarkable shortage of data and general information on the breeding of the Little Corella in captivity, despite it being abundantly clear that the species has been successfully bred, many times. It may very well be that aviculturalists do not write articles for avicultural publications when the breeding of a species is so commonplace that a report of a given breeding will most likely not expand upon what is already known about the species and its life cycle.

While there is little documentation regarding Little Corella breeding in aviary captivity, there was an (inadequately) detailed account of a successful breeding reported by F.E. Blaauw in *Ibis* in 1927 under the title "On the Breeding of the Bare Eyed Cockatoo of Australia (*Cacatua gymnopsis*)." Other information can be obtained by contacting Bird Care in Victoria, Australia.

When acquired by Blaauw, his pair of Little Corellas were already older birds and were well known to him, the birds previously having been resident at the Hanover Zoological Gardens. After introducing the pair to a large sized aviary (size undisclosed) with a hollow log in it (position of log undisclosed), the bonded pair began whittling away at the log's hollow entrance. A single egg was laid.

While Blaauw's report on the breeding was undoubtedly an honest attempt to document the event, some of his observations must be held suspect in regards to their accuracy. For example, he described the single egg as "big round white egg," and concerning the incubation, wrote that "after three weeks *exactly* the egg hatched" (emphasis added).

After the nestling hatched, the cock began entering the nest site "presumably to feed the little one." At three weeks of age the nestling was the size of a "woman's fist" and was sprouting white feathers; its beak was white and its back covered with yellowish down. By the fifth week, it was completely covered with feathers, the beak seemed short and wide, and there was already pink coloring to the lores. By the seventh week the juvenile was fully feathered, its periophthalmic ring was bluish, and the juvenile was beginning to peek out of the nest log. At approximately nine weeks of age, the juvenile fledged, identical in appearance to the adults except for the periophthalmic ring, which had not yet acquired its elongated shape. Although the juvenile appeared quite capable of feeding itself upon fledging, the parents continued feeding it for some time afterwards (time not disclosed). Mr. Blaauw concluded that both parents were quite dutiful in their parental responsibilities.

In regards to breeding the Little Corella, Bird Care (2012) recommends an aviary approximately 4 to 5 meters long × 1.5 meters wide, and about 2.1 meters high (13'–16' long × 4.5' wide × 6' high). A heavy-gauge wire mesh is recommended. The enclosure should be amply furnished with several natural wooden branches of different sizes to serve as perches, situated at various locations and heights. Nesting boxes should be placed within the aviary at three or four prospective breeding sites; these should range from hollow logs to grandfather-clock-type nesting boxes, with internal dimensions of approximately 300 mm (12″). Decomposed sawdust and wood shavings should line the bottom of the nests. Once the bonded pair have shown a preference for one of the nesting sites, the others should be gradually removed. Since the Little Corella is known to use the same nesting site year after year, and to use that site for non-brooding when not in breeding season, the preferred box should be left in the aviary once the young have fledged.

While the Little Corella breeds in the company of other Little Corellas breeding in the immediate vicinity, a breeding pair still require living space apart from other pairs. It is hence advisable to breed only one pair to an aviary.

Because the species likes to chew, and chewing is emotionally healthy for the Little Corella, providing the pair with live, nontoxic tree branches to chew on and/or debark is essential. Hanging ropes provide considerable diversion for this agile, acrobatic species. Additionally, to keep the inquisitive, intelligent corellas active, various wooden or vegetable-dyed-leather toys should be available for them to chew on and play with. As with all of the toys, branches and perches are gradually demolished day by day, and require periodic replenishment.

Because the Little Corella feeds primarily on the ground, the feed and water dishes should not be placed in areas where they may be contaminated by bird droppings from a perch overhead. The floor of the aviary needs to be cleaned regularly. Where possible, hose flushing is advisable.

Because the Little Corella is amenable to most of the foods offered it, feeding the nesting pair is not problematic, as it is with some other cockatoo species. Various seeds such as wheat, millet, corn, and hulled oats are popular, among other seeds. Safflower and sunflower seeds should be sparingly given because of their high fat content. Vegetables are readily devoured: carrots, peas, bean, broccoli, and fresh corn on the cob, as well as celery, zucchini, and chard. A variety of fruits such as apples, pears, and peaches, cut into chunks, are welcomed. There are others. The corellas also have a fondness for nuts such as pecans, walnut, roasted peanuts.

Pet Companion

Although the Little Corella is plentiful in Australia, it is not often encountered for sale either in its native country or elsewhere. A search for the species for sale in Australia provided two sources, one of them in NSW asking AU$550 for hand reared juveniles, and the second for a young specimen for AU$300. A search in the United States resulted in one Corella for sale—whether it was a Little Corella or whether it was a Western Long-billed Corella (*Cacatua pastinator*) is unclear. The species' availability in Europe or Great Britain is unknown.

While the Little Corella is for the most part considered a pest, a nuisance, and is generally believed to be undesirable as a pet, those that have the species as a pet companion have nothing but praise for it. A search of YouTube on the Internet will result in a number of home videos of this corella in a wide variety of intriguing behaviors.

Despite its overall homeliness, the Little Corella has numerous positive qualities as a pet bird. Of all the cockatoos it is considered the best mimic, it dances, and it has a legendary propensity to talk and acquire large vocabularies, a quality recognized well over a century ago when the species was captured in the thousands at the time for exportation to satisfy the pet trade. Additionally, the corella is a docile bird and more tractable than some other cockatoo species. When captured from the wild, it is easily tamed; and as is true of most cockatoos, it thrives on affection and reciprocates it. However, it is not as emotionally demanding of the owner's attention as other cockatoos. But it is an intelligent bird that, as an escape artist, if given the opportunity, will ultimately learn how to unlatch the door to its cage.

The Little Corella is a gentle bird, playful, an acrobat, and not overly noisy or possessive.

For all the above reasons the Little Corella proves itself an ideal pet companion.

Because of the corella's size, a large cage is not required: a cage the size of a cubic meter (3' × 3' × 3') will provide the bird with ample space to stretch its wings and to occupy itself. Two or three different sized wooden perches should be randomly attached in the interior of the cage. A note of good husbandry: because the species generally feeds while on the ground, the food and water dishes should be placed away from the perches to avoid being contaminated by droppings from the perched corella. Also, the bottom of the cage is best lined with paper, with a barred flooring is positioned two or three inches above the paper used to collect droppings and food debris: the barred bottom of the cage will keep the bird from walking on its own droppings.

Because the bird likes chewing, several chewable wooden toys should be provided it. Expect to have to replace the toys and perches periodically as they become systematically demolished. A short, hanging rope can provide the pet with another diversion from boredom, as can fresh branches from nontoxic trees. A cockatoo that demolishes its toys, hangs and swings from a rope, or chews apart the very perches on which it stands is an emotionally healthy bird.

Because of the Little Corella's temperament, the pet should be allowed out of the cage for two to four hours a day, providing an excellent opportunity for interaction and play— but not allowed unsupervised freedom, because this inquisitive bird may encounter dangerous items or toxins, or chewable electrical wiring, or may simply decide to chew on some prized mantel ornament that once belonged to your great-grandmother.

Feeding the Little Corella is a delight, because the bird is not a finicky eater and will accept almost every type of food offered it, as noted in the previous discussion on aviary birds.

Finally, all corellas enjoy a shower. Spraying the pet companion with a light mist of water is not only healthy for the corella's plumage, but also provides an important facet of interaction between owner and pet. The corella can be allowed to dry in direct sunlight, or can be gently blown dry with a hair dryer.

11

Red-vented Cockatoo
Cacatua haematuropygia (Müller, 1776)

COMMON NAMES: Philippine Cockatoo, Kalangay (in the Philippines), Agay (on island
        of Palawan)
SUBSPECIES: NONE[1]
LIFESPAN: (estimated) 40 years[2]
IUCN RED LIST OF THREATENED SPECIES: Critically Endangered
CITES: II

Description

The Red-vented Cockatoo, endemic to the Philippines, is one of the smallest of cockatoo types found within the family *Cacatuidae,* excluding the Cockatiel (*Nymphicus hollandicus*). In overall appearance it is white on both upper and lower parts, and as with all white cockatoos its white plumage makes it extremely conspicuous when in the foliage of mangrove habitats, lowland dipterocarp (*Dipterocarpus*), or in flight. While the species is strikingly white, there are some color deviations: the undersides of the flight feathers are a pale yellow, and the tail feathers are a bright sulphur yellow on the outer webs and white on the inner. The yellow coloration may vary in intensity from individual to individual. Another departure from the overall striking white appearance are the bright vermillion colored feathers around the vent, those feathers tipped white (the red vent coloration is what provides the bird its name).

The cockatoo measures approximately 33 centimeters (13") long, has a wing span approximating 34 centimeters (13"), and weighs on average 300 grams (10.5 oz.). The inner thighs appear greyish and the feet are mealy black. The species has a white crest, helmet shaped, short and stubby, the crest feathers having a yellow suffusion in the basal parts. The crest is so short that it does not even reach past the occiput and extreme upper nape area when lying flat. Its yellow suffusion is faint at best, and barely discernible. The crest can be erected at will and is erected when the bird is frightened, threatened, curious, or in any other emotive state. The Cockatoo's hooked beak is medium sized, a light grey at the base and ivory horn colored at the tip of the upper mandible. The bird's periophthalmic ring is both bare and white.

The sexes can be easily differentiated by the coloration of their eyes: males have brownish black eyes whereas the female's eyes are reddish brown. While the difference in eye color is assumed to be sufficient evidence of sex, that color difference is slight, and if the sex of the bird is important, a DNA test or surgical testing should be obtained for assurance.

Juvenile birds closely resemble adults, except that their eyes are brown.

Behavior

The Red-vented Cockatoo is a gregarious, social bird and can commonly be found in small flocks, except during the breeding season (Katala Foundation 2012). When flying in flocks, the Red-vented Cockatoos are deafening, but generally they are considered quiet compared to most other cockatoo species. Their calls range from "eeeeek" to "owwwwwk" to "torouuuuuk," and various assorted other calls (Katala Foundation 2012). The species is also known for making a characteristic bleating call and occasional whistling sounds.

The cockatoo's flight behavior has been described variously. Porter in 1953, for example, described the flight as being direct with rapid wing beats, whereas Whitehead, almost a century earlier, described the flight as "slow flapping." Flight is usually accompanied by constant and harsh shrieking (Whitehead 1890; Porter 1953).

During midday, when the day's heat is most intense, the birds will frequently sit motionless on a bare tree limb for hours, only occasionally emitting a shriek (Rand and Rabor 1960). According to Lowe's observations (1916), when roosting the species habitually favors the same roosting tree from the night before. When not in trees, the cockatoo is considered somewhat nomadic at times, particularly in its search for seasonally available food, and as a strong flyer, it has been known to fly up to eight kilometers (five miles) from one island to get to another where it can roost, feed, or even breed (Lambert 1994; Birdlife Species Fact Sheet 2012).

The Red-vented Cockatoo forages a wide variety of different foods on a daily basis. In the wild, its native food variety and availability are determined by seasonal changes, insofar as each seasonal change makes one or another food type available, while another becomes scarce. For the most part, the cockatoo depends on these seasonally available foods (BirdLife Species Fact Sheet 2012), making it unnecessary for the birds to scrounge about searching for something to eat. And, while the species is partial to native grass seeds, the conversion of forests and clearings to agricultural activities reveals the species' adaptability, in that the cockatoo now also forages on corn and unripened rice. At the time when the species had an abundant population that was widely distributed, flocks would appear when seeds had just recently been sown, or were just beginning to sprout, or when ripened crops were ready to be harvested. The birds would alight onto the field to feed and consequently cause considerable damage to the recently planted fields or to the crops ready to be harvested (Lowe 1916). Frequently, as observed by Whitehead over a century ago, flocks from other regions would arrive at a planted field, their numbers adding to the cockatoos that inhabited the immediate terrains near human settlements and the planted fields, and that were themselves already plundering those fields. Because of the extensive crop damage, the cockatoos were considered pests, and every effort was made by indigenous farmers to kill them. Because of the massive reduction of their numbers over the past century, there are no longer any similar flock foraging spectacles.

As it is a herbivore, the Red-vented Cockatoo's diet in the wild consists of various native flowers, or fruits, nuts, and buds, soft tree bark, and even nectar. It was reported that the species also had a partiality for banana seeds, but during the 1880s Rabor in his field studies could find no evidence of the species foraging in banana plantations, although he found ample evidence of their presence in other cultivated crops, namely rice and corn fields.

The species is nomadic or migratory, insofar as it is known to fly considerable distances to feed, particularly because of seasonally fluctuating food availability. It scavenges in rice paddies and corn fields, outside the breeding season, and is adept at finding food resources in regenerating forests. (Note that the above description of their feeding behavior is based on reporting from that period decades ago, when the species was numerous and large flocks were common. Given the species' critically diminished numbers today, many of these feeding behaviors no long apply, realistically, anywhere.)

Habitat and Distribution

The Red-vented Cockatoo is endemic to the Philippines and is the only cockatoo species to be found there. It was once common throughout most of the Philippines; it was

This delightful, popular pet companion, endemic to the Philippines, is all but extinct in the wild now. Once numbering in the hundreds of thousands, the population has been reduced to approximately 4,000 birds throughout the species' entire former distribution. Poachers who normally earn approximately $1 an hour as a laborer can sell a poached nestling Red-vent for $500 (photograph by Nakane Manjón, courtesy BirdPark Avifauna, Netherlands).

so numerous that its depredations on rice and corn crops proved a serious economic problem. The cockatoo was widely distributed on all the larger islands, as well as on many of the smaller ones, excluding central and northern Luzon (Collar et al. 1999; Widmanm and Widmann 2008). Many islanders soon discovered that there was a cash value associated with these "pests" because of the demand for them as pets both in the Philippines' urban centers and abroad. With rampant harvest of nests for young birds, the species' numbers declined so much that by 1994, Lambert estimated that there were only 1,000 to 4,000 birds remaining in the wild, and by 2006 it was estimated that the population was fewer than 1,000 birds (Widmann and Widmann 2008).

The number of Red-vented Cockatoos a century ago was large, but had never been quantified. Early field researchers encountered considerable difficulty in determining the birds' exact population centers because the species preferred heavily forested areas in remote regions, difficult to access, and the birds were also somewhat nomadic. As well, birds were often captured by local inhabitants in remote areas, and then bartered or sold to persons living where the species was unknown. Ornithologists bartering or purchasing specimens of unknown origin were subsequently faced with both confusion and misunderstanding regarding the species' actual distribution and numbers. For example, in 1872 Walden and Layard had obtained several specimens during an expedition on the island of Negros. After several subsequent expeditions into the same area, they reported in *Ibis* that "the exact habitat ... itself has never been accurately determined, for the bird does not appear to have been seen wild by any trusted traveller."

Similarly, in reporting on birds collected in southern Palawan by a Mr. E. Lamprier, Sharp curtly dismissed the species in 1887 by noting simply "New to Palawan." Whether Sharp was implying that the Red-vented Cockatoo was new in the sense it had been introduced there is uncertain, but the fact that he chose that particular word ("new") to describe its discovery there strongly suggests the infrequency with which the species was encountered due to irregular distribution and/or random localizations. At a later date, in 1916, Lowe was to describe the Red-vented Cockatoo as being "one of the commonest birds" on Palawan.

Although there are but a scarce few of these cockatoos now left surviving in the wilds, earlier observation and study of the species when it was common everywhere, prior to its rapid population decline, provides some insight into its life habits. The cockatoo by nature prefers secondary forests, or lowland primary forests, particularly at altitudes below fifty meters (about 150'), although it has been known to frequent higher-altitude terrains. As well, it was also found in mangroves along the coast, particularly when logging had reduced inland forested habitat, and frequently it was found near habitat that had nearby riverines.

Prior to the wholesale harvesting of the species for the domestic and international pet trade in the eighties, and to the present, the species was normally found in small flocks of ten or so individuals, but larger flocks were by no means uncommon. While the species primarily inhabited heavily forested regions, the cockatoo could frequently be found near agricultural clearings. Grant, for example, collected specimens from the islands of Mindora, Samar, and Leite, and in each instance the specimens were obtained at low attitude-forest areas, terrain that for the most part was already being agriculturally exploited (Grant 1896a, b, c). It should be noted that the islands the species inhabited are mountainous, with elevations as high as 2,900 meters (approximately 9,500'). Similarly, during the 1950s Rand and Rabor collected specimens at altitudes as high as 300–400 meters (900–1,300'). To what degree the cockatoo inhabited higher altitudes was undeterminable a century ago, and is certainly undeterminable today given that few individuals still remain at large in the wild.

Previously, while the species was never quantified a century or so ago, it would be reasonable to assume that the bird numbered in the thousands, for in historical field notes and published materials, the species is not described as rare. Today, however, throughout the species' previously extensive inhabited terrains its numbers today are few, a handful here and there at best, and in most of the terrain it once previously inhabited, it is now unquestionably extinct.

Aside from the fact that the species is critically endangered, and that it is already extinct over much of its previously inhabited terrain, accurate, reasonably reliable population figures are still unavailable. The bulk of the Red-vented Cockatoo population is now restricted to Palawan at the island's St. Paul's Subterranean River National Park, at the El Nido Marine Reserve, and at Pandanan Island; a promising conservation program is currently underway at the Rasa Wildlife Sanctuary, where a small population of approximately 25 individuals was recovered to 280 individuals by 2012 (Widmann and Widmann 2008), due to the vigorous conservation efforts implemented by the Katal Foundation,[3] an encouraging success.

In 2009, Philippine Conservation Program officials estimated that on Palawan Island there were approximately 750–2,800 individuals. Remnant populations are also believed to exist on Tawitawi, Masbate, and Mindanao. While exact population numbers are unknown, and can only be assumed to exist on non–Palawan islands, there are probably few mature cockatoos of breeding age on these islands. It is generally believed that there are some other small isolated sub-populations here and there, elsewhere, but the populations of these small localized groups, if they exist, are too small to ensure those local populations' long-term viability.

The sharp decline in the numbers of Red-vented Cockatoos in the wild can be attributed to a variety of factors. The principal cause for the decline is abusive exploitation for the pet trade. It is believed that the population declined about 80 percent, over the past ten years or so (Philippine Cockatoo 2012). In addition to the species' over-exploitation for the pet trade, the decline in territorial availability for the species and the degradation in habitat quality have also contributed to the species' jeopardized future. Due to logging and agricultural activities, there are fewer mature trees to provide nesting sites (BirdLife Species Fact Sheet 2012). Moreover, despite the fact that the Philippine Cockatoo, among other species of wildlife, is protected by the Philippines' Wildlife Conservation and Protection Act, and the fact there are few individuals extant in the wild, brazen poachers are still poaching nestlings. Poaching young birds has an immediate, twofold effect: first, it obviously contributes to the decline in population numbers; and second, more importantly, poaching deprives the existing wild stock the recruitment of young eligible birds—candidates for future breeding stock—and contributes therefore to a population that is aging without minimal replacement by younger birds.

In the illegal pet bird market, a Red-vented Cockatoo that could realize a poacher c. $160 in 1997 in Manila (Birdlife 2012) can now realize a minimum of $500 for a young specimen: $500 is a substantial amount of money when compared to an average hourly wage of one dollar an hour earned by Philippine laborers during 2012.

To combat poaching, the Katal Foundation has recruited former poachers and trained them as wildlife officers (see below), a strategy providing the poachers the opportunity of earning a liveable income while concurrently utilizing their poaching skills in being able to locate nests and monitor the growth of the nestlings inside (Philippine Cockatoo 2012, Birdlife 2012), and hence protect the young birds from human predation.

Propagation

While the Red-vented Cockatoo once numbered in the countless thousands, and many were captured for the pet bird trade, there is a scarcity of field studies pertaining to the species' reproduction in the wilds.

What is known is that the mating season for the Red-vented Cockatoo is from January to July (BirdLife Species Fact Sheet 2012), although many cockatoos begin pairing up as early as October. They are often seen together near what will be their nest area, grooming and preening each other (Katala Foundation 2012). The species prefers towering trees at least as tall as 30–35 meters (100'–115'), often dead and in clearings (Rabor 1977; Lambert 1994), and frequently near rivers—but they will nest in younger trees, if need be. They have also been known to nest in coconut plantations. The actual nest hollow will generally be chosen by the end of December. Frequently, the hollow had previously been the nest site of a woodpecker, or some other species of bird, or perhaps even another cockatoo pair.

There is no evidence to suggest whether the same pair of cockatoos will return to the same nest site the following year(s), or whether the same pair breeds annually (Lambert 1994).

In view of the general paucity of suitable nesting trees, it may very well be that a suitable nest site is occupied by another pair of cockatoos the following year, or by another species of bird. When the existing nesting sites familiar to a breeding pair are already occupied, and there are no other breeding sites available in the pair's familiar habitat, it is not known how the birds respond to this circumstance: for example, do they postpone nesting until a site becomes available? Or being nomadic, do they search other areas? Do they forgo nesting that year?

Breeding generally occurs from March to June, but the laying of eggs can begin in early February and peak before mid–March or early April (Katala Foundation 2012); egg laying as late as June, while uncommon, occasionally occurs. Normally, only two eggs are laid (World Parrot Trust 2012), but occasionally there are three eggs, or even a singleton.

The incubation time is 28 days, the weight at hatching is 10 grams (a third of an ounce!), the weight at weaning is approximately 260 grams (circa 9 oz.), and the juveniles fledge in about 11 weeks (World Parrot Trust 2012). Both the male and female share in the incubation, which generally begins with the second egg, which is typically laid three days after the first. It is not clear whether juveniles remain in a family group after fledging, or precisely how long the young remain dependent on the parents after leaving their nest.

Aviary Notes

The Red-vented Cockatoo is considered by some aviculturalists to be a difficult species to breed in captivity. One of the problems relates to the pairing of the male and the female.

It was generally believed that the species did not reach sexual maturity until approximately its eighth year. In effect, too frequently, older males were sometimes paired with younger, unreceptive females. Another major obstacle to successful breeding seems to be a shortage of females available for breeding purposes (Low 2012). (No one has provided a reasonable explanation of why there would be more males than females available.) If so, this situation is compounded by the fact that since the species is protected due to its diminished numbers in the wild, obtaining females is a formidable obstacle to overcome.

Since the species is popular as a household pet in the Philippines, most of the birds captured for the bird trade were and are (although illegally) destined for the domestic pet bird market, and to a smaller degree for international sale. Historically, the species was not popular in either the United States or Canada, particularly since there were and still are available in the avian pet trade far more colorful and flamboyant species such as the Sulfur-crested Cockatoo (*Cacatua galerita*), the Umbrella Cockatoo (*Cacatua alba*) and the Molluccan Cockatoo (*Cacatua moluccensis*), as well as numerous Central and South American parrot species, such as the Yellow Nape Amazon (*Amazona ochrocephala*) or the Blue Front Amazon (*Amazona aestiva*). Consequently there were few efforts expended on importing Red-vented Cockatoos, keeping them in North American aviaries, and in breeding them. Similarly, in the Philippines, few individuals bred the birds in captivity, because wild-captured birds were relatively inexpensive, and since the majority of captured wild cockatoos were domestically sold, new stock could be readily obtained by nabbing them from their nests to replace sold birds.

Additionally, when birds were more abundant, individuals could simply locate an occupied nest, monitor the growth of the nestling, and at the appropriate time remove it from the nest. Thus not only is the literature on the breeding of the species sparse regarding reproductivity in the wild, but also there is virtually no information regarding captive-breeding activities. There is, however, considerable literature regarding the various efforts being employed to prevent a further decline in the birds' numbers, and to make every effort to increase their population, hopefully sufficiently enough that in the future they can be reintroduced to some of their rehabilitated former habitats.

Whether in fact the bird is difficult to breed in captivity because of its psychological make-up, or whether its poor success at breeding while in captivity is a consequence of the breeders' lack of expertise in providing the breeding pair the conditions essential for success, is speculative at best. Indeed the species' reputation as a poor breeder in captivity may be more fiction than fact.

As an interesting historical note, there was so little known about the bird's breeding, nesting, or brooding, that there were few reports in the avicultural literature regarding the birds' propagation until almost fifty years ago, despite various field observations and reports regarding this species. Indeed, Harrison and Holyoak were finally able to locate a Red-vented Cockatoo egg for examination in 1970, an egg they noted had been laid in captivity (the egg was in the British Museum), just so that they could see what it actually looked like.

While there is little captive breeding of the species in North America or the Philippines, captive breeding in Europe has had a limited success over the years; a log "stud" book is maintained by cooperative European zoos and private breeders in an attempt to maximize breeding success by providing a means to pair up cockatoos of breeding age that are genetically unrelated.

In Great Britain, Rosemary Low reported on the successes of a private breeder named "Ken" (he did not want his identity divulged), who was a lifelong breeder. She reported that he became involved with the species in 1989 when he purchased a male. Five years later he purchased a female, a bird that had formerly been a pet companion. Two months later, the pair were incubating. His avicultural interest piqued, he began purchasing females as they became available.

He reported the following:

1. One pair had fourteen infertile eggs over the years before producing their first fertile eggs in 2002.
2. In 2002, he bred two pairs. In total they laid eleven eggs, ten of which were fertile. All hatched and survived but one. (One female laid six eggs, the other five.)
3. He monitored the weight of eggs, and began artificially incubating them, successfully.
4. Since 1994 "Ken" and his wife successfully reared 29 Red-vented Cockatoos.
5. He found that the compatibility of the male and female is essential—hence by having more males that females, and by careful observation of the birds' interactions, it was possible to match together a female and male when the hen began showing interest in a particular male.

In regard to his aviaries, Mrs. Low reported that they were approximately 5 meters (16′) long, covered, quite secluded, and with paving slab floors. The nest boxes were T-shaped with an entrance at each end of the T, thus providing the female an opportunity to escape should the male become too aggressive. The birds were fed a variety of fruits (oranges and pomegranates) and assorted vegetables (such as sweet corn, carrots, peas), and seeds soaked in water.

Female needs to be at least seven years old before she lays her first egg, and the male at least six years old before he can fertilize them, although copulation had been observed when the birds were as young as four years of age. The nest box is constructed with an escape exit for the female lest the male becomes too aggressive. In the sixteen years that they have been breeding the species, they were only once forced to hand rear one. Once the birds are incubating, they are fed dandelion leaves, sprouted seeds, various green foods, eggs, and corn-on-the cob (Low).

The World Parrot Trust (2012) advises that this species accepts a diverse diet; besides the foods provided by the breeders above, the Parrot Trust recommends a diet consisting of a mixture of seeds (millet, canary, oats, safflower, sunflower), a variety of vegetables and fruits, various nuts (roasted peanuts, pecans, walnuts, hazelnuts), and complete kibble.

Australia is a country that subscribes to CITES and hence permits no importation of the endangered species from the Philippines or elsewhere.

Pet Companion

While cockatoos are notorious for their loud calls, described usually as very noisy, the Red-vented Cockatoo is reputed to be considerably less raucous than other species of cockatoos, but still loud enough to be disturbing to neighbors, and therefore for the most part rendering them unsuitable as apartment pets, depending on the tolerance levels of neighbors. But since it is not as noisy as other cockatoo species in general, especially when compared to Moluccan or Umbrella cockatoos, the Red-vented Cockatoo proves itself a desirable pet, if one can find one to purchase. Additionally, the species is particularly appealing because it is noted for its ability to mimic the human voice.

As is common to most cockatoos, the Red-vented Cockatoo is inquisitive, and while it too likes to chew objects in its surroundings, and is adept at demolishing them, it is not quite as destructive to its perches or cage toys as are other cockatoo species.

While the Red-vented Cockatoo is not as well known as a pet in North America as it is in Europe, Asia, or the South Pacific, its popularity as a pet companion throughout the Philippines and southeast Asia is legendary. For citizens of countries that do not subscribe to CITES, or that turn a blind eye to illegally trafficked birds, the shortage of Red-vented Cockatoos has now made it an expensive purchase.

A comprehensive search (February 2013) of the Internet for Red-vented Cockatoos for sale resulted in two advertisements. One advertisement was for a seven-year-old pair available in the Philippines (city undisclosed) for P$60,000 (US$1,475), a sizeable amount for that nation. The second was for a male in New York: it was part of a pair that had not bred successfully, and the female had already been sold. The asking price for the male was not disclosed.

The cockatoo is popular because of a number of personal traits it exhibits. As noted earlier, compared to other cockatoo species it is reputed to be quieter and hence does not become a constant annoyance. It is well known for its ability to mimic sounds, particularly the human voice. It is intelligent, mischievous and demanding of human attention and involvement. And it is also affectionate. Rosemary Low confesses, "Seldom have I seen a parrot breeder with a happier expression on his face than Ken with five young cockatoos jostling for position on his head!" Certainly a sight to behold, and a marvellous experience for Ken.

Given its rarity, it is certain that the cockatoo will rarely be available for sale to the general public outside of the Philippines, and with just as much certainty, despite serious efforts to preserve the species in the wilds, continued poaching could conceivably make the species extinct in the few areas still remaining where their small, isolated populations tenaciously fight for survival.

Conservation Notes

A variety of efforts have been embarked upon to conserve the few extant small populations to prevent them from also plummeting into extinction. Because the cockatoo *will* breed in captivity, even should these current conservation efforts fail and the bird finally succumbs to extinction in the wild, there are probably enough captive cockatoo specimens in private aviaries and zoos to prevent the Red-vented Cockatoo from going extinct altogether. Near Manila, there is a captive population being bred by the Antonio de Dios Birds International for ultimate release to the wilds (Boussekey 1995; Ibolandia). This organization is reportedly the largest captive exotic rare bird breeding facility in the world, and is believed to have over 6,000 different specimens of some of the world's rarest birds.

Currently, in addition to legislation prohibiting the harvesting of this species, a number of other programs have been initiated, demonstrating some success. Efforts are being made to preserve and/or rehabilitate habitat favorable for the breeding and nesting of the species. Five protected zones in the Philippines have been established. Additionally, because so many towering trees have been felled, leaving a paucity of suitable breeding sites, various nest boxes of different designs have been installed on Palawan Island and its satellite islet Rasa.

As well, nine former poachers on Palawan Island were conscripted for their assistance. As was the custom for poachers on the island and other islands, a poacher would identify one or several nests with brooding hens. The poacher would then lay claim to those nests and that claim would be honored by all other poachers and would-be poachers, and at the appropriate time the poacher would remove the nestlings for sale. In exchange for training and a well paid permanent job as a wildlife officer, the poachers were hired to continue using their poaching skills in finding and monitoring brooding pairs, and protecting their nests and their young; but this time, rather than harvest nestlings and selling them, the former poachers now ensured that the juveniles fledged into the wild (Widmann and Widmann 2008). From all reports, these new conservation officers zealously protect the nests, and the program is considered a success story. Furthermore, the protected areas on Palawan are now attracting eco-tourists, bird tourists enthralled with the opportunity of actually seeing and hearing rare cockatoos in the wild (Widmann and Widmann 2008; Katala Foundation 2012).

Notably, already there are significant population increases in several of the protected areas, notably on Rasa Island (Katala Foundation 2012; Bird Life Species Fact Sheet 2012; Palawan Council 2012). In fact, the food resources on the islet were too limited to support the increased population, and it became necessary to capture some of the birds for release elsewhere (Widmann and Widmann 2012). The Katala Foundation has also established the Philippine Cockatoo Conservation Program. The foundation began the construction of an institute designed for research, education, and the breeding of captive birds, and by 2009 a number of buildings had already been constructed. A national education program has also been implemented (Katala Foundation 2012).

While these efforts may not be enough to restore the Philippine Cockatoo to its former awe-inspiring numbers and presence, it just may be enough to ensure its long-term survival (Birdlife Species Fact Sheet).[4]

ENDEMIC TERRITORIES OF NON-AUSTRALIAN SPECIES

Endemic Territory of Non-Australian Cockatoo Species (Bruce Jones Design).

PART TWO

THE GREY/PINK COCKATOOS

Genera *Eolophus* and *Lophochroa*

12

Galah Cockatoo
Eolophus roseicapilla (Viellot, 1817)

COMMON NAMES: Galah, Rose-breasted cockatoo, Roseate, Galah Cockatoo, Rose
Cockatoo, Roseate Cockatoo, Pink and Grey. (These common
names are recognized and used in all English-speaking countries.)
In Australia it is also referred to as the Willi-Willock, the Willick-
Willick, or Pink and Grey. (In South Australia, the Gang-gang Cock-
atoo (*Callocephalon fimbriatum*) is sometimes mistakenly called the
Galah.)

SUBSPECIES
1. *Eolophus roseicapilla roseicapilla* Nominate Race (Viellot, 1817)
2. *Eolophus roseicapilla kuhli* (Mathews, 1912)
3. *Eolophus roseicapilla assimilus* (Mathews, 1912)

LIFE LONGEVITY: (estimated) 40 years[1] (in the wild)
IUCN RED LIST OF THREATENED SPECIES: Least Concern
CITES: Unlisted

Description

The Galah is endemic to all of Australia and is considered one of the most beautiful
birds in the world. It is virtually impossible to mistake this cockatoo for any other species:
it is medium sized, colored pink and grey, weighs 275–425 grams (9.7 oz.–15 oz.), is approximately 35 cm (13.7″) long, and has a wing span 249–270 mm (9.8″–10.6″).

The forehead and crown feathers are whitish with pink bases, while the cheeks, neck,
nape and throat are a deep pink color. The breast and the abdominal areas are also deep
pink. This rosiness includes the outer webs of both underwing coverts and secondaries.

The crest is recumbent, colored similarly to the forehead and crown feathers, a pinkish
white, and lies flat on the head most of the time, unless the cockatoo is excited, at which
point the crest is raised.

The beak is horn white and the periophthalmic region is bare. The male's periophthalmic area is rose red, and his iris is brown; the female's periophthalmic color is pinkish,
and her iris is mid-brown/red. The species is sexually dimorphic, but the eye color and
orbital skin differences are the full extent of that differentiation. The sexes' appearance,
including overall color, is not affected by seasonal changes.

The upper part of the body is hoary grey, with the upper wing plumage darker at the

The Galah is known for its awesome flocking behavior, the flocks often numbering in the hundreds and even thousands. Despite being an agricultural pest, it is believed to be increasing in numbers even though it is severely persecuted for its crop damage. Nevertheless, observers never fail to comment on their awe when seeing these beautiful cockatoos in flight (photograph by Tatiana Gerus).

terminal ends than the intermediate or basal portions. The upper tail feathers are similarly colored, but the under coverts are a lighter shade. The lower back, vent, and rump are considerably lighter colored grey than the upper parts. The feet are a mealy grey.

Juveniles are duller colored on both upper and lower parts, their rosy pink breasts washed in grey.

Differentiating between the races can best be done on the basis of size, coloration of the periophthalmic region, and the general coloration of the plumage. However, it should be emphasized that *there exist considerable variations in these characteristics within any given race of the species.*

The western race, the *E.r. assimilus*, can be distinguished by its somewhat larger crest, which is also considered by some to be pinker than in the other two races, and by the periophthalmic ring, which is almost a white-grey. Additionally, the overall appearance is somewhat paler.

The *E.r. kuhli* is also somewhat lighter in color than the nominate race, the *E.r. roseicapilla*, but there is additionally an absence of the darker coloration on the feather extremities. Another difference is that the *E.r. kuhli* is somewhat smaller than the other two races.

This cockatoo is considered one of Australia's most beautiful birds. It is endemic throughout the entire Australian continent, is one of the most populous of the cockatoo species, and is a common sight, even in urban areas (photograph by Cyndy Sims Parr).

In respect to juveniles, in his studies of the various subspecies during 1951, Mayre observed that while the young of the three races have some grey washed through their rosy pink breast plumage, it is only the young of the *E.r. kuhli* that are markedly grey; consequently, *kuhli* juveniles are clearly distinguishable from the adults, which is not true of either the *assimulus* or *roseicapilla*. Overall, the color of the juvenile Galahs is duller than that of the adult, their crests are greyish, and they have brown irises and whitish periophthalmic eye rings, although Forshaw notes they are not carunculated.

Albinos are not at all uncommon to the species. The most common genetic mutation is the total substitution of the grey upper parts with white. A rarer mutation—one that has nevertheless been encountered on several occasions—is the replacement of the rosy coloration with a pure white. Such mutants in the latter case, Lendon notes, however, retain the grey of their upper parts.

Behavior

The Galah is a gregarious cockatoo, its behavior loud and bold, and while most other cockatoo species are known to form at the minimum small flocks of a few individuals to occasionally larger flocks of one to three hundred or so, the Galah will form flocks in the many hundreds, and even thousands on occasion, a phenomena witnessed and written about over a century ago, and that is still common today. Of course, it also forms small groups, ranging from family sized groups, to twenty or thirty individuals. Normally, the Galahs pair off and join others to form larger loose flocks: ultimately, these minor flocks can become flocks of hundreds if not thousands of birds, depending on feed, water, and seasonal variations.

In general, the Galah is a species that rapidly responds to environmental conditions: specifically water and food variances, due to inland Australia's unpredictable climate. The large flocks congregate and migrate in search of more favorable living conditions when the water and food resources become precarious. Because of this migratory behavior in response to environmental conditions, it has established itself permanently in areas where it was hitherto previously unknown—especially where modern agricultural practices have converted entire regions of previously valueless terrain into vast tracts of grain cultivation. Australia's agriculture has provided the species the means by which it has colonized virtually the entire country.

While this beautiful bird in the wild is now so numerous that it is considered a pest by farmers because of its damage to crops, its aerial behaviors are delights to behold, even by jaundiced opponents of the Galah, as some early documented descriptions reveal.

The literature is filled with references to the species. The multiplicity of references are obviously related to its abundance throughout all of Australia. However, one suspects that the real reason for the immense interest of both ornithologists and naturalists alike and their need to publish voluminous materials on the species can be traced to its outstanding beauty in the wild, particularly when the Galah is encountered in large flocks milling in the air.

This beauty inspires awe. A random selection of some descriptions produces observations such as "in the half light they indulged in some wild pre-roosting acrobatics, flying low and at a high speed singly and in pairs in and around the trees," written by Warham in 1957; and the description half a century earlier by Stone in 1912 when he wrote, "Wheeling in flight with wonderful precision, their rose colored breasts suddenly coming into view simultaneously, and then as suddenly dissolving into a mass of grey, and the sun shining all the time."

The most descriptive observation, a poetic one, was written by an anonymous correspondent to the *Emu* in 1909, an abbreviated version worth reading:

> A large flock of Galahs on a partially dead myall tree has a most wondrous effect.... The grey and pink clothe the bare branches, and give them an appearance of bursting into blossom, almost the shade of some double peach blossoms....
>
> Have you ever seen a proper flight of Galahs? It is a wondrous sight, and once seen, never to be forgotten. I will endeavor to describe such a scene.... Usually, when the weather is broken or unsettled ... it would seem that all the Galahs in the vicinity had gathered into one flock, shrieking and screaming as they circle high in the air, all beating their wings in unison. So, as if it were given a given signal, instantaneously the delicate rose colored breasts are all turned the same way, making a beautiful glow of color as the birds veer round; then, with one beat, the flock seems to have disappeared, just a glimpse of silvery-grey flashing as they turn their backs; then a mere speck where each bird is flying, so small that one would hardly believe it to be a bird, so almost invisible does the grey become; then again a flash of silvery light before the glow of their breasts flash into view again. The whole time there is an incessant screaming as they beat backwards and forwards in the same place for perhaps half an hour; then swooping with a rush of wings cleaving the air, reforming into flocks—all at a tremendous pace, and flying so close together that one constantly expects to see a collision, but never does one bird make a mistake; simultaneously every bird turns and twists in mid air, until, wearied out, the flock disperses into small groups, which drift away to settle in the grass or trees about. Sometimes, the Galahs keep this up off and on all day, for days at a time. Another such flock ... it must have been over a quarter mile long and one hundred yards wide, inside which space were crowded fluttering, flashing forms, alternating in their rose and silver splashes of splendor as they beat backwards and forwards.

The correspondent's description of the last flock would place the number of Galahs in the thousands. While there are some skeptics who believe such estimates to be overzealous, such massive flocks were in fact by no means uncommon. Jackson, in 1919, when writing about one of his encounters described their numbers "in flocks of thousands"—his reference is to *many* flocks, and all of them numbering in the *thousands* of individuals. These larger congregations appear to gather primarily during the wet season.

Most sightings of the Galah, however, past and present, are of flocks numbering under 500 individuals. Observation and analysis of flock behavior soon reveals that flocks are composed of pairs of birds. Pairs are known to mate for life, and in the event of the death of a mate, the surviving Galah is known to acquire a new partner (Galahs Australia 2005). Pairs are known to maintain permanent territories.

Aside from the dramatic, aerobatic wheeling and cavorting flying, the flight of the Galah is characterized by strong, rhythmic beats. During the summer months, the species does much of its flying and cavorting during the cool of the morning and evening hours, but during the midday heat when temperatures become uncomfortably warm, the Galah perches, resting quietly in pairs or small groups in the shade of tree branches. Nesting and roosting sites are almost always situated near water. When roosting, they roost communally. At times, for no apparent reason, the entire congregation will suddenly rise above the tree upon which they were perched, float momentarily above it, and then quietly resettle again. The Galahs aerial dances are remarkably eye pleasing.

Water plays a critical role in the habits of the species, especially in the interior of the continent where deserts and quasi-desert habitats predominate. During the summer, when watercourses have all dried up, leaving but a few ponds scattered here or there, distances apart, the Galah continues to faithfully cling to its habitual locality so long as some water is reasonably nearby. When water becomes exceedingly scarce, the Galah by necessity is compelled to migrate (Sedgewick 1952). The search for water often takes it to terrains where the species is uncommon (Lord 1956). The massive agriculturalization of the country noted earlier included the development of ponds and water resources to support heavy agriculture; this provided the Galah the means to permanently colonize almost the entire country: the previous persistent migratory search for water was no longer regularly needed because permanent water supplies were assured. In fact, there are some ornithologists who are of the opinion that the Galah is now beginning to displace the Leadbeater Cockatoo (*Lophochroa leadbeateri*).

The Galahs' heavy reliance on water is accompanied by interesting and colorful behavior. Macgivillray (in Mathews 1916) reported that when watering, "these bird love to cling to a post or fence or dead tree in the water; sometimes a whole crowd of them will alight on a post, and then a great screaming and flapping of wings ensues as each tries to get a position near the water.

I have seen a partly submerged post and wire fence covered with Galahs this way." Warham's field notes in 1970 on their watering habits record this delightful spectacle:

> They [i.e., Galahs] had two favorite spots—dead limbs from riverside gums that stretched out over the water and only about nine inches from the surface. The birds would alight five or six at a time on these branches, and then waddle sideways, Parrot-wise, until well over the water, eventually bending down until their bodies were vertical and their beaks immersed. Their powerful feet held them in position, with remarkably little wing flapping, ... When one bird had finished drinking it would be shouldered aside by the next in queue.

While, like most birds, the Galah is arboreal and spends much of its resting and roosting time in the trees, almost all of its feeding takes place on the ground. Their feeding behavior is just as much a spectacle as their flock flying behavior, particularly when the species is feeding in large flocks.

Austin (in Mathews 1916) writes, "I have seen enormous flocks.... While crossing a large plain, I saw acres and acres of the ground just simply a mass of pink and grey with these birds."

The Galah is not partial to any specific foods; it eats a wide variety of seeds from ground-level native plants, as well as the seeds from the acacia, and Lea and Gray in 1935 noted that the species also consumed grit; now, with intensive agriculture, particularly domesticated grain crops such as wheat, corn, and oats, which attract large Galah flocks, its foraging has become a matter of considerable concern to farmers.

In feeding, watering and roosting, the Galah is frequently in the company of the Sulphur-crested Cockatoo (*Cacatua galerita*) and the Red-tailed Black Cockatoo (*Calyptorhynchus banksii*), but the Galah always outnumbers the other two species. Since the Sulphur-crested Cockatoo posts sentries to warn the other birds of impending danger, the Galah benefits by their presence. Nevertheless, when Galahs are feeding, even when not accompanied by other sentinel cockatoo species, there will be at least one bird that will keep watch, and if disturbed by a possible threat will warn the rest of the Galah flock to flee. The flock is realistically unapproachable at that time.

The Galah is unusual in many ways, for not only is it an expansionist species, despite its constant persecution as a pest; it is not wary, shy, or timid. Many view the species as being somewhat stupid, undoubtedly because of its failure to automatically flee from an obvious impending danger, as one would expect it to do when threatened. But it is perhaps not as stupid as some would describe it. Currently, the species frequently also inhabits urbanized areas and is often found nesting in suburbs, even in heavily populated urban areas such as Adelaide (Lendon 1973), and has been doing so for almost a century. It could be argued that the species, despite its persecutions, has learned to tolerate human presence. These urban, acclimatized cockatoos are often so tame that heavy human traffic does not overly concern them. (Their lack of fear is undoubtedly related to the fact that in urban environments the birds are not being shot, for shooting the birds could conceivably lead to one's arrest because there are few cities anywhere in the world where gunfire is tolerated. Think of the countless pigeons in every city in the world, as an example, or the Canada Goose in urban Canadian and American cities, which are never shot, and with good reason.) Even as early as 1916 the Galah had already become accustomed to the human presence.

A Mr. W.B.B. Alexander (1916), for example, was to write, "A flock of some size was observed to drink regularly at a raised horse-trough close to the homestead (about 50 yards distant ... although it was a busy place, as horses were constantly being brought to drink, and wagons and other vehicles constantly passing within a few feet." Similarly, in a story worth repeating, one that generally reflects the widespread recognition of the Galah's general tameness, even though the incident may be somewhat exaggerated, in 1903 a certain H. Kendal wrote to *Emu*:

> Last week, as a lady was proceeding ... to her home, she saw a bird pursued by two hawks.... This turned out to be a Galah Cockatoo, which flew almost immediately on to her dress and accompanied her home. Though at first it would allow no one but its rescuer to touch it, it afterwards proved so tame that it would perch on shoulder or arm of any member of the family, and though at liberty, came regularly to be fed. One morning it was missing, but on "Cocky," being called two or three times, it surprised the young lady looking for it by answering "Here I am, close to her."

It sounds like hyperbole, but believe this tale as you will.

When threatened the Galah reacts with what Goodwin (1974) described as a "threat display," a display often used at a distance. Goodwin argues that the display is a reaction to a "conflict between fear and aggression":

> The bird typically stands upright, leans back a little and raises its wings, often one wing more than the other. Then it suddenly swings its head and the forepart of its body forward and downward, raising its wings fully above it and uttering a harsh, hissing screech as it does so. As it utters this sound the mouth is wide open but the cheek feathers still completely cover the lower mandible when viewed from the side. This display usually incorporates a rocking side-to-side movement.... The screech may be uttered as the bird leans back and raises its wings and the forward movement may be omitted.

Goodwin identified another form of behavior common to the species:

> The other display I termed the "nodding display." In this, the crest is fully erected ... and the bird quickly bows forward, uttering a sharp "*ink*." This display was often seen from one or both birds of pairs perched in roosting trees or, more specifically, near a nest site. Sometimes, it alternated with the screech display. Although the birds were probably motivated by fear ... one had the impression that the nodding ... indicated an intention of holding ground—"Here I stay"—rather than fleeing.

The Galah's crest is a marvelous communication attribute, the crest being erected whenever the species is alarmed or excited. But the crest also serves other useful communicative purposes: a raised crest can be a display for its mate, or for defence of its territory or its flock, or a means of alerting its flock; or it may be erected by the bird because it is curious about something, or because of some excitement, surprise, frustration, or fear. Anyone approaching a wild Galah can expect a raised crest, which in itself is a warning that by approaching further the transgressor will be bitten. When the crest is lowered, the bird is most probably calm, friendly, and approachable (Marshall 2012).

As noted earlier, the Galah has been described as a shrieking and screaming cockatoo when in mass flock flying behavior. They are a conspicuous cockatoo particularly because they are noisy, and active. Their vocalization has been described as that which only a noisy cockatoo would do, a voice which can be best characterized as metallic, disabyllic, grating and high pitched. When seriously alarmed the Galah shrieks. Galahs Australia describes their voice as "Clear, two-noted contact call 'chi-chi' or 'che-che.' Harsh alarm screech." Jackson in 1918 blatantly described their vocalization as "the uproar from their screeching frightful."

Habitat and Distribution

The Galah occupies virtually the entire island continent of Australia and most of the small adjacent Australian islands, including Tasmania, where it was introduced. Initially, the species was more common inland than along coastal regions, particularly in the eastern and southern reaches of the country. Following the expansive development of wheat and other cereal agriculture, the species underwent a concurrent spread both eastwards and southwards. The creation of ponds and waterways essential for extensive farming also assured the species an ample water supply. Serventy and Whittell attributed some if not all of the Galahs' expansion to inland climate changes and to other variables currently undefinable.

The *E.r. roseicapilla* occupies most of Queensland, New South Wales, Victoria and a significant portion of South Australia. The species' expansion was downward to both the coastal plains along the eastern seaboard and southwards into the coastal plains of Victoria, and similarly into the coastal plains of South Australia.

The subspecies *E.r. kuhli* is found throughout the Northern Territory, the entire northern reaches, and eastern portions of Western Australia.

The subspecies *E.r. assimilus* occupies most of Western Australia, having expanded southwards in 1904 from as far north as the Murchison River to as far south as Hatanning (Serventy and Whittell 1962), and now occupies the entire state barring the southwestern coastal regions.

There is no clear and recognizable line of integration between the three subspecies.

In regards to Tasmania, the species in early ornithological literature was considered a "vagrant" by some ornithologists such as Mathews. Early speculation regarding its presence on the island was attributed to mainland forest and plains fires, and escaped birds from a ship moored in Huon Harbor (Sharland 1952). It is still speculative whether the species should be considered native to Tasmania. The Galah was introduced to Kangeroo Island[2] where it is now firmly entrenched due to its rapid expansionism.[3]

Except for the heavily forested tropical rain forests of Cape York Peninsula, and three or four extremely arid inland areas where life is difficult at best, the species inhabits almost every type of conceivable terrain on the continent. The species, while it has some preferences, shows a remarkable ability to breed in almost every circumstance imaginable, from towering trees, to shrubs, to caves and even hollows on cliffs. Given Australia's extensive farming of cereal crops and the creation of numerous artificial waterways and ponds by which irrigation is assured, the species has become a permanent resident in regions where it was rarely seen before, if ever.

Propagation

The Galah is a prolific breeder, a distinct advantage in that it is considered a pest in the agricultural industry, and is consequently persecuted vigorously. Because of the birds' reproductivity, the killing of large numbers of them appears to have little effect on their population health. Although the Galah prefers eucalyptus trees for its nests and lines its nests with eucalyptus leaves (the only cockatoo to do so) and refreshes the nest each day with new leaves, it is adaptive enough to choose other trees for its reproduction requirements when forced to by shortages of eucalyptus-tree breeding sites; when choosing other trees for nesting, however, it still requires access to eucalyptus trees. Because the cockatoo's breeding requirements are not negatively impacted by deforestation, and because expansive cereal agriculture creates favorable breeding conditions, the Galah's population growth is assured despite its being vigorously persecuted for crop damages. Galahs Australia (2005) reports that the Galah will nest virtually anywhere, even in a "hole in a rock face or cliff."

The Galah's seeming indiscrimination—despite its preference for the eucalyptus trees for its nest sites—may not be so much indiscrimination as a pragmatic adaptation to a scarcity of nesting sites during the breeding season, when there are large numbers of various cockatoo species competing for a limited number of breeding sites. The Galah, however, whenever possible, will chose a tree located near water, preferably a gum tree.

Competition being what it is, given the large numbers of house hunting pairs[4] not only of Galahs but other avian species, and the premium therefore placed on the limited gum tree sites, a possible nest site may be a matter of "catch as catch can," especially in those regions where gum trees are not commonly encountered. In some regions, for example, such as in the northwest Cape York region, the Galah is content to nest in the mulga or gidya shrubs. Of course, any type of nesting site is better than none; while more fortunate pairs may locate a site seven or eight meters (23'–28') up in a tree, making the nest "difficult to access" (Lawson 1905), some other nests may be located as low as only two to three meters (6'–9') from ground level as reported by Dr. J.B. Clellan (1916).

Competition for nest sites is also intensified by other cockatoo species coexisting in the same locality. Macgivillary (1916) writes, for example, "Many were the disputes and altercations over hollows within the sight of our tent door, both between different pairs of Galahs and other cockatoos. A pair of Sulphur Crests (*Cacatua galerita*) had taken possession of one hollow, and were treated with the greatest respect; not so for a pair of Blood Stained Cockatoos [i.e., Little Corellas] (*Ducorpsi sanguinea*) whose chosen nesting site was occupied by Galahs during their absence, but the usurpers were always rejected on the rightful owners return from their feeding grounds."

When fortunate, the Galah will locate its nest in a hollow limb or hollow trunk of either a dead or live tree. The pair will use the same nest hollow year after year, if possible. The entrance is generally gnawed at, and the bark stripped away; chips that fall into the hollow do not appear important as nesting material, a matter that has caused speculation and debate as to the reasons for the gnawing at the entrance and the stripping of the bark. Initially it was argued that the gnawing was to create a smooth surface so that iguanas and other predators would be prevented from obtaining footholds and hence access to the nest's contents. However, aside from the fact that the Galah has few natural enemies, the iguana is quite capable of climbing trees, bark or no bark. Additionally, it could be argued that had the iguana been a natural enemy and therefore a constant threat to Galahs, the evolutionary process would have resulted in a more discriminatory process of nest selection by the species in order to optimize the survival rate for the young. Otherwise, its trend to increasing numbers would stabilize, or even conceivably decline. Moreover, there is no report in the literature citing an actual occurrence of an iguana raiding a nest site.

The Galah reaches sexual maturity usually by its fourth year, and rarely breeds before then. In southern Australia the birds begin pairing from July to December while in the north, the pairing occurs from February to July. The courtship display of the Galah is a simple ritual. The male struts along a tree branch towards the female, his crest erect and his head slightly weaving from side to side. This behavior may be followed by the pair's departure to another tree where the male repeats his ritual. Often, there is mutual preening between displays. The Galahs, like most other cockatoo species, forms lifelong bonds with their partners.

As noted earlier, the Galah Cockatoo is a prolific breeder. Often the species will raise two families a year. But according to Macgillivarys in 1910, three families a year are by no means unusual. The typical clutch is four to five eggs, the last egg laid approximately two weeks after the first (Whitlock 1909). The eggs are white, lustreless, and moderately varying in size and shape. Egg dimensions are approximately 34.0–36.0 mm × 25.2–27.0 mm (1.3"–1.4" × 1"–1.1").

Eggs are incubated in approximately 30 days, the male participating in the incubation but only during those times when the female has departed the nest. During brooding, however, both male and female share in the care of the young. By the seventh week, the young have usually fledged (Alderton 2003), at which point they are moved to a treetop creche that may be as much as two kilometers away (approximately a mile), a creche in which there are other juveniles awaiting their parents, who are out foraging (Stang 2012); the parents arrive in intervals to feed them. The juveniles remain dependent on the parents for as long as five or six weeks after fledging. Once abandoned by their parents, the young Galahs form large flocks that disperse over the countryside, where they become nomadic, wandering extensively.

Aviary Notes

The Galah is such an amenable breeder in captivity that a complete itemization of the countless successful breedings and the breeding details would involve needless repetition. Suffice it to say that the species is an excellent candidate for both novice and professional aviculturalist interested in breeding the species, not just because it readily accepts captivity, but because its needs are relatively simple and it is willing to accept almost any type of nesting site provided it.

Regrettably, as beautiful as the bird is, its reputation as a pest condemns it to general public disinterest at best and persecution at worst. Fortunately, despite being a common species that is not of interest to many folks—specifically in Australia, where the Galah is generally perceived negatively—there are still enough Galah admirers in Australia and worldwide that it is not only bred in captivity by avicultural hobbyists but is also adored as a companion pet. Because the cockatoo is so numerous in the wild, few professional aviculturalists breed them for sale: the commonality of the bird and the ready availability of legally captured wild birds has depressed their market value. But while the Galah has a depressed bird value in Australia, it is admired and desired in most other nations with avicultural histories, and commands a high value therefore.

The species was first bred in captivity somewhere in the late 1870s (Prestwick 1951). The Marquess of Tavistock was the first to breed the species in England, somewhere during the 1950s, and F.H. Rudkin was the first to breed it in the United States, in 1929. These successes have been duplicated a myriad of times in a host of different nations.

During the first early attempts to breed the Galah in captivity, most of the interest was focussed on producing albinos or various mutation combinations. This interest, it should be noted, resulted from the fact that the breeding of the species in captivity was not very challenging compared to breeding other avian species, other cockatoos included. Moreover, it was discovered that the Galah readily bred with other cockatoo species with the result that interesting hybrids were produced: e.g., Galah × Gang-gang Cockatoo (*Callocephalon fimbriatum*) (Dr. L.J. Clendinem); the Galah × Greater Sulphur-crested Cockatoo *(Cacatua galerita)* (Cosgrave); Galah × Yellow- crested Cockatoo (*Cacatua sulphurea*) (British Naturalist 1913); Galah × Leadbeater's Cockatoo (*Lophochroa leadbeateri*) (Lendon 1950); Galah × Long-billed Cockatoo (*Licmetis tenuriostris*) and the Galah × Little Corella (*Ducorpsi sanguinea*) (Aviculture Magazine 1966). In short, it appears that the Galah has been bred with virtually every species within the "White Cockatoo" group. Additionally, cross-breedings separated by two or three generations have produced interesting and beautiful color variations. At this point, there is no reported success of cross breedings between the Galah and the six types of Black Cockatoos.

Because of the ease with which the Galah accepts captivity, and because it breeds well in captive conditions, the aviary, nest box, and feeding conditions are not necessarily elaborate. Depending on the breeder, the Galah is described as either totally destructive of its nest box and/or aviary and its contents, or as a cockatoo that is notably *less* destructive than other cockatoo species: In 1950, Boosey, for example, described the Galah as having "chewed up the first nest box ... reducing it to a pile of sawdust," whereas Rudkin writes of the cockatoo, "They are not very destructive ... not when I compare them with the Lemon Crested Cockatoos [*Cacatua sulphurea?* Subspecies?]."

What many individuals decades ago did not fully realize is that chewing is an essential component of the cockatoo's emotional well-being. The numerous anecdotes in the literature suggest that that avid chewing habit that often demolishes aviary environments on a regular basis is not so much a matter of the species' disposition towards destruction *per se* as it is the result of an emotional need to chew, or at worst, is a particular destructive characteristic of an individual bird.

Regarding the aviary itself, while the general principle that "the larger the better" is always a wise dictum to follow when providing an aviary for larger species of parrots, the flight cage size for the Galah Cockatoo need not be too large, if space is in limited supply. Rudkin in 1933, for example, after trying several sized flights, states that an aviary 10' × 8' × 7' (approximately 3 meters × 2.5 meters × 2.5 meters) is quite satisfactory. A one-inch-gauge wire netting is considered appropriate for the Galah. Contemporary practices, nevertheless, encourage aviaries to be a minimum of 5 × 1.2 × 2 meters high (16' × 4' × 6').

In respect to their courting and breeding behavior in captivity, Boosey recollected one experience he had with a pair he owned in 1953:

> Roseates ... are more demonstrative and therefore more amusing, and if the meeting is a success—as it usually is—they go through the strangest tactics; raising and lowering their crests; preening each others crests; and the cock, apparently desiring to admire his fiancé's profile from either side, never climbs or flies *over* her, but invariably tries to climb *under* her, often falling off in the process, this being the signal for much raucous screaming and agitated raising of crests!

Similarly, Dr. Greene, a century earlier, who admitted he had an bias against the species, did nevertheless succumb to the delightful mating antics of the Galah, and proceeded to describe the ritual in his just-as-delightful writing style:

> The love making again of a pair ... is a sight to be seen: What a series of bows and capers, what self contained warbling! To hear him "coo" to his lady love, you would never suppose him to be the pink fiend whose piercing shrieks but just now drove you from his presence with your fingers in your ears; but he is: when he is teased he screams, when he is angry he screams, when he is hungry or thirsty he shrieks, but when he is jealous he yells like a demon—or as demons are supposed to yell.

Given the species' general acceptance of almost any type of nesting arrangement, either a hollow tree trunk or a grandfather-clock-type nest box can be provided the pair. Rudkin (1933) favored the grandfather clock construction, measuring approximately five feet (1.5 meters) long made of 1" (25 mm) × 12" (300 mm) boards,

> at the sides forming a long spout, over one end nail one half inch wire cloth, this is the bottom, stand upright on this end, cut a hole 3 or 4 inches (75–100 mm) across the top, nail a strip of wire cloth from this hole on the inside about eighteen inches (.5 meters) down, fill with earth up to this and firm it down and then put 2 inches (50 mm) of sawdust on top of this earth. Put a lid on top of this long case, nail a step just below the hole on the outside.

For incessant chewers, Boosey lined his nesting boxes with zinc. In order to make the birds feel "more at home," the Marquess of Tavistock even covered the top of his nesting boxes with a layer of bark.

Because the Galah is not a finicky eater, feeding the species with nutritional foods is not problematic for the aviculturalist. Striped sunflower seeds, corn, peanuts, oats, canary seeds, diverse grass seeds, and various greens and fruits, and even meal worms and grubs for animal protein, are all readily devoured, although it should be pointed out that the Galah, as is true of many caged livestock, may develop a preference for one food type over another. Given individual differences, however, it would be a rare Galah that would present feeding problems.

Providing the aviary-housed birds with fresh, nontoxic branches to chew on es entertainment, hence preventing boredom and ultimately neurotic behaviors such as feather plucking. In countries warm enough for the eucalyptus to grow, the cockatoos should be provided fresh branches regularly. Finally, because the Galah is genetically prone to chew, the water dish should be sturdy and situated so that it cannot be easily destroyed and overturned. Expect to replace perches and toys regularly, as well as chewable branches—all of which will be ultimately chewed into shreds.

The Galah proves a hearty cockatoo in captivity and if properly acclimatized, can endure the types of climates common to countries like Britain without much duress. *The young, however, are susceptible to chills and must be protected from inclement weather for five or six months after hatching and, most preferably, until after their first moult.*

Some caution in regards to meddling with a nesting pair: While the parents will not neglect their responsibilities to their young, or abandon them, they will aggressively defend their family if intruded upon by the aviculturalist, a matter which should concern no one but the overzealous breeder anxious to peek now and then at his Galah family.

Breeders will be delighted to know that some pairs will produce two successful nests a year, regularly (Rudkin 1929; Kendall 1984), and despite the fact that the species generally reaches sexual maturity by its fourth year, some Galah hens have even successfully bred and reared a brood before they were one year old (*Aviculture* 1944).

Pet Companion

As can be garnered from the above, the Galah readily adapts to human presence and to captivity, and is hence easy to care for because it is does not have specialized needs. It is not a finicky eater and will accept most foods ranging from seeds and nuts to fruits, vegetables, and dandelions.

The bird makes an exceptionally friendly, delightful, affectionate and amusing pet. In addition, it is a colorful species. In Queensland, at the time of this writing (summer 2012) a wild-caught young bird can be purchased for as little as AU$100, and an aviary-raised bird certified free of Psittaccine Beak and Feather Disease (PBFD) will cost up to AU$300. (Cockatoo Heaven 2012).

Its popularity is so well established that even as early as 1840 it had already become the most popular of Australian parrots as a household pet. Some Galahs are noted for their limited mimicry, but for individuals seeking species that can acquire extensive mimicked speech, the Galah is not the best choice: Sulphur-crested Cockatoos or corellas are much better talkers. For non–Australians interested in obtaining a parrot with mimicry ability, some of the Amazon parrots such as the Blue-fronted Amazon (*Amazona aestiva*) prove to be excellent mimics that can acquire extensive vocabularies (Mulawka 1983), are more readily available, and are less expensive than American-bred cockatoos.

As a companion pet, the Galah exhibits the personal attributes most desired in a parrot. Galahs have remarkable dispositions. An excellent example is the Galah owned by the southern California Rudkin family (a family well known in avicultural circles). During a tour of the Rudkin Jr. Collection during 1974, Sedley observed the Rudkin pet Galah, of which he wrote:

> Opening the aviary before him, he [Rudkin Jr.] thrust in his arm. Immediately a lovely Rose-Breasted Cockatoo flew to his wrist. Withdrawing his arm, he cuddled the bird against his

cheek. Her delight was plain to see as she rubbed her face against his face and gave vent to soft little sounds of endearment.

"Aren't you afraid she might fly away? I asked.

"Not a bit," he answered. "If she did she'd turn around and fly back again."

In addition the birds are playful, intelligent and readily bond socially with their owners. There are some reports that the birds can become unpredictable as they mature (Cockatoo Heaven 2012), but the manner in which this unpredictability manifests itself is not disclosed, and neither are the sources that have led to this indictment.

Because the Galah is intelligent, it requires both the stimulation from interaction with its owners and from chewing toys, branches, and the like. Hence, owner participation in the bird's daily life is an important element that cannot be ignored. Finally, the Galah is not an excessively noisy species, although some birds may enjoy vocalizing early in the morning and/or in the evening.

Some Historical Notes

Despite the Galah's attractiveness, and the fact it is widely considered one of Australia's most beautiful birds, it has been ruthlessly persecuted and exterminated in great numbers during the past century. The persecution of the species is somewhat of a logical paradox insofar as the bird is a beautiful asset contributing to Australia's uniqueness and desirability as a tourist destination, and it makes itself a desirable companion pet. Despite those qualities, the Galah is concurrently a destructive species that causes considerable damage to agricultural crops and therefore financial losses to farmers.

The cockatoo is most especially destructive to cereal crops, particularly just after the seeds have been sown. Not only does it relish freshly sown seeds, but its damage to agriculture persists after the grain has been harvested. Warner in 1970 wrote, "I have seen them perched on bags of wheat, helping themselves freely to the contents. With their powerful beaks they find it an easy matter to tear a hole in the thick hessian of which the sacks are made." In an interesting and illuminating study conducted during 1950, it was calculated that the average flock of 5,000 birds would consume between 25 and 35 tons of cereal grains per annum (Allen 1950).

Another reason the species was persecuted—although not relevant today—was that the species often perched on telegraph wires when telegraph communication was the only means by which one side of a massive country could instantaneously communicate with the other side. The birds would grab the telegraph wire in their beaks, thereby breaking the continuity of the wired message. Or, as Bernsey in 1906 reported, there were so many Galahs sitting on the top telegraph wire that their weight would bend the wire down until it touched the lower transmission line, thereby disrupting communication for extended times, particularly in remote areas where the problem could not be immediately dealt with. The communication problems could not be quickly resolved given the vast stretches of the country and the very sparse servicing population available.

Also, Austin (1916) wrote that the Galahs "have been so destructive to crops that they have been poisoned and shot in thousands; ... around the cultivation paddock ... enormous heaps of dead galahs ... many being shot to feed the dogs in rabbit packs."

Poisoning has been a common practice, despite its disastrous consequences to other species of wildlife. Bounties were paid. In some regions, the bird was used for target practice by hunters and shooters alike.

The contempt for the Galah even extended to the sport of trap shooting—the birds were captured in the hundreds and then released one by one for shooters at various trap shooting clubs.

Complaints of the practice by the Royal Australian Ornithological Union to clubs such as the Ararat Gun Club elicited no response (Dickson 1951).

To deal with agricultural "pests," shooting, trapping, and gassing is legal under the Wildlife Act of 1975 (Department of Primary Industries 2011)—in addition to the Galah, Sulphur-crested Cockatoos (*Cacatua galerita*) and the Long-billed Corella (*Cacatua tenuirostris*) are included as legal "pests" targeted for eradication.

There is no question that the Galah causes considerable damage to Australia's agricultural economy. Poisoning is a poor choice for a solution because of its indiscriminate death sentence on other desirable species of fauna, particularly those that are not agricultural threats. Whether trap shooting the species is an ethical solution to the problem of Galah damage to the agricultural industry is a matter of debate, although there is an emotional distaste for this practice.

While the agricultural industry views the Galah Cockatoo as a serious threat, there are some students of ornithology and environmental studies who argue that the species is beneficial to agriculture at large because it feeds a great deal on saffron thistle seeds, thereby acting as a natural restraint to the proliferation of that noxious weed, an argument first made by Christian as early as 1916.

Regardless of whether the species is shot, poisoned or gassed in the war to protect the agricultural economy, the Galah Cockatoo nevertheless, fortunately, continues to prosper in numbers.

13

Leadbeater's Cockatoo
Lophochroa leadbeateri (Vigors, 1831)

COMMON NAMES: Major Mitchell's Cockatoo, Pink Cockatoo, Wee Juggler (Australia), and Inca Cockatoo (archaic).

SUBSPECIES:
1. *Lophochroa leadbeateri leadbeateri* Nominate Race (Vigors, 1831)
2. *Lophochroa leadbeateri mollis* (Mathews, 1912)

LIFESPAN: 79+ years ("Cookie": born c. 1933, still alive at Brookfield Zoo, Illinois, September 2012)

IUCN RED LIST OF THREATENED SPECIES: Least Concern

CITES: II

Description

Endemic to Australia, the Leadbeater Cockatoo is unquestionably one of the most beautiful of all the species composing the family *Cacatua*. Its outstanding loveliness rests on its uniqueness in coloration and in the extraordinary shape and coloration of its crest. It is the only cockatoo that has a multicolored crest. It is a medium sized, stocky cockatoo, ranging from 35 to 40 cm long (13.6"–15.6"), and weighing 300–450 grams (10.6 oz.–15.8 oz.): it is slightly larger than the Galah (*Cacatua roseicapilla*) and somewhat smaller than the Sulphur-crested Cockatoo *(Cacatua galerita)*, both popular in Australia as pet companions.

The cockatoo is fundamentally pink and white, with gorgeous hues and blendings of colors, all soft textured. The entire back, wings and tail are white except for the inner webs of the tail feathers, which are a bright rose hue. The two central feathers are white.

The head region—including the hindneck, sides of the face, breast, and upper sides of the body—is a salmon pink color, a coloration also common to the underwing coverts. The stomach is similarly salmon pink. The crown of the head and the occipital crest area feathers are pink at the base and white at the ends. The nuchal crest is elongated and white with the intermediate regions of each feather tinged with crimson and yellow.

While the crest is a plain white when it is recumbent, and nondescript, when erected it becomes immediately obvious why the cockatoo is considered the most beautiful; the crest is stunning for both its delicate beauty and in the manner in which it is displayed. Alexander (1916) described its magnificence when he wrote, "By opening their wings partially they exhibit the pink color beneath, at the same time spreading the magnificent crest with its bands of yellow and scarlet until it forms a perfect semicircle. If I had not seen it done repeatedly, I could not have believed that the crest could be spread so far forward, the front feathers seeming almost to touch the beak."

The species' bill is light horn in color, of intermediate size, and with an upper mandible that does not project far below the lower mandible as is common to other cockatoo species. Juvenile Leadbeater's closely resemble the parents.

There is little sexual dimorphism. Yet the female is slightly duller in color with a whitish upper belly, and her crest can sometimes have a slightly larger yellow band than the male's, but these differences generally require an experienced, discriminating eye. The feet are mealy grey for both sexes. The male's eyes are darkish brown, almost black, whereas the female's are a lighter shade of reddish brown. For both sexes the periophthalmic ring is narrow, white, and bare.

The two subspecies can be differentiated by their coloration. The *L.l. mollis* has a much deeper hue to the underwing coverts than the nominate race; this is also true of the inner webs of the primaries. Since color differences are often subtle and subjectively interpreted, the crest coloration provides the best identification of subspecies: the *L.l. mollis*'s crest has little or no yellow in the intermediate zone of each feather, as is the case with the nominate race.

Behavior

During the non-breeding season, the Leadbeater is generally found in small flocks of six to eight individuals. Such flocks are believed to be composed of family units, but this belief has to date been unconfirmed, Occasionally they can be seen in the company of the Galah Cockatoo (*Eolophus roseicapilla*), or Little Corellas (*Cacatua sanguinea*).

Leadbeater pairs often interact with other pairs, forming flocks approaching 50 or so individuals. Rarely, the species has been encountered in large congregations numbering as many as 300 or so individuals (Hall 1974), although such gatherings are not commonly encountered today, as the species' habitat has been dramatically altered by deforestation and agricultural development. Even a century ago, large flocks of comparable size were rarely encountered; Captain White in 1913 is one of the very few individuals to have had the opportunity, past or present, to witness large flocks. He wrote, "They were feeding in large flocks on bare ground, and when alarmed they took flight with such screeching. But alighted again soon. They often alighted on a dead tree, which they covered in such a mass as to give it the appearance of wool."

Living in the interior of the island continent where it is arid for a significant portion of the year, the Leadbeater can be found wherever there is some water available, especially watercourses by which scrubs and gum trees can be found growing. Whenever there is a permanent water supply the cockatoos will remain in the immediate vicinity. As water sources dry up, the birds will fly increasingly longer distances from their feeding grounds to locate water supplies. Any water soon attracts birds, all kinds. Keartland (1916) noted that whenever he sank a well in the Great Desert in northwestern Australia, it was soon visited by Leadbeaters even though there had been no sign of them during drilling.

The cockatoo hydrates twice daily: early in the morning and again in the evening. When watering, each member of a pair awaits its turn—the second bird hydrating itself as long as an hour after the first (Grant 1916). Because water is so scarce in such terrains, their flights to the watering hole are both habitual and predictable. The Leadbeater is therefore easily captured at whatever watering hole the species frequents.

Because of the sparsity of vegetative growth over much of the Leadbeater's geographical

The Leadbeater is considered perhaps the most beautiful of all the cockatoo species. As well, it is noted for its longevity. A Leadbeater named Cookie at the Brookfield Zoo in Illinois was born circa 1933 and was still alive and healthy in September 2012 (photograph by Drew Avery).

distribution, the species has developed a diversified diet. Often it embarks on local migrations in search of food (Del Hoyo et al. 1997). The cockatoo is diurnal. It feeds primarily on the ground, but will also feed in trees and shrubs, depending on which fruits, seeds, nuts or berries are available. It eats the seeds of various pines, and because of its strong beak it is able to extract seed kernels from the hardest of nuts. It is fond of the seeds from the eucalyptus, ground water melon, yellow cotyledons (Hall 1974), tuberous roots, grasshopper eggs (Sandland 1916), various beetle larvae (extracted from acacias or eucalyptus trees), and even ant eggs. It also feeds on a wide variety of plants, the *Callitris* spp. and acacia seeds in particular (Environmental Protection Agency 2007). When native foods are in short supply, the species may resort to foraging agricultural grains.

In the wild, after feeding, the cockatoo is sedentary, often engaged in diverse routines. In 1912 Bennet described one of these routines:

> When its hunger is appeased it has the habit of cutting off the smaller branches of the trees or shrubs in which it may be resting. It also tears off the bark of the larger branches, or the trunks of trees, until the ground below is strewed with small branches, leaves and fragments of bark. This destruction is particularly noticeable in the vicinity of the trees in which they may be breeding, and I have frequently seen an old male engaged for hours at this pastime in the tree where his mate was engaged in the duties of incubation.

The Leadbeater's call is a somewhat more plaintive one than that of most other species, whose calls are usually loud, raucous, or piercingly harsh. The Leadbeater's call is disyllabic, a somewhat wavering, characteristic call resembling a "creek-ery-cree," which can be heard from some distance away. Others describe the call as a "distinctive stammering whinny" (Avianweb 2010). When disturbed or alarmed, however, it will utter several sharp shrieks in a row. The frequency of the calls indicates the degree of stress.

The Leadbeater's crest is important to its communication. Usually, the crest lies flat on the head, but if the male is courting, it may erect its crest in full, and if the cockatoo is suspicious, alarmed, distressed, or excited, or warding off an opposing male, it also raises its crest. The erecting of the crest is often accompanied by strong vocalizations.

Like most cockatoos, the Leadbeater's flight seems almost labored. It is slow, with wing beats that are shallow. It frequently glides, and if it travels longer distances than normal to forage for food, or acquire water, it frequently takes short flights from one tree to another. It normally flies at or near treetop level.

The Leadbeater is a wary species. Chandler in 1913 wrote that the species would abandon its nest when an intruder was 50 or more yards away. When he, also an avid photographer, attempted to photograph the species a quarter of a century later, his efforts were so frustrated by the cockatoo's wariness that he confessed, "I used every method of dealing with the birds that I could invent to outwit them. However, the alert cockatoos were aware of the danger, and fighting adverse weather conditions in addition to the nervous birds I retired practically beaten after seven or eight trips to the nest and over forty hours spent in a hide."

Of the pictures he did take, he said with some hyperbole, "Most of the photographs were taken at one three hundredth part of a second but the eye of the bird saw the opening of the shutter, and the crest in every photograph was slightly blurred."

Habitat and Distribution

The Leadbeater inhabits a significant portion of Australia, but although the species has declined in numbers in some areas, it is considered common in most other regions of its distribution; the nominate subspecies has an estimated population of c. 50,000 individuals, and the *L.l. Mollis* is believed to have a stable, equally large population (BirdLife Species Fact Sheet 2012), although its numbers have never been quantified. The species is distributed in all Australian states, except Tasmania. Because of its general uncommonality, and the fact that it is not found along coastal regions, it was not discovered until 1832, which is considerably later than the discoveries of most other Australian species of cockatoos.

For the most part, the species inhabits the central regions of central and western Australia. The Leadbeater lives primarily in arid terrains, as noted above, but also in scrublands, savannas, and wooded grasslands; during the breeding season the cockatoo relies on forested habitats where there are tall enough trees with hollows for nests. Its northern boundaries are marked by a line drawn from the Fritzroyi in Western Australia to Tanami in Northern Territory. Its most eastward distribution is contained west of the line drawn from Tanami to the Macdonnell Ranges and Alice Springs regions, and from Alice Springs to the southeastern corner of Queensland, appearing as far east as the western fringe of the Darling Downs (Environmental Protection Agency 2007). Its numbers have declined considerably in the most eastern and southern reaches of its geographical distribution.

The species is encountered infrequently and in small numbers in the coastal urban areas of Melbourne in Victoria and Sydney in New South Wales, regions that are not part of the species' normal geographical distribution.[1] It is believed that these small populations are either aviary escapees or individuals that have been deliberately released (Hindwood 1966).

The *L.l. leadbeateri* inhabits the eastern portions of the species' distribution, while the *L.l. mollis* is found in the central and western areas of its distribution (Rowley; del Hoyo, et al.).

Propagation

The Leadbeater, while relatively rare throughout its extensive range, is a reliable breeder in that it breeds consistently without requiring specific, specialized environmental conditions. For example, at the Hattah Lake District, Jones, during 1952, found that breeding Leadbeater pairs were more or less equally distributed between mallee, pine and open areas, although the species favors forested areas.

The species prefers a gum tree located near water, when available, for its nest site. The nest may be constructed just a few meters above ground level to as high as ten or fifteen meters (30'–50') above in a towering tree. Unlike the Galah, whose distribution encompassed almost the entire continent despite the extensive logging and clearing of forests and shrub lands, the Leadbeater cannot tolerate fragmented and partially cleared lands, which have limited nesting sites and few breeding opportunities. Additionally, the species is territorial and will not tolerate another pair attempting to nest within a kilometer (half a mile) or thereabouts. While there may be several pairs nesting within the same general area, each pair maintains more or less that distance from its nesting neighbors, which is socially expected.

The Leadbeater's courtship display is interesting. The male struts along a branch towards the female, bobbing his head up and down, swishing his tail in a figure-eight movement. At times he may lift his wings to reveal the coloration of his under coverts. The female, in return, with raised crest, bows low in response (Forshaw 1977). They chatter softly together, and if the female accepts him, they allopreen and sometimes feed each other (Del Hoyo, et al. 1997).

The Leadbeater is monogamous, bonding with its mate for life, and is known to continue using the same nest for years. After breeding, and once the young are independent, the pair remain together. The cockatoo breeds from August to December, with most egg laying taking place in August and September. In the northern regions of its distribution, the species often begins breeding as early as May. The eggs are white and oviate, measuring 35.0–40.0 mm × 26.0–30.0 mm (1.1–1.5" × 1.0–1.2"). A major study of the species by Rowley and Chapman during 1991 found that the effects of winter or annual rainfalls did not affect the timing of the egg laying. Regarding clutch size, the same research showed that of the 63 clutches involved in the study, the average clutch was three or four eggs per nest, and that 84 percent of the eggs hatched, with 64 percent of the young fledging successfully. They noted that that particular group of Leadbeaters in their study added 127 individuals to the species' regional population.

The nest is normally situated in a hollow within a branch or stump, anywhere up to a meter deep (3') into the cavity. Grant (1916) reported that the bedding was frequently up to 127 mm (5") deep, lined with decayed leaves and rotted wood. The birds can often be found enlarging the hollow and/or its entrance, an activity that adds wood chips to the bedding already there.

Incubation lasts approximately 24 days, with the female roosting at night and the male during the day. Because the chicks hatch altricial, blind and without down, they require substantial care. The chicks remain in the nest for nearly two months, fed by both parents. It may take up to a month before they can fly competently. After fledging, the young remain with their parents, forming a familial flock for three or four months. The young will continue to be fed, but mostly by the male. Juveniles closely resemble adult females but their eyes are lighter brown, they have paler plumage, and a duller frontal band (Forshaw and Knight 2010; Del Hoyo, et al. 1997). Juveniles reach sexual maturity about three to four years of age (Del Hoyo, et al. 1997).

Aviary Notes

In Australia the Leadbeater is infrequently bred in captivity. The disinterest in captive breeding is due in part to the species' general unsuitability as a pet companion (and hence unsaleability by a breeder); additionally, should someone want a Leadbeater, a nestlings can be legally harvested from the wild (BirdCare 2008).

Nevertheless, the species is an excellent subject for anyone interested in breeding it. It is quite hardy, is not a finicky eater, and is relatively inexpensive for an adult pair—approximately AU$500 for a breeding pair in Victoria (BirdCare 2008). It does not require quite as expensive an aviary investment as many of the other cockatoos. It breeds well, regularly each year, and produces (if all goes well) three or four fledglings. And while the bird does not reach sexual maturity until about its fourth year, some males can be bred as early as two years of age, and females by four years (Vane 1951). Additionally, some bonded pairs have been known to produce a successful family year after year until they are in their thirties (Oboiko 1941; *Aviculture* 1940).

Furthermore, the Leadbeater interbreeds with other species of cockatoos. It has been successfully bred with the Orange-crested Cockatoo (*Cacatua sulphurea citrinocristata*) (Kendall 1964), and Cumming reports it breeding with the Sulphur-crested Cockatoo (*Cacatua galerita galerita* ?), among others.

The one major difficulty in breeding this species is that the male can be aggressive both to its partner and its offspring; it is essential to provide the hen means of escape in the event of the male's aggression, and a means for protecting the young, if need be. Additionally, the Leadbeater's disposition does not make it well suited as a pet companion. For those individuals still interested in breeding the species, it is preferable to acquire a pair already bonded, rather than acquiring a male and female and wait (hopefully) for them to become bonded.

The aviary itself should be at least 4–5 meters (13'–16') long, and at least 1.5 meters (4.5') wide × 1.5 meters (4.5') high, although Quist reported breeding success with an aviary measuring approximately 2 meters (6') long × 1 meter (3') wide × 2 meters (6') high. A heavy-gauge meshing is required because the cockatoo can quickly destroy light-gauge mesh enclosures. While a grandfather-clock type of nest box can be used, it is preferable to provide the pair a solid log with a hollow. Several potential nest box arrangements should be concurrently provided the pair; once they begin showing special interest in one of the nest box offerings, the others should be gradually removed. The internal dimensions of the nest box (or hollow) should be approximately 300 square centimeters (76 square inches) by approximately 1,000–1,200 mm (one yard) deep. And, because the male can be overly aggressive to the female, a double-entry nest box arrangement is essential to provide the female an escape route. The bottom of the nest box should be layered with rotted, nontoxic wood sawdust, wood shavings and any other type of suitable nesting materials.

The cockatoos should be provided wooden perches and ample fresh branches to chew. Chewing provides the cockatoos with an activity, thereby avoiding boredom, which often leads to self mutilating behavior such as feather plucking. Chewing also provides it with exercise and the means to control the growth of the beak by wearing growth down. These branches and perches need regular replacement, as they are invariably chewed into slivers.

Pairs interested in breeding will display their interest by chewing and enlarging the entrance to the hollow. Once the eggs are laid, the pair will alternate the incubation with the female assuming the responsibility during night and the male during the day.

In the Northern Hemisphere, egg laying normally begins towards the end of spring, generally in late May. Both adults will participate in feeding the young. A wide variety of food is favored by incubating and brooding pairs: sweet corn, various seeds (especially sunflower and canary), hulled oats, millet, wheat, almonds and other nuts, peanuts, various fruits, and vegetables such as peas and broccoli. In Australia, in addition to the above foods, native foods are always welcomed: acacia seeds, pine seeds, diverse wild grass seed, eucalyptus, and others.

After fledging, the young may take up to a month before they can fly competently.

While the Leadbeater Cockatoo can be an excellent, responsible parent when allowed to rear its young without interference, disturbances in the vicinity of the nest area can have dramatic consequences concerning the adequacy of the care provided the young. Not only may the male abandon the nest at the slightest provocation (Lendon 1973), but under stress the male may maim or even kill his young. Ezra, for example, reported in 1940 that his cock bit one of his nestlings through the beak. Similarly, Vane found that after his pair had successfully hatched a clutch of three, the nestlings were almost immediately abandoned after a neighbor's bailing machine disturbed them. (The same pair, incidentally, upon losing their first clutch, immediately attempted to incubate a second, but that second clutch proved unsuccessful because the male refused to sit.)

The Leadbeater male at times kills its offspring *without* cause. Oboiko reported in 1941 that he had a pair that between 1922 and 1939 annually produced a successful clutch but when hatched, the male killed the nestlings before their first feathers began to sprout.

The problem of infanticide is perplexing, given that the species has no reluctance to breed in captivity, and will even tolerate some exposure to human presence during nesting.

In attempting to understand this phenomenon and rationalize the bird's behavior towards its offspring, Oboiko offered a plausible explanation concerning the etiology of the behavior. He suggested that the young birds are conditioned to respond to specific patterns of behavior each time an adult enters the nest site. When the adult's behavior differs from its usual behavior (such as when it may have been alarmed by Oboiko's example of the noise from a bailing machine), the adult's distress evokes a different kind of response from the young (a response to a disturbed set of behaviors). Since the young now have reacted to the adult's behavior in a non-normative fashion, the adult bird, not recognizing the new pattern of behavior and relating it to his young, kills them. This explanation does have a degree of plausibility. However, it does not totally explain the phenomena. Reports indicate that it is always the cock that does the killing. Additionally, as observed by Ezra in 1940, juvenile males are more likely to be killed than juvenile females. On the other hand, it may be only the male that possesses the infanticide reaction. Whatever the case, the aviculturalist breeding the Leadbeater Cockatoo is best advised to keep intrusions and disturbances to the barest minimum.

Pet Companion

While the Leadbeater Cockatoo's attractiveness enhances any and all avian collections, there is general agreement that the species is not desirable as a pet in a household environment—at least not in the traditional view of what constitutes a good cockatoo pet companion. Dr. Greene well over a century ago, accurately described its liabilities: "Beyond its beauty, and that is great, there is nothing to recommend this bird to the notice of amateurs, for he is not very intelligent, nor is he docile! He never learns much, and invariably remains wild and suspicious, even after years of captivity, and much patient effort to convert him to a better frame of mind."

While a few Leadbeater Cockatoos can be taught to mimic, by and large the species fares poorly as a mimic. It comes poorly qualified in other ways, also. Because it is so highly suspicious, it neither responds to affection, seeks it, nor returns it. And the older the bird, the less likely it is to have an emotional interaction with it. Attempting to develop reciprocal emotional bonds with the Leadbeater is difficult at best. Yet they demand a great deal of effort and time to keep them happy with a semblance of tameness. Although the species does not have a harsh, unpleasant vocalization, some individuals become quite noisy. It is not considered intelligent (Avian Companions 2012). Parrot Link (2012) describes it as "one of the less suitable Cockatoos as a pet, very cuddly as babies becoming quite dominate as they age." Like all cockatoos, of course, they can be expected to be destructive of woodwork in the cage, and of perches. As noted earlier, feeding the cockatoo is not a problematic exercise. Finally, the cockatoo exudes a powder that can prove to hazardous for those suffering breathing problems.

In short, the cockatoo is ill suited for someone seeking an avian pet companion.

PART THREE

THE BLACK COCKATOOS

Genus *Callocephalon,* *Probosciger* and *Calyptorhynchus*
Subgenus *Calyptorhynchus* (Zanda)

14

Gang-Gang Cockatoo

Callocephalon fimbriatum (Grant, 1803)

COMMON NAMES: Helmeted Cockatoo, Red-headed Cockatoo, Red-crown Cockatoo, and Galah ("Galah" is a localism used in South Gippsland and should not be confused with the Galah *Eolophus roseicapilla,* a distinctly different species); the Gang-Gang Cockatoo has also been called, both in archaic English and French, the Ganga Cockatoo, a term rarely heard today.

SUBSPECIES: None

LIFESPAN: (estimated) 60+ years[1]

IUCN RED LIST OF THREATENED SPECIES: Considered Vulnerable in NSW, Endangered in certain regions, Extinct in previously occupied islands.[2]

CITES: II

Description

The Gang-Gang Cockatoo is a small cockatoo, similar in size and shape to the Galah (*Eolophus roseicapilla*), ranging in size 32–37 cm (12.5"–14.4") in length (Higgins 1999), and weighing approximately 280 grams (10 oz.) on average. A sexually dimorphic bird, it is endemic to Australia.

Overall, the male is larger and is far more brightly plumaged than the female. The male has a bright flaming red in the head region, which includes the forehead, crown, face, hindneck, and nuchal crest. Exercising a bit of poetic licence, Bell in 1956 described the Gang-Gang Cockatoo as having a "rosy countenance, topped by an uncombed, careless crest which gives the Gang-Gang a high forehead, weirdly intellectual look, which is enhanced by the penetrating white-rimmed eyes." Poetry aside, its crest is wispy, recumbent, recurved, and bright red, and can be erected at will. The bird's irises are dark brown and its bill is a greyish horn color.

The remainder of the upper parts of the male's body are a slate color with pale margins to the feathers, the margins being particularly more noticeable in the head region, upper wing, back, and tail coverts. The lower feathers and underparts are slate brown, a coloration that is considerably duller than that of the upper parts. The feathering, including the underwing and under tail coverts, is more lightly margined, with some feathers of the lower abdominal area having reddish-orange tips and white bars. The feet are grey.

The Gang-Gang Cockatoo is rarely seen in captivity, even in Australia. To obtain a license to own one is virtually impossible (photograph by David Cook).

The female is far duller in appearance. While in general she resembles the male, she lacks the bright red to the head region. Additionally, her grey crest is smaller and fluffier. Her head and crown are almost a uniform black, but with some orange ventral scalloping; the margined edges to the feathers are just barely discernible. As is the case with the male, the female's remaining head feathers are slate grey, but again the margins are less pronounced. The back feathers are mottled in bars of a lighter shade of grey. The lower abdominal area feathers are barred with white and are margined more widely with salmon.

All other features are more or less alike between the sexes, any color differences being subtle variations.

Juvenile males closely resemble adult females in overall body plumage coloration and patterning. Young males, however, have their nuchal crests tipped in red, and there are some minor red markings to the cheeks, hindneck, and forehead areas. The juvenile male acquires full male adult coloration after its first moult.

This cockatoo is now frequently seen in urban settings, where it is actually welcomed. It is a heavily protected species. Capturing one from the wild can result in a fine up to AU$29,313, plus confiscation of the vehicle used (photograph by P.S. Jeremy).

Behavior

The Gang-Gang Cockatoo shows no particular preference for one type of terrain over another and appears to be quite content wherever it is currently living so long as there is an abundant supply of food. It appears to have a diversified diet, although at times it shows a distinct preference for certain foods when they become seasonably available; hawthorne berries and the seeds of the acadia and pyracantha are particular favorites when ripe. In addition, the species feeds on the seeds of the eucalyptus and other trees, wattles, assorted fruits and nuts, and even specific insects: the larvae of wood boring insects, especially a grub known as spitfires (Lendon, in Cayley 1973) are favorites. The species is almost completely arboreal and is predictable in its feeding habits; groups of the birds will continue to feed in the same tree until the tree has been totally stripped of all its fruit or seeds, particularly the eucalyptus: White (in Mathews 1916) noted that the birds would devour such quantities of the trees' seeds over a period of time that the smell of the seeds' oils would permeate the bird's flesh.

The species has a marked tendency to be nomadic, and it frequently appears in areas where it has been previously unknown (Russel 1921). During 1946 Barrett observed that occasionally in search of food the species would "even enter the streets of country towns where the hawthorne grows in parks and gardens," particularly in the suburbs of Canberra and Melbourne. These wanderings appear to be directly related to availability of traditional food supplies, which at a given time may be in short supply. For example, the NSW Scientific Committee (2008) reports that during the winter months the species can be commonly encountered eating seeds of introduced shrubs and trees around human settlements.

In addition to these nomadic movements in search of foraging opportunities, the species' annual cycle is characterized by seasonal movements in which there are population shifts from one region to another depending on seasonal ripening of diverse tree berries or seeds.

The Gang-Gang Cockatoo flies in a slow manner, and similar to some other species of cockatoos, its flying appears labored. The flight is often accompanied by a low-pitched wheezing. It also has a distinctive call, when and if it calls, that can be best described as the sound of a creaking gate.

During spring the birds are found in pairs, but by the end of summer, after a successful nesting, the young accompany their parents on food foraging excursions and nightly roosting. Usually the cockatoo is then found in small groups, mostly family units. By the autumn and winter months, many of these family groupings unite with other birds, forming flocks numbering up to fifty or so individuals, particularly during hawthorne berry season.

The species is naturally quiet, and it is said that one can walk under a tree in which the birds are perched and not be aware of their presence.

Unlike most other species of cockatoos, the Gang-Gang Cockatoo is neither wary, shy, nor suspicious. It often proves itself exceedingly tame in the wild and can be approached without difficulty, especially when feeding (Frith 1969). It would appear to have virtually no normal instincts of caution or fear, in that often it does not effectively respond to immediate dangers confronting it: when fired at, for example, the Gang-Gang Cockatoo will rise into the air above the tree upon which it was perched, or feeding, will mill about above the tree for a few seconds, as if confused, even though one of its fellows may have already fallen to the gunfire, and then will either alight on the same tree or upon another immediately adjacent. Mellon (in Mathews 1916) chronicles one such incident in his correspondence to

Mathews: "The birds were very intent on feeding on the wattle.... the birds settled on the large eucalyptus trees and then came down to the smaller acacias underneath; they were quite tame, ... so that I could pick and choose my birds, so as to get pairs."Similarly, in the *Australian Museum Special Catalogue*, Grant (1912) was to write, "On one occasion my brother and I shot eighteen from one tree, which were attracted by the cries of two of their wounded mates lying on the ground."

For all readers distressed at the plight of the cockatoos being shot at, they may be cheered somewhat by an additional comment Mr. Grant had to make about the birds that had been killed that day: he cautioned his readers, "These birds inflict a nasty bite. A wounded female I attempted to pick up fastened on to my right thumb, the top of it nearly bit through."

Much of the cockatoo's leisure time is spent in mutual preening. Cayley described one such session: "I have seen a bird lying along a branch with its wings spread, while its neighbor went carefully over its feathers as if seeking vermin in a monkey like fashion."

The Gang-Gang Cockatoo exhibits unexplicable behavior at times. Sometimes, during feeding or preening, the birds will abruptly and without apparent cause take flight above the trees on which they have been perched, wheel and circle, and then descend back down to them to resume their previous behavior—all as if nothing happened. At other times the cockatoos will simply sit quietly for hours on end on the highest branches of trees.

Habitat and Distribution

The Gang-Gang Cockatoo inhabits the extreme southeastern region of Australia in both New South Wales and Victoria. In New South Wales it is limited to the south seaboard areas and to the central regions (Shields and Chrome 1992), and as far north as Newcastle. In Victoria the species is common as far westward as the Mount Dandedong region. The cockatoo is restricted to the coastal plains, including terrains leading into the high country, and can be considered common in such areas. It is believed by some—a matter that has not been confirmed—that it also inhabits the extreme southeastern corner of Australia. The species inhabited King Island in the Bass Straits until recently, but it is now considered extinct there; the bird occurs on Kangeroo Island off the coast of South Australia, where it was introduced in the recent past. It is thought to be an occasional visitor to Tasmania.

The species was also once numerous and widespread in the area now constituting Sydney and environs, but the loss of habitat to urbanization during recent years has dramatically resulted in what is believed to be a decline in its population in that area. While this decline in the immediate Sydney environs is due to the extensive loss of the species' former normal habitat, the general fragmentation of the remaining woods and forests does not seem to have dramatically affected its aggregate population numbers and its overall distribution. In fact, the species is suspected of now actually increasing in numbers; some of the cockatoos are reported even to be overwintering in the suburban Canberra environs (Birdlife 2012).

During the summer the Gang-Gang Cockatoo can be found in cooler and wetter mountain woodlands and forests, while during the winter months it inhabits the forests and woodlands in lower elevations. The species occurs in a variety of forests and wooded habitats in more open woodland regions in both southern New South Wales and Victoria (NSW Environment and Heritage 2011). It prefers to inhabit open Eucalypt forests and woodlands that have a widespread acacia under storey, both kinds of trees being important to their foraging. Although there are numerous pine plantations in the region, the species is rarely encountered therein.

Propagation

The Gang-Gang Cockatoo reaches sexual maturity at approximately four years of age (Chambers 1995). On the onset of the breeding season, which is from October to January, the birds begin pairing up.

A preferred nesting site is normally in a hollow of a live eucalyptus tree (Beruldsen 1980) in a thick sclerophyll forest with a dense understory, preferably composed of acacias. The ideal tree will be located near a watercourse and will be a mature tree of considerable height. The cockatoo prefers a nesting hollow that is situated high above the ground, as much as twenty or more meters (60-plus feet), and that may be as much as two meters deep (6') from the entrance. The hollow may be in the trunk of the tree or in the stump of a broken limb (Gibbons and Lindenmayer 2000).

The entrance to the nest hollow is enlarged by both adults' actively chewing at the entrance. According to a naturalist acquaintance of Howe, the cockatoo will also chew off many of the branches in the immediate vicinity of the nest so that the ground below is littered with debris. While the rotting wood within the nest hollow usually suffices as the nest material, the shreds of wood resulting from the entrance and nest cavity chewing simply adds more to the nest bedding.

Before descending into the nest itself, the female exhibits another one of its many rituals common to the species: she perches at the entrance, raises her crest, and bows to the right and then to the left. In 1924 Howe timed one such ritual performance, which proved to be eleven minutes long.

The female will normally lay from one to three eggs, two being the normative clutch. The eggs are laid two to three days apart, and are reported by Frith as measuring approximately 34 × 28 mm (1.3" × 1.1"). Forshaw gives the range of the eggs in the H.L. White Collection as 33.5–36.4 mm × 26.6–28.2 mm (1.3–1.4" × 1.0–1.1"). Should the nesting fail, the pair will often attempt a second brood (NSW Scientific Committee 2008). Both adults take turns incubating the eggs; when the female leaves either for food or water (Hedges 1926), the male will enter the nest to continue the incubation. The Donpaulna Aviaries (2012) reports that males take the night shift when incubating and the female the day shift, with the female spending a longer time on the nest overall. The incubation period is approximately 29 days. On hatching, the nestlings have a rusty colored down. Hart found that both parents participate in the feeding of the young.

The young fledge at approximately eight weeks, but the newly fledged offspring will still be fed by the parents for about two months after the nest has been abandoned, at which point they become completely independent. The juveniles remain with the parents as a family unit until larger congregations begin forming in the autumn. It is not clear whether the family remains together once it has joined a large flock, although it is known that the adult pair maintain a multi year bonding. The Gang-Gang Cockatoo is believed to have a strong nest site fidelity (NSW Environment and Heritage 2011), and is known to breed semi-colonially when the cockatoo's population density is high (NSW Scientific Committee 2008).

Aviary Notes

Unlike some other species of cockatoos, the Gang-Gang Cockatoo breeds readily in captivity, provided some minimal, common sense provisions are taken to ensure optimal encouragement for the pair, and suitable environmental conditions for nesting, brooding, and fledging. Despite this encouraging generalization, there are regrettably some matters of serious concern that cannot be ignored for both Australian and non–Australian breeders. One principal concern is the availability of the cockatoos. While numerous birds were exported from Australia prior to the country's prohibition of fauna exportation during the seventies, and they were bred, and their descendants are still being bred in non–Australian aviaries and zoos, there is no longer any opportunity to obtain the cockatoo from Australia; and there are not enough birds bred in captivity to satisfy even a small percentage of aspiring Gang-Gang Cockatoo purchasers interested in breeding them.

For Australians, the Gang-Gang Cockatoo is protected; robbing a nest for a nestling is illegal, and there are heavy financial penalties for violating the prohibitions; specifically, the fine for taking a Gang-Gang Cockatoo, adult or nestling, from the wilds is AU$29,313 per specimen, and/or up to two years imprisonment (Berwick Leader News 2012); as well, Australians require a license to obtain and own a Gang-Gang Cockatoo, a license that is difficult to obtain. Moreover, the cost of the cockatoo cannot be ignored: at the time of this writing (September 2012) an Australian in Queensland can expect to pay at least AU$2,500 for a pair. And, at this writing, an examination of Gum Tree did not reveal even one advertisement across Australia advertising a Gang-gang Cockatoo. In the United States, there was only one classified ad, in Texas, offering Gang-Gang Cockatoos for sale (although there may be other advertisements over the course of a year), and although the breeder advertised them, he had none for sale.

Then there is the question of pair bonding. Even if both a male and female can be obtained, they may not necessarily bond, and even if they do, many pairs do not breed regularly; plus, should one of the bonded birds die, it may take the surviving mate several years to bond with another bird, before recommencing breeding. While the Gang-Gang Cockatoo is an exceptional species, it is notorious for being a feather plucker, a behavior probably motivated by, among other things, boredom. Regardless, it is expected that anyone attempting to breed the bird, assuming they can or have acquired a pair, will have an Advanced Specialist Breeder level of knowledge (BirdCare 2012).

Similar to other species of cockatoos, the Gang-Gang Cockatoo exudes a white powder that it uses in its regular grooming of its feathers. Anyone suffering from asthma or other breathing difficulties would be well advised to avoid this species.

And finally, despite all the discouraging issues raised above, almost everyone intimate with ornithology and aviculture strongly advise against pet ownership of the Gang-Gang Cockatoo: while the species is not yet threatened with extinction, the continued diminishing of its regular habitat does not bode well for the species' population numbers in the long term.

As noted earlier, the species breeds well in captivity despite the negative tone of the paragraphs above. The Gang-Gang Cockatoo has been bred many times since 1921, and such breedings are no longer considered exceptions or rarities, as they oft are with some other cockatoo species. They have been bred in a number of different countries, some as far north as the British Isles. The first publically noted non–Australian successful breeding was accomplished by Mme. Lecallier in France in 1921 (Prestwick 1951). She reported that two eggs had been laid in June, and the first hatched on July 4, and the second two days later. By September 4, the youngsters were fully feathered, flying well, and feeding themselves.

In Great Britain, the first breeding award went to the Marquess of Tavistock in 1938[3]; in Australia to a Miss S. Merriwell in 1945 (Lendon 1947); and in the United States the first recorded breeding was in 1973 by Velma Hart. There are countless others successes with the Gang-Gang Cockatoo, far too many to individually acknowledge.

While there are several written accounts on the successful (or failed) breeding of the cockatoo in captivity, few provide the exacting details that characterize the F. George Hedges report, written in 1926, an accounting still used extensively as an invaluable reference. A brief summary of Hedge's report might prove useful to an aspirant breeder.

Hedges housed his pair in an aviary measuring 16 × 14 × 12 feet (approximately 5 meters × 4.5 meters × 4 meters): the aviary was built higher than usual because he wanted to ensure the pair a semblance of the wilds. The nest box, a barrel, was fixed high in a dead pear tree erected in the middle of the aviary. Apparently, though, a high aviary with a high nest box is not necessarily critical to encourage breeding interest. Lendon in 1947 reported of a pair in the Halstrom Collection that "bred in a log lying on the ground" (Lendon, in Cayley 1973). His comment about that particular breeding, perhaps made with tongue in cheek, was, "This species was bred, one might say accidentally." That pair, incidentally, was housed with several other cockatoos of different species.

In regards to Hedge's aviary, he attached to it an additional, covered, accessible enclosure approximately 14 feet long × 3 feet wide (about 4.3 meters by 1 meter).

The pair were first observed copulating in May and two eggs were laid in June, the second egg two days after the first. He checked on the nest regularly, reporting that his regular intrusions to check on the brooding and nestlings did not disturb his nesting pair; Hart, however, found her birds considerably distressed by her similar intrusions to monitor the nesting progress.

Of Hedge's pair of nestlings, one died before the fourth week. At four weeks the surviving nestling was covered in bluish grey quills, and by the chick's sixth week, its crest was beginning to reveal some red; at the time of fledging the juvenile was almost identical to the adult female except for the spotted red in the crest.

Every reported breeding stresses the ease in feeding both the parents and their young. Daily diets normally consist of some concoctions of sunflower and canary seeds, bread and milk, oats, wheat, diverse greens and fruits, and in southern climes, eucalyptus leaves. Compared to some other species of cockatoos—the Glossy Black Cockatoo (*Calyptorhynchus lathamii*), for example—the Gang-Gang Cockatoo is neither a finicky eater nor an eater evolutionarily limited to a few specific seeds, nuts, or fruits.

As can be gathered from above, the Gang-Gang Cockatoo is a hearty bird and can be acclimatised to colder climates in the Northern Hemisphere providing, of course, that suitable shelter is available to the birds during days of inclement weather.

Professional experience recommends an aviary at least 5 meters × 1.5 meters × 2.1 meters (16' × 5' × 7'), with only one pair inhabiting the aviary (BirdCare 2012), and in northern climes the provision of shelter, the bigger the better. There should be an ample supply of nontoxic, leafed tree branches for the cockatoos to chew upon, and wooden perches. Since the species is primarily an arboreal feeder, feeders should be at least a meter (3') above the floor. (But some Gang-Gang Cockatoos have been reported to occasionally feed on the ground in an aviary.) Because the cockatoos will demolish the tree branches and perches in short order, expect to replace them regularly. Similarly, while many food trays and water containers are constructed of thin-gauge galvanized metal, those that are provided the birds should be sturdy enough to withstand the constant chewing, or otherwise, similar to the branches and perches, they too will have to be replaced.

The constant chewing provides the cockatoos with exercise, reduces boredom, and helps control beak growth. By providing the cockatoos with ample objects to chew upon, these intelligent cockatoos will be diverted from boredom and from the consequential feather plucking for which they are known. In this connection, a heavy-gauge galvanized mesh should enclose the aviary; birds clinging to the mesh of the enclosure will also tend to chew on the mesh, another positive distraction from feather plucking, and also helpful in controlling beak growth.

The preferred nest housing is a log with a hollow, but the cockatoos will accept nest boxes. Depending on the available space within the aviary, several nest boxes or logs should be provided. Assuming the pair is bonded, they will begin taking an interest in one or another of the proffered nesting accommodations; the others should then be gradually removed. The nest boxes should be approximately 275 square mm (circa 10"), with an entrance hole approximately 75 mm (3"). Bird Care recommends the log nest box option should be at least 600–1,200 mm long (24"–48").

In addition to the foods mentioned above by earlier breeders of the species, BirdCare recommends feeding the birds local insects, meal worms, crickets, and even some meat, especially during the breeding season to supplement the birds' protein requirements, and concurrently recommends restricting the provision of too much sunflower and safflower seed, because a heavy daily diet of these favorite seeds leads to obesity in the birds. In southern climates, eucalyptus, acacia and cones from introduced pines, and fruits from the hawthorn and cotoneaster bushes are favorites that provide the birds with both mental stimulation from the chewing required and variance in the daily diet. Various nuts such as peanuts and almonds, and fruits such as apples, and even dry dog food are generally accepted. And, for those breeders who are not too squeamish, commercially raised mice should be offered. In short, since the Gang-Gang Cockatoo readily accepts a wide range of foods, feeding the birds is the least of the aviculturalist's concerns. (The reader is referred to the 2008 BirdCare technical data sheet for more comprehensive detail and information on Gang-Gang Cockatoo husbandry; the data sheet also includes a substantial bibliography of publications relating to the breeding of the species, and can be downloaded from the Internet.)

Pet Companion

The Gang-Gang Cockatoo is considered by some to be an ideal pet, if they could only obtain one. While the species is uniquely attractive, and is as intelligent as most other cockatoo species, it carries with it a negative history related to its purported tendency to feather pluck, and "personality" problems, a negative reputation dating to the mid–1800s. Some historical perspectives might be helpful to understanding its current negative reputation.

The first Gang-Gang Cockatoo in Britain was acquired by the London Zoo in 1859. Because it was considered rare, it had been an expensive acquisition, particularly since the exporters argued that the species was fragile and rarely survived long ocean voyages. Dr. W.T. Greene, who published three separate volumes on parrots between 1884 and 1887, and who was considered both a parrot expert and a leading chronicler of parrot aviary and field studies, and who had never before seen a Gang-Gang Cockatoo outside the London Zoo, took it upon himself to resolve the controversy already developing regarding the species' disposition and hence its desirability, or lack of it.

Dr. Greene wrote, "Authors ... declare that it makes a most charming cage bird and pet while others ... give it a character of peevishness, moroseness, and in fact everything that a pet should not possess." He quoted a certain Dr. Max Schmidt—first establishing that Dr. Schmidt was an authority on the Gang-Gang Cockatoo—who not only insisted that the species was more "moroser" (*sic*) than other cockatoo species, but that it was also "insusceptible of being tamed, and teachable." Dr. Greene also opposed the idea of the species' being a desirable pet because—according to a certain Dr. Karl Russ, who Dr. Greene also considered an authority because he had written a book titled *Die Papagien*—the cockatoo "killed and ate guinea pigs" (Greene 1979).

Ironically, even though Dr. Greene admitted he had rarely seen the species, or interacted with it, and hence considered himself neutral despite quoting extensively from negatively oriented parrot authorities, wrote, "They are shy birds, consequently, nervous, and require patience and perseverance."

Finally, Dr. Greene's observations concluded with some remarks from the Honorable and Reverend F.G. Dutton—an avicultural crony of Dr. Greene's who frequently collaborated in Greene's publications. The reverend described the Gang-Gang Cockatoo thus: "The bird was neither brilliant in color, nor graceful in shape; but it was decidedly sulky in temper, and its name Gang Gang was music in itself compared to its note, which is the more rasping and aggravating of all the Cockatoo cries, and that is saying a great deal" (Greene 1979).

All of this kind of historical nonsense provides, of course, interesting and amusing reading. But the authorities of one hundred and fifty years ago chronicled as best they could given the limitations of knowledge and experience concerning the species they were trying to understand.

In more recent times, both our knowledge of the species and our views towards it have changed considerably. The species can be tamed easily, so much so that it can be left at liberty and allowed freedom to fly about at will (Bedford 1952). Lendon (in Cayley 1973), who had several over a period of years, wrote of one of his Gang-Gang Cockatoos, "It became very friendly, enjoying having its crest scratched and always performing its quaint display, consisting of a purposeful advance along the perch, culminating in a hop with the crest erect whenever spoken to."

There are many now who praise the species, but there are still others who find the species better left in the wild, zoos and what few aviaries have them for show or breeding. The Donpaulna Aviaries says, "They are a very special cockatoo with their character and unique sound ... a great companion bird," and Avion Companions states, "They make excellent pets." They have been described as tame and gentle. In 2006, John McGrath reported having a few birds with limited vocabularies, and Molliercocks (2012) states that his pet Raymond has been taught various tricks such as rolling on his back and waving his feet in greeting.

There are numerous accounts referring to the cockatoo's tendency to pluck itself bare of feathers, a behavior that almost always results from sheer boredom, boredom caused by the owner's failure to provide his cockatoos with a stimulating environment and probably also by his failure to interact with his charges. The species is notoriously known for being a "feather plucker," but how much of that notoriety is a snowballed stereotype based on a handful of previously disappointed pet owners? Notable aviculturalists such as the Marquess of Tavistock, Velma Hart, Donpaulna Aviaries and other well established breeders and authorities have not experienced the feather-plucking, self-mutilating behavior. And what percentage of Gang-Gang Cockatoos in captivity are "feather pluckers" would be nothing more than a guess.

Whatever the case, much of what was written above is an academic exercise of little value to bird lovers hoping someday to acquire a Gang-Gang Cockatoo. A scant few will ever have the privilege of owning one.

Some Historical Notes on Taxonomy

The Genus *Callocephalon* is a monotypic genus accorded genus status within the Family *Cacatuidae* because of specific characteristics that make it unique and separate from all other cockatoos.

Because of its specific and unique coloration, it had been separated from the White Cockatoos; however, it had traditionally been considered closely related to the Black Cockatoos. Even though it is also separate from them, a century earlier Mathews expressed reservation about relating the *Callocephalon* to the Black Cockatoos, arguing that color in this instance may be superficial, and that eventual study in skeletal structures might prove the Gang-Gang Cockatoo to be more closely related to the White Cockatoos than was generally believed. He also argued that because of the Gang-Gang's color similarities to the immature Yellow-tailed Cockatoo (*Calyptorhynchus funereus*), it might be more appropriate to include the Gang-Gang under the Genus *Calyptorhynchus*.

More recently, Lendon (in Cayley 1973) suggested that the *Callocephalon* might be a link between the so-called White and Black cockatoos. Forshaw considered a more specific relationship of the *Callocephalon* to other groups within the Family *Cacatuidae*: he likened the Gang Gang Cockatoo to the Galah (*Genus Eolophus*), primarily on the basis of hybridization between the two species, and particularly because of the similarity of their flight behavior. While the genus *Callocephalon* no longer provokes debate regarding its relationship to other cockatoos, there are still some within the avian community who harbor doubts.

15

Palm Cockatoo

Probosciger aterrimus (Gmelin, 1788)

COMMON NAMES: Goliah Cockatoo, Black Cockatoo, Black Palm Cockatoo, Great
Palm Cockatoo, Goliah aratoos

SUBSPECIES:
1. *Probosciger aterrimus aterrimus*—Nominate Species (Gmelin, 1788)
2. *Probosciger aterrimus goliah* (Kuhl, 1820)
3. *Probosicger aterrimus stenolophus* (Van Oort, 1911)

LIFESPAN: 80–90 years[1]

IUCN RED LIST OF THREATENED SPECIES: Extinct along coastal areas of New
Guinea's southern coast. Near threatened
in Cape York, Australia.[2]

CITES: Appendix I

Description

Most descriptions of the Palm Cockatoo describe it as a slate black, but in fact its color
is closer to a glossy black. The slate coloration is due to the powder the cockatoo applies to
its feathers during grooming and which distorts the overall shading.[3] This blackness is uniform and the only deviation from its glossy black appearance is in the cheek lories areas,
which are bare and pinkish toned, and which will change color depending on the bird's level
of stress: this color can change to a pink or even beige, or scarlet red when the bird is excited.
The bird can hide its lories with coverlet feathers. The Palm Cockatoo is the only cockatoo
species to have a bare cheek patch that is used to signal conspecifics. The feet and mandibles
are both black. The thighs are blue-grey in color, and bare. The cere is feathered. The crest
is best described as exceptionally long and filamented, backward curving, and plume-like.
The irises of both sexes are dark brown, and the eye rings are bare. Aside from some differences in weight between the sexes, the cockatoo is basically monomorphic and cannot be
sexed by eye color, plumage color, or size; confirmation of sexes necessitates either DNA
analysis or surgical testing.

The species' beak, however, is outstanding, deserving some elaboration. First of all, it is
extremely imposing in size, and of the various species composing the parrot tribe, only the
Hyacinth Macaw (*Anodorynchus hyacinthinus*) has a larger beak than the Palm Cockatoo's; the
cockatoo's upper mandible is considerably longer than the lower mandible, and substantially

The Palm Cockatoo is the only cockatoo species that lives primarily year round in tropical rain forests. It is also one of the very few wildlife species known to be skilled in tool-making. The bird is known to fashion a tool from a branch that it uses to drum against a tree trunk, the sound carrying for a considerable distance. The sound is believed to tell eligible females the suitability of the male's proffered nest hollow during breeding season (photograph by Peter Stubbs).

narrower at the base than the former. Because the two mandibles do not match together, the black tongue with its reddish tip is always clearly visible, even when the mandibles are closed. Considering the overall size of the Palm Cockatoo, and most especially the enormity of the beak, the tongue appears disproportionately small. In fact, the *Probosciger* was originally named genus *Microglossus,* namely "small tongued." Curiously, the tongue is cylindrically shaped.

In addition to its enormous size, the beak is unique in both its construction and in the dexterity with which it is employed during feeding, a matter which has drawn the attention of numerous students of ornithology. Structurally, the beak is unique in part because the upper mandible is corrugated on its inner surface, much as the jaws of a pair of pliers are corrugated to provide gripping power. Such corrugation is a definite asset during feeding, when hard nuts form a staple part of the cockatoo's diet. Additionally, the beak can exert considerable pressure so that even the hardest of nuts cannot remain inviolate, a strength which Eastman and Hunt observed can effectively "snap fencing wire with the ease of pliers." The upper mandible corrugations also help hold the nut firm while the lower mandible moves back and forth crushing the nut's shell.

In overall appearance, the beak appears unwieldy, massive, and clumsy. This appearance is deceptive, however, for the Palm Cockatoo can employ its beak with delicate dexterity as well as crushing strength.

The smallest seeds can be efficiently manipulated and their shells removed with remarkable ease. The deftness, ease, and delicate manipulation of the beak in the shelling of the smallest of seeds is so astounding that Rand in 1942 was compelled to write, almost incredulously, "It is amazing that the Black Cockatoo could have removed and husked these seeds, only a few millimeters across, without breaking them." It should be noted that close examination of gizzard contents revealed virtually no chaff.[4]

While there is no observable sexual dimorphism between males and females, except for occasional variations in size, this minor variation is consistent over the total distribution of the species' range. The individual birds average in length from 55 to 60 cm (21.5"–23.5"), and weigh approximately 910–1,200 grams (32–42 oz.). Finally, the tail of the Palm Cockatoo is comparatively long when compared to other cockatoo species, whose tails tend to be blunter and shorter. The Palm Cockatoo's tail and the wing have a rounded appearance. Additionally, the cockatoo's tail is distinctive because it does not have a color band as do the other Black Cockatoos.

Regarding the subspecies, there is little significant variation between them, and the question of what differences there are has over the past decades caused considerable debate and disagreement regarding the exact number of subspecies. Over the years, there have been as many as eight subspecies identified and considered as part of the Palm Cockatoo family. Almost all of the disagreement centred on size differences in the birds from one region as compared to another, and even within a given region itself. For example, the *P.a. stenolophus* is considered by some to be similar to the *P.a. goliah* in overall size, but to have a somewhat narrower crest. The *P.a. goliah*, on the other hand, is somewhat larger than the *P.a. aterrimus*. Some have argued, however, that the *P.a. goliah* and the *P.a. aterrimus* may not be separable because there are significant size differentials between individuals in each population and such variations lack constancy. And so on. Currently, the recognized subspeciation of the species is as follows. The differences, the reader will note, are based mostly on the contentious size differentials:

P.a. aterrimus: both adults are black with a greyish tinge due to the white powder the cockatoo uses in grooming; it has bare, crimson cheek patches, and bare, blue-grey thighs. The male's black beak is larger than the female's. The eyes are dark brown, and the eye ring is grey.

P.a. goliah: identical to P.a. aterrimus, except notably larger in size.

P.a. stenolophus: both male and female adults are as large in size as the P.a. goliah, except that this subspecies' crest feathers are narrower.

Behavior

Unlike most of the other cockatoos, which at times form large flocks sometimes numbering in the hundreds and occasionally in the thousands, the Palm Cockatoo tends to prefer its own company to that of others, and when it does flock, it is typically in a loosely gathered group of a few individuals, which might number five to seven birds. It is not known whether the birds in these loose groups are related or unrelated.

In the morning, the cockatoo is quiet and quite leisurely about leaving its roosting tree for the feeding grounds. It is only well after sunrise that it begins stirring, preening itself, and responding to the calls of several other individuals who might be in the immediate area, or even in the same tree as itself. After an hour or so of preening and calling, singly, individuals may fly to join others in a tree in the open. Such congregations of a small handful of birds normally occur well after sunrise, in open woodland, or at a rainforest's edge (Parrot Tag 2012), and rarely number more than six or seven individuals. When not in small groups, they are invariably seen singly or in pairs. At night they roost singly, although there may be more than one Palm Cockatoo separately roosting in the same tree (Wood 1984); the roosting tree is always the tallest tree in a sheltered area of the forest.

In the morning after the preening or display activity, the entire group departs for the feeding grounds. While the cockatoos embark to a feeding area more or less together, they are not "flock eaters"—that is, each bird feeds independently from the others in its small, loosely gathered group. Their feeding behavior is similar to that of several strangers entering a restaurant at the same time, but each of whom sit and eat separately from all the others.

The Palm Cockatoo feeds on various seeds, leaf buds, diverse berries, fruits, and nuts, particularly the *kanari* nut, its favorite, a nut that, incidentally, has a hard shell and is difficult to break. Departure en masse takes place immediately after one of the birds departs alone, for whatever reason. The flight consists of several slow wing beats, punctuated by considerable gliding, a flight conveying the appearance of being heavy and strained. Forshaw was to write that they "make a most impressive sight as they float through the rain forest tree tops.... The glide is also employed as they come in to alight after a normal flight. They always glide directly into the tree and do not adopt the spiral course characteristics of many members of the *Cacatuinea.*"

On windy days the birds rarely leave the shelter of the thick forest, but it has been observed that on calm days the species often makes flights to the coast, where on one occasion a maximum of thirty individuals were actually seen in a flock. Because of the dense nature of the forest and its general inaccessibility it is unknown precisely what attracts the cockatoo to the coastal regions, but it is speculated that the trip to the coast may serve some social function (Wood 1984).

Calling generally begins at sunrise. The cockatoo carries in its repertoire of vocalizations a variety of whistles, and even a striking "hello" sound that is almost human sounding. Its calls have been described in a variety of ways.

While some observers such as Rand and Gilliard in 1967 have dismissed the bird's call simply as "loud whistled calls," or as "a loud shriek and various whistling noises," other field workers have provided more elaborate and analytical descriptions of the call. Slater has analysed their call as disyllabic, a whistle in which the first note is mellow and deep and the second a shrill and prolonged call terminating in an upward inflection. Diamond described the call in the following terms: "a rapid series of alternative upslurs and downslurs '... whik-whik-whik ... ,' at a rate of four per second. Occasionally, a melodious, whistled, jumbled call with quality similar to the Dominella lory." In 1933, Dr. D'Ombrain described his pet Palm Cockatoo's vocalizations thusly: "a peculiarly loud and not unusual whistle, which is uttered at all times of excitement, or when in a merry mood.... When alarmed, especially when the bird is in the dark, it emits a most blood curdling loud and drawn out growl or scream.... While uttering these calls, the mandibles are opened to their widest, and the larynx can be seen working. The call is of such a clear, carrying nature that it can be heard upwards of half a mile away [one kilometer]." In his studies of the Palm Cockatoo in the Cape York rain forests, Wood noted that the bird's vocalizations were complex. He distinguished three basic calls given in considerable variation through the changing of the modulation and arrangement of their eight syllables. He discovered that cockatoos as distant as 200 kilometers had exactly the same calls, but the modulations were constantly different. The reporters of the Palm Cockatoo describe these vocal differences as "dialects."

Vocalization often accompanies ritualistic behavior. For example, Lendon observed that when his Palm Cockatoo whistled, it not only cried out in a shrill "undescribable whistle," but would stamp its foot—and concurrently, its bare cheek area would flush redder. When frightened, the Palm Cockatoo often stamps its foot—unlike other cockatoos, who hiss when frightened (That Bird Blog 2008). In 1964 Forshaw observed interesting display behavior associated with diverse vocal activity:

> As the first note of the call is emitted, the bird adopts an upright stance with the crest half raised.... On giving the high pitched drawn out note the cockatoo lunges forward, extends the wings, raises the crest and the tail.... The display was performed two or three times in rapid succession by different birds in the tree.

According to Forshaw's account, this display and vocal activity was not related to courtship behavior. In his field work studying the species in 1987, Wood observed various displays. He writes of one: "Displays involve crest erection, bowing, outstretching of wings and swaying. In these situations, mock combat may be observed, birds chasing each other from branch to branch." He notes, however, that these mock combat displays lack the raucous screeching and body contact common to combat between males during territorial disputes.

Aside from its various vocalizations, the species is distinct from all other cockatoos, and indeed from almost all other bird and animal species: it *utilizes a tool, a stick that it manufactures* (approximately an inch [25 mm] in diameter by about 6" [15 cm] long) and which it uses to beat on a tree or bough. The stick is clearly bitten off a living branch, and its severance is noticeable once the cockatoo peels off the bark (Wood 1984). The beating against the tree is loud enough that the noise can be heard 100 meters distant (circa 300 yards). The use of this manufactured tool was observed by Wood on several different occasions, and by other field workers. The purpose of the drumming is not known, but it has been suggested that females can assess the desirability of a given nesting site based on the resonance of the drumming display (Palm Cockatoo).

Habitat and Distribution

Of all the members of the *Cacatuinea*, the Palm Cockatoo is the only tropical rain forest adapted species. Most of the other species of cockatoos prefer dry and often sparsely vegetated terrains. The birds are not easily studied in their natural habitat because of their relative inaccessibility due to the heavy forestation, and also because their population density is low. The Palm Cockatoo is hence a tropical dwelling species of which little is known. When they are seen, they are usually in a clearing, in the open, always perched atop the highest of eucalyptus trees, unless they are feeding on seeds on the ground (MacGillivray 1916).

While protected by conservation laws, the Palm Cockatoo is believed to be declining in numbers. A century ago, in 1911, Bernard recounted how he had first visited the peninsula in 1896, and then again in 1911, and wrote that the species had been common in the region. But an acquaintance of his, a certain Mr. F.L. Jaredine, apparently a resident on the peninsula, had made the observation that the species in fact appeared to be diminishing in numbers, and this he attributed to "the frequent visits of sportsmen from Thursday Island who shoot everything that comes their way." In this connection, incidentally, when Rothschild and Hartert were in New Guinea in 1901, they learned that the Palm Cockatoo was considered sacred and was therefore safe from human harm because it was believed that for anyone to kill one of these birds meant certain death for himself.

When the Palm Cockatoo is found outside the depths of the rain forests, it is usually in the tallest of trees, which may be found in small clearings or along the edge of a forest. Because tall trees growing in the open are generally scarce, once a large one has been located, it will be favored day after day. Since the cockatoo is sedentary in its behavior, it may remain in the same district for months. In general, unless the cockatoo is in a forest clearing or minor savannah area, it is seldom conspicuous in behavior due to the thick tropical forestation in which it is normally found and which effectively conceals it, especially given its dark coloration.

In Australia the species inhabits the far northern Cape York territory, where their preferred choice of terrain is dense rain forests. Their distribution is widespread over New Guinea, where they can be found from the lowlands up to 1,300 meters (approximately 4,200'), tropical savanna, pure rainforests (Juniper and Parr 1998), monsoon woodland, and forest edges. In New Guinea the cockatoo appears to be more tolerant of degraded forest habitat, mostly in the foothills and low lands (Birdlife 2012).

The subspecies are distributed as follows:

P.a. aterrimus: The upper tip of Cape York Peninsula region in northeastern Australia, the Aru Islands in Indonesia, southern New Guinea, and Misool in the West Papua Islands.

P.a. goliah: West Papua Islands, except Misool, Indonesia, Central New Guinea from Vogelkop, Irian Jaya, east to southeast Papua New Guinea.

P. a. Stenolophus: Geelvink Bay, Irian Jaya, and north New Guinea, from Mamberamo to south eastern Papua (World Parrot Trust 2012).

The numbers of the various races have not been quantified, mostly because of the difficulty of gathering data in the terrains in which they are found.

Propagation

Countess field observations have established that aside from the Cockatiel and the Galah, most cockatoo species usually lay only two eggs, occasionally one or three; but the Palm Cockatoo, among its numerous other distinctive characteristics, lays only *one* egg. While it is possible that a two-egg clutch may on occasion be laid, such clutches have to be rare indeed. For example, MacGillivray (1914) wrote that of the seventeen nests that McLelland inspected during his 1911 field expedition into the Cape York area, not one nest was found to contain more than one egg, nestling, or fledgling. All ornithological literature based on scientific study to date notes this one-egg consistency. Yet, in 1966 Eastman and Hunt in their book *Parrots of Australia* describe the typical clutch as consisting of two eggs, a claim that is in obvious error.[5]

As with all other species of cockatoos, the Palm Cockatoo's eggs are white. They are elliptical, somewhat pitted and reveal tiny excrescences. Forshaw found the eggs in the H.L. White collection and the Australian Museum measured 44.7–54.9 × 34.5–39.9 mm (1.7–2.2" × 1.3–1.6"). The World Parrot Trust (2012) gives the eggs' dimensions as 50 × 37 mm (1.9 × 1.5").

Because of the dense forests the species generally inhabits, and the fact that the population density is very low, observations regarding the courtship behavior of the male and female are infrequent, and there is scant information from the wilds on brooding, or the solitary egg, or the rearing of the (sole) nestling. What firsthand information there is has been obtained with considerable, mostly unproductive, field study and observational difficulty, and is understandably sparse.

In respect to courtship behavior, the Marquess of Tavistock, an avid and notable aviculturalist in his time, referred to two incidents that he described as "courtship behavior." On the first occasion he observed a male feeding a female, which he inferred was courtship. Regarding the second occasion, he wrote an article for *Aviculture Magazine* (Tavistock 1928) in which he provides a description of the courtship behavior of a pair of Palm Cockatoos in his collection: his observations, although lengthy and having erroneous conclusions regarding courtship display, provide a delightful read:

> I have had a pair of Palm Cockatoos in my collection for about a year. In the spring they were turned into a large aviary. But they had been so shy and secretive, spending nearly all their time in the shelter, that ... one might almost have said of them they had no habits. This afternoon, they were both in the flight and the hen ... began to make advances on her companion. With her crest partly erect, she walked up to him in a jaunty manner, and when quite close puffed out the feathers on her breast. She then faced in the same direction as the cock and stamped either foot alternatively, posturing and bowing and rocking her head in a ridiculously affected manner in which she evidently considered quite becoming. The performance was enlivened by two distinctive calls—a kind of snarling croak and a crescendo scream which I can only describe as indistinguishable from that uttered by a housemaid engaged in bandage with her swain. During the performance the bare skin on the hen's face became a much deeper pink. The cock ... did not respond to her advances, but made no attempt to drive her away.

At the time of his writing there were scant means to differentiate male from female Palm Cockatoos—DNA and surgical sexing technology were still decades away. The courtship behavior Tavistock provides is that exhibited by males, and not by females, as he believed: succinctly, it was the male who tried to entice the female and it was the female who "did not respond."

While it is difficult at times to discover and access Palm Cockatoo nests for study, details of their construction have nevertheless been documented. The species prefers savanna terrain over rainforest as its breeding habitat (Murphy et al. 2003), although it will nest within the rain forest itself (Wood 1984). Nesting sites are almost invariably in the highest of trees, usually a Eucalypt species, with hollows as high as 45 meters from the ground (140'), although the cockatoo has infrequently been found to nest as low as four meters (13') above the ground, again usually in a eucalyptus.

The pairs normally may have up to a dozen nesting hollows in their territory (Wood 1984), vigorously defending each of them. As the breeding season approaches, the pair regularly and with increasing frequency visit their nesting hollows: territorial displays, nest usurpation, and competition by conspecifics indicate competition for nest sites; a male's successful nest monopolization results in a shortage of nesting sites for some breeding females, and the consequential result is that there are fewer occupied nests in a given area, and ultimately fewer fledglings.

The nest is constructed within a deep hollow of the trunk of a towering, huge tree where it is inaccessible to snakes; the nest may be more than a meter (3') down in the hollow cavity. Although there may be numerous hollows in the various towering trees, alive or dead, not all of the hollows may have the necessary configuration for the construction of a suitable nest. Fires are an important element in the creation of nest hollows. But severe or numerous fires can also destroy hollow nest sites. Fires do, however, provide an opportunity for termites and microorganisms to colonize a cavity. In doing so the insects and microorganisms hollow out the area from the inside, which will at a later date transform the hollow into a suitable nest site. Regrettably they also provide feral bees an ideal hive location, hence even further limiting nesting opportunities.

At the bottom of the hollow, the cockatoos construct a bedding of wood splinters, the bedding actually forming a platform of considerable thickness upon which the solitary egg will be laid. The adults carry shredded branches of wood into the cavity, where they then chew them into match-sized splinters. The depth of the shredded bedding appears to be dictated by the depth of the hollow (Wood 1984). Since the nest is constructed in the hollows of upright trees, it has been conjectured that the bedding of wood splinters serves a twofold purpose: first, since the nests are typically in rain forest terrain, there is considerable rainfall, and there is therefore the danger that a nestling could drown in the eventuality of a heavy downpour; the bedding hence serves as an elevated platform. Second, the wood splinters serve a hygienic function in that they permit the excreta to filter downwards.

It is believed this nest may be used for several years by the same pair, although there is no confirmed evidence supporting his belief.

The solitary egg laid is incubated for approximately 28–31 days, the female incubating at night and the male during the day. The hatched chick is totally naked and, unlike other cockatoos that are hisuated, it does not develop down. The female alone feeds the chick (Wood 1984). The young Palm Cockatoo juvenile leaves the nest 100–110 days after hatching, an extraordinary period because it is the longest nesting period of any parrot species (World Association of Zoos and Aquariums 2012). On leaving the nest, the chick is still unable to competently fly for approximately two weeks, and will continue to be fed by its parents for about six weeks. Wood found that the fledged juvenile often remained with its parents until the next nesting period, but always flew well behind its parents wherever they went.

Juveniles are similar to their parents in appearance, except that their crest is shorter, their periophthalmic ring is white, and the underpart feathers have a pale yellow edging.

In the Cape York Peninsula area, the Palm Cockatoo breeds in August but often as late as January: nestlings can be found as early as the first week of August, but some as late as the later part of January. In a 2006 field study of 27–28 nests studied in the Cape York Peninsula, Murphy et al. found the peak of the egg-laying period actually occurred in September. Evidence suggests, however, that the principal breeding months are from September to November. Reports from the New Guinea region indicate that the breeding season may be slightly later than that in Australia. Archbold (in Rand 1942) reported finding specimens that had enlarged gonads during August, but Ripley reported in the same year that from his observations the *P.a. goliah* breeds primarily in December.

From breeding studies in the wild, such as the three years of field studies by Murphy and his colleagues, it has been concluded that the cockatoo was a weakly seasonal breeder. While there were 41 breeding attempts at 28 nests which the ornithological team monitored for three years, 81 percent of the nests failed to produce a single fledgling (Murphy et al. 2003). Since females lay only one egg, and since the females nested only once on average every 2.2 years, the probability of fledgling success is low. Given that some nests fail due to predation and infertility, nesting pairs only fledge one youngster per year—a mean of 0.11 (Heinsohn et al. 2009).

Aviary Notes

The Palm Cockatoo is known to be difficult to breed in captivity. Yet there have been a number of successful breedings by both public and private institutions in Europe, North America, and elsewhere. Low in 1993 reported on the first documented breeding by Bob Lynn of Sydney, Australia, in 1968. In Europe, eggs have been laid in all twelve months and in the United States in ten months of the year. The cockatoo has been primarily bred in a variety of American research centers, such as the Avicultural Breeding and Research Center in Florida, and the New York Zoological Society's Palm Cockatoo Wildlife Survival Center in Georgia. Egg laying is reportedly sporadic, however, and while the researcher aviculturalists prefer that the pair raise their nestling themselves, if there is concern regarding the parenting the egg will be placed in an incubator.

Despite a poor history of breeding in captivity, there are aviculturalists who would welcome the challenge.

There are various reasons that may motivate an aviculturalist to acquire specific birds: their beauty, their rarity, the challenge, the prestige of having bred a species known to be difficult to breed in captivity, and the prospect of selling some birds. The Palm Cockatoo, because of its rarity (and hence inaccessibility to all but a privileged few) and its beauty, is a most desirable cockatoo to possess, a magnificent species that few bird lovers or naturalists will ever have the opportunity to acquire, let alone see.

The Palm Cockatoo is problematic for the average aviculturalist who may have one or more aviaries, several species of parrots or other avian species, a driving passion for his hobby or livelihood, and who would like to include this cockatoo in his breeding programs. More frequently than not, aviculturalists finance both their operational costs and the acquisition of additional birds by selling young birds hatched and reared in their aviaries.

For serious aviculturalists interested in acquiring Palm Cockatoos, this interest is fraught with a host of serious issues when the breeding of the cockatoo is a primary goal. The first obstacle in acquiring this species is its rarity, and hence its overwhelming unavailability. Rarity, of course, makes acquisition expensive. And acquiring the species is not simply a task of identifying someone with a Palm Cockatoo for sale: one bird may be eventually purchased, but then another must be identified as also available for sale. While the cost of a pair may not be a prohibitive concern for the affluent breeder, there are other more basic concerns that cannot be conveniently ignored. Since the Palm Cockatoo is not sexually dimorphic, there is the burden and cost of identifying the sex of the bird via surgical means or DNA analysis.

As noted earlier, while the exact number of this species in the wild is unknown, what is known is that this cockatoo is anything but a prolific breeder. It does not breed regularly or annually, and it only lays one solitary egg when it does. And should that nesting fail, unlike many other species of birds, the Palm Cockatoo will not lay a second egg until two years later, if in fact it does lay another egg.

There is also the uncertainty associated with putting two cockatoos together with the expectation that they will copulate, and subsequently lay an egg. For any number of subtle reasons the pair may not be compatible. Think in terms of human incompatibilities and divorces.

Breeding a captive Palm Cockatoo necessitates an aviculturalist who is thoroughly knowledgeable in the cockatoo's psychological and biological constitution, an avian expert who can create the exact kind of environment that will encourage nature to take its course. This is not an easy, reachable goal when the cockatoo is not known to breed readily, even in the wild.

For those able and determined to embark on a breeding program, some information concerning the aviary would be helpful. The Palm Cockatoo is a large bird, and while it has been bred in smaller aviaries, the best rule of thumb for aviary construction is "the bigger the better." The World Parrot Trust (2012) recommends the aviary should be at least 7 meters long × 4 meters wide × 2.5 meters high (approximately 23' × 13' × 8'). The larger the aviary the more opportunity there is for the birds to deal with their confinement, the exercise an essential ingredient in preventing boredom. Several perches should be provided throughout the aviary at various heights, preferably higher, and varying in thickness and length. Since part of the male's repertoire of behaviors includes strutting and displaying, a perch at least a meter (3') long should be included. All the perches should be so situated that they do not obstruct flight space. In addition, an upright log or tree trunk is also monotony relieving.

Because the Palm Cockatoo has such a powerful beak that it easily can chew through twelve-gauge wire, the mesh surrounding the enclosure should be composed of at least a fourteen-gauge mesh. Because the cockatoo is a tropical bird, and will tolerate for short periods of time temperatures as low as -4C (25 degrees F), aviaries in northern Europe or North America need provision of indoor warm shelter in the event of cold weather. Conversely, during extremely warm weather during the summer months, such as can be experienced in California or Arizona, for example, some provision for shade must be provided these black birds from direct sunlight.

In respect to nest boxes, several should be provided the pair, despite the fact that they will only use one if breeding. In the wild, the cockatoo possesses several nest sites and defends each of them; this is a natural behavior for the species and it is believed that the pair's regular visitation to one or the other of the nest sites strengths their bond. Providing several nests encourages the bonding.

Logs with hollows are not essential: nest boxes with open tops are quite acceptable, and are the preferred nesting *modus operandi* of North American breeders. The box nest site should be no deeper than 1–1.3 meters (3–4') deep. There is no need to place nesting materials in the nest boxes. An ample supply of fresh, nontoxic tree branches placed near the nests will provide the birds with opportunity to shred them into nesting materials. As the branches are gradually converted into nesting bedding, additional branches can be introduced to supplement them.

Because the birds breed infrequently, and often unsuccessfully, the nesting pair should be monitored as a routine necessity. This can be accomplished by establishing a video camera near the nest that provides the breeder instant information concerning nesting issues that might arise and conceivably jeopardize the egg/or nestling's viability. The camera negates the need to regularly inspect the nest, an inspection whose intrusion can be distressing to the nesting pair. In the event an egg has been laid, and there are some disturbing behaviors exhibited by the nesting pair, the egg can be removed from the nest and placed in an incubator. While the incubator is an additional cost, it is a trifle when compared to the aggregate expenditures already expended to obtain a Palm Cockatoo pair and have them lay an egg. In regards to mechanically incubating the egg, and hand feeding the nestling, there are numerous informational resources available to provide the breeder the necessary information in sufficient detail necessary to rear the nestling to fledgling age.

Because the species is an intelligent bird, every effort should be made to ensure that the birds do not become bored. Enrichment opportunities should be provided: branches and sticks to demolish, hanging ropes on which to swing. These will all need to be replaced regularly.

Feeding the birds is not a problem. Their food should be placed in a bowl that is inside a hanging wire basket, which permits the birds to access the foods without upsetting the bowl's contents. These are large birds. Provision should also be made to ensure the birds have constant access to fresh water.

Pet Companion

The Palm Cockatoo is rarely encountered as a caged household pet, or even as a resident in a zoo or in private or public bird gardens in Australia, Europe, North America, or elsewhere. This cockatoo, among other species of Australian birds, parrots and otherwise, has since 1976 been protected by the Australian government—it is illegal to capture them, possess them without a license, or to sell them without a license. Further, the species is protected by CITES, which makes it difficult for poachers to illegally traffic in non–Australian Palm Cockatoo subspecies from New Guinea, West Papua, Indonesia, and a variety of smaller islands north of Australia. Nevertheless, they do: black market pet traders plunder the species' nests for nestlings and then sell them on the pet trade black market.

Although some cockatoo species in Australia are bred and sold legally under license, there are no breeders licensed to have Palm Cockatoos, despite the fact that the species' numbers in the wild are not believed to be disturbingly declining. Yet there is a smattering of specialist breeders of the Palm Cockatoo in the United States, Europe and elsewhere (Dubai, for example) who have the occasional Palm Cockatoo available for purchase. The cockatoos in the possession of these breeders are the offspring of Palm Cockatoo acquisitions prior to Australia's prohibition against capture and exportation of exotic species, and CITES' intervention in the trafficking of wildlife, although it is highly probable that some Palm Cockatoos currently in the possession of some breeders are birds that entered the pet trade via the black market, and others from non–Australian distributions.

As noted earlier, the cockatoo is anything but a prolific breeder in the wild, and its fecundity with specialized breeders and zoos is similarly poor, if not worse: the Denver Zoo, for example, in 2011 proudly reported that they had two fledglings from two separate pairs. These fledglings were the second and third in the zoo in twelve years.

Since many Palm Cockatoo eggs are now hatched in incubators, which marginally increases the percentage of surviving fledglings per nest over the number reaching fledgling stage in the wild, nestlings hatched in captivity are almost always fed by hand until old enough to feed themselves—a demanding and labor intensive activity. For these reasons, and others, the Palm Cockatoo is not only difficult to acquire, but expensive.[6]

Because of its size, intelligence, color, and rarity, it is a species that has always commanded a higher price than other exotic forms. Its overall scarcity, no doubt, is what prompted Dr. Greene to write over a century ago that the "Arara Cockatoo"[7] was one of the few birds that maintained a consistently high price—a price that he did not feel at the time was justified; he noted, however, that when encountered in captivity, the Palm Cockatoo appeared to be quite docile and "respecting in character, which is good, we might even say excellent." It is not an accomplished mimic of human sounds. It has long been noted that hand fed cockatoos, and other parrot types, prove to be more affectionate pets than if captured and brought into captivity after they have already fledged. Through hand feeding the nestling is imprinted by humans, and hence the bird assumes it is human, and responds accordingly. Human imprinted birds are fundamentally failures for breeding.

While most cockatoos prove to be adorable pets, even though they might chew the house apart if given the opportunity, they respond emotionally to their owners and seek both affection and interaction. Perhaps because the Palm Cockatoo's size may inhibit more cautious bird fanciers, there are some who hold the view that this cockatoo lacks the personality attributes of other cockatoos, such as the Moluccan Cockatoo (*Cacatua moluccensis*) or the Sulphur-crested Cockatoos (*Cacatua sulphurea*), among other cockatoo species; in fact, Palm Cockatoos that have been hand fed as nestlings are reported to be significantly more emotionally responsive, to have a more emotionally colorful personality, and to be more responsive to their owner's overtures than many other cockatoo forms, including the White Cockatoos.

The cockatoo proves to be gentle, despite its ferocious-appearing beak. Because of its size, it is bold, almost assertive, and a respectful relationship between owner and bird therefore requires a bold owner who can inculcate in the bird a bond that is mutually satisfying.

Taking care of this pet companion is not difficult. Because the Palm Cockatoo is an inquisitive, active being, the bird should be provided ample wood materials, besides perches, on which it can chew at will. Chewing and splintering the wooden playthings serve important functions in the maintenance of the cockatoo's overall health, both physical and emotional: the chewing keeps its beak in trim, provides it with the pleasure that comes with chewing, entertainment, if you will, and it provides it with something to do, thus avoiding the boredom that cockatoos have difficulty coping with. These chucks of wood are soon reduced to splinters, however, requiring regular replacement; similarly, galvanized feed containers are rendered useless within a short time. In short, to maintain a Palm Cockatoo in sound physical and emotional health necessitates a dedicated (loving) owner willing to respond to the pet's needs.

As in the wild state, the Palm Cockatoo enjoys bathing. Its manner of bathing is unusual but nevertheless an obvious pleasure for the bird, and undoubtedly just as pleasurable a spectacle for the owner. If sprayed with a garden hose, the bird will hang upside down in the downpour. Opening its wings and ruffling its feathers, it allows the water to trickle into its down layer. D'Ombrain (1933) found that when using his grinding wheel at certain speeds, which produced a sound akin to rain falling onto a tin roof, his pet Palm Cockatoo, Old Tom, would hang upside down in anticipation of a downpour, and presumably D'Ombrain would feel compelled to oblige his pet with a bath.

A household pet Palm Cockatoo living indoors in a residence requires at minimum a macaw-sized cage: minimum dimensions 48" × 36" × 60", and that is just the minimum— the bigger the better—constructed with bars able to withstand destruction by the bird's powerful beak. Note that while Palm Cockatoos are beautiful cockatoos, and may be much admired by apartment neighbors, their loud vocalizations may conceivably alienate those same admirers. In short, Palm Cockatoos are not suitable candidates as apartment pets. The cockatoo's diet should include a variety of nuts such as pine nuts, walnuts, almonds, and (especially) the *kanari* nut—if available; wheat; sunflower seeds; fresh corn; and nutritionally complete kibble (World Parrot Trust 2012), as well as some greens. There are some aviculturalists and pet owners who report occasionally feeding their cockatoos boiled eggs, even small quantities of meat.

As is true of some other species of exotic birds, the Palm Cockatoo at times shows a preference for one sex over another among its human owners. The D'Ombrain family's 'Old Tom,'[8] for example, so thoroughly hated women and was so clever at differentiating between men and women that even a pair of slacks worn by any woman in the family, or a visitor, could not deceive the wily old codger.

In 1933 D'Ombrain wrote, "Of late ... it [Old Tom] has been observed to have developed a dislike to all females young and old! ... [and] will chase my wife and children (girls)." Twelve years later, in 1945, the younger D'Ombrain, the doctor's son, wrote, "Tom is still a misogynist and has never shown any desire to make an exception to my wife who looks after her during the day." And that Palm Cockatoo had already been in the family for over twelve years.

The Palm Cockatoo is one of nature's most remarkable creations. It is a delightful bird but not appropriate for everyone. This imaginative, intelligent bird requires an owner who has the time, patience, and willingness to regularly involve himself, devote himself, on a daily basis to a bird whose well-being emotionally and physically is dependent on the owner while it is in captivity. One can put a horse into the pasture, and once every few days check the pasture to ensure the horse is still there, still alive, and then go on with one's business, knowing that the horse is quite content with its life condition. An owner of a Palm Cockatoo simply cannot treat that bird as if it were a horse in a pasture.

16

Red-tailed Black Cockatoo

Calyptorhynchus banksii (Latham, 1790)

COMMON NAMES: Banksii, Banksian Cockatoo, Black Cockatoo, *Calyptorhynchus banksii,* Forest Red-tailed Black Cockatoo, *Calyptorhynchus magnificus,* a former Latin nomenclenture used in the ornithological literature until the mid 1990s.

SUBSPECIES:

1. *Calyptorhynchus banksii banksii*—Nominate Species (Latham, 1790)
2. *Calyptorhynchus banksii graptogyne* (Schodde, 1989)
3. *Calyptorhynchus banksii macrorhynchus* (Gould, 1843)
4. *Calyptorhynchus banksii naso* (Gould, 1837)
5. *Calyptorhynchus banksii samueli* (Mathews, 1917)

LIFESPAN: (estimated) 29.3 years[1]

IUCN RED LIST OF THREATENED SPECIES:

1. *C.b. graptogyne:* Threatened with Extinction
2. *C.b. naso:* Vulnerable
3. *C.b. banksii:* Critically Endangered[2]

CITES: II

Description

Endemic to Australia, the Red-tailed Black Cockatoo is an imposingly large cockatoo, as are all of the other four cockatoos species constituting the genus *Calyptorhynchus.*

The Red-tailed Black Cockatoo comprises five subspecies, the smallest being the *C.b. naso,* weighing 565–730 grams (20–26 oz.), and ranging in overall length from 53 to 60 centimeters (20"–23") (Department of Environment and Conservation 2009); the bird's tail constitutes approximately half the bird's total length. According to Forshaw's studies, the larger subspecies weigh 670–920 grams (23–32 oz.). Both male and female adults are blackish appearing, but the female's starkness of black is subdued by a wash of dark brown. The male's plumage has a glossy appearance that is more noticeable in the upper parts and those parts where there is a wavy appearance to many of the feathers.

The crest of both sexes is somewhat recumbent and long. As with all the other species of cockatoos, the crest can be erected at will and is usually erected in response to surprise, fear, or other emotive states. When the bird is at peace with the world, the crest remains recumbent.

Comprising five subspecies, the Red-tailed Black Cockatoo is rarely owned as a pet in Australia, or in the United States where a few are bred each year; the cost per individual bird is between $15,000 and $40,000. In Australia poaching or illegally killing one can result in a fine of up to AU$10,000 per bird (photograph by Jerrod Amoore).

The eye ring is dark grey and the iris brown. The feet are mealy black.

Both sexes have a subterminal red band across the tail that includes all but the middle two feathers and the outer webs of the outermost lateral tail feathers. Males are readily distinguished from females by the broad red tail panels that are clearly visible when the cockatoo is either alighting or taking off (Higgins 1999).

The Red-tailed Black Cockatoo is noticeably sexually dimorphic. In addition to the overall features noted above, the female's crown, occipital area, crest, under wing coverts and primary feathers are mottled in yellow; breast and tail feathers are lightly margined with the same coloring; the outer tail feathers, in addition to being barred with a subterminal red band, have yellow-orange barrings that are narrower at the terminal ends of the feathers than at the intermediate zones; and unlike the male's beak, which is black, the female's is white with a brownish tip.

The five subspecies differ in various ways, including beak size and shape, some coloration variances, and body size, the latter being significant:

C.b. banksii: as outlined above in the cockatoo's description.

C.b. macrorhynchus: the male is similar to *banksii* but has a broader and heavier bill. The female is also colored like the *banksii*, but the pale yellow or orange on the tail may be either severely limited or absent; the spots on the upper wing coverts, neck or head are smaller.

C.b. samueli: both sexes are as *banksii*, but the *samueli* bill is smaller, as is the bird overall.

C.b. graptogyne: the male is similar to *samueli*. The female is more brightly marked by broader pale yellow margins to under part feathers, and larger pale yellow spots on upper wing coverts.

C.b. naso: both sexes are similar to *samueli*, but the crest is smaller and more rounded; the wings are longer and pointed; and the bill is larger and broader.

Immature males closely resemble adult females until they are sexually mature at about their fourth year. Juvenile males differ slightly from immature females in that they are less spotted with yellow, but except for their eye ring, which is white, they are similar to adult females (Johnstone and Storr 1998).

Concerning the color metamorphoses of immature males approaching maturity, a matter that caused considerable confusion to earlier field workers, there is a gradual transformation after each moulting that is worth recounting in detail. Ornithology and aviculture is indebted to Mr. J. Grogan, a successful breeder of the species for several years, who had carefully documented the stages of color transformation. His observations were reported by Serventy and Whittell (1962):

First Year: the head and wing coverts are spotted with yellow and the breast feathers are barred with yellow or buff; the tail feathers, instead of the entire red band, are crossed by yellow or orange bars, a quarter to half an inch wide.

Second Year: following the annual moult, the yellow flecks become fewer in number; the breast barrings are less conspicuous; the tail bars become broader and more reddish and the beak is darker and harder;

Third Year: very few yellow flecks remain and many of the narrow black bars subdividing the orange-red bars on the tail disappear;

Fourth Year: the whole plumage is now shining black, the tail band an unbroken red and the beak black [World Parrot Trust 2012].

Behavior

As is common in most other species of cockatoos, the Red-tailed Black Cockatoo is a gregarious species, almost always found in the immediate company of its own kind. In the early morning the birds leave their communal roosting area to drink at a nearby water site. They then disperse individually to a variety of feeding areas. Midday they seek shelter from the day's heat in a tree's foliage, where they remain until late in the afternoon, at which time they return to their feeding haunts. By the end of the day the birds return to their watering site, and then to their roosting tree.

In the more southern regions of its habitat range the cockatoo tends to flock in smaller groups of three to six or eight individuals. Occasionally, small groups along the southeastern regions will mingle with small flocks of the Yellow-tailed Black Cockatoo (*Calyptorhynchus funereus*). At times, particularly in the savannah, or in the north at a food source, there may be 500 birds or more in a flock, though such large flocks are now no longer common.

Whether the bird gathers in small flocks of six or eight individuals, or in larger flocks, an individual within that flock will fly ahead of the group as a scout for it, searching for food and water resources. Although it is illegal to hunt the species or to shoot them for sport, because they are protected under the Conservation Act, selected farmers are given permits by the Queensland Department of Environment and Heritage to shoot up to thirty so called "scout" birds when the farmers complain that the species, along with the Sulphur-crested Cockatoo (*Cacatua sulphurea*), cause considerable damage to various crops, in particular peanuts and corn (Parrot Society of Australia 2012). If convicted of illegally killing this cockatoo, on the other hand, offenders face confiscation of firearms and a fine of up to $10,000 for each offense (Department of Environment and Conservation 2009). It is similarly illegal to capture birds, or to take nestlings from nests for purposes of obtaining a pet, or to illegally traffic in wildlife.

Several decades ago, in the northern reaches of its range, the cockatoo was often encountered in flocks of 200 or more, and large flocks of 500 were by no means uncommon. Now, as noted earlier, such large flocks are considered uncommon, even in the northern parts of its range in Australia where its populations are still relatively healthy in numbers.

The Red-tailed Black Cockatoo enjoys an extensive array of foods. To some degree its preferences depend on what is available in the region of the country it inhabits. While it is fond of the seeds of the Casurina, Banksia, eucalyptus and acacia trees, it is also fond of beetle grubs, which it searches out much in the manner that Nichols describes in his discussion of the Yellow-tailed Black Cockatoo (*Calyptorhynchus funereus*); the species is also fond of various berries and fruits, as well as the nectar from the blossom of the *Barardius semiorquatus*.

Although the Red-tailed Black Cockatoo is primarily arboreal, ground-level foods are nonetheless important. Two subspecies, the *C.b. graptogyne* and the *C.b. naso*, are almost exclusively arboreal feeders. Seeds of various ground grasses and creeping plants are important additions to the other three subspecies' diets. Besides feeding on wild seeds, corn, peanuts, wheat, and other non-arboreal foods, they have been observed feeding on the rice knocked from stalks by other species of feeding birds (Crawford 1972), and have been seen feeding on water lily bulbs at their favorite watering holes.

Arboreal feeding deserves descriptive elaboration. The birds call to each other regularly with a high pitched "creeeee creeeee" and a flock of the birds will soon settle noisily in the high branches of a favorite food tree. The cockatoo will neatly cleave off a small branch on which there are some seeds or fruit; "A branch when severed is held in the bill, then passed to the foot, then the berries or nuts picked. If the branch ... is close to the bird's present perch, the fruits are picked without severance of the branch" (Hall 1974). Within a short time the ground beneath the tree will be littered with the debris resulting from a host of cockatoos feeding in the branches. It has been speculated that this feeding behavior saves the bird the mistake of going over an area in search of food when that area has already been harvested. This feeding behavior is always accompanied by harsh cries. Similarly, visitations to the water site are also always accompanied by constant shrieking.

The cockatoo is a cautious and wary bird that at the slightest hint of danger will sound cries of alarm and immediately flee to safety. When alarmed, it cries out a sharp "krur-rak." Hall described the cockatoo as a conspicuously noisy bird whose calls were accompanied by "much flapping about." Its most characteristic vocalization, "krurr," or its loud, grating, rolling "kree," are always given when the bird is flying; and the sound can carry for long distances (Forshaw 2002): the call can be heard long before the cockatoos can be seen. For some observers, the cockatoo's call is considered metallic sounding, harsh and grating (Hall 1974). In 1996, Courtney described the vocalizations of a displaying male as a soft growling followed by a repetitive "kred-kred-kred-kred."

In a somewhat more poetic vein, however, Bell (1956) four decades earlier was to write of the bird and its vocalizations: "In lonely country I have surprised hundreds of the birds. Wave after wave, they rose in scores and fifties on hurried rounded wings that made the air alive, as with the vibration of clashing bells. In full massed chorus, the sounds have a wild melody; but the solitary call—a grating 'krurr'—is not pleasant."

The Red-tailed Black Cockatoo's flight is best described as labored and slow, their flapping wing beats deep and intermittent. The birds generally fly at treetop level, and when they have reached their feeding grounds they will glide with motionless wings for hundreds of meters (yards) before finally dropping down to feed. On occasion, the species has been observed to fly at night, its flight accompanied by a cry (Hall 1974). In 1926 the Marquess of Tavistock, a dedicated aviculturalist and ornithologist, prolific in both his studies of birds and his published articles, had a pet Red-tailed for several years that was permitted complete liberty just outside the city of London. Concerning this cockatoo, he writes, "It has the unexpected habit of flying about on moonlight nights uttering his weird, wailing flight call."

Habitat and Distribution

The Red-tailed Black Cockatoo enjoys an extensive, varied range in Australia. While it is more common to drier areas, it inhabits a wide variety of habitats ranging from humid, dense tropical forests to grasslands and shrub lands, eucalypt through sheoak and acacia woodlands. It favors eucalyptus woodlands and trees along waterways. The water source is regularly visited each morning and evening for drinking. The cockatoos' distribution is pervasive across most of the northern reaches of the country, and it is so abundant in some regions that it is considered an agricultural pest (Lim et al. 1993). While some farmers can apply for a license to legally kill some cockatoos, particularly the "scouts" (see above), there are undoubtedly some birds killed illegally despite the severe penalties if caught doing so.

In the southwestern portions of Western Australia the species is considered common as far north as the Murchison River and eastwards towards central Australia. It is clear that the species is common from a line projected northwards from Esperance on the south coast of Western Australia to the east-west axis using the Murchison River as the baseline. Prior to European settlement the species was mainly confined to watercourses in the dry and arid stretches in the state. With settlement, however, the introduction of the weed doublegee (*Emex australis*), which has become a favorite food to the species, and the provision of agricultural watering holes encouraged the increase of its distribution into what was once arid and semi-arid Eucalypt woodlands, and partly cleared farmlands and acacia scrub land (Department of Environment and Conservation 2009).

On the western coast of Western Australia the species is not encountered between the Murchison and Fitzroyi river regions, although it is found north of the Fitzroyi in a line more or less projected southeastwards to the Finke River and Alice Springs in the state of Northern Territory: it is commonly encountered north of this line. Alice Springs appears to be the most southerly reach of the species in Northern Territory.

In regards to the northern half of the continent, therefore, the Red-tailed Black Cockatoo can be considered to occupy all of the northern portions of Western Australia, most of Northern Territory from its central-southern regions northwards, and all of Queensland, except in the Brisbane region, where it is no longer reported. The species is commonest, however, in those regions where the rivers empty into the Gulf of Carpenthia.

In New South Wales, it is now found only in the state's more western regions, and it is infrequently encountered in Victoria. Isolated and rare populations occupy a small area straddling the southern borders of Victoria and South Australia in the immediate coastal region.

Cockatoos are known to be migratory, but their migrations are regular seasonal population movements and differ from one part of Australia to another. For example, in Northern Queensland the cockatoo tends to follow food sources as they become available, whereas in some parts of Northern Territory, the cockatoos migrate to escape the high humidity in the summer wet season (Storr 1967). Subspecies *samueli* migrations in the wheat belts of the country are irregular and appear to have no relationship to the season or food supplies (Sedgewick 1949). In southwestern Western Australia, the migrations follow a north-south pattern, northwards in the case of subspecies *naso* after breeding (Ford 1965).

While each subspecies appears to be somewhat regionally nomadic, their presence in a specific locality is not always predictable or dependable. Since so much of this nomadic or migratory behavior is conditional on breeding, climatic conditions, and food availability, it is not clear what the patterns of movement are, the distances of the migratory movements, and the degree of permanence they hold in the various subspecies' repertoire of instincts and habitual, seasonal behaviors.

Currently, while the above discussions suggest that the various subspecies have the semblance of healthy populations, there are some serious concerns regarding numbers and population viability. A general summary of their distribution and commonality is as follows:

C.b. banksii is commonly found in northern Queensland but is considered critically endangered in New South Wales. Its numbers there are unquantified.

C.b. macrohynchus is common to northern Australia. Its numbers there are also not quantified.

C.b. samuelii is found in small, patchy populations from western Queensland to the west coast. Similarly, its numbers are unquantified.

C.b. graptotyne is an isolated, endangered subspecies found in southeast South Australia and western Victoria. It is estimated to number fewer than 1,000 birds. It is considered endangered.

C.b. naso. This subspecies is a threatened, small, isolated population in southwest Western Australia. Its numbers are so few that it is considered likely to become extinct.

Propagation

The breeding season for the Red-tailed Black Cockatoo varies depending on the latitude. Southern populations breed from October to March, the breeding beginning after the coldest and wettest part of the season is over; Attiwell in 1960 found a nestling as late as April. In the north the season occurs from May to September, and in the west from July to October.

There appear to be two distinctive breeding seasons: in Northern Territory the season actively begins in March and may stretch into July, whereas in Queensland eggs are laid as late as May with the nesting season ending in September, and from July to October in the west (Storr 1977).

In an interesting field study conducted on the breeding seasons of *C.b. samueli* in Western Australia during 1967, Saunders reported discovering two distinct breeding seasons: he found that while the cockatoo breeds during the spring–winter period, it also breeds during the autumn–winter, a period that is the hottest and driest and that has conditions completely the reverse of the former season. It is not known whether this dual breeding season is characteristic of the entire *samueli* population and/or whether some pairs attempt two broods in one year. This reported phenomenon is unique for, unlike the northern populations of the Red-tailed Black Cockatoo, which may be separated by thousands of kilometers east–west from one end of the country to the other, a separation representing two distinct climatic and geographical environments that affect breeding cycles, the Western Australian subspecies is confined to a limited geographical area that is approximated 600 kilometers (approximately 400 miles) north–south by 300–400 kilometers east–west (about 185–250 miles), an area that does not always exhibit extremes in ecological and climatic conditions.

Once the birds have migrated to their preferred breeding areas, and pairing has taken place, an interesting courtship display occurs: the male fans out his tail, puffs out his cheek feathers to cover his bill, and then raises his crest—and immediately afterwards he lets the crest fall over his upper mandible. During this courtship ritual, as is also characteristic of the Yellow-tailed Black Cockatoo (*Calyptorhynchus funereus*), the male struts back and forth before the female, bowing more or less continuously. Red-tailed Black Cockatoos mate for life, and it is believed that if one of the pair disappears the other may not mate again.

The cockatoo's favored nest site is a hollow in a tree trunk, preferably a dead tree, especially one found in a forest clearing or open field, and whenever possible with a hollow that is a considerable distance from the ground. When towering trees are unavailable, or when preferred nesting sites are a premium, the species will choose a hollow closer to the ground. For example, one already well-incubated egg was taken by Cosgrave (in Harrison and Holyoak 1970) from a nest hollow only 20 feet (6 m) from ground level.

Nesting materials consist of wood chips that drop into the cavity during the cockatoos' enlargement of the entrance to the hollow and/or nest cavity itself, and the decaying wood generally found in the bottoms of such hollows.

As with the White-tailed Black Cockatoo (*Calyptorhynchus baudinii*), it is the female alone who incubates the eggs. The clutch is normally one or two eggs, two being usual. If two eggs hatch, one nestling invariably perishes. The incubation period is one month, and the post-nestling period is at least three to four months. The brooding continues for approximately three weeks after the egg(s) have hatched, at which time the young are generally abandoned for most of the daytime hours, except for feeding periods during mid-morning and early evening (Saunders 1974).

During the incubation period, the male feeds the female both in the morning and late afternoon. Feeding is via regurgitation, during which time the male's head bobs up and down, a behavior that assists in the transfer of food. It is only during these feeding times that the female will be found outside the nest during the incubation period. Once the young are partially fledged, both adults participate in the feeding of the young. As early as 1903 Cochrane observed that during the feeding "they [the adults] would fly to the nest hole and enter without out a word."

The young fledge when about ten weeks old, but they continue to remain with the adult pair for some months afterwards, during which time they remain totally dependent on them.

A final note about the brooding of the young. It is noted above that the young are abandoned for the better part of the day. This daily abandonment begins when the nestlings are about three weeks old. This abandonment is undoubtedly a learned survival mechanism, for during those months when the weather is extremely hot there is the danger the young would smother during the midday period should the female occupy the nest with her young.

Aviary Notes

The species was not frequently bred in captivity in the past, even though the literature of several decades past recorded a number of laid eggs over the years by one reporting agency or another; most of the reportings pertain to the infertility of the eggs. The Red-tailed Black Cockatoo was a popular bird, especially hand fed, captive-raised males, and while they became excellent pets, it was discovered that they concurrently became poor candidates to mate with females: the imprinting on the male somehow diminishes its natural breeding interest or ability to copulate and fertilize a female's ovaries; no similar imprinting has been noted in females. The effects of psychological imprinting on the cockatoo were a century ago unknown to avid aviculturalists.

For example, the Marquess of Tavistock had a total of thirteen Red-tailed Black Cockatoos during his distinguished career as an aviculturalist, and on several occasions had hens that had been incubating eggs; until the time of his death, however, the marquees was never fortunate enough to have one female hatch even *one* egg, although a number of eggs had been laid over the years. Ironically, just after his death, one of his females that had faithfully laid eggs year after year—all of them infertile—laid a fertile egg on October 24, which was later hatched on December 26.[3]

A brief note in *Aviculture Magazine* (1940) had the following observation to make about that particular breeding success:

> Though its mother did not seem very devoted, the chick lived.... In spite of the cruel weather it grew until it was four weeks and six days old and well feathered. Then "brittle bone" rickets appeared, and the poor bird was found to have both legs and both wings broken. Mr. Gorman took charge, has hand reared it to the present day, fifteen weeks and two days from the time it was hatched. It is still unable to feed itself, even though fully fledged.

It should be noted that the nestling hatched at the beginning of England's winter. There is very little further information available concerning the event itself, regarding the nesting arrangements, feeding, or whether the egg was hatched indoors or outdoors. While Tavistock's numerous disappointments over the years with this species were the norm and not the exception, Red-tailed Black Cockatoos have been successfully bred countless times since Tavistock's era: all of these successes, of course, result from our studied understanding of the species and the particular requirements associated with its breeding cycle, the effects of imprinting, the bird's biological and emotional constitution, and environmental matters such as satisfactory aviary conditions.

Breeding the species in Australia requires licensing as a "Specialist Breeder Only." The license can be acquired from the state of residence. But not many licenses are rationed out. There are successful specialist breeders: World Parrot Trust (2012) reports one breeder who had a prolific Red-tailed Black Cockatoo that raised thirty young in twenty years.

A brief historical sketch of successful breeding events leading to contemporary aviary practices might be helpful to aspirant aviculturalists. In Australia, Hallstrom (in Preswick 1951) achieved his first breeding success in 1943, and by 1948 successful nests were a common event in all his aviaries. In 1950, in a report written in the parrot records of the Adelaide Zoo Gardens, Lendon reported on several successful nests. The species has since been bred in a variety of zoos, including the San Diego Zoo in California (Lint et al. 1993), an exceptional event in that the species was (and still is) rarely encountered in the USA.

For the reader interested in breeding the Red-tailed Black Cockatoo in an aviary, the first major considerations are the acquisition of birds suitable for breeding, and their cost. Regarding Australians, Australian laws prohibit the harvesting of the cockatoo from the wilds; the sale or trade of the species bred in captivity require the seller to be a licensed breeder, and the buyer is obligated to acquire a license to own a Red-tailed Black Cockatoo. Having a license does not permit the holder to export the cockatoo. A licence is not only difficult to obtain but is rarely issued: hence, obtaining a suitable pair for breeding purposes becomes a formidable task. In the late 1990s Red-tailed Black Cockatoos could be purchased in Australia for $1,750, and for $8,000 or more elsewhere (Rural Industries 1997). Currently (2013), in Australia the cockatoo can be purchased in the AU$1,200 to $1,500 range (whether these birds would be suitable for breeding is unknown).

Elsewhere in the world, Red-tailed Cockatoos hatched in aviaries and hand raised command much higher prices. For example, during that same period in the United States hand raised birds cost $15,000 to $40,000 (Baker 2012), and at the time of this writing are substantially more. But in the United States and elsewhere the cockatoo is rare and is seldom available for sale, and hence is far more expensive. Those few fortunate aviculturalists who have this species in their aviaries are understandably inclined to hand raise young birds—despite the resulting additional labor costs—because the fledged young command a much higher price than birds that are raised naturally in the nest by the hen and the cock. And even should an aviculturalist be willing to pay the higher cost per specimen because of the premium associated with hand raising, there is always the problem that while the male may be a delightful pet companion, it may also be imprinted and hence be unsuitable for breeding purposes.

For those wishing and financially able to embark on this exciting and challenging adventure, and having the time and the financial and human resources to locate and acquire a suitable male and female, some mundane but essential logistics require attention. Firstly, it is highly recommended that the male and female belong to the same subspecies to assure that all offspring are genetically identifiable. Finding two possible, suitable candidates from the same subspecies is in itself problematic, particularly for non–Australian aviculturalists.

The aviary should be about 8 meters long, approximately 2 meters wide, and about 2.5 meters high (26' × 6.5' × 7.5'), enclosed in a heavy-gauge (preferably welded) wire mesh. Perches can be branches, and there should be ample leafy branches for the birds to chew on: chewing branches reduces boredom, provides beak exercise, and gives entertainment. Feed bowls should be immovable, and should be of a material that cannot be destroyed through play.

The nesting accommodations are preferably logs, the nesting hollow at least 700 mm (2.3') deep, the internal dimensions 350–400 mm (14–15") square, and the entrance hole approximately 200–300 mm (7–9"). There should be a climbing structure outside the entrance hole so that the birds can access the nest. The bedding materials in the nest should consist of rotting sawdust, wood shavings, and nontoxic, leafy materials. Several nesting accommodations should be offered the pair, and once they have shown a preference for one or another nest site, the others should be gradually removed when it is becomes obvious which one the pair have finally chosen. The log should be placed close to the covered area of the aviary, but not too close to the roof where the summer's heat can negatively impact the brooding female, or the nestlings.

The birds should be fed various leafy vegetables, seeds, soaked or sprouted seeds, nuts, and even chick weed and dandelions. Native foods, such as Banksia, Acacia, Hakea, Eucalypt, and Causuarina seeds, as well as diverse fruits and other nuts familiar to the cockatoos (if available, depending on where the aviculturalist has his aviaries) will provide the birds a healthy, adequate diet (BirdCare 2008).

Breeding the Red-tail Black Cockatoo necessitates intimate familiarity with the requirements of successfully breeding the species. The cockatoo proves to be a good candidate for aviary breeding if the conditions provided the pair are both adequate and appropriate for the species' needs.

The above notes are only an approximate indication of some of the complexities involved, and the hurdles ahead. The reader is encouraged to explore additional information before embarking on this investment and adventure. The reader is recommended to obtain the comprehensive information guide on the bird's husbandry, titled *The Red-tailed Black Cockatoo*, from BirdCare.com, P.O. Box 126, Mitcham, Vic 3132 (Victoria, Australia). This document not only provides detailed instructions helpful to the aspirant aviculturalist, but also provides an extensive bibliography of published articles in *Australian Aviculture* and *Australian Birdkeeper*, from which the condensed manual was compiled. This brief manual is a summation of the content of the important articles pertaining to the husbandry of species; the articles provide considerably more detailed information based on breeders' experiences, procedures, and failures—matters of important interest not necessarily covered by the compiled document.

Pet Companion

Having a Red-tailed Black Cockatoo as a pet is a pleasure few people will ever experience, even in Australia where this cockatoo is endemic. The only experience most people (including many Australians) can have with this species is seeing one in a zoo, if there is one nearby with the species midst other avian charges, or by (rarely) seeing one on television: there are a few delightful personal videos on the Internet's YouTube that one can access easily (a pleasant rainy day project searching them out). Because the cockatoo is a protected species in every state it inhabits, adult cockatoos cannot be harvested to enjoy as household pets, and it is equally illegal to plunder nests for eggs or nestlings. For an Australian, obtaining a Red-tail necessitates applying for a license to own a wild species. Not all Australian exotic birds require licensing in order to have one as a pet. Sulphur-crested Cockatoos, for example, are exempt from licensing permits. But some species require a license, and those species (animals as well as birds) that are considered rare or vulnerable are prohibited from private ownership, except through licencing. The licensing protocols differ from state to state. In New South Wales, for example, there are two licenses: Bird Keeper's Licence and the Companion Bird License. These licenses require a basic knowledge of bird care, and must be renewed every five years. Any protected species, such as the Red-tailed Black Cockatoo, can only be obtained by purchasing a bird from an aviary that is licensed with the particular state's version of the Advanced Aviculture License: the breeder is prohibited from selling a protected species—even though the bird has been legally bred in captivity—to a potential buyer unless the buyer can prove he is in possession of a license permitting him to own one. Similarly, a private individual advertising a Red-tail for sale will require the prospective buyer to prove that he/she is licensed to own a Red-tailed Cockatoo.

While obtaining a cockatoo involves some governmental formalities, and modest costs for the appropriate license, an Australian can purchase an aviary-raised cockatoo for approximately AU$1,200–AU$1,500 at the time of this writing. By searching classified advertisements one can always find a smattering of licensed birds for sale. And while birds are not available in overabundance, there are sufficient numbers available due to the limited but successful private aviaries and their breeding programs.

For individuals residing in other countries and interested in owning the Red-tailed Black Cockatoo, the cost per individual bird is extravagantly expensive for the average pocketbook, if a cockatoo can even be found available for sale. Since Australia prohibits the exportation of its cockatoos, and has for several decades, there are few Red-tailed Black Cockatoos available in industrialized countries such as Britain, Germany, Canada, the United States, or elsewhere such as Singapore, where there are strong traditional aviculture interests.

In addition to the Red-tailed Black Cockatoo's rarity, and the resulting cost involved in acquiring a bird, anyone interested in obtaining one needs to be aware that the species are "powder down" birds—i.e., they exude a powder from a gland, which they use in their grooming. Anyone with asthma and/or allergies would be best advised to consider another species of exotic bird.

Anyone owning a Red-tailed Black Cockatoo will be astounded at its loving personality, particularly one that is imprinted, and its intelligence. Because of these attributes, the very ones that make the cockatoo so attractive and endearing, the cockatoo needs a dedicated owner, an owner able and willing to provide the bird with the love and attention it needs. The bird will be more than anxious to reciprocate. Being involved with one's pet means that the owner should consistently train the bird to reduce its tendencies to engage in normal but annoying habits, such as excessive vocalizations or destructive chewing. The bird should be engaged enough so that it does not become bored. It has long been noted that intelligent birds, when deprived of a challenging, interesting environment become "feather pluckers."

No one is quite sure precisely how long Red-tailed Cockatoos live, although there are records of several who have lived into their forties; there is considerable speculation on their life expectancy, which may range anywhere from 25 to 100 years. In the right environment it will learn to "talk" and while parrots are notoriously good talkers,[4] some are much better than others. The Red-tailed is generally considered to be a moderate talker, and over time, with a dedicated owner, the bird will imitate its owner, and various other interesting sounds from other sources.

The cage requirements for the Red-tailed Black Cockatoo that will be resident indoors can be summarized as "the bigger the better." Given the cockatoo's size, the cage should be at minimum a macaw-sized cage: 18" × 36" × 60" (.5 m × 1 m × 5 m). It should be furnished with wooden perches, provided with various nontoxic branches to chew on, and an attached food container, preferably one that cannot be easily mangled and destroyed by vigorous chewing. Expect the branches and perches to be shredded and requiring replacement regularly as part of routine cage maintenance chores: a bird demolishing replaceable cage furniture is a healthy sign of a pet companion enjoying its life.

Depending on the size of the caged accommodations for the parrot, it needs to exercise. A cage inside a house cannot by virtue of its size provide the flying (and exercise) opportunities of an aviary. A close physical, reciprocal bond between the bird and its owner allows the bird opportunities to flex its wings.

The bird should be fed a wide variety of nuts, seeds (both sprouted or otherwise), and various greens, as indicated earlier. Some birds can be fickle in their feeding preferences. The Marquess of Tavistock observed that of the thirteen Red-tailed Black Cockatoos he owned, only one would eat fruit. Other owners, however, have demonstrated that while the Red-tailed Black Cockatoo prefers nuts and seeds, it will also eat various greens and fruits when gradually introduced to them. Additionally, there are available in the pet trade market a variety of foods specifically formulated to provide caged birds with the necessary nutrients essential to the bird's good health.

Finally, whether owning an expensive Red-tailed Black Cockatoo, or another exotic species, it is important to identify a local veterinarian who specializes in bird health problems, or at least one who has some experience in dealing with avian ailments.[5]

17

Glossy Black Cockatoo
Calyptorhynchus lathami (Temminck, 1807)

COMMON NAMES: Glossy Black Cockatoo, Leaches' Red-tailed Black Cockatoo, Casaurina Black Cockatoo, Casaurina, Casaurine, Nutcracker, Latham's Cockatoo

SUBSPECIES[1]:

    1. *Calyptorhynchus lathami lathami*—Nominate Species (Temminck, 1807)

    2. *Calyptorhynchus lathami erebus* (Schodde and Mason, 1993)

    3. *Calyptorhynchus lathami halmaturinus* (Mathews, 1912)

LIFESPAN: (estimated) 30+ years[2]

IUCN RED LIST OF THREATENED SPECIES:

    In Queensland and New South Wales: Vulnerable

    In Victoria: Threatened

    In South Australia: Endangered

CITES: II

Description

Endemic to Australia, the Glossy Black Cockatoo is the smallest of the several species and subspecies of the Black Cockatoos, excluding the diminutive Cockatiel (*Nymphicus hollandicus*). Its overall length ranges up to 50 cm (12.8"), and its weight may reach 430 grams (15 oz.). Because from a distance it appears entirely black, and because it has a red tail, as does the Red-tailed Black Cockatoo (*Calyptorhynchus banksii*), it is sometimes mistakenly misidentified as a Red-tailed Black Cockatoo on field census expeditions, and vice versa.

The Glossy Black Cockatoo is sexually dimorphic. The upper parts of the male are black and brown tinged. This coloration includes the wings, back, and central tail feathers. The entire head area is a smoky brown with the intermediate portion of each head feather slightly darker than the terminal ends. The underwing coverts are more smoky colored than stark black, a softer shade than that of the upper coverts and primaries.

The Glossy Black Cockatoo's bill possesses a gibbous quality, giving the bird the appearance of it being swollen. As with all other cockatoos, the Glossy Black Cockatoo has a crest, but it is short compared to that of other species, both black and white, and can be best described as being almost a nonentity. But, as is the case with the other cockatoo species,

Glossy Black Cockatoos are rare. Their reproductivity is extremely low. Research shows that as few as 18 percent of nests actually fledge a juvenile. Additionally, the bird breeds poorly in captivity because for food it is reliant on the seeds from specific pine cones, and it is not willing to accept unfamiliar foods such as fruit, greens, or nuts (photograph by Richard Fisher).

the Glossy Black Cockatoo can erect its crest at will, and it usually does so in response to an emotional state such as fear or curiosity.

The bird's feet are mealy black and the legs are dark grey.

The tail feathers, excluding the two central ones, have a vermillion sub-terminal band stretching across the intermediate parts, including both webs on each feather excepting the outer feather, which is totally black. There is some yellow suffused through the red, but the male's tail is conspicuously and predominately red.

The female's color differs in several ways from the male's. Females are more dark brown, and they have some yellow feathers scattered over the head and neck regions. The female's bill is whitish and not grey, as is the case with the male. The female's tail differs from the male's in that the outer edges of the primaries are edged faintly with yellow, and the orange-reddish tail coloration is crossed with four or five quite narrow black bands. Like the male's tail, the female's is suffused with some yellow within the orangish-red swath, although not conspicuously. This yellow is more pronounced on the underpart of the tail.

Juvenile birds closely resemble the adult female in most respects, except that they have no yellow markings in the head region. Llewelyn (1974) noted that juvenile males and females can be easily identified: young females have varying amounts of yellow coloration scattered over the underparts, particularly at the edges of feathers, whereas there is an absence of yellow on the immature male (Forshaw and Cooper 2002).

Behavior

The call of the Glossy Black Cockatoo has been variously described—generally in poorly executed imitations—but as Lendon (in Cayley 1973) has noted, "the call is unmistakable, but difficult to describe." It is a wailing cry, low toned; an "arr-red." When flying, the cockatoo often utters a particularly mournful note, a plaintive cry. In 2008, the New South Wales Scientific Committee summarized the species' calls as being similar to those of the Red-Tailed Black Cockatoo (*Calyptorhynchus banksii*), but not as loud and discordant.

Little is known about the Glossy Black Cockatoo in the wild for a number of practical reasons. Historically it was always quite rare, even during the bonanza days of Australian exploration and settlement well over a century ago, when adventurists, naturalists, scientists and innumerable others flocked to Australia; the island continent was unlike any other newly discovered lands for a wide variety of reasons, especially its dramatically different fauna. While ornithologists scoured the continent in their quest to discover new species—the more spectacularly different the better—they rarely encountered the Glossy Black Cockatoo, because it was a rarity even at that time. Complicating the rarity, the cockatoo chose extremely tall trees for nesting and roosting, and was not only not visible but generally silent.

In fact, at a time of vigorous, almost frantic, specimen and egg collecting for university lab study and museum collections in Europe, by 1916 Mathews lamented that to date not one single Glossy egg had been collected and measured. A second factor contributing to the lack of field notes is the species' similarity in appearance to the Red-tailed Black Cockatoo (*Calyptorhynchus banksii*), the latter frequently encountered and hence not always warranting a field worker's attention unless there was a particular peculiarity to note.

The Glossy Black Cockatoo is not as shy and wary as other cockatoo species. It is a gregarious bird, but rarely found in flocks numbering more than ten. The cockatoo is almost reckless when faced with impending danger, perhaps even a relatively "stupid" species. For example, more frequently than not, when a cockatoo was shot for scientific study or for sport, and had fallen to the ground, its companions did not flee as might be expected; rather, after being initially startled by the gunfire sounds, the entire flock, usually small, would mill about briefly in the air in the immediate vicinity of the fallen companion, and then soon alight on the branches of a neighboring tree so that "everyone can be procured" (Mathews 1916). And so they were.

While killing the cockatoo has no doubt also contributed to its rarity, it is doubtful that human predation has been the sole source of the species' population predicament. For example, there are in the literature no historical accounts reporting mass sporting slaughters of the Glossy Black Cockatoo, as is the case for other avian species such as the Sulphur-crested Cockatoo (*Cacatua galerita*), thousands of which were slaughtered for entertainment in an afternoon's shootings for sport, on a variety of occasions.[34] Capturing Sulphur-crested Cockatoos in large numbers and then releasing them singularly as live targets for an afternoon's shooting entertainment was normal for the times, but ultimately there was sufficient opposition to the killing of these birds in these sport shootings that the shooting galleries approach fell out of popularity.

In respect to the Glossy Black Cockatoo, there were simply not enough of the birds available to capture for such wholesale sport shootings, even though the occasional hapless individual cockatoo was opportunistically shot for sport. Additionally, as discussed shortly, the species is neither a prolific breeder nor a species easily adaptable to diverse foods, specifically cultivated grain crops. All of these issues contribute to its rarity.

The Glossy Black Cockatoo is almost exclusively arboreal in its habits, but it is equally comfortable in open country and heavily forested areas. When it does leave the trees it is usually only for a drink of water, particularly midday during hot weather, and then again only later during evening hours, or to seek food. The cockatoo feeds almost exclusively on the seeds extracted from the wooden cones of various species of She-oaks, especially the Drooping She-oak (*Alloasaurina verticillata*), the Forest She-oak (*Allocasuarina torulosa*), and the Black She-oak (*Allocasuarina littoralis*) (Higgins 1999; Chapman 2007), depending on the region a subspecies inhabits. In his field studies during 1982 Joseph found the cockatoo occasionally feeding on the Sugar Gum (*Eucalyptus cladocalyx*), but because of its highly specialized feeding requirements, particularly its reliance on the various She-oak species, the cockatoo is rarely encountered in those regions where the *Allocausarina* does not grow.

The Glossy Black Cockatoo forages in trees of varied density and size, but it prefers larger trees that have large seeds. An individual may forage in a tree for hours on end, often returning to the same tree at a later date.

When it feeds on wooden cones from the She-oaks, the cockatoo pulls the cone off a branch, then strips away the tough outer hull with its beak, rotating the cone in the left foot, and once the seeds are exposed removes them with the tongue for eating. Chrome and Shields (1992) surmise that the opening of the cone to expose the seeds is a learned behavior, because their field observations indicate that juveniles have considerable difficulty in manipulating the wooden cones. Because of this exclusive dependence on the She-oak, and the Gum Tree, any tree in the region that has ripening cones will be visited daily until all of the cones have been stripped from the tree. The grounds surrounding the tree soon become littered with shredded cones, twigs, and other debris.

The cockatoos are locally nomadic in that they roam for food and water in local areas where they usually communally roost: that roosting site may be used for extended periods of time regardless of where they may have roamed for food. Cayley (1973), for example, found the birds would often fly fifteen to twenty miles (24–32 kilometers) to find feeding areas of ripening pine cones and then return to their usual roosting site. At times, as a result of fire or drought, the cones are no longer easily available because fires have destroyed the trees. On Kangeroo Island, for example, where the Glossy Black Cockatoo depends on the Drooping She-oak (*Allocasuarina verticillata*) and the Sugar Gum (*Eucaplyptus cladocalyx*), and where there had been several forest fires in succession, the cockatoo was observed meandering haplessly over the island in search for new supplies of cones (Wheeler 1959).

The Glossy Black Cockatoo flies in a labored and heavy manner, as is common to many of the Black Cockatoo species. It usually flies at an altitude only slightly above treetop level, unless it must cover considerable distances to reach either roosting or feeding grounds. During flight, it sometimes has a loud, wailing cry that can be heard long before the bird comes into view.

The species is generally found in small parties ranging from two or three individuals—which are usually considered family groups (Pepper 1996)—to groups of seven or eight, and it has been on rare occasions encountered in larger congregations of up to fifty birds or so (Wheeler 1959). How long those larger flocks remain cohesive is unknown. Small groups of juveniles are occasionally encountered (Pepper 1996). At times, the species has been observed near flocks of Yellow-tailed Black Cockatoos (*Calytorhynchus Zanda funereus*), but the two species do not mix well together, unlike the familiarity the species at times exercises with the Red-tailed Black Cockatoo.

Habitat and Distribution

The Glossy Black Cockatoo prefers woodlands with hollow bearing trees, open Eucalypt forests, timbered watercourses, and places where ample She-oaks (*Allocasauarina*) grow as food sources. In New South Wales the bird prefers brigalow scrub or hilly, rocky country. At one time, the species, while not overly abundant, was widely distributed throughout the entire southeast of the country. Now, it is sparsely distributed from the east coast of Evangella in eastern Queensland to Mallacoota in western Victoria to Rockhampton in Queensland (Chrome and Shields 1992), and is now considered extinct in most parts of West Victoria and southeast South Australia, excluding a few isolated pockets in mountain ranges. Because the species relies so heavily on She-oak trees for its food, the population distribution is dependent on the availability of the food trees, and that in itself is dependent on agricultural practices, logging, and wild field fires, which often kill many cone bearing trees.

The Glossy Black Cockatoo prefers forest terrains that are drier, characteristically forests with low soil nutrient components, and that are favorable for the She-oak *Allocasaurina*.

Currently, the different subspecies inhabit the following terrains:

C.l. Lathami: This subspecies is primarily found wherever there are *Allocasaurina* woodlands; there are isolated pockets of the cockatoo in Eungella in central Queensland; and a separate pocket in Riverina, New South Wales, where it is considered an endangered population. Its overall habitat stretches from Mallacoota in Victoria to southeastern Queensland. The species is considered rare throughout its range, but since 2007 the *C.l. lathami* has been listed as vulnerable in both Queensland and in Victoria. (Historically, its range included Tasmania and King Island; it is now extinct on both islands.)

C.l. erebus: Farther north in east-central Queensland, it can still be readily encountered. Its status there is currently considered least concern.

C.l. halmaturinus: It is rare on Kangeroo Island, and there are a few isolated, small populations on King Island in Bass Strait (Schodde et. al. 1993). On

Kangeroo Island, it is limited to the eastern and northern parts; while the subspecies is listed as endangered, a major long-term Australian Government (Biodiversity 2012) study on the effects of an ongoing rehabilitation program to prevent the subspecies from sliding into extinction has been encouraging.

Based on these ongoing field studies, the cockatoo's Kangeroo Island population has been quantified as follows:

- 1979–80 census gave a population estimated at 115–150 birds.
- 1987–88 censuses revealed a total of only 25 and 50 birds observed, respectively.
- 1993—a total of 136 birds were counted in the census.

In 2006, the annual census provided a counting of 310 to 330 birds (Biodiversity 2012; Pedler and Mooney 2005).

In their studies, the NSW Scientific Committee in 2008 reported that occasional vagrants from the island occasionally visit the mainland. To what extent they remain there is unknown.

Propagation

A century ago, according to Ashby (in Mathews 1916), a field avian naturalist and a correspondent of Mathews, the Glossy Black Cockatoo clutch almost always consisted of only one egg (Biodiversity 2012), and the species was known to have the low reproductive rate characteristic of several cockatoo species, particularly all the Black Cockatoos. Overall, little was known of the species and its propagation because of its general rarity, and when an encountered Glossy Black Cockatoo was suspected to be nesting, it was difficult to obtain data given that the nest was typically inaccessible.

From aviary studies, it is known that the species reaches sexual maturity at about two years of age, but males do not begin breeding until they are approximately five years of age (Mooney and Pedler 2005); females are not receptive until they are at least three years old (Pedler 2003). Like the other Black Cockatoos, the Glossy Black Cockatoo chooses a towering tree, preferably a Eucalypt, dead or alive, that has a large hollow, often as deep as a meter (3'), in the trunk or in the stump of a broken branch, either which will serve for nesting purposes (Cayley 1973). The nesting hollow may be 12–14 meters (40'–45') or more from the ground. The nest bedding is composed both of rotted wood and the wood chips that the bird creates when enlarging the nest hollow to make it more habitable (Chrome and Shields 1992).

The clutch, invariably only one egg, is laid in autumn or winter. Incubation takes approximately one month, generally twenty-nine days. In 1959, Hallstrom reported the nestling having a "fluffy," cream colored down, a first for that observation. The female is totally dependent on the male for food during the incubation period. After the egg hatches, for approximately three weeks following, the male continues to feed the female, who in turn feeds the nestling, but because the nestling's rapid growth requires constant feeding, the female now departs the nest and joins the male in foraging.

The nesting period is approximately three months, with the juvenile fledging at approximately 60 days after hatching. After fledging, the juvenile remains dependent on its parents for up to four months, and continues being fed by both parents (Garnett et al. 1999); it may remain with them until the next breeding season a year hence, even "sometimes until the next year's young fledge" (NSW Scientific Committee 2008). The cockatoo normally only nests once a year, but Garnett reports that the female may lay up to three separate consecutive clutches in a single season should the first breeding fail. There is no published documentation concerning the success of the subsequent clutch laying and their hatching and/or fledging.

The decline in population is attributed to a variety of environmental factors, and especially to the fact that the species only has one fledgling, even if the nest is successful; human activities play a prominent and often negative role in altering the environment. On Kangeroo Island, for example, the nesting success of the small population has been monitored since 1995, at which time the cockatoo's nesting success (i.e., the proportion of nesting attempts that were successful) was a bare 18 percent. That poor record increased to a mean of 51 percent during the 1997–2004 period. The increased success is attributable to an effective management and recovery program designed to reverse the population decline (Mooney and Pedler 2005).

Nesting failures are attributable to several factors: other cockatoo species interfering at the nest (e.g., Little Corellas, Sulphur-crested Cockatoos, or Galahs); competition for the limited available tree hollows by other avian species, possums, and the introduced honey bees (*Apis mellifera*) (the limited nest opportunities are particularly aggravated and diminished by major forest fires consuming mature trees); predation by possums; and loss of nest contents due to flooding, fire, or in the instance of long dead trees, their collapse (Garnett et al. 1999).

Aviary Notes

As discussed earlier, the Glossy Black Cockatoo is almost exclusively monophagus, dependent on the cone seeds of several species of *Casaurina* and *Allocasuarina* pine cones, an exclusiveness that makes its exceptionally difficult to keep the species alive and healthy in captivity, especially for the very few which may be scattered about the world in a few zoos or exclusive avian collections. Even in Australia, where there are sufficient *Casaurinas* and *Allocasuarina* food resources, the task of feeding the bird in captivity can be difficult at best.

Sir Edward Hallstrom, a wealthy Australian, managed to keep several in his aviaries and was the first to breed the species in captivity in 1950, an endeavor that demanded exceptional effort and determination, and only after an experimental program that he embarked upon in which there was a concentrated effort to find a diet acceptable to the cockatoos—which ultimately proved only moderately successful. Since Hollstrom's first attempts, there has been some progress achieved in creating a daily food regimen that is acceptable to the birds, a diet composed of various seeds and fruits, that provides the cockatoos with sufficient nutrients. But the diet *also* includes seeds from pine cones.

Because of the species' unique evolution towards an exclusive dependence on the *Casaurina* and *Allocausaurina* seeds, departure from this exclusive diet has direct negative consequences on the cockatoos' health and general life. First, the restrictiveness of the diet has genetically predetermined the cockatoos' feeding habits so that it is difficult to encourage it to eat the *seeds alone:* Pine cones must first be crushed and then the seeds eaten *if the upper mandible is to be kept from overgrowing.* Secondly, the thousands of generations of reliance on the pine cone has probably resulted in the species' metabolic adaptation to a biological dependence wherein the oil from the seeds is primarily essential to the cockatoos' health. Denying the cockatoo these seeds in an attempt to force it to eat foods foreign to its needs is contrary to the species' health.

In addition to the feeding conundrum, the species does not readily breed in captivity. For example, not only was Hallstrom the first aviculturalist to achieve a captive breeding, which occurred in 1950,[4] but it was not until over sixty years later that there was another captive breeding: on July 21, 2011, the Taronga Zoo in Sydney, Australia, announced with considerable fanfare the hatching and survival of a fledging Glossy Black Cockatoo (Taronga Zoo 2011). *There appears to have been no other captive breeding in the sixty-one years between those two successes.*

The major obstacle to maintaining the bird in captivity has historically been the problem of guaranteeing an adequate supply of pine cones. Any other foods provided the birds were categorically rejected, and the birds would ultimately starve. Hallstrom was compelled to deal with this monophagus because he was having difficulty acquiring sufficient quantities of seed cones, despite his considerable financial and human resources. His solution was something of a compromise. He provided his cockatoos with sufficient pine cones each day to keep their beaks in trim, but he concurrently *force fed* them a mixture of canary seeds, striped sunflower seeds, peanut butter and peanut oil. Although the birds were forced fed, and were probably quite distressed by the ordeal, they eventually became accustomed (undoubtedly reluctantly) to the new diet and its administration. It took Hallstrom almost six years to accomplish this feat.

At approximately six years into his conditioning the birds to accept some different foods, he took two pairs and placed them in separate aviaries, in both instances providing hollow logs. He observed that one pair had copulated. The other pair showed no interest in nesting, on the other hand. The mated pair produced an egg, which was followed by a second a few days later. The female sat closely, hatching an egg after 29 days, but the male began losing condition and Hallstrom was compelled to remove it from the aviary because the cockatoo was starving himself in order to keep the hen fed. Hallstrom reported that his female rarely left the nest.

Based on the brief outline above regarding the Glossy Black Cockatoo and the challenges that present themselves to anyone attempting to breed, or even maintain, these cockatoos in aviaries, it should be abundantly clear that the level of knowledge required is substantial, and that the challenges presented are for Specialist Breeders only.

There are a number of other concerns that the reader should be aware of: first, the Glossy Black Cockatoo is a species protected by CITES, and any trade, sale, or traffic of this species is not only illegal but could conceivably result not only in heavy fines, but in confiscation of transportation, and perhaps even imprisonment. Secondly, for aviculturalists outside continental Australia, obtaining a license to import the species is virtually impossible, and even should one somehow obtain one or two of the species, legally or illicitly, the problem of providing the cockatoos with a sufficient quantity of pine cones becomes formidable. Finally, for those few Australians who are fortunate enough to obtain a licence to own one or a pair of Glossy Black Cockatoos, there is a substantial cost to be considered and endured:

for a pair in Victoria, circa 2005, the price was AU$15,000 (Birdcare 2012); today, in the spring of 2013, that cost would be substantially higher. And once the birds are acquired, the prospective breeder will have significant obstacles to overcome, the same issues that challenged Sir Edward Hollstrom. Again, the feeding of the birds is a major concern.

Given all that historical context, and the current status of the species, for those aviculturalists embarking on a Glossy Black Cockatoo breeding program (and who can obtain a legal pair), some basic, current breeding information might be helpful.

Although the Glossy Black Cockatoo is the smallest of the Black Cockatoos, its aviary should be at minimum—like those for other Black Cockatoos—at least 5 meters long by 1.8 meters wide and at least 2.4 meters high (16' × 5' × 7'). The bigger the aviary, the better. Because of the power of the cockatoos' beaks, and their propensity to chew actively, a heavy-gauge mesh is recommended, preferably weld mesh (Birdcare 2012). Perches of different lengths and diameters should be installed at several locations throughout the aviary, as well as leafy branches, all of which give the cockatoo opportunity to chew and entertain itself, elements that are most important for its emotional health. Of course, the perches and branches will have to be replaced regularly as they soon become shredded into floor litter. Water containers should also be sturdy enough to withstand vigorous chewing.

The cockatoo requires an upright log in which there is a hollow for nesting purposes.

Initially, several potential nesting logs should be provided the birds from which to choose, and when it becomes obvious over some time which nesting log is the pair's preference, the others should be gradually removed. The log should be situated in a sheltered area of the aviary, but not so close to the ceiling as to overheat during hot days, and the log should be stabilized to keep it vertical. The interior of the hollow in the log should be up to 1000 mm deep (3') and at least 300–450 mm (11"–17") in diameter. For nesting materials, rotted sawdust, leaves, wood shavings and other nontoxic nesting materials should be provided. The female will produce wood chips when enlarging the nesting hollow to her preferences (BirdCare 2012), thus adding further to the nesting materials.

Currently BirdCare recommends that a daily diet should include grey striped sunflower seeds, almonds, fruits, and vegetables. This diet should be daily supplemented with some *Casaurina* seed cones. That recommended diet is an ideal diet, and would assume that the birds have been weaned from their monophagus. But, as Hallstrom has indicated, considerable experimentation was required to achieve that state whereby the birds accepted different foods. . Hence, each aviculturalist will experiment accordingly, so that not all aviary daily diets for captive Glossy Black Cockatoos will be identical. The diet provided in a given aviary may differ from another aviary's inhabitants' diet based on the cockatoos' acceptance of non-*Casaurina* foods. The final diet in each instance will be determined through trial and error, and a great deal of patience.

For more detailed information and solutions to specific breeding problems, contact with BirdCare is recommended.

Pet Companion

Unlike other species of exotic birds, particularly the cockatoos, for which there is usually ample literature of both scientific and personal observational data, there is a noted absence of information on the Glossy Black Cockatoo. Of particular interest is that on the Internet, particularly on popular Web sites such as YouTube, there are almost no videos relating to the Glossy Black Cockatoo species, aside from a few brief videos of the species' behavior in the wild. There was one exception: an entertaining one and a half minute video of a young man and his delightful, wonderful interaction with a young female cockatoo perched on his arm. The video was shot at a professional, commercial aviary, and (presumably) was entered there as part of that aviary's advertising program.

On the Internet, as well, a search for Glossy Black Cockatoos for sale on Gum Tree showed there were no birds offered for sale, and no one was advertising to purchase a Glossy Black Cockatoo in all of Australia during September 2012. Furthermore, the advertisements of a number of professional aviaries and breeders were searched, and while almost all of them had the species listed, there were none currently for sale or forthcoming.

In the published literature there are numerous references to the Glossy Black Cockatoo's rarity, and to the fact that persons should not own them for pet purposes because of this rarity. Interestingly, almost ironically, several correspondents commented on the qualities that made this species an ideal candidate for a pet cockatoo: e.g., Avian Companions (2012) described the bird as being "Pet Quality—A very exceptional pet with an unusual repore [*sic*] with their owners. They are very loving and are very intelligent." Of course, these same qualities are applicable to almost all of the cockatoo species.

To summarize, the Glossy Black Cockatoo's rarity makes this exceptional bird an impossible (legal) acquisition for virtually everyone, Australian or otherwise. It is equally almost impossible for internationally recognized zoos anywhere in the world to acquire specimens either for display or for breeding. And sadly, because of the species' rarity, and the difficulty in maintaining the bird in captivity, few people will ever enjoy the opportunity of seeing a live specimen.

18

White-tailed Black Cockatoo

Calyptorhynchus baudinii (Lear, 1832)

Common Names: The Long-billed Black Cockatoo, Baudin's Black Cockatoo, White-tailed Cockatoo, White-eared Black Cockatoo
Subspecies: None
Lifespan: (Estimated) 60+ years[1]
IUCN List of Threatened Species: Least Concern[2]
CITES: II

Description

Endemic to the state of Western Australia, the White-tailed Black Cockatoo is among the largest of the cockatoo species. On average, they are 56 cm (31") long, have a wing span of approximately 110 cm (42"); Biodiversity (2012) and the World Parrot Trust (2012) report that the species weighs on average 630–750 grams (22–26.5 oz.).

Overall, the White-tailed Black Cockatoo's coloration is brownish black. The feathers are edged in dusty white, almost a light grey, giving the cockatoo a scalloped appearance, the scalloping notably visible on the belly, throat, back, nape and breast. Similarly, the feathering on the sides of the body, on the abdomen, and both the under tail and under wing coverts is faintly margined in buff. The side tail feathers have a broad white band near their terminal ends. The birds have a short, rounded crest that is erected at will, most often when the bird is alarmed, frightened, or in some other emotive state, and or even when alighting on a branch after flight. Their legs are scaly, brownish grey, and their irises are dark brown.

Both sexes have a large bill with an elongated upper mandible, a beak that is significantly longer and narrower than that of the Carnaby Cockatoo (*Calyptorhynchus latirostris*), a species for which it is often mistaken (Forshaw 2006). While on initial inspection males and females appear almost identical, there are some minor differences. The male is marginally larger than the female. His periophthalmic ring is bare and pinkish, and his elongated beak is dark grey. His ear coverts are a dusty greyish white.

The female's beak is bone colored with a black tip. Her periophthalmic ring is grey. Her ear coverts are a brighter yellowish white. Both sexes have the ability to fan their cheek feathers forward enough to cover the base of the bill, an ability few other birds have.

For all intents and purposes, juvenile White-tailed Black Cockatoos closely resemble adults, except that juvenile males have a beak color similar to adult females. By the end of their second year the young male bird's beak begins to darken (Johnstone and Storr 1998).

Behavior

Like all other cockatoos, the White-tailed Black Cockatoo is noisy and raucous, especially outside of breeding season. Its call is distinctive but difficult to imitate, regardless of one's well intentioned efforts. The call has been described variously: as a short "whicher whicher" and "bunyip- bunyip," a flock call (Johnstone 2010). Its most common call has also been described as "wy-lah ... wy-lah." It is also heard to whistle "whee-whee," and to

The population of the White-tailed Black Cockatoos is believed to be between 10,000 and 15,000. Of that estimated population, it is concluded that approximately 1,000 to 1,500 are breedable adults. On the basis of these figures, the species is considered endangered, particularly since that their natural habit is being logged and converted to agriculture, there are fewer native foods available, and fewer tree hollows are available for nesting (photograph by Graham Ringer).

utter a low "chuck" (Oiseaux 2012). A variety of other sources have used the catch-all term "very noisy." It is said that Australian Aborigines have even named the species "OO-Lak," a name ostensibly imitating the cockatoo's call.

As is the case with the Yellow-tailed Black Cockatoo, the White-tail flies well above the forest canopy, usually in pairs, or a pair with a singleton (assumed) juvenile, a grouping that strongly suggests family units. The species is known to pair for years. Field observations have identified the odd bird in these threesome groupings as an immature birds because of the baby-like qualities of their bird calls (Milligan 1903).

The cockatoo's flight is slow, almost labored, consisting of slow, flapping wing beats. On alighting, the White-tail Black Cockatoo spreads its long, blunt tail and raises its crest. Lenden (in Caley 1973) reported that flocks of twenty or more individuals are rare, although he also reported once seeing a flock of approximately 100 individuals; more recently, in 2010, Johnson notes that while rarely witnessed, the cockatoo has been at times seen in flocks containing as many as 300 individuals. He reported that such flocks are often a mixture of the White-tailed Black Cockatoo and Carnaby's Black Cockatoo (*Calyptorhynchus lastiros*), and that while the birds are primarily arboreal in habit, they have been observed foraging at ground level when there is ample availability of various seeds.

There is some evidence to believe that the species undergoes seasonal movements of populations to and from the coast. The phenomenon was first noted by Orton and Sandlord in 1913 when they reported, "All birds leave during November or December, and go out on the sandy plain country"; more recently, in 1948 Perry noticed that the birds left the pine tree plantations during August and September in the Perth region and that they would annually return during February and March. While it is clear there is a distinct population shift either east or westwards, the migration is never so complete that entire regions are left bereft of any individuals. That some individuals remain behind while others migrate may be related to the species' breeding cycles: the species breeds infrequently and it is estimated that only 10 percent of sexually mature adults breed seasonally (Planet of Birds 2012). Notably, it is estimated that there are only 10,000 to 15,000 White-tailed Black Cockatoos extant. These population estimates are based on a field census taken from 1995 to 2004. Of that number it is believed that there are only about 1,000 to 1,500 mature breeding adults (Birdlife 2012).

The White-tailed Black Cockatoo appears equally at home in dry woodlands, open country, and humid tropical forests. The species is diurnal. It forages at all levels, from ground level to forest canopy, feeding on a wide range of native seeds and nuts, and the fruits of diverse shrubs and trees introduced by the agricultural industry. In respect to native foods, the cockatoo heavily depends on the flower and seeds of marri, as well as the seeds of the *Hakea, Banksia,* and *Dryandra* species, *Erodium botrys* and jarrah (Birdlife 2012). It also has a fondness for the grubs of the cossid moth (*Xyleutes boisduval*) and the long horned beetle (*Trphocaria aeanthocera*). When choosing forested areas for a seasonal haunt, it shows a distinct preference for woods composed primarily of Eucalypti and Banksia trees, especially when there are major grub infestations, or where Banksia seed cones are ripening.

The grubs are a special delicacy. The grub worms its way into the bark of the tree and may tunnel inward several inches from its point of entry in its search for food and concealment. The White-tailed Black Cockatoo has an uncanny ability to uncover the exact location of the concealed grub. When a large infestation of grubs infest a forested area, the infected trees are soon left in tatters after a small party of the cockatoos have vigorously stripped off great quantities of bark in their quest for the grubs.

The species is therefore important in controlling beetle infestations, and hence has considerable commercial value from that function; but the cockatoo is also responsible for killing many trees, and is consequently considered a pest, and subsequently a number are shot every year under the authority of a licence to do so.

Additionally, when traditional food sources are in short supply, when beetle grubs are at a premium, and when pine cones (*Pinus radiata*) have yet to ripen, the cockatoo will forage in commercial pear and apple orchards (Perry 1948) much to the distress of orchardists: the cockatoo has acquired an appetite for the pips of the pears and apples.

The cockatoos will tear down great quantities of the pears or apples to get at those pips; they totally ignore the fleshy parts of the fruit. Moreover, alighting on branches already heavily laden with ripening fruit, the birds break many branches (Mathews 1916; Serventy and Whittell 1962). The ground beneath invaded fruit trees is soon littered with damaged fruit and branches. In the past, damage to orchards was so extensive that an open season was unofficially declared by farmers against the cockatoo. Since the mid-nineties, however, the Australian government has enacted various programs making it illegal for farmers to shoot cockatoos without a license. Nevertheless, in Western Australia the cockatoos are still persistently perceived as pests (Chapman 2007), and even though this species has been vigorously protected since 1996, it is still illegally being shot (World Parrot Trust 2012), a practice that contributes to the continued decline in their numbers, in addition to the loss of a significant portion of their breeding habitat to agriculture and logging, and their slow reproduction rate.

Habitat and Distribution

The White-tailed Black Cockatoo is endemic to the extreme southwestern area of the state of Western Australia in Australia, an area that could be best described as coastal. In terms of distances, the territory inhabited by the cockatoo is approximately 500 kilometers (300 miles) north and south, and approximately 100–400 kilometers (60–250 miles) east–west. To the north, the cockatoo occurs as far as Wundowie, approximately 75 kilometers (50 miles) northeast of Perth. While the species appears to inhabit a relatively large area, the fact is that according to Western Australia's Department of Sustainability, Environment, Population and Communities (DSEWPC), approximately a third of the cockatoo's alleged territory is only territory in which the "species may occur." The cockatoo is known to breed in the area mostly from Perth in the northwest, to Albany to the far south and Margaret River (Biodiversity), and it has been noted to breed as far north as Lowden and Harvey (Higgins 1999).

In 2009, the DSEWPC estimated that while the species can be regularly found, or at least seen occasionally, throughout its range of distribution, its actual known breeding areas are few in number, infrequently encountered, and to some degree unknown. While the department identified some specific areas where the cockatoo has been known to breed consistently, and while it is known to breed as far south as Albany and as far west as Margaret River, breeding pairs in those terrains are widely dispersed and are from year to year irregularly encountered.

The species prefers southwestern, humid and sub-humid, heavily forested areas, particularly where the marri tree *Corymbia calophylla* is common, as well as the jarrah (*E. Marginata*) and the karri (*E. diversicolor*) trees, and where the average annual rainfall is 750 mm (30") or more (Saunders 1974). During breeding season, the cockatoo is found in wet *selerophyll* forests. Outside the breeding season, the cockatoo resides in open *wandoo* woodlands, and even in orchards; the habitat in which it is found is determined by the availability of food. The non-breeding range in which the cockatoo may reside may also be a function of the availability of marri, upon which the cockatoo depends, its flowers being a major food source.

The species is not entirely predictable in its migrations and/or nomadic wanderings: it is not at all uncommon for the White-tailed Black Cockatoo to heavily populate a region for a number of years, and then to be totally absent from that area for one or more subsequent years. Additionally, the month of arrival at any given locality favored by the species, when such a favoritism occurs, varies from one year to another (Davis 1970). Such phenomena are most probably shaped by weather conditions, breeding requirements (e.g., nesting hollow availability), the abundance or shortage of local foods, and other considerations, some too subtle perhaps to be easily identifiable.

Propagation

The White-tailed Black Cockatoo's breeding season extends from August into December, with some pairs beginning nest preparations as early as July. It is a species long known for its strong pair bonding, an observation first made by Carter in 1916 (in Mathews), who wrote in a personal communication of a mailman who had observed a pair that had "bred there the same nest site for several years between October and November."

In his field studies of the species during the 1970s, Saunders found that the pair exhibits an interesting courtship behavior, often before the nest construction begins. The female emits a begging call, a call that he describes as similar to the call of hungry nestlings. The male responds by bobbing its head up and down, touching the female's beak. Upon contact, both beaks then move up and down for approximately fifteen seconds at which time he transfers food to the female.

While there are some reports of nests being constructed in tree hollows as low as three to five meters (10–17') above ground level, most preferred nest sites are in towering trees with a greater diameter than 1.5 meters (4.5'), and that are 230–300 years old, usually marri trees. However, the hollows in trees on which the cockatoo minimally depends for its nest building are at least 130–220 years old (Birdlife 2012). The birds particularly prefer the hollows that form after a large branch has broken off and fallen to the ground.

Once the nest site is chosen, the pair gnaw at the entrance to the hollow itself, many of the chips falling into the nest site and forming part of the nesting materials upon which the eggs are laid. According to Milligan in 1903, nest bottoms may be as much as three meters (10') below the entrance, although contemporary observers note that the nest itself is generally only one to two meters (3–6') deep. Completion of nest construction takes four to six weeks. Copulation occurs about a week before nest completion.

The White-tailed Black Cockatoo on average lays only two eggs, although a single egg or three eggs are not uncommon. The ovate eggs are dull white, measuring 45.0–54.0 × 32.0–37.5 mm (1.7"–2.1" × 1.3"–1.5"), the second egg being laid anywhere from two days to one week later. The second egg is definitely smaller than the first, and since it will hatch at a correspondingly later date, the nestling will be comparably smaller than the first hatched, and will hence be disadvantaged in the competition to be fed. Consequently, regardless of the number of eggs laid and successfully hatched, only one nestling will be raised to fledgling age. The incubation period is approximately thirty days, and the young fledge at approximately the 77th day.

The incubating hen is fed twice a day by the male, at mid-morning and then again in the evening. The female alone broods the young, the cock never entering the nest cavity itself except during that period when the nest was being prepared. Aside from leaving the nest to be fed, or to get water, the hen is constant in her brooding duties. Given the species' low reproductivity, her refusal to leave the nest during brooding ensures the nestlings the necessary attention essential to survival. The species may have a weak instinctual reproductive drive, for Saunders in his field studies found that when a nest had failed, there was no further attempt by that pair to begin a second clutch.

In this connection, the recognition of the cock's call undoubtedly plays an important role in ensuring that the female will not leave the nest unnecessarily, thereby exposing the clutch or nestlings to intruders or danger. Even when there are several nesting pairs in the area, she will respond and leave her nest only at the call of her own mate.

After the nestling is approximately two weeks old, the hen begins leaving the nest at dawn and does not return to feed the youngster until some time mid-morning; also, the male no longer feeds the female. When the nestling is approximately four weeks old, at which point it can make both threatening noises and postures, it may not see the adult pair from mid-morning to evening. These are the only times when the nestling may be fed, especially if the day is hot, when the parents will rest in the shade of the trees rather than forage for food.

In this connection, young birds are quite demanding, often taking several months before they are fully independent, even though they may have fledged weeks before and are quite capable of feeding themselves. This dependency has led to some speculation that the species may not be an annual breeder. However, this does not appear to be the case. Whether or not the species breeds each year may not be a function of just genetics and instincts, but also of seasonal weather variations, food supply, and nest availability. Saunders found that in one locality near Manmanning a pair would fledge only one nestling in a period of three years, while at Cormalla Creek the ratio of nestlings produced was two every three years.

It should be noted that during the breeding months, and during the entire nesting period, it is only breeding pairs that are to be found in the area; sexual maturity of the species is believed to be reached by the fourth year, but it is not known where sexually immature birds can be found during the breeding season.

Aviary Notes

When researching the literature, or perusing information on the Internet regarding birds in general, or a species in particular, one is confronted with reams of data, some scientific and some informal, as is the case of numerous anecdotal materials shared on Web sites such as YouTube.

When one peruses information sources regarding the breeding of birds, whether domestic or wild, one is invariably confronted with similar but more specialized reams of information, regardless of species. But not so when researching the White-tailed Black Cockatoo: data on its aviary breeding and care is disappointing at best. Published literature is equally sparse. In fact, there is very little confirmed data on the breeding of the bird in the wild, and what information there is can be questioned as being conceivably speculative.

The reasons why there is little real data on the species are varied. First of all, the White-tailed Black Cockatoo was considered a pest for much of its history by Australian farmers because of its destructive foraging in orchards and in its killing of valuable trees. As a "pest," it was systematically destroyed, a persecution that persisted until the species, among numerous others, had to be protected. There was little interest in the species because of the public perception that the species was of no value. The cockatoo, besides being considered destructive, is a wary bird, difficult to approach, and because it normally nests in especially high trees, in heavily forested areas, it was and is difficult at best to get access to the nest to really observe nestlings and the brooding female. Additionally, the species has a reputation for being difficult to breed in captivity.

Moreover, when the species fell under governmental protection, a punitive fine of AU$4,000 was levied against anyone found guilty of being in the possession of a White-tailed Black Cockatoo captured in the wilds. In the meantime, while orchardists and farmers in general were subject to being fined for killing the species, regardless or not whether the cockatoo was destructive to crops or forest, the cockatoo was still considered an undesirable fauna appropriate for target practice; the species fell victim to the shotgun, and still does today.

In short, there are few of the species in captivity. There are small captive populations held at the Healesville Sanctuary in Victoria, some at the Perth Zoological Gardens, and a few at the Melbourne Zoo (Garnett 1993). (The number of private aviaries licenced to possess and breed the species is unknown.)

While there is little information available, anecdotal or otherwise, regarding the species and its aviary history, BirdCare (2008) does publish information on the breeding of various species of birds, and on the White-tailed Black Cockatoo. Much of the information on the species provided by BirdCare for potential breeders of the species, or interested avicultural hobbyists, is of the general type. The cockatoo is described as difficult to breed, although it is also described as the least aggressive of the cockatoo species. Its aviary should at minimum be 8 meters (26') long by 1.5 to 1.8 meters (4.5 to 5. 7') wide, and about 2.4 meters (7') high. Because the species likes to chew a great deal, an activity that not only provides exercise for its beak but is essential to the bird's emotional health, there should be ample leafy branches available throughout the aviary, as well as wooden perches of diverse lengths and diameters situated at various heights. All of these will periodically have to be replaced as the birds demolish these aviary accessories.

The cockatoo is particular about its nesting site, preferring upright logs with a diameter wide enough that it can easily contain a nesting hollow of 350–400 mm (14"–16") in diameter. While logs are preferred, a nest box might tempt a pair interested in nesting. BirdCare recommends placing several nest boxes, besides logs, in the aviary; should the birds begin showing a particular interest in one potential nest site, the others should be gradually removed from the aviary.

The nest boxes should have an interior diameter similar to a log hollow. The entrance to either type of nesting choice should be approximately 200–300 mm (8–12"). In respect to nesting materials there should be a provision of decomposed sawdust, wood chips, and other suitable materials such as nontoxic leaves.

The birds should be fed the types of foods with which they are familiar in the wild. In addition, various seeds such as striped sunflower, canary seed, pine cones, Banksia nuts and cones, and almonds are welcomed by the birds.

While there are countless sincere, avid bird hobbyists who would welcome the challenge of breeding this wonderful cockatoo in captivity, there are but a scant few Australians who will ever enjoy that opportunity. As for aviculturalists in the rest of the world, obtaining a pair or even one solitary White-tailed Black Cockatoo is virtually impossible.

First of all, the cost of a (true) pair is high; at least $5,000, a considerable expense even should one have the capital resources with which to indulge a costly hobby. There is also the problem of too few cockatoos to supply avicultural hobbyists: the cockatoo is rarely available from licensed aviaries because of the cockatoo's poor reproductive performance in captivity. The construction of a suitable aviary is also a cost to consider. If one is Australian, capturing a couple of specimens from the wild may be an interesting challenge, but so will be the grief associated with considerable legal problems, fines, and possible imprisonment for violating conservation prohibitions. And finally, hobby clubs of bird enthusiasts would agree with BirdCare that the breeding of the species should be left to specialist breeders.

As for non–Australian hobbyists, they will have to content themselves by reading about the species, or watching videos of the White-tailed Black Cockatoo on television or on YouTube.

Pet Companion

Although there is some interest in the White-tailed Black Cockatoo because of it plight vis-à-vis the loss of habitat due to logging and farming, its previous vigorous persecution as a destructive pest, a persecution still persisting today to some degree, and its abysmal reproduction rate, there is little information available regarding this species as a pet. The stereotype of the bird historically considered a pest has no doubt negatively affected its desirability as a household pet. What little literature there is regarding this cockatoo as a pet is in itself confusing.

First of all, there are very few of this species bred in captivity, largely due to the fact that in the public's mind, the White-tailed Black Cockatoo is a pest and hence is less desirable than other species of birds. In addition, conservation laws prohibit the capture of the species, and while aviary bred cockatoos can be legally owned, there are few bred in captivity and therefore correspondingly very few available for purchase.

During preparation of this book, research was conducted on the availability of the cockatoo. On the Internet, internationally, there were a number of breeders who advertised various species of aviary bred, exotic birds for sale, many of them rare, and many purportedly hand fed. The White-tailed Black Cockatoo was among those advertised as being available.

However, on various breeders' Web sites, those purporting to breed this species among other species, the White-tailed Black Cockatoo was in every instance listed as being unavailable. A perusal of Gum Tree, a popular Australian Web site on which individuals can place classified advertisements for any variety of items, there was a classified advertisement of a "White Tail for sale—tamed male, talks, very friendly. Must have bird keeper's licence. $1,500. Not Negotiable." That ad appeared in the Moora Boolarea region. Another Gum Tree classified advertisement appeared in the Perth region in which a male cockatoo, eighteen months old, aviary bred, was offered for sale for AU$1,500. It was not specified in either instance whether the cockatoo was *Calyptorhynchus baudinii* or *Calyptorhynchus latirostris*.

While the species' reputation as a pest may have prejudiced cockatoo fanciers against acquiring them as pets, they are variously described as wary, easily stressed, intelligent, and like other cockatoos, equally demanding its owner's attention and companionship. But, there is virtually no anecdotal descriptions of the bird's behavior, temperament, intelligence, and suitability as a household pet, the type of informative opinion that results from months if not years of involvement with the bird(s).

Because of the legislation prohibiting the ownership of the species, unless it is legally aviary bred, the White-tailed Black Cockatoo is a species realistically unavailable to most bird fanciers in Australia. And based on the fact it is considered endangered, it will most definitely remain unavailable to the general public outside of Australia in the foreseeable future.

Threats to the Species

As noted earlier there is an estimated population of ten to fifteen thousand White-tailed Black Cockatoos in Australia, and although numerous sources have cited that figure as a reliable estimation, it is not quite clear whether in fact there are indeed that number of this species existing in the wild. Since the government issues licences permitting possession of the species, it is possible to determine how many are in captivity. But there is no accurate way of estimating the White-tailed Black Cockatoo's population in the wild, given that it frequents heavily forested areas, that it is thinly spread over a wide terrain both during and after breeding, that its breeding terrain has been dramatically reduced, and that the species' reproductivity is low. In addition, some birds are killed annually, either legally or illegally.

In the literature figures are often provided without any identification as to the source of that data; frequently, not only specific data, but entire paragraphs have been lifted from other publications without identifying those publications, or even acknowledging that the information came from another source: the concern here is not that there is or might be plagiarism, but rather that a figure or "fact" is automatically considered accurate if more than one source cites the same data; even though one source after another may be copying materials from sources that may have derived that information by plagiarizing still other sources. Hence, exactly what is the population of the White-tailed Black Cockatoo?

BirdLife (2012) reports, "The 1995–2004 surveys of the species suggest the total population at probably still 10,000–15,000 individuals." Note that those figures published in 2012 are already over a decade old. Those figures are constant regardless of the reporter.

The same document reports that there are only 1,000 to 1,500 mature birds.

P. Matheson (in Litt. 2004) is of the opinion that the bird is declining in numbers because of illegal shooting, feral bees, logging, and the loss of suitable nesting and feeding habitat. Because of the changes to the habitat, it is estimated that the rate of population decline is 5 percent over three generations—approximately 58 years (Garrett and Crowey 2000).

In the IUCN Red List, the species in 1988 was listed as "Lower Risk/Less Concern." The following year it was listed as "Vulnerable," and by 2005 it was categorized as "Endangered." It has remained so until and including the present (BirdLife 2012).

Disregarding the species' categorization as "Endangered" for the moment, a figure of ten to fifteen thousand would not necessarily suggest the species is faced with extinction in the near future. However, there are a significant number of factors that are a threat to the species' population numbers, whatever they may currently be, and hence its population stability.

First, it is estimated that approximately 40 percent of the habitat used by the birds during their breeding season has already been logged. The species require tall trees that are up to 300 years old: younger (smaller) trees cannot usually produce the hollows that the species depends upon for its nests. In short, there are fewer nest opportunities available. Some of the logging, of course, is for the provision of wood for housing, furniture, and the like. Much of the logging, however, is also for agricultural purposes, orchards and wheat and other grain crops.

Second, despite laws protecting the species, farmers can still obtain so called "Damage Licenses," which permit them to kill the birds when they are found foraging agricultural crops. While individuals can be fined AU$4,000 for having in their possession a wild caught cockatoo, farmers are rarely fined a comparable sum for killing one, or even a number of cockatoos. There is some evidence, however, that since this species, is in danger of extinction, the government is becoming more stringent in prosecuting individuals who are killing the birds.

Third, given the loss of numerous nesting sites to loggers, the species is now competing with feral bees, which have found tree hollows ideal for their hives. There are reports that some nestlings and brooding hens have been lost to bee attacks, but that information is difficult to confirm, particularly since the nests (and hives) are difficult to access.

Fourth, and most important, it is clear that the species is not producing at least one nestling per mated pair per breeding season. The actual figure is .6 young per nest. Since the species does not breed well in captivity (Garnett 1993), captive breeding programs are not a solution to the declining population of the species. The laws make it extremely difficult for individuals to obtain the cockatoo and attempt aviary experimentation leading to the development of avicultural practices that could conceivably prove successful in breeding the species. Currently, the cockatoos' future is uncertain, but it is not entirely bleak. Various recovery actions have been implemented, completed, or are underway: the species is now protected from wholesale shooting by orchardists protecting their crops under the Open Season Notice (1989), and the identification and listing of threatened fauna under the Wildlife Conservation Act in 1950, and then again in 1996 (Mawson and Johnstone 1997). (Because there are cockatoos still being shot in violation of protective conservation legislation, it is not clear whether losses by shooting exceeds the species' annual reproductivity output.)

In addition, a recovery team has been formed to research and develop techniques to protect orchards and diverse fruit crops without doing harm to cockatoos (Chapmann and Massam 2005).

A variety of various other recommendations have been made, which include assisting orchardists develop nonlethal means of protecting their fruit from foraging cockatoos, monitoring populations more closely across the range of habitat common to the species, and encouraging more detailed field studies of the birds in the wild, particularly their detection, surveys regarding their foraging behavior, and the identification of their nesting and roosting sites.

19

Carnaby's Cockatoo
Calyptorhynchus latirostris (Carnaby, 1948)

COMMON NAMES: Carnaby's Black Cockatoo, Carnaby's Cockatoo, Mallee Cockatoo,
Rigoolark, Short-billed Black Cockatoo, Slender-billed Black Cock-
atoo, White-tailed Black Cockatoo, White-tailed Cockatoo
SUBSPECIES: None
LIFESPAN: (approximately) 25 years[1]
IUCN RED LIST OF THREATENED SPECIES: Endangered
CITES: II

Description

Endemic to Australia, Carnaby's Cockatoo is a large black cockatoo weighing on average 520 to 790 grams (18.3 oz. to 28 oz.), measuring 53 to 58cm (20–22.5″) in length, and Higgins (1999) reports its wing span as approximately 110 cm (42″). For all intents and purposes, the bird is mostly black, a black that may be washed brownish-black or greyish-black.

The species is sexually dimorphic. In terms of similarities between the sexes, body feathers of both adult males and females are narrowly edged in a vague dull white at the tips of the feathers, suggesting a scalloped appearance. There are broad white panels in the tail: the central tail feathers are all black, however, whereas the lateral tail feathers are white with black tips. The panels appear quite distinct when the bird is flying.

As is true of all other cockatoo species, the Carnaby's Cockatoo has a crest; its crest is short and recumbent and can be erected at will depending on whether the bird is excited, alarmed, surprised, or in any other particular emotional state. When the cockatoo is not in a state of excitement, the crest lies back on the head, almost unnoticeable. The species' beak is broad, short and curved, and strong. The eyes are dark brown.

In terms of fundamental sex-determinate differences, the male's beak is black, whereas the female's is an off-white color and is tipped in black. While both sexes have distinctive round ear coverts, the female's covert feathers are bright white while the male's are distinctly dusky white. The female's patch is also usually slightly larger than the male's. The periophthalmic ring is a fleshy pink for males and darkish grey in females.

In respect to their legs and feet, there are variances in degrees of color differentials between the sexes. Depending on the individual bird, a male's legs may vary from grey to greyish black, and the soles of its feet may be slightly lighter, and even occasionally tinged

The Carnaby's Cockatoo is often mistaken for the White-tailed Black Cockatoo. It was not until the 1940s that ornithologists determined that there were two different species of white-tailed black cockatoos. There is some concern over the Carnaby, for its numbers are few and it is estimated that only 15 percent of fledged juveniles survive their first year (photograph by Jerrod Amoore).

in pink. There are some variances in female leg coloration also, but the color is typically paler than that of the male's legs. In fact, the female's legs may be pinkish or pinkish brown, depending on the overall paleness of the upper feathering. In darker colored females, however, the leg coloration will resemble that of the males (Higgins 1999; Johnstone and Storr 1998).

Young Carnaby cockatoos closely resemble the adult female in respect to their plumage. However, there are some minor differences between the adult and juvenile: young birds have smooth, bone colored beaks, and their periophthalmic ring is greyish (Forshaw 2006). Their tails also have less white. Juveniles can often be easily recognized by their raspy vocalizations when begging for food. During their second year of life, young males can be distinguished from females whose beak has acquired the horn color and black tipped upper mandible (Higgins 1999), and by the end of the second year the juvenile females closely resemble the adult's coloration.

Note: There are two white-tailed black cockatoo species in southwestern Western Australia: they are the Carnaby's Cockatoo and the White-tailed Black Cockatoo (*Calyptorhynchus baudinii*), also known as the Long-billed Black Cockatoo. There are slight differences between the two species, differences that are not always obvious to an inexperienced eye. *C.b. baudinii* has a marginally longer wing and a skull that is broader, higher, and has a longer culmen. The upper mandible extends below the lower (Juniper and Parr 1998; Birdlife International 2011; Saunders 1974; Australian Government 2011). *C.b. baudinii* also differs behaviorally in that it prefers regions where there is significantly more rainfall than that preferred by the Carnaby Cockatoo (Saunders).

Behavior

Carnaby's Cockatoo is a mobile, gregarious, social bird, historically known to congregate in large flocks outside of the breeding season. During the breeding season, however, the cockatoo is normally encountered in pairs, or in small flocks of just a few individual birds. Given the reduction of habitat still available to the species and the bird's low reproductive rate of only .6 chicks every year or every two years (Johnstone and Storr 1998), there are far fewer birds now than previously, and larger flocks are hence now an exceptionally rare occurrence.

A century ago there were numerous field reports of large flocks of black cockatoos observed in the southwestern regions of Western Australia, but at the time there was no ornithological knowledge that there were more than two white-tailed black species (i.e., *C. lastirostris* and *C. baudinii*); and, in reviewing early field notes from a century or more ago it is not possible to accurately quantify earlier estimates of numbers (of Carnaby's), or to be confident that any particular sighting of a large flock at the time was indeed that of Carnaby's Cockatoos as opposed to a flock of Long-billed Black Cockatoos (*C. baudinii*), or even the red-tailed form (*Calyptorhynchus banksii*), unless the Red-tailed Cockatoo was reported as such in those early field notes. Indeed, both white-tailed species co-occupied similar regions with the Red-tailed Black Cockatoo (*Calyptohynchus banksii*), but at a distance it is difficult to accurately differentiate the Red-tailed Black Cockatoo from the white-tailed forms. Given this history—i.e., the early historical reports of large flocks—it would be reasonable to argue that Carnaby's Cockatoo probably never did number in the many thousands; moreover, given their small numbers, modern agricultural practices began to seriously reduce the amount of available native habitat that the birds required for both feeding and nesting, a major environmental transformation that precipitated their steady downward decline in population numbers from whatever they were historically, for within a short period of time the Carnaby's Cockatoo stood on the brink of extinction.

During the breeding season, and post fledging, the cockatoos are usually seen either in pairs or small family units, the average number of surviving young birds per clutch being almost always one. After the breeding season, some family units move to post breeding areas, where there are ample food supplies, and where they are joined by other family units, including small flocks of several families; but in many instances, some birds remain behind to forage locally in heath land, near their familiar roosting sites.

Other birds gather in larger flocks and migrate locally to coastal regions where pine plantations have become an important food source since the late 1920s, and which provide the birds secure roosting sites until the next breeding season.

When in flocks, whether large or small, the birds are noisy and are conspicuous by their raucous calls. Their most common call, if it is possible to mimic it, consists of a "whay-lay, whay-lay" or a "whee-whee," or sometimes a low "chucking" sound (Oiseaux 2012).

The species is by nature arboreal, spending most of its waking hours during hot weather in the shade of treetop canopies, most often quite well out of sight, but occasionally it can be found low in stunted bushes. When not in breeding season, and on the coastal plains, the Carnaby's Cockatoos can normally be found roosting in towering river gums, native or introduced eucalyptus, or pine plantations if the seed cones have ripened.

The birds typically leave their roosting site in the morning; with considerable clamour they depart to their foraging areas, leaving one site for another as it suits them, depending on how much food is available. After a day's feeding they return to their roosting site. It has been observed that a flock will use a roosting area over several consecutive years. Johnstone and Kirby (2008) believe that the communal roost of several hundred birds serves an important social value insofar as it provides unmated birds opportunity for mate selection.

The Carnaby's Cockatoos enjoy a varied diet. When food is abundant, they can often be seen in the company of the Red-tailed Black Cockatoos (*Calyptorhynchus banksii*) or with Baudin's Black Cockatoo (*Calyptorhynchus baudinii*) (Saunders 1974; Higgins 1999). The birds scavenge on remnant native vegetation, the original habitat fragmented primarily for urbanization and agriculture; they can also be found on adjacent farmlands, where they feed on pine nuts, and occasionally on canola. The birds can also be found feeding on introduced weeds in pastures or along roads. Given the loss of much of the species' habitat to the plough, the search for sufficient food negatively impacts the cockatoo. Annually, numerous birds are injured or killed by vehicles when they are feeding along roadsides.

During the 1920s, the planting of pine plantations in the Perth vicinity provided a new, important source for food and roosting opportunities for the cockatoo (Birdlife International 2011; Australian Government 2011).

For over seventy years the pine plantations near Perth became increasingly a major food basket for the species and other cockatoo forms; the birds readily adapted to the diminishing native food availability that invariably accompanies habitat fragmentation (Cale 2002). These pine plantations are situated within the humid and semi-humid zones of the Swan Coastal Plain. As native vegetation feeding opportunities diminished, the species began foraging on the seeds from the cones of the *Pinus* spp. in the pine plantations. When foraging in the plantations, the birds begin on the outskirts of the plantation, and as the cones' availability along the perimeter of the plantation is exhausted, the birds gradually work towards the center of the plantation, foraging in each tree until there are no cones left. The birds then glean from the ground whatever seeds may have fallen from the trees (Saunders 1998).

This important food source will in the near future become increasingly in short supply as the pine trees gradually die off or are cut down for their lumber: the pine plantations consume vast amounts of water, all of it derived from the underlying aquifer, which is rapidly becoming depleted (Valentine and Stock 2008); to conserve the remaining underlying water supply Western Australia has prohibited any further plantings of the pine. Within eighteen years, all pine plantations are scheduled to be agriculturally decommissioned (Government of Western Australia 2008).

The loss of the pine plantations as a food source in the very near future will be a major threat to the species' population viability (Cale 2002; Garnet and Crowley 2000), especially considering the species' poor reproductive history. To complicate the species' survival predicament, the loss of the plantations will also further limit the availability of suitable roosting sites.

In respect to other food alternatives, of particular importance to the birds' food needs are their preferences for the seeds from proteacous plants such as the *Banksia, Alloscasuarina, Dryanda, Hakea,* and various *Eucalyptus* species, among others (Department of Environment and Conservation 2007); in fact, they are known to feed on the seeds of over 52 varieties of native plants (Valentine and Stock). Carnaby's Cockatoo is even known to feed on the larvae of wood-boring moths. The bird is also fond of the nectar of a variety of flowers, and when a flock has descended to feed on a flowering tree, the ground is soon littered with the color of fallen flowers.

When arboreal, and feeding, the cockatoos can be found at treetop crowns cracking seeds or cones, and from time to time fluttering down to forage on the ground beneath a tree for fallen seeds. The birds continue to feed at a given location until the food is exhausted. When feeding, like some other species of cockatoos, one or two birds can be observed perched high in nearby trees where they act as sentinels, and as soon as there appears a predator or some other type of potential threat, the sentinels begin screeching loudly; within seconds the entire flock will abandon their feeding in the pursuit of safety.

Their flight is best described as strong, almost laborious, their wings flapping slowly. When flying their white tail feather panels are conspicuous, making them difficult to overlook.

Habitat and Distribution

Carnaby's Cockatoo is endemic to the extreme southwestern corner of Western Australia. It is mainly found in pockets of small populations between the Murchison River and Esperance, and inland as far as Lake Cronin (Bird Life 2012; Juniper and Parr 1998; Saunders 1990; Australian Government 2011; Cale 2002). Carnaby's Cockatoo is known to occupy a wide variety of terrains; during the breeding season it is common in the Wheat Belt, and during the non-breeding season in higher rainfall terrains. When not migrating to more distant regions after breeding, during the non-breeding season some Carnaby's Cockatoos can now be found inhabiting suburban orchards and gardens, and even urban parks. In essence, however, a large proportion of the species migrates short distances to and from the Wheat Belt and the southern and western regions of the Swan Coastal Plain, a twice annual migration determined by the breeding cycle.

The cockatoos are common to the Swan Coastal Plain during the non-breeding season, which is from January to July, the region considered important to the species' viability because of its native vegetative food abundance (Saunders 1990). During the breeding season, the cockatoo prefers regions where there is from 350 to 700 mm (9–17") of annual rainfall; the Wheat Belt's climatic environment makes the region ideal for their breeding purposes (Saunders 1980; Berry 2008). The normally high annual rainfall in the Wheat Belt region assures abundant vegetative growth upon which the birds forage for food to feed their young.

The species is difficult to quantify in part because of its small numbers, but mostly because it is both regionally migratory and locally somewhat nomadic. As a consequence, quantifying the species becomes problematic because it is difficult to anticipate specific locations where the birds can be found in numbers large or small at any given time during the course of the year (Biodiversity 2012). Population numbers are crude estimates, therefore. What is obvious is that the species is no longer found breeding in approximately a third of its former range where nesting pairs could be commonly found forty-five years ago, and for all intents and purposes it can now be considered extinct in those regions; moreover, the population has declined significantly during that period throughout its entire remaining distribution (Saunders 1990; Biodiversity 2012).

Carnaby's Cockatoo is considered highly mobile, insofar as the breeding birds are frequently resident where native vegetation has been cleared and cultivation provides non-native vegetative foraging opportunities (Saunders and Ingram 1998). When the breeding season is complete, however, most birds migrate either to the south or the west, to areas that are not arid, where the birds can feed on native vegetation that thrives on heavy rainfalls (Johnstone and Kirby 2008). In some areas, the species assumes a limited nomadic life, wandering locally, but once the rains begin in April, the birds disperse widely in their search for food (Saunders 1990).

Although Carnaby's Cockatoos have been reported in flocks numbering up to 10,000 individuals during the non-breeding season on the Swan Coastal Plain, such flocks are actually rarely encountered. The general migration west and southward during the non-breeding season is normally composed of smaller flocks numbering fewer than a thousand birds, which can at times aggregate into larger foraging gatherings on the Swan Coastal Plain.

As noted earlier, however, while Black Cockatoo flocks consisting up to an estimated 10,000 birds were reported a century ago, and while at times there was a distinction made that an observed bird or flock was probably either a Red-tailed Black Cockatoo (*Calyptorhynchus banksii*) or a White-tailed Black Cockatoo (*Calyptorhynchus baudinii*), it was not until 1948 that it was confirmed that the White-tailed Black Cockatoo actually consisted of two species: Carnaby's white-tailed taxa was identified as being distinct from the White-tailed Black Cockatoo (*Calyptorhynchus baudinii*), which had been first identified by Lear in 1832, well over a century earlier, despite a predominance of similarities between the two forms. An untrained eye would have difficulty differentiating them. The two species are so similar in overall appearance that it was not until the late 1940s that it was generally agreed that there were two species of white-tailed cockatoos, and not just one species with a wide variance in specific biological and behavioral parameters.

In 1948 Perry recorded flocks of Carnaby's Cockatoos that he estimated to number from 5,000 to 6,000 individuals foraging in four different pine plantations in the Perth Area; by the late 1970s Saunders encountered only one large flock, and that flock numbered only an estimated 1,200 birds (Saunders 1980). More recently, in 2006, with the aid of volunteers, Shah (2006) took a census of the birds, a flock comprising sixteen roosts on the Swan Coastal Plain during the non-breeding season, a flock that he estimated contained at least 4,500 individuals. While it is believed that that number is underestimated, and larger flock gatherings have been reported, *these reports of large numbers derived from census taking should not be interpreted as evidence that the Carnaby's Cockatoo population is numerically thriving and increasing in numbers.*

The Carnaby's Cockatoo has historically occupied Western Australia's Wheat Belt during the breeding season (July to December), but that territorial occupation has declined significantly since 1948 concurrent with a precipitous decline in population. As early as 1980, it was already obvious that the species had disappeared from at least a third of its former habitat (Saunders 1980). It is estimated that because of this habitat loss their population declined by approximately 50 percent (Garnet and Crowley 2000; Mawson and Johnstone 1997; Saunders & Ingram 1998). As agriculture, urban development, and mining claimed more land, and native vegetative food and nesting sources were lost consequential to these environmental changes, there were subsequential declines in population throughout its entire distribution (Saunders 1980).

Much of the original habitat has been severely fragmented and degraded, so that in effect there is little remaining native habitat except that found on some large coastal reserves. In 1998 Johnstone and Storr suspected that this shortage of suitable habitat might be triggering a gradual redistribution of the species towards both the west and south. Recently, data from the Storr-Johnstone Bird Data Bank suggests that the species is now expanding its territorial distribution into the Jarrah-Marri forests and concurrently into the Tuart Forests on the Swan Coastal Plain (Johnstone and Kirby 2008). Because the species is migratory, additional field work is required to determine if in fact there is a permanent redistribution resulting from the loss of traditional habitat. This fragmentation and dimunization of available habitat may have in effect divided the species into three to four subpopulations: a subpopulation in the northern region of the Wheat Belt, another in the southeast Wheat Belt corner, a third subpopulation in the upper part of the southern Wheat Belt, and finally a fourth separate subpopulation along the coastal area near Esperance (Garnett and Crowley 2000).

The clearance of native habitat has not only reduced food availability but has also diminished the number of nesting hollows available, a matter of some concern because of the competition for nesting site hollows from feral European honey bees (*Apis mellifera*), the Galah (*Elophus roseicapilla*), the Western Long-billed Cockatoo (*Cacatua pastinator*), and the Australian Wood Duck (*Chenonetta jubata*). The shortage of nesting hollows is especially worrisome because the species does not produce sufficient numbers of surviving young birds to replace its aging population. Consequently, as the native habitat has been dramatically reduced, Carnaby's Cockatoo not only has become extinct in some specific localities where it was previously common, but also is now in diminished numbers in those areas it is still known to occupy.

With the assistance of hundreds of volunteers, BirdLife Australia conducted what is fondly called the "Great Cocky Count," a census of the Carnaby Cockatoo, during April 2010 and April 2011, and then again in 2012. Similar counts had been conducted several years earlier, but these three recent ones were governed by more stringent guidelines. When the final figures were tallied, it was found that the population had dropped 37 percent in just one year: in 2010 a total of 12,954 roosting cockatoos were counted, whereas in 2011 the final tally was 8,365 cockatoos (Platt 2012). The 2012 tally showed no significant variance from the 2011 data.

Propagation

Because of concern regarding the Carnaby Cockatoo's severely declining numbers over the past five decades, there have been a number of studies focusing on the species' distribution and the environmental and human factors affecting its reproduction; these studies were motivated by the belief that the data will lead to the development of conservation strategies to prevent the species from going extinct. While the Carnaby's Cockatoo is a protected species, and there has been considerable effort expended to mobilize public support for its protection, the studies have demonstrated that the species' declining numbers are strongly correlated to the dramatic loss of suitable native habitat; fewer nesting hollows, less food availability, more failed nests, and higher rates of fledgling mortality. Because of these critical impediments, the cockatoo's normally low reproductive rate is threatening to decline further because fewer breeding-age cockatoos are able to nest or to provide sufficient food for their offspring's healthy development.

As noted earlier, the breeding season begins in July, at which point those Carnaby's Cockatoos that have migrated to the Swan Coastal Plain and elsewhere begin migrating back to the Wheat Belt to find suitable nesting hollows. Pairs will return to a nesting hollow they had utilized before, but if their nest ended in failure during the previous breeding season, the pair will normally seek a new hollow.

An early, heavy, autumn rainfall is important to the Carnaby's Cockatoo. If it is a light rainfall, the birds postpone the laying of the clutch: shortfalls in rain results in poor vegetative growth and hence diminished food availability for offspring, resulting in the possible failure of the nest. A late laying of eggs, on the other hand, exposes the sitting hen and the eggs to the detrimental effects of hot weather, and hence the success of a nesting is also jeopardized.

The Carnaby's Cockatoo prefers smooth eucalyptus trees with large hollows for its nesting, the hollows preferably higher up in the nesting tree, as high as ten meters (32'), regardless of whether the tree is alive or dead. While a eucalyptus is the preferred tree for a nesting site, the cockatoo will nest in other tree species when nesting opportunities are limited due to deforestation and competition from other avian species.

The eggs are creamy white and are usually laid on a mat of wood chips in the nesting hollow from late July to late September. The normal clutch size is 1–2 eggs (average of 1.7 eggs); when the clutch consists of two eggs, the second egg will have been laid anytime from one to eight days following the first (Saunders 1982). Only one nestling is usually raised to fledgling age, despite the fact that there are numerous two-egg clutches. Saunders reported in the eighties, based on his field study conducted on clutch size and nesting success involving 222 nests that had two eggs, that the second nestling usually died within 48 hours of hatching, and of those few that survived that critical two-day period, only eleven survived past the third day.

The survival rate of the second nestling appears to be directly related both to how much time elapsed between the two hatchings and to the availability of food; a longer period between hatchings translates into the first hatched nestling being fed more often, growing, and becoming larger, stronger, and hence more competitive for foods that arrive at the nest, advantages a younger nestling is unable to compete against; the consequence is death. Additionally, the severe fragmentation of the remaining native habitat necessitates the male having to fly increasingly longer distances to obtain sufficient food, and given the longer flights, and the availability of food, which may or may not be bountiful, the male is often unable to adequately feed both the hen and the nestlings as often as they need to be fed, particularly the nestlings. When food is difficult to garner, and there are longer periods between feedings, the younger nestling is the first to become malnourished and then perish; earlier field studies have shown that when the adults must fly longer distances to obtain food, the singleton was frequently found malnourished and ill prepared for fledging. Losing a nestling, some females may re-lay a second clutch, and Saunders reported one female actually laying a third clutch after experiencing failure with her first two attempts. These are exceptions, however.

It is believed that the Carnaby's Cockatoos pair for life, but there is no evidence confirming that belief. It is known that both parents are religious in their parenting responsibilities. The female alone incubates the eggs for 28–29 days (Saunders 1982), and will continue to attend to the nestling(s) in the early stages of brooding, during this entire time being fed by the male. As the nestling grows, both adults begin jointly leaving the nest to forage during the day, returning to the nest mid-morning to feed the nestling juvenile, and then later at dusk to again feed it (Department of Environment and Conservation 2007). The larger the young bird becomes, the greater its food requirements and demands. It has been found that when food is scarce and the female must also spend increasing amounts of time away from the nest in her search for food, the result is reduced fledgling weight, and ultimately reduced breeding success for the pair.

During the nesting season the species relies heavily on native vegetation, much of it foraged in kwongan heathlands (Saunders 1982). Now, because of loss of native habitat and its effects on food availability, it is estimated that on average the food foraged is obtained up to twelve kilometers (7.5 miles) distant from the nest (Saunders 1990); the native habitat is severely fragmented, the fragments are unconnected by habitat corridors, and because there are insufficient food resources within the fragments, food must be gathered from where it is available in abundance, usually at some distance. The Western Australia Department of Environment and Conservation (2007) reports that during the 1970s in a major study of a local population of Carnaby's Cockatoos, the cockatoos ceased breeding in the area once the loss of the bird's native habitat exceeded three quarters of its original availability.

Given habitat loss, the survival rate of nestlings is problematic. The juveniles fledge from eleven to twelve weeks (World Parrot Trust 2012), but after fledging, the juvenile continues to be fed by the parents. The young bird remains with the parents for several months, often until the next breeding season, and it is believed that some yearlings still linger in the vicinity of their parents while they are raising another nestling. While the survival rate of adult Carnaby's Cockatoos is believed to be from 61 to 69 percent, upon fledging the highest survival rate recorded for juveniles is 86 percent, but the average survival rate is barely 63 percent. It is estimated that only 15 percent of successfully fledged juveniles live longer than one year. Assuming this estimate is reasonably accurate, the loss of young juveniles is a major threat to the overall Carnaby's population stability insofar as the remaining population is aging and is without sufficient numbers of young sexually mature birds to replace them. The average age of adults is estimated to be fifteen years old. Moreover, young females are believed to be at least four years old before they begin breeding (Department of Environment and Conservation 2007).

Given the low reproductivity of the species, and the loss of native habitat, the current survival rate of successfully hatched Carnaby's Cockatoos is insufficient to maintain the population.

Aviary Notes

One of the major obstacles confronting the aviculturalist—Australian or otherwise - interested in breeding the Carnaby's Cockatoo is the virtual impossibility of legally obtaining a pair, particularly due to their rarity. Because of CITES, illegally captured birds are also rare in the international black market pet trade. Because of its rapid decline in population and the international interest that its dire circumstance has generated, the species has become an important Australian icon representing Australia's unique fauna to the world at large. The numerous postings on the Internet regarding this species give the impression that this cockatoo has captured the Australian public's heart, and that its possible extinction is of concern to just about everyone, as is true also of its protection.

The species is protected by law, and there are severe penalties for poaching individuals from the wild. A search of the Internet was conducted to identify any birds that might be for sale, anywhere. There were absolutely none advertised in North America, Europe, Australia, or even Asia, particularly Singapore. That is not to imply that there are never any Carnaby's Cockatoos available for purchase, legal or illegal; but at the time of the search there were none available. Almost twenty years ago, Mawson in 1997 reported that illegal birds were at the time selling for AU$3,000 per bird, and AU$5,000 per pair. Because the birds breed so poorly in captivity, the price for illegal birds has declined somewhat, as breeding interest in them waned (Garnett and Crowley 2000; Cale 2002). The current (2012) price for illegal, or legal birds, is presently unavailable, and hence unknown.

In Australia, there are few Carnaby's Cockatoos in private collections, or kept as pet companions. Two decades ago in 1993, Garnett estimated that in Australia there were approximately only 400 of the species held privately (Garnett 1993). Recent figures are unavailable (BirdCare 2002).

When field research made it clear by the mid-eighties that the Carnaby's Cockatoo was in a spiraling population decline, a captive breeding program was established in 1996 by the Western Australian Department of Conservation and Land Management (CALM). Staff from CALM collected eggs from the wild for incubation, as well as nestlings; the primary purpose was to form a sustainable captive population available for the re-introduction of the species to the wilds should the existing wild population collapse into extinction (CALM 1999; Mawson and Johnstone 1997; Cale 2002), and/or suitable habitat became available as a result of conservation efforts.

The eggs and nestlings obtained from the wild were distributed to licenced professional aviculturalists and to the Perth Zoo. Additionally, injured birds from the wild were rehabilitated and were either released to their normal habitat or incorporated into the existing stock of captive cockatoos. This incorporation also served to broaden the genetic diversity of the captive birds (Biodiversity 2012; CALM 1999).

In addition to the cockatoos under professional aviculturalists' management and those in the Perth Zoo, the cockatoo is now also held at Taronga Park (Sydney Zoo) and at the Adelaide Zoo. Captive birds are also now being held by eight institutions and zoos worldwide.

The Perth Zoo also maintains a stud book for all captive breedings, conducts a DNA analysis on each bird, and microchips each bird to ensure that anyone with a Carnaby's Cockatoo obtained it legally (Birdlife International 2011; Biodiversity 2012).

Although there is no schedule governing when or where the captive birds are to be released, or how many, the primary present goal is to ensure that the species does not go extinct, and when suitable and/or rehabilitated habitat becomes available, decisions will be made.

Pet Companion

While working on the White-tailed Black Cockatoo (*Calyptorhynchus baudinii*) chapter, I explored the Internet with the expectation of being able to garner personal anecdotes from individuals who had the species as a pet companion. Usually, a brief exploration of the Internet provides prompt results: there's invariably at least one YouTube video of someone and his/her pet, the particular pet species in which one has an interest at the time. Or failing a video, at least a blog or two concerning experiences with the species in question, be it a wild bird or captive pet companion. That Internet search was a failure.

There appears to be little non-scientific information on the species, that it is endangered, aside from the fact that it is considered a pest both by farmers and the general public, that professional (and hobbyist) aviculturalists do not breed it because unlike some other cockatoo species, there is no consumer demand for it as a pet companion. And although the species is endangered, like the Carnaby's Cockatoo, there was little concern expressed for its possible impending extinction. And there were many informational entries. It was even possible to locate two White-tailed Black Cockatoos for sale in Gum Trees classified ads.

While the search for specific information on the White-tailed Black Cockatoo evoked what may be described as a blasé public attitude, quite the opposite attitude emerged when exploring issues concerning the Carnaby's Cockatoo.

Although to the inexperienced eye the Carnaby's Cockatoo is not significantly differently from the White-tailed Black Cockatoo, and even though it is now defined as a species unique to itself, it has acquired a totally different persona, an entirely different reputation, a public sympathy. While there is still the occasional shooting by an irate farmer who is distressed by the Carnaby possibly damaging his crops, his canola, there is considerable expressed public sympathy and concern for the plight of the Carnaby's Cockatoo. There have been numerous news stories about its plight by the Australian Broadcasting Corporation (ABC), articles in *Australian Geographic Magazine*, videos on YouTube (Department of Conservation and Land Management). There has also been considerable public support, as best witnessed by the countless volunteers involved in the annual "Great Cocky Count." Murdock University has devised an action plan for protecting the local birds in its immediate area. There are considerable scientific, avicultural and financial investments made by the Perth Zoo, and affiliated institutions, to ensure this species' survival. Even the prestigious journal, *Scientific American*, published an article concerning the species' predicament.

In searching the Internet for Carnaby's Cockatoos for sale, there was not one classified advertisement offering one for sale, anywhere. Nor was there any Internet blog regarding someone's pet companion Carnaby's Cockatoo. In short, there is no experiential information that can be helpful in informing the reader concerning the bird as a suitable, or unsuitable, pet companion.

There are some generalizations that can be made, however, that are most probably accurate. Like the other cockatoos, excepting perhaps the Cockatiel, the Carnaby's Cockatoo is probably intelligent, can learn to become an escape artist, easily bonds, is emotionally demanding, reciprocates interaction with its owner, and requires at least two or three hours of attention devoted to it daily. If given enough time and training, it can also probably learn to mimic people or to whistle. It would be a strangely unique cockatoo if those predictable traits were inapplicable to the Carnaby's Cockatoo.

Given all of the above, the reality is that the Carnaby's Cockatoo will rarely be available for purchase to the Australian public, and almost as rarely encountered on an Australian outing in the outback. And, regrettably, most persons throughout the world will never have the opportunity of viewing one of Australia's remarkable birds.

We wish it well in its struggle to survive.

20

Yellow-tailed Black Cockatoo
Calyptorhynchus funereus (Shaw, 1794)

COMMON NAMES: Yellow-eared Black Cockatoo, Wy-la (Aboriginal), Funeral Cockatoo (archaic), Southern Yellow-tailed Black Cockatoo, Eastern Yellow-tailed Black Cockatoo.

SUBSPECIES:
1. *C.f. funereous*—Nominate form (Shaw, 1794)
2. *C.f. xanthanotus* (Gould, 1838)

LIFESPAN: (estimated 60+ years); Rotterdam Zoo 41 years (Higgins 1999)

IUCN RED LIST OF THREATENED SPECIES: Least Concern

CITES: II

Description

Endemic to Australia, the Yellow-tailed Black Cockatoo is one of five Black Cockatoo species comprising the genus *Calyptorhynchus*. From a distance, the cockatoo appears to be a large black bird, similar to a crow, but upon closer inspection its plumage is dark brownish black with a slight greenish tinge to it, the underparts decidedly more brown. The underwing coverts have slightly yellow margins, as is also true of the under tail coverts. The body feathers are marginally scalloped in yellow, as is also the case with some feathers on the nape, wings and neck. The tail, quite long but somewhat roundish, has its blackness broken by a band of yellow in the middle portions of the lateral tail feathers. The inner webs of these feathers are flecked in black, most of the flecking occurring in the basal regions. The central two feathers are pure black, however. The feet are an ashy grey.

Both males and females have prominent yellow cheek patches behind each eye, but the male's patch is smaller and a duller yellow than the female's. Both sexes have a short, black mobile crest on the top of their heads that can be erected at will, particularly if the bird is emotionally distressed or excited. The cockatoo's bill is medium sized, grey-black, and is more elongated than that of other cockatoo species, excluding the White-tailed Black Cockatoo (aka Long-billed Black Cockatoo); the beak's elongated, pointed upper mandible is a useful adaptation in its search for grubs, a main food source.

In general, while the species is sexually dimorphic, the differences between the sexes are not immediately apparent to the inexperienced eye. Males are marginally smaller than females. In respect to their color, the males have a more blackish appearance with less yellow

margining to the feathering. The male's periophthalmic ring is pinkish/reddish while the female's is a pale grey, although for both sexes the eyes are brown. The male's beak is black whereas the female's is bone colored.

The species is composed of two subspecies. Besides weight and slight size differences, there are some minor physiological differences in coloration distinguishing one race from the other. The *C.f. funereous* has a very dark brown/black overall color as compared to the *C.f. xanthanotus*, which in turn has its underparts scalloped more brightly yellow (Higgins 1999; Saunders 1979).

Of the two subspecies, the *C.f. funereous* is decidedly larger than the *C.f. xanthanotus*: its tail averages approximately 33 cm (13"), about two centimeters, or approximately an inch longer than the other race. In additional to a longer tail, it also has a much larger bill and claws, and its wings are considerably longer (Higgins 1999). In overall length, Forshaw (2006) notes that the cockatoo averages from 55 cm to 65 cm (21.5–22.1").

The *C.f. xanthanotus* race inhabiting the mainland is larger than its subspecies brethren on Tasmania, a difference that led to some considerable professional disagreements regarding subspeciation: tasmanian females average 585 grams (20.5 oz.) and males average 583 grams (20.5 oz.); that same subspecies on the mainland on average weighs 637 grams (22.5 oz.) for females and 630 grams (22.2 oz.) for males (Higgins 1999). While there is a slight difference between the average weight of the subspecies on the mainland and that of the same birds on Tasmania, there was insufficient overall evidence of difference to argue that there were in fact three subspecies. In 1979, Saunders had argued that in addition to the weight difference the Tasmanian birds also had wider mandibles than did their mainland form. Those differentiations have to date not proven to be a convincing subspecies norm characteristic of the southern Yellow-tailed Black Cockatoo (Christidis and Boles 2008).

Juveniles for the most part resemble adult females. In general, the juvenile's upper mandible is a horn colored shade that darkens to adult coloration by the second year; the lower mandible does so by the fourth year. Overall, the juvenile's plumage is considerably duller. As well, their eye rings are grey upon fledging (Forshaw 2006; Lendon 1950), but the data pertaining to the change to adult color is sparse and poorly documented.

Behavior

The call of the Yellow-tailed Black Cockatoo has been described in a variety of ways, as is common to naturalists attempting to replicate an original, actual sound. Without exception, however, field workers agree on one thing: the Yellow-tailed Black Cockatoo's call is so loud that it can be heard long before the bird can be seen, despite the fact that the cockatoo is a large bird. Its call is most often described as harsh and discordant. There is also common agreement that there is no possibility of mistaking the call for that of any other species. Howe, in Mathews (1916) described the call as a " … kee-ow, … kee-ow … ," a description

Opposite: **The Yellow-tailed Black Cockatoo is considered a wary species. When a flock is foraging on the ground, there are always a couple of individuals high in the tree tops acting as sentinels. At the first sign of danger, the sentinels screech out alarm calls, and the flock immediately flees to safety (photograph by David Cook).**

contemporary observers persist in utilizing to describe the cockatoo's vocalizations. More recent and contemporary naturalists have described the call in a variety of other ways: Lendon in 1950 described the call as a "distinctive wailing cry." It has been described as a high pitched screaming whistle; Slater in 1970 referred to the call as "harsh shrieks" and Forshaw (2006) notes a "peculiar grating note" when the birds are eating.

Needless to say, as is true of many other cockatoo species, the Yellow-tailed Cockatoos are noisy and raucous (Forshaw 2006). While in flight the birds are constantly calling to each other, the calling also common during their roosting. They are also known to make harsh calls when disturbed, presumably alarm calls. While the species are generally quiet when feeding, juveniles frequently making food-begging calls (Higgins 1999).

The cockatoos frequently make long journeys in small groups comprising both parents and their young (almost exclusively a singleton), or in a small flock of several birds. When flying long distances the birds fly at high altitudes well above the tree canopy. Although their flight has been described as fluid, slow, and undulating, it also gives the impression of being labored because of the bird's slowness in flying. When flying in larger flocks, it appears to struggle a great deal; Littler (1910), at a time before negative stereotypes became taboo, described the flight as a "Chinamen's procession." Outside of the breeding season, the Yellow-tailed Cockatoo may congregate in larger groups numbering up to a hundred birds or so. While in these larger groups the familial relationship of a mated pair, and their offspring, if there is one, is maintained (Forshaw 2006).

Upon landing on a bough of a tree, the cockatoo raises its crest, maintaining this for a period before allowing it to gradually return to its normally reclined position. Roosting sites are generally towering Eucalypts; the cockatoos come to the ground only to drink or to feed on fallen Banksia or pine cones. Because they are generally wary, most of their non-flying time is spent high in the trees either to escape the heat of the day or to roost. Interestingly, Forshaw has observed that the Yellow-tailed Cockatoo appears to many observers to be less wary when in suburban or urban areas.

Because the Yellow-tailed Black Cockatoo can be found in a wide variety of environments ranging from alpine heights to coastal plain forests or grassy woodlands, even heavily populated urban areas,[1] it should not be surprising that the cockatoo enjoys a wide variety of foods. Unlike many other species whose diet is limited to a few different seeds or fruits, who therefore rely on specific sources for foraging, and whose population stability is therefore dependent on an unchanged habitat, the Yellow-tailed Black Cockatoo eats a wide variety of foods; consequently, environmental changes affecting one food source or another does not threaten their ability to find sufficient food. Some authorities hold the view that the cockatoo is primarily an arboreal feeder. Yet numerous field observers from Howe (in Mathews 1916) to Lendon (1950), and more recent observers, have reported that flocks will congregate on the ground to feed on ground-level plants or cones dropped from trees. Dissection and examination of gizzard contents reveal seeds of diverse grasses. When the cockatoos congregate in larger flocks, they forage together, altogether the various individuals are usually spread over a wide area, where they are nevertheless always in contact with each other through their loud and constant vocalizations.

Their diet varies considerably, which protects them from losses of traditional native foods resulting from the degradation of the habitat and the consequences to food availability. Much of their diet depends on the seeds of various native trees, such as the She-oaks (*Allocasuarina* or *Casuarina* trees), as well as the *Torulosa* and *Eucalyptus*. The cockatoos are also fond of various flowers, green seed pods, *Banksia* seeds as well as the seed pods and seeds of *B. Serrata, B. Marginata,* and various species of the *Hakea*. They are partial to pine cones in plantations of the introduced *Pinus Radiata* (causing damage to the trees), among a wide variety of other seeds from introduced trees (Barker and Vestjens 1984). On the Eyre Peninsula, where the species is identified as endangered, various trees have been planted, among them the introduced Aleppo Pine, whose cones are popular with the cockatoos there (Van Weenen 2009); it is expected that the plantings will assist the birds in restoring their numbers.

The cockatoos drink from whatever water sources are available, such as puddles or stock troughs—they usually hydrate themselves late in the afternoon or early in the morning. When alighting near water, the birds will land several feet from the source and then slowly proceed to walk towards it. A sentinel is always posted.

The cockatoo is particularly fond of tree-boring beetle larvae such as the cossid moth (*Xyleutes boisduvali*) and the long horn beetle (*Tryphocaria acanthocera*). While the Yellow-tailed Black Cockatoo searches for these larvae throughout the year, it is during June and July that the larvae are plumpest, and concurrently the young cockatoos have recently fledged. The adults search the trees for signs of the larvae, often pausing to listen intently to sounds that might be emanating from within the tree. If the cockatoo estimates there are larvae within, it begins to strip away the bark, stripping away a piece big enough so that it can stand on it. The cockatoo will continue to gouge and excavate the tree where the suspect larvae are burrowed until they can be extradited from the heartwood (Mcinnes et al. 1978). North (in Littler 1910) describes the manner in which the grubs are located:

> It strips and cuts away, i.e. the Eucalyptus tree bark, with its powerful bill, ... Probably by tapping, the bird detects the distance down the limb the grub has bored, for it is generally about eight inches below the hole where it has entered the wood in its search for the grub, and it may be another foot before it obtains it.

The stripping away of the bark to get at the grub leaves the tree in tatters. A century ago Littler (1910) described this tattered appearance aptly when he wrote, "The trees have the appearance of having been well worked over with strong rakes." Invariably, of course, both in the instance of orchards or pine plantations, large numbers of trees are killed, all leading to the persecution of the species despite the great beneficial effect the cockatoos have in controlling beetle infestations.

The cockatoos are also fond of Banksia cones, when the follicles have opened. In the pine plantations, the cockatoos nip off green cones, and holding the cone with the left foot, they extract the seed from each segment, a process taking about twenty minutes per cone (Dawson 1994).

Habitat and Distribution

The Yellow-tailed Black Cockatoo is found throughout most of southeastern Australia, including Tasmania and the various islands of the Bass Strait. It is common throughout New South Wales, where it inhabits regions along the Great Dividing Range to the coastal areas, and across Victoria to southern Queensland (Forshaw 2006). Specifically, the nominate race, known on the mainland as the Eastern Yellow-tailed Black Cockatoo, inhabits central Queensland south into New South Wales and into eastern Victoria. There are a scattered few birds on Eyres Peninsula, the only region of their traditional habitat where their population is considered vulnerable (Cameron 2008): much of the original habitat was destroyed by a bush fire, crippling foraging and nesting availabilities.

The *C.f. xanthanotus* race occupies Tasmania, the various islands of Bass Strait, and parts of the mainland in western Victoria and southeastern South Australia.

The Yellow-tailed Black Cockatoo frequents a wide variety of terrains, ranging from heathland to subalpine environs, from riparian forests to grassy woodlands, and higher alpine regions from sea level up to 2,000 meters (6,500'). There is sufficient evidence from field observations to conclude that as winter approaches the cockatoos move towards lower lying coastal areas (Dawson 1994). In short, the birds migrate nomadically to occupy habitats at any given time when food is sufficiently abundant. They have even been found in pine plantations (where they cause some damage to the trees) and orchards, especially when there are large infestations of beetles and cossid moths; surprisingly, they are also frequent visitors to heavily populated urban and suburban areas, particularly parks and golf courses, notably in and around Melbourne (Melbourne Parks 2012) and suburban Sydney (Higgins 1999). Since the cockatoo is known for its wariness, it is not clear whether in fact the birds have lost some of their fear of humans, whether they are driven to search for food in heavily populated urban areas because of the loss of natural habitat as a result of urbanization, industrialization, and deforestation, or whether the birds have found they can find sufficient foods in urban environments without fear of persecution.

The question of its reputed wariness is in itself a quixotic one regarding its reliability.

Most contemporary field observers are consistent in their opinions that the cockatoo is extremely wary and will flee at the slightest provocation. Yet despite this consensus regarding its wariness, there are numerous reports of observers approaching the birds without them becoming unduly alarmed. A Mr. Mellor (in Mathews 1916) wrote that when the birds were not harassed by shooting at them, "they became very tame." Similarly, North (in Mathews 1916) wrote, "Usually they are shy and wary and difficult to approach, but occasionally I have, without difficulty, walked beneath the tree on which they were perched." Comparably, Hall, himself an astute and accomplished ornithologist at the turn of the last century, observed that flocks he encountered while in the mountains were "very tame." What is not clear, however, is precisely how much stealth these field workers employed to get that close to the birds.

Interestingly, the Yellow-tailed Black Cockatoos have developed a "sentinel system" similar to that of the Sulphur-crested Cockatoo (*Cacatua galerita*) in Australia, or the common American Crow (*Convus brachyrthybchos*) in North America. During feeding and drinking, one or more sentinels are posted in neighboring trees. At the slightest hint of danger, the cockatoo sentinels emits a harsh shriek, and the entire flock wheels into the air and towards safety. It is not clear from examining early field notes whether in fact the sentinel system employed by the species is a learned behavior resulting from its persecution at the hands of the first Australian colonists or was common to the species long before the advent of Australian colonists and their firepower in persecuting "pests."

Propagation

The Yellow-tailed Black Cockatoo's breeding season varies depending on the latitude in which the bird lives. The cockatoo limits its breeding to forested areas with towering trees (Forshaw 2006). The breeding season in southern New South Wales is from December to February, whereas in northern New South Wales, it is during January through to May; it occurs from October to February in South Australia, Tasmania, and Victoria, and in Queensland from April to July. Studies have shown that the species chooses nesting trees measuring as high as 58 meters (185') with a mean diameter of 2.5 meters (8') at breast height (Higgins 1999). It is near the top of the tree that the mated pair normally prepare their nest. Generally, the birds choose an isolated tree so they can fly from one tree to another without hindrance. The pair may use that same nest for several consecutive years. While the Yellow-tailed population is not currently considered vulnerable, industrialization and deforestation for agriculture and lumbering developments are in the long term major threats to the species' population stability as these huge trees are felled.[23]

Despite deforestation, the cockatoo has not approached vulnerable status, even though there is but a precariously small population of the species remaining on Eyre Peninsula. It would appear that the species may be adapting to the changes in its habitat; specifically, the species may be adapting to nesting opportunities in trees that earlier would not have been considered. Other wise, if in fact the species has not slipped into the vulnerable category, it may be because the species is annually reproducing sufficiently enough young to maintain its population despite reduced numbers of suitably sized nesting trees. There is no hard evidence to support this, however.

Yellow-tailed Black Cockatoos sexually mature by their fourth year. During courtship, the male spreads his tail feathers, thereby displaying the yellow tail feathers, extends his crest, and bows several times while concurrently "softly growling" (Higgins 1999). A towering tree is chosen, either dead or alive, usually a Eucalypt, in which the nest is prepared. The pair begin working on the nest about a month before egg laying.

Preparation involves scraping and/or peeling the inner walls of a hollow, the chips forming the basis of the nesting materials, to which are often added gum leaves. The hollow may be as much as two meters (6') deep and 0.25–0.50 m (1.2–1.5') wide. Both the male and female prepare the hollow. There are usually only two eggs laid, anywhere from two to seven days apart; the eggs are dull, oval and lustreless. It is not unusual for a nesting pair to have only a singleton egg, or even three eggs, but it is rare for more than one nestling from a clutch to survive to fledgling age. The first egg is larger than the subsequent eggs, and of course, given that the second egg is laid a few days after the first, the first hatched nestling has already a size and weight advantage over the later-hatched sibling nestling. Additionally, in the competition for food from the parents, the elder sibling will be more aggressive to ensure it is being fed, thereby receiving more attention from the parents—and hence having a distinct advantage over its less developed sibling. While all eggs may be successfully incubated, there is yet to be reported one instance of more than one nestling from one clutch being raised to fledgling age in the wild. It is believed that the second nestling perishes due to parental neglect, which results in starvation and malnutrition leading to the nestling's death.[3] There is no hard data to confirm this hypothesis, however.

The first egg is normally about 47–48 mm long × 37 mm (1.8" × 1.5") in diameter. The second egg is marginally smaller. While there is little known of their breeding in the wild (most probably because the nests are so high above the ground, even though they are quite visible from below), from studies done of the cockatoo in captivity the incubation period is 28–31 days (Cameron 2008). New hatchlings are covered in yellow down and have pink beaks (Higgins 1999). By the time the young fledge, that pink fades to a greyish white. Fledged juveniles closely resemble the adult female, but their plumage is duller overall.

Concerning brooding, an interesting pattern of behavior appears to typify the species as reported by a Mr. A.J. Campbell (in Littler 1910). He noted that while the female was brooding, the male would punctually appear at the nest site each morning, noon or thereabouts, and at night. Before approaching the nest, the male would call from a considerable distance away, at which point the female would respond by appearing at the entrance to the nest and replying with a "scream." Once the cock was in sight, she would fly to a dry branch near him, at which point he would proceed to feed her via regurgitation. Once fed, she would preen herself, then return to the nest, always entering the entrance backwards. Interestingly, although there might be several brooding pairs in the immediate area, she would only respond to the calls of her own mate, regardless that several other males would be similarly calling.

Aviary Notes

The Yellow-tailed Black Cockatoo has proven itself difficult to breed in captivity. Whether the birds are too nervous, the aviary is not suitably built to encourage breeding, or any other host of reasons, some subtle and others obvious, the hatching of the cockatoo's eggs is an event that draws considerable interest. For example, Lendon in 1950 reported that of the several cockatoos that had been in the Adelaide Zoo over several decades, there had been no successful hatchings, although he also noted there were several eggs laid at various times. On one occasion eggs were laid in a hollow log, but there was no interest in incubating them. Lendon did not speculate on the cause for this disappointing history.

In 1973, or thereabouts, Lynn (in Cayley 1973) reported he had a pair that had laid eggs, had shown an interest in incubating them, and had actually reared two youngsters on at least two occasions, but such rare successes were interspersed with years in which laid eggs were reported infertile.

Lynn's pair were housed in an aviary 40' × 10' × 9' (12 meters × 3.3 meters × 3 meters), and the birds were approximately four years old when the first clutch of two infertile eggs was laid in 1961. The male was replaced in 1962, but another two infertile eggs were laid. In 1963 the female again showed interest in the nest box. The entrance to the log was enlarged and the birds continuously chewed the interior of the hollow. Two more eggs were laid, but this time a chick hatched exactly thirty days later. That nestling proved somewhat fragile, and from the onset Lynn had to take an increasing greater responsibility in rearing it by feeding it by hand. Although that hatchling fledged at ninety days after hatching, it regrettably died before the year was out.

In the following year, the pair successfully reared a second chick, a nestling that proved itself quite healthy. In 1965 the pair laid another two eggs, but one of the eggs proved infertile and the other contained a youngster that had died within the egg. Lynn noted that the hatched birds were extremely frail and special care had to be taken to rear the nestlings to fledgling age. He also observed that while both parents fed the nestlings, a juvenile would continue to remain dependent on the male for almost a year afterwards.

While there is a scarcity of information on Yellow-tailed Cockatoos being bred in captivity, Rob Marshall of the Avicultural Society of New South Wales reported on his experiences with the species. He purchased a pair in 1984. They were put in an aviary measuring 40' × 18' (height not provided) (12 × 6 meters), an aviary the pair shared with some other 30 assorted avian inhabitants. He found a suitable log, placed it in the aviary, and began to tempt the birds with a variety of foods. The cockatoos destroyed the nesting log that year, and for the following five years destroyed each replaced nesting log until finally, finally, two eggs were laid, six days apart. The eggs were fertile, and the female brooded until the 20th day, at which time she abandoned her eggs. The following year—the eighth—the female again laid two eggs, but this time Matheson incubated them himself. A nestling, named Jackson, was successfully raised to adulthood, and is fondly described by his owner as "mischievous." Marshall also reports that since Jackson's hatching he has reared several other chicks from the same pair; the hen laid between 5 to 12 eggs annually! (A questionable annual egg output, if it is from one pair of a species of cockatoo that breeds but once a year and rarely has more than two eggs per clutch. Perhaps there was more than one mated pair in his aviaries.) Regrettably, Marshall did not discuss the essential ingredients to account for his successes, aside from the fact that he hand fed the young birds.

Since the birds are large, the aviary should be approximately 8 meters long × 1.5–2.0 meters wide × 2.5 meters high (approximately 26' × 6' × 8'). Because the species enjoys chewing and has a powerful beak, the mesh enclosing the structure should be heavy gauge. Several natural wooden perches should be provided: sturdy branches of different lengths and thicknesses, at various heights throughout the complex. One or two short lengths of hanging rope provides interesting diversions for the birds.

Because the Yellow-tailed Black Cockatoo enjoys chewing, an activity that is both normal and essential to its well-being, suitable nontoxic, live branches should be provided the birds, the chewing a beneficial entertainment, a relief from boredom, and important in ensuring that the beak receives both sufficient exercise and growth control.

Four or five different nesting arrangements can be interspersed throughout the aviary: hollow logs or grandfather-clock-styled nest boxes. The nest boxes should be close to a ceiling, but far enough away to protect the young from heat. They should be 700–900 mm × 350–400 mm in diameter (approximately 28–35" × 14–16"). The entrance hole should be approximately 100–150 mm (4"–6") in diameter. There should be an ample amount of decayed sawdust, wood chips, or other suitable materials upon which the hen can lay her clutch (BirdCare 2012). Once the pair begin favoring one of the nest facilities, the others should be gradually removed. Since the species is known to utilize the same nest site over successive years, if a pair have fledged young from a particular nesting arrangement, it should be left in the aviary.

Because the birds find both pleasure and exercise in chewing, most wooden contents in the aviary are soon shredded into oblivion. They need to be replaced, regularly.

The species proves it can co-exist with other species of smaller parrots, but it does not handle disturbances while breeding.

Pet Companion

The Yellow-tailed Black Cockatoo is rarely seen in zoos outside of Australia. While the species was occasionally seen in captivity prior to the late 1950s, a few birds entered the world pet trade market for a short period before the Australian government placed an outright ban on the exportation of wildlife species in 1959. While the species is not considered endangered, it is protected by CITES (Convention on International Trade in Endangered Species of Wild Fauna and Flora). It is placed on the Appendix II of species considered at risk, which makes it illegal to trade, export, or import without CITES approval, and that approval is contingent on the understanding that the legal transaction is related to the species' conservation, as opposed to the private sale of the species in question for profit.

The Yellow-tailed Black Cockatoo has also not been a popular aviary or household pet. For the most part, in Australia, the bird was, and still is, historically and currently perceived as a pest. Because of the damage done to gum trees due to the cockatoo's fondness for cossid moth larvae, the species was considered responsible for extensive damage to plantation trees. In some areas of New South Wales they were shot as pests until the late 1940s (Higgins 1999). Bird fanciers rarely took an interest in this species, in part undoubtedly not only because of this perception but also because they required large cages, or aviaries, to prevent apathy of captive birds, and the usual neurotic behavior that often develops in cockatoos that are bored and/or deprived of emotional reciprocity.

Although the species is not considered vulnerable because of its wide dispersion over a variety of habitats, except for Eyre's Peninsula where the birds are considered endangered, the species is everywhere protected from capture and sale, or from being shot by irate farmers. There are few Yellow-tailed Black Cockatoos outside of Australia due to Australia's ban on trade in this (and other) exotic bird species. The few that do exist outside of Australia are generally in zoos. In Australia, outside of the wilds, the cockatoo can be found in the aviaries of licensed specialist breeders who sell young birds to exclusive aviaries and wealthy bird collectors. In short, the species is an expensive investment, if one is available to acquire. A detailed search of the Internet, particularly YouTube, shows no blogs or videos of the Yellow-tailed Black Cockatoos as pets, or of bird fanciers who are in possession of this species. However, there are multitudes of other videos on YouTube that deal with a host of parrot types in captivity that are pets, not only in Australia but throughout the world. In essence, the species is not common to the general avian-interested public.

Before Australia banned the exporting of its exotic bird species, some Australians and a few individuals internationally had acquired one as a pet. Porter, for example, in 1940, wrote, "They make the most delightful pets and are extremely tame and familiar. In fact, there is no bird I would rather have ... but alas they are difficult to rear and still more difficult to procure, as it is only by cutting down some giant forest tree." The Marquess of Tavistock during the 1920s had a female for several months, but while she proved tame, he described her as "vicious" (Tavistock and Delacour 1926). The cockatoo is generally considered high maintenance and prone to stress. It is considered not as desirable as other cockatoo types.

Even given these negative attributes, there are those aviculturalists and bird pet owners who would welcome the opportunity to own one. Given the status of the species in the wild, CITES restrictions, and Australian prohibitions concerning harvesting wild specimens, few individuals will ever have the opportunity of owning one, even illegally. And unless an individual visits an Australian zoo, or travels off the beaten track in the species' native habitat, most people will never see one, particularly non–Australians.

PART FOUR

SMALL COCKATOOS

Genus *Nymphicus*

21

Cockatiel

Nymphicus hollandicus (Kerr, 1793)

COMMON NAMES: Weero. Quarrian, (both common to Australia), Cockatiel, common in both Australia, and North America. (Cockatoo-Parrot and Cockatoo-Parakeet: now archaic).
SUBSPECIES: None
LIFESPAN: 36 years (longest known in captivity)
IUCN RED LIST OF THREATENED SPECIES: Least Vulnerable
CITES: Not Listed

Description

Endemic to Australia, the Cockatiel is the smallest member of the cockatoo family, weighing on average 80 to 100 grams (1.8–3.5 oz.), and measuring from beak to the end of the tail 29 to 33 cm (11.31"–12.9") (McCaffery 2009; Kavanau 1987).[1] The tail constitutes approximately half the length of the cockatiel, at about 15 cm (6") long; the wing span averages 30–35 cm (12–13.5". The species is a sexually dimorphic monotype: in terms of obvious similarities between sexes, the males and females are for the most part grey both above and below in overall appearance, with the underside feathers having a brownish tinge.

The upper part of the male is quite distinctive from the female's, however: the forehead, face, and throat are a lemonish yellow, as are the basal parts of the crest feathers. The ear coverts are a distinctly bright orange, bordered by white; the female, on the other hand, is primarily a simple grey coloration throughout the entire head region, excepting for the ear coverts, which are a dull, burnt orange, but which lack the white border.

Despite its size, like all other cockatoo types the Cockatiel has a crest. The crest is long, narrow, wispy and tapering, approximating 5 cm (2") long, and composed of several feathers in linear order from front to back. As with all other cockatoos, the crest is used communicatively; the position of its crest, that is whether erect or flattened against the crown, is indicative of the bird's emotional state, a form of communication complementing its vocalizations, which also indicate the bird's current mood.

The beak for both sexes is a grey color with the lower mandible primarily horn colored. The pointed upper mandible moderately projects over the lower. The eyes are dark brown.

The wings of both sexes are mostly grey but are conspicuous with white flashes on the

Because of their head coloration, male Cockatiels are preferred over females, although both sexes make wonderful household pets. Because it breeds prolifically it has been hybridized so that there are now more than thirteen different recognized patterns and coloration combinations (photograph by Jim Brendon).

This pair (male to the right, female to the left), if provided the opportunity, will lay up to three clutches of eggs per year, 4–6 eggs per clutch. They breed so prolifically that they are inexpensive, proving to be an ideal companion pet, and they can be purchased in just about any city in the world (photograph by Jim Brendon).

outer edge of each wing. During flight, this patch of white clearly distinguishes this species from other, similarly sized, grey avian species.

The Cockatiel's tail is unique among the cockatoo forms, for it is the only cockatoo whose tail comes to a point. When flying, the tail is spread out, resembling a large fan. The female's tail is greyish brown, speckled with white. The two outermost feathers are mottled in yellow and barred intermittently in a lemon yellow. The male's tail is a plain dark grey, with the underside decidedly darker than above.

For both sexes, the feet and the thighs are grey colored. The Cockatiel's feet are zygodactyl, as is common to all parrots, with two toes facing forward and two backwards.

Juveniles are phenotypically female appearing, and virtually indistinguishable vis-à-vis their sex until their first molt, beginning at about six months. Until that molt, they are predominately grey with the ear covert patch the adult female's dull orange. With molting, however, immature males begin to acquire the adult male's distinctive head coloration: the dull orange cheek patch is replaced by a bright orange, the face and crest feathers become a bright lemon yellow, and the yellow or white tail bars on the underside of the tail are lost. The female makes no observable changes in color with that first and subsequent molts.

Behavior

The Cockatiel is ordinarily an arboreal species, but it feeds almost exclusively on the seeds of ground-level plants, particularly the seeds of the *Danthonia* and *Asistida* sp. It is also fond of *Acacia* seeds (Pizzey and Knight 1997) and is attracted in large numbers to terrains where the shrubs grow in abundance. At times, it will feed on diverse herbaceous plants, or on various localized fruits or berries common to shrubs and low-level trees. It is also known to feed on ground-dwelling insects.

When feeding on the ground the birds are difficult to detect because their plumage blends remarkably well with the earth and ground cover, and they forage quietly, camouflage and silence protecting them in large part from aerial predators. Forshaw (1977) reports that sometimes the Cockatiel can be seen feeding in the company of Red-rumped Parrots (*Psephotus haematonotus*).

The Cockatiel is also known to raid cultivated fields of sunflowers, sorghum, wheat and millet. Regarding sunflowers, the birds directly land on the flower's head and deftly pick out ripened seeds. When these raids are carried out by flocks often numbering in the thousands, the resulting damage to the crops is significant. While the Cockatiel is by law a protected species, there have been open seasons declared against the species, particularly in Queensland, to control the damage. Pesticides have also been used against the birds as a means of protecting crops (Kavanau 1987). These efforts to protect crops are for the most part unsuccessful and do not appear to affect the Cockatiel numerically.

Because the Cockatiel is a gregarious, social bird, its crest serves an important communicative function. As with other cockatoo forms, the position of the crest indicates the bird's mood. Generally, when the bird is content, the crest is slightly raised, perhaps to as much as a 45 degree angle. But when the bird is alert to a possible threat, or if startled, the crest is erected upright, and should the bird be directly threatened, the crest is held close to the head, as it is during flight, to escape the perceived or impending threat. In addition, the Cockatiel's vocalizations can indicate a variety of moods. For example, the male uses prolonged singing to woo a female during the breeding season. A shrill call, on the other hand, indicates danger, and often accompanies evasive flight (Kavanau 1987; Pizzey and Knight 1997). These calls can be heard at considerable distances, and can also serve as courtship songs or warnings to other cockatiels, among other specific communications.

The species thrives well because of its fecundity, its adaptability to diverse terrains and climates, and its ability to escape from predators. During droughts, the birds may daily fly as distant as thirty kilometers (18 miles) to watering holes or to feeding grounds.

When the birds are stressed or flushed, they immediately fly directly from the ground to a nearby tree, usually a dead one, if one is available, where they perch on the ends of dead branches. While they are at times found at the tops of trees, their preferred perch is found in lower portions of a tree. The species rarely perches on a living tree unless there are several dead branches on it.

When perching, the Cockatiel has the unusual communal habit of perching side by side, several in a row, and engaging in mutual preening. Such preening is normally accompanied by a quiet chattering (Christholm). In a habit common to this species only, when the Cockatiel needs to scratch its head, it does so indirectly by scratching over the wing.

The Cockatiels' flight is direct and straight, at times protracted. They are known to fly an estimated sixty-plus kilometers (approximately 35 miles) an hour, faster than any aerial pursuer. Their flight is often accompanied by a specific distress call that was described by Mellor in a personal communication to Mathews (1916) as a "crale-e-eek." Frequently, Cockatiels can be found flying in the company of Budgerigars (*Melopsittacus undulates*) (MacGillivray 1910). The Cockatiel's flight invariably evokes awe. Amazed at their flying, Grant in 1912 wrote of one such flock in flight:

> Sometimes in the early morning they would assemble in flocks of about thirty or forty, and when on the wing their evolutions were carried out with such precision, it gave one the impression that each bird knew its place and kept a certain distance from its mate. They never flew very high, sometimes sweeping the ground, when they would give one of their graceful side turns.

Habitat and Distribution

The Cockatiel is endemic to almost the entire Australian land mass and is widely numerically distributed, despite the fact that in some regions there are more Cockatiels than in others. They are found mostly in arid and semi-arid terrains, but are uncommon in desert terrains unless there is an available nearby water source. Though the Cockatiels are nomadic and at times can be found along coastal areas, they prefer open areas provided there is a nearby water supply; this monotype is rarely found in heavily forested terrain.

While the species is common to most of Australia and many of its offshore islands, it was previously unknown in Tasmania, and when an infrequent Cockatiel was encountered there, it was normally considered an occasional vagrant, or an escaped pet. It is now found in small numbers in Tasmania, and is believed to have been accidentally introduced (Kavanau 1987), although its numbers and distribution have not been satisfactorily quantified.

In Queensland, in general, the Great Dividing Range appears to be its most eastern range of distribution, although there are variously reported individuals and small flocks observed in some coastal areas from time to time. Similarly, while the species does not inhabit the Cape York Peninsula, Brigadier H.R. Officer (in Cayley 1974) had reported seeing small flocks as far north as the Princess Charlotte Bay during its unpredictable nomadic movements.

The species is common throughout most of New South Wales, Victoria, and South Australia, excepting the fertile southeastern coastal regions. In Western Australia, it is common throughout the entire state, and is particularly populous in the southwestern portion of the state. In North Australia it is found throughout the state except for Arnhem Land.

The Cockatiel is a social, gregarious bird commonly found in flocks numbering from as few as half a dozen individuals to flocks numbering in the thousands, particularly in the northern reaches of its distribution. Because the bird is so numerous, it is impossible to quantify or even roughly estimate its numbers. Suffice it to say, the species enjoys a healthy population.

The Cockatiel is both migratory and nomadic; its nomadicism even surpasses that of the Galah Cockatoo (*Eolophus roseicapilla*). But while all cockatiels are nomadic, various localized populations of the species are not migratory; the migratory patterns of behavior are region or locality specific and directly related to regional water availability. Whether migratory or not, Cockatiels are confronted with wide daily and seasonal variances in temperature, as high as blistering heat during the summer and near freezing temperatures during winter (Allen and Allen 1981).

The distance the Cockatiel travels from one region to another varies considerably, correlated with the weather and the particular part of the country the bird inhabits. In general, Cockatiels inhabiting both the drier interior and more southern latitudes of the Australian continent, where weather patterns are more consistent, predictably migrate annually on a north–south basis. At the end of each long-distance migration, however, the birds resume local nomadic behavior at their new destination, much of this local nomadism again shaped by both food and water considerations.

Populations in the northern latitudes of Western Australia, Northern Territory, and Queensland are not migratory but are primarily opportunistically nomadic in behavior, their movements taking them into more hospitable coastal regions when climatic conditions are unfavorable in the northern interior. Movements of northern populations cover shorter distances in their search for water and do not reflect any given seasonal regularity of movement on a north–south basis. The extent of migration and nomadism is for the most part conditioned by the adequacy, or lack of it, of seasonal rains in the interior regions of the continent. While a significant proportion of the species' population is migratory, in general these migrations are both unpredictable and intermittent, the unpredictability being directly correlated with the severity of drought conditions and the fact that the birds do not always instinctively migrate to a specific region. For example, in 1907 Batey observed that the species was completely unknown in his area prior to 1853, but that a few years later they bred in large numbers in his region, only to be absent again for some years afterwards. Then, again, a few years following later, a small number of individuals were once more observed in his region. Batey's observations of the infrequency of the species' migrations to his area are typical of numerous other similar observations made by field naturalists over much of the country during the course of the past century.

Because much of Australia is arid and droughts are common, the Cockatiel's widespread distribution throughout the continent has proven the species' adaptability.

In South Australia, for example, during prolonged and severe drought conditions, Cockatiels can be found in coastal regions (Frith 1969), so close to the ocean that they can be found near sand dunes (J.W. Mellor, in Mathews 1916), areas that are not part of their normal habitat. Similarly in the north, in the Cape York Peninsula, which the species does not usually inhabit, Crawford (1972) found after six years of field observations of northern Cockatiel populations during the 1970s that nomadic excursions into northern Cape York terrains were directly related to water supply in the immediate south.

But while seasonal rains are unpredictable in many arid regions of Australia, contemporary agricultural practices to increase farm production have resulted in the proliferation of permanent ponds, some streams, and otherwise permanent water resources, ensuring year-round water availability in many regions, all which benefit localized populations.

Migration into regions where the species was hitherto unreported led some naturalists to argue that the species was gradually extending its range of distribution into the eastern and southern regions of the continent. Lendon (in Cayley 1974), for example, cited recent incidences of breeding pairs in the Adelaide area as evidence of expansion.[23]

Propagation

In the wild, the Cockatiel is believed to pair for life, the male and female developing a strong bond with each other early in their relationship, a pair bonding that may be life long and quite stable, although this is not well documented (Smith 1978). It is estimated that in the wild males reach sexual maturity at approximately thirteen months while females reach theirs at approximately 18 months. (Spoon and Milliam 2006).

The courtship behavior of the species is ritualistic. When looking for a mate, the male whistles various mating calls and songs, and interested females respond in muted chirps. The male approaches the female with his wings lifted up and away from the body, his crest depressed, and his head lowered, accompanied by a constant whistling call. The courtship behavior is reminiscent of the begging sounds that are associated with a Cockatiel's soliciting a preening from another. An accommodating female's tail is held erect, indicating her willingness and readiness. The female's head is usually preened during the courtship. This behavior is part of the pair bonding process (Smith 1978), which implies a monogamous pairing: a hen already paired will raise her crest to discourage other would-be suitors. Copulation takes place shortly after head preening, and continues later throughout incubation and brooding.

The biological mechanics of copulation and later egg laying are interesting phenomenon. As noted above, there are several copulation couplings. The female's oviduct tract provides the male's spermatozoa an environment that encourages its longevity for over a month therein, thereby enabling the hen to continue laying eggs even should the male be absent. Once a nest location has been decided upon, the hen will lay an egg every other day (Spoon and Milliam 2006; Kavanau 1987). The average clutch is four to seven eggs, and it has been found in aviary breeding that once a clutch has hatched, since both adults contribute to the feeding of the young, some females may begin laying a second clutch if there is another nesting box nearby. Because the female is a determinate bird in its egg laying, and spermatozoa are still viable in her oviducts, she will continue laying eggs, the nest box, acting as a catalyst. (In captivity, the hen is usually not provided a second nest box in order to allow the bird to rest from the chick-raising ordeal.)

The Cockatiel's breeding season varies significantly according to the time of year, the amount of daylight, and the onset of rains. When the seasonal black clouds begin developing, indicating the beginning of the rains, "cockatiels call excitedly to one another as they fly from perch to perch. The excitement ... usually elicits a frenzy of sexual display by the males ... who search for nest holes accompanied by the hen" (Smith 1978). Depending on the region, breeding may begin as early as July and as late as November or December. If there has been an abundant autumn and winter rainfall, MacGillivray noted in 1910 that breeding often begins as early as May.

While breeding generally takes place in the latter half of the year, irrespective of latitude where the species is located, nests can be found almost any time following rainfalls. Moreover, within a given locality the breeding season of the species may stretch over several months.

Since the species is known to produce successive clutches in captivity, successfully fledging their young, it is highly probable that in the wild numerous pairs attempt more than one clutch per season, even though there appears to be no field evidence to support this assumption.

As the migration of hundreds to thousands of birds begins to reach its final destination, paired birds drop off wherever there is some promise of ample food supply (MacGillivray 1913), nest opportunities, and fresh water nearby. By the end of the flock's migration, the population of breeding pairs may be dispersed considerably, given that their preferred habitat is not heavily forested and hence nest sites are more infrequent. Usually a given locality will be populated by numerous breeding pairs. Because of suitable nesting site shortages, at times more than one pair may choose to nest in the same tree (Austin 1967). The choices of possible nesting sites will vary accordingly to the trees available to the Cockatiels.

Generally, dead trees are preferred, particularly those found along creek beds. While the Cockatiel tends to prefer taller trees when they are available, given the wide variation of terrains to which the species migrates, particularly when forced into alien localities because of drought, the Cockatiel can be found nesting at almost ground level in mallee shrubs (MacGillivray, in Mathews 1916). Grant in 1912 wrote that he "found them breeding in the dead Box Trees almost at water level."

A suitable nesting site is normally a hollow in a dead limb. The eggs are laid on the rotting wood and earthy materials usually found at the bottoms of such hollows. Frequently, the Cockatiel chooses a nesting site that is commodious enough to admit larger birds, such as the larger species of cockatoos. Both adults alternate during incubation, the male normally sitting during the daylight hours from early morning to late in the afternoon, and the female sitting at night, the male perched close by. The eggs begin hatching 21 to 23 days after the sitting begins. Feeding the young is equally shared by both parents via allofeeding; parents are as attendant to their feeding responsibilities as they were to sitting their clutch. As soon as one adult has alighted at the nest to regurgitate food to the young and flies away to forage more food, the other parent is shortly thereafter there to feed the young (Bennet 1912). In 2006 Spoon and Milliam concluded that clutch size, number of successful fledglings, and the psycho-social elements comprising reproduction strongly correlate with the compatibility, or lack of it, of the mated pair.

The young fledge three to five weeks after fledging and become totally independent four to five weeks later.

Aviary Notes

The Cockatiel is an ideal aviary subject. It is has a delightful personality, which makes it an endearing bird as a pet companion, and which makes it easy to sell, if that is an objective of the breeder; and, if breeding the species is not considered a business venture, the sales of a few young over the course of the year help offset the operational costs, particularly of seeds.

The Cockatiel is a prolific breeder: it is hardy, not too demanding, and it can be bred peacefully in colonies, even in the company of other avian species. The species has been bred countless times in captivity, everywhere around the globe where there are aviculturalists. Next to the common Budgie, the Cockatiel is the second most popular bird companion in captivity. Indeed, anyone interested in breeding the species will be delighted to know that avicultural expertise is not essential to assist nature taking its course, except for the commonsense provision of adequate accommodations, and food and water for the birds, just as one would provide the necessities of life for a pet cat or dog.

Uniquely, the Cockatiel is a species of a bird that has been hybridized into a remarkable variety of colors, patterns, and diverse color mutations. The species has been color-and-pattern mutated into a host of distinctive combinations rarely encountered in nature: the most common and immediately recognizable of the color mutations is the Albino Cockatiel, a hybrid either distinctly pure white or yellow washed, and which is extremely popular as a bird companion. Numerous other "wild" or "pied" mutations have been developed through selective breeding; these mutations involve a variety of color combinations, dramatically differing from the normal grey color or color patterns of the Cockatiel in the wild. There are at least twelve to thirteen color mutations and patterns, many of them now considered legitimate hybrids.

While the genetics of hybridization is an interesting and challenging avicultural pursuit, a full discussion of the topic cannot be herein explored: it is simply too complex and diverse to be adequately attempted.[3]

A few additional words on the species' breeding history may be interesting to consider. While it is not known exactly where or when the first captive breeding occurred, Prestwick believes that it was in France prior to 1850. Confirmed successes in France were reported in number by the 1870s, in Britain in 1863, in Belgium in 1876, in Germany in 1858, and in the United States in 1909. Indeed, the species' commonality and prolificacy as an aviary subject motivated Edwards in 1935 to cynically write, "Now there are so many bred in California [alone] that there is almost an oversupply."

As noted above, the Cockatiel is a prolific breeder in captivity. A small sampling of the literature will suffice to provide the reader with some indication as to why they are so popular: five mated pairs gave Mrs. Oliver Cilmer a total of sixty fledged young in one year; Moore, in Auckland, New Zealand, had a pair that had 100 surviving offspring over nine breeding seasons; Seth-Smith had a pair that raised sixteen young from March to September; Sumner Marriner reported that his pair from 1910 to 1911 had five nests of four hatchlings each, and in 1911 alone raised eighteen young from 22 eggs; Professor G.A. Hubbard wrote of a hen he had that over ten years gave four clutches of four to six young each year. Clemitson wrote that his pair had 33 young over three seasons.[4] These kinds of reproductive successes are common.

While obviously not all pairs produce as many young as the pairs cited above, the simple unblemished fact is that the average cockatiel is not only a prolific breeder, but is also a responsible attending parent. Two or three clutches per year consisting of three or four surviving juveniles per clutch are average reproduction rates. In large-scale Cockatiel breeding farms, particularly Cockatiel factories, hens that do not consistently produce clutches of four to five eggs minimally are routinely weeded out.

On the individual basis, some hens are extremely fecund. There are a number of confirmed reports of hens laying nine or more eggs per clutch, of which most of the young are successfully hatched and reared to fledgling age.[5]

The Cockatiel will breed year round, and in northern climates such as found in Europe or the United States and Canada, the birds can be successfully bred indoors during the winter months, providing of course the birds are given lengthy (artificial) daylight hours, as would be the case during the breeding season in the wild. While there are some Cockatiels that will mate as young as five months of age, most breeders discourage premature pairing and wait until the birds are minimally eight months old, or older, an age lower than the generally held view that males are sexually mature at thirteen months while females are at eighteen months.

As with many game birds, Cockatiel hens will begin laying fertile clutches long after the initial copulation (Smith 1978). Once a clutch has hatched, and just prior to the juvenile's fledging, a second nest box placed near the first will usually act as a catalyst stimulating the hen's reproductive drive, and be sufficient inducement for her to abandon her first already-hatched clutch to the care of the male, and begin laying a second clutch. Again, this is possible because the pair copulates regularly, even during brooding, and the spermatozoa deposited in the hen's reproductive tract remains viable for at least four weeks. Most breeders, however, as noted earlier, prefer to rest the hen between clutches.

The Cockatiel will accept almost any type of nest facility. It has even been known to lay clutches on the bare ground, successfully rearing the clutch. Most breeders provide their birds with a nest box hung in the upper reaches of the aviary. In colony breeding, a number of nest boxes are placed throughout the flight, and after a brief period following the nest boxes' introduction to the aviary, the pairs soon begin showing signs of interest in breeding and nesting.

The nest boxes should be approximately 15 cm × 15 cm × 22 cm (6" × 6" × 8.5") high, preferably covered by a roof that is hinged, and with an entrance hole placed about 7–8 cm (3–4") from the top of the nest box; a thin layer of nontoxic sawdust can be placed within to serve as nesting material. A suitably sized aviary for one or two pairs including both the flight and shelter—in climatic areas where shelter is essential—would be approximately 3 meters long by 1.5 meters wide, and 2 meters high (9' × 5' × 6').

In colony breeding, several pairs can be introduced into the flight without the possibility of aggressive behavior developing, provided the flight is big enough. For example, in 1937 Bauer placed eight pairs in a pen that was 7 meters long × 3.5 meters wide × 2 meters high (23' × 12' × 6'). In colony breeding, all nest boxes should be alike in order to minimize quarrelling between pairs. Note, also, there should not be an excessive number of males in such colonies if the birds released therein are not yet paired.

For serious amateur aviculturalists with limited space for aviaries, the Cockatiel easily lends itself to breeding in mixed company and can usually defend its nest site quite successfully against more aggressive species such as broadtails, so long as the aviary is long enough.

After the introduction of the nest box and the pair's acceptance of it, the first egg is usually laid within a day or so, that egg followed by a second, an egg each second day following, until the clutch is complete. Since the hens are determinate egg layers, broken or lost eggs are soon replaced until the hen reaches her genetically programmed number of eggs laid to complete her clutch. Since the male never enters the nest until the entire clutch is complete, it is easy to calculate how many eggs are in the clutch, by the number of days that have elapsed before the cock first entered the nest.

Because the Cockatiel is a determinate layer, removal of eggs will not induce the hen to lay more eggs than would be her normal clutch. When a hen appears to be brooding but is unable to lay eggs, for whatever reason, if eggs are provided for her to sit and brood, she will frequently be induced to lay her own clutch after the foster young have fledged. Some hens will even begin laying if provided foster eggs when the hen appears actually brooding but has not yet laid eggs.

As noted earlier, the male sits during the day, and the female at night. The eggs begin hatching in two-day intervals after the 21st and 23rd day after being laid. Both parents brood the young. After approximately ten days after the eggs have hatched, the parents begin leaving the nest for extended periods, leaving the young unattended. The hen will continue to brood during the night, however, until the young fledge.

When hatched, the young are sparsely clothed in wispy strands of yellow down. Their eyes remain closed for approximately a week. Within a few days after hatching, their crests become quite noticeable. Young nestlings, when frightened, will hiss and sway back and forth. At approximately 35 days of age, the juveniles fledge, but they do not always fly upon fledging. When first flying, the juveniles prove to be strong flyers, and it is not unusual for a youngster testing its wings to kill itself by flying against the aviary mesh.

Those fledglings still unable to fly but now out of the nest will often cluster in a corner of the flight, huddled against each other. Juvenile Cockatiels become totally independent approximately three weeks after fledging.

The feed normally offered the young consists of canary seed, oats, sunflower seeds and bread soaked in milk. Some breeders provide a limited amount of greens for brooding pairs. There should always be fresh water, as well as cuttlebone.

For the most part, Cockatiels prove to be dutiful parents. At times, however, first-time parents may throw out either their young or the eggs from the nest. In such instances, if placed with an older and experienced pair, the rejects will be reared by the foster parents.

Some hens prove to be incorrigible. In 1931 Macklin lamented about one hen he had that produced several clutches consisting of 36 eggs in total—all which were either thrown out of the nest or totally ignored. Some Cockatiels are known to pluck their nestling's plumage, and have also been known to pluck them once they have fledged whenever they are perched nearby. Also, at times, if a second nest is not provided while a pair is brooding its current young, the hen may begin a second clutch in the same nest box before the first round of juveniles have fledged. At times, some hens have been known to chew at their young. Such problems, however, are the exception and not the rule.

Pet Companion

The Cockatiel makes an ideal pet companion, regardless of the age or sex of the owner. It proves itself not only a delightful companion, but compared to other cockatoos species, or other parrots, in fact, its needs are simple: while it proves itself friendly and can be trained to perform some minor tricks, it is not emotionally demanding, requiring three or more hours of daily interaction as needed by other species to ensure that it does not develop neurotic behaviors out of sheer boredom—behaviors such as plucking out their breast feathers, or shrieking uncontrollably at various times and completely alienating all neighbors near and far, including often family members.

Its housing needs are modest: a cage a meter cubed (3' × 3' × 3') is more than enough to provide ample living space for the bird, and if one's household is limited in size, an even smaller cage will suffice. Additionally, because of its size the Cockatiel is not as destructive of toys and branches as are other species of cockatoos.

Its personality attributes are legendary. They are hardy, and enjoy a marked longevity given their size: Colleen Clancy of California, for example, had a cockatiel that lived to be 29 years old. And her cockatiel was not an exception. They can be taught a variety of tricks, an ability that was recognized in the late 1800s: Dr. Greene, concerning a cockatiel he had, wrote, "He will perform all matter of little tricks, such as kissing his mistress, pretending to be dead, flying out the window and returning at the word of a command."

Cockatiels are not recognized as accomplished mimics, but if acquired as young birds, preferably as pre-fledglings requiring some hand feeding, the young Cockatiel can occasionally be taught a limited vocabulary. As a general rule, however, adult birds rarely learn to mimic human sounds, although they do have a reputation for being excellent whistlers.

The Cockatiel proves to be an exceptional pet companion, and a strong bond can be developed with this diminutive bird. Over the years this writer has had several, two of which immediately come to mind. One, a lutino, named Sylvester, was always free to come and go out of his cage. On my arrival home from running some errand or another, Sylvester would immediately fly from his cage to sit on my shoulder. Another cockatiel, named Tweedy Bird, often became distressed when there were guests visiting, and would fly about the house looking for me, and once having found me, would land on my shoulder and insist on remaining there until the guests departed. She was so completely attached to me that she would permit herself to be gently placed in my coat pocket with only her head showing.

While many Cockatiel owners keep their birds locked in their cages most of the time, a bird that has some freedom outside the cage—if it is trained to view its cage as its sanctuary—will rarely depart from its immediate vicinity. The trick is to clip two of the leading primary flight feathers from a wing: clip only halfway down to their base so that the blood vein is not cut. By clipping the flight feathers, the bird will be unable to fly, and should it fall from its cage or its perch, it will be able to glide to the floor without injury.

Once the bird tries to leave the cage by flying away, it will realize that flight is no longer an available option. It learns quickly that its place is either on or in its cage. As the bird is sitting on its perch, if a finger is thrust perpendicular against its breast, if will reflexibly step onto the finger, as if stepping onto a branch. Then, transfer the bird to your shoulder. It will step off. It will soon discover that being on your finger, or shoulder, is natural and comfortable. Give it a treat, a seed. Walking about the house doing one's chores with your pet companion on your shoulder is an excellent opportunity to talk to it, to whistle, and to gently scratch its crest. It will soon be begging for the scratch. When returning the bird to its cage, either offer it your finger, or bend over to allow the bird to climb onto its cage. You will find after a while that locking the bird inside will not be necessary. And your pet Cockatiel will be a pleasant companion.

Chapter Notes

Chapter 1

1. Carol Highall, Dr. Bob's All Creatures Pet Health Site, http://www.petdoc.ws/.

2. Dr. Greene was a significant contributor to literature on avian issues, was an avid collector with extensive aviaries, and had a wealth of experience. As was his custom, confirmed by observers reporting on some of Dr. Greene's activities in various avicultural publications, Dr. Greene permitted some of his more tamed cockatoos freedom to fly about freely, like domesticated pigeons—and this in Great Britain, not too far from London.

Chapter 2

1. International Association of Avian Trainers and Educators, http://www.parrots.org/index.php/encyclopedia/wildstatus/moluccan—cockatoo.

2. The Moluccan Cockatoo makes liberal use of the powder its gland copiously produces to groom itself. If house dusting is not a regular daily chore, evidence of the powder will be found throughout the house, or bird room, within a few days.

Chapter 3

1. AnAge: The Animal Aging and Longevity Data Base, "Cacatua Sulphurea," 2012, http://www.genomics.senescence.info/species/entry.php?species_Cacatua_sulphurea.

2. See Habitat and Distribution, later in this chapter, concerning the state of the four subspecies in the wild.

3. CITES protects species by making the trade of wild-caught birds illegal. Any rare bird bred in captivity is given a CITES certificate, ostensibly proving it is captive bred. The certificate must accompany the bird's sale or resale (Innskipp et al.).

4. Early field ornithologists usually captured birds in the field, measured them, noted their colors, etc., and released them. But some of the time birds were simply killed and sometimes skinned for detailed measurement and study at a later date in a laboratory, usually in a European university or museum setting. Once a sufficient set of data had been acquired through these methods, a portrait emerged based on the number of birds studied: typical wingspan, coloration, weight, male–female differences, and so on. The bird type was then given a name by the field worker (usually a European) who first "discovered" it. Once the biological parameters had been ascertained, other similar-looking cockatoos discovered elsewhere were also collected and studied, and those new sets of data were compared to the original set of compiled statistics; if there was a similarity between the two populations, but some minor differences between them, the second bird type would be taxonomically classified as a subspecies of the first. If not, it was identified as a different species. At times, there were heated disagreements concerning the bird's classification, based on the interpretation of the differences and/or similarities.

5. While estimates vary significantly, depending on the scientists and the diverse scientific communities, it is believed that in the Amazonian rain forests alone there are at least a million undiscovered species, from insect to mammal to plant. And that is considered a conservative estimate. Not a week goes by without a new insect being discovered, an orchid, a fish, and so on.

6. One need only compare the meager field data on non–Australian cockatoos, as an example, with the voluminous materials compiled on Australian species at the beginning of the last century to note a marked dissimilarity.

7. All species of the Lesser-crested Cockatoo are common only to Indonesia.

8. All four races of the Lesser-crested Cockatoo are fully protected in Indonesia. Under the country's laws, it is illegal to capture, trade or possess any of the species. Infraction of the laws can result in a liability of up to 200 million rupiahs fine (approximately $21,000), and up to five years' imprisonment (Convention). That is a substantial amount of money for the average Indonesian. Because so few birds still remain in the wild, and the penalties for poaching are so heavy, there are fewer birds being illegally captured for the pet trade. However, ironically, it is reported that since the birds are so rare, they are still being illegally poached, but now for government officials because owning such a rare bird bestows upon its owner

considerable prestige (Indonesian Parrot Project 2012).

9. The scientific community has long looked askance at aviculturalists for their lack of scientific inquiry and questionable record keeping, an assertion that has some merit given examples such as the Lesser-crested Cockatoo, which has been bred successfully countless times, and yet various important details pertaining to those breedings are neither recorded nor publically shared if they are recorded. This is of critical importance given the possibility of the Yellow-crested Cockatoo's extinction in the wilds, and of other comparable rare birds facing a similar fate. For an examination of this issue, see Edward J. Mulawka, "Responsible Aviculturalism," *Bird World*, July/August 1979, pp. 27–28.

Chapter 4

1. The cockatoo called Cocky (subspecies undisclosed) died at age 82+ as resident of the London Zoological Gardens, where it had lived for many years. The age of the bird was authenticated from zoo records (Bird Facts, http://www.weird facts.com/animal-facts/3241-birdfacts-html).

2. In 1899 Gurney published an article titled *On the Comparative Ages of Which Birds Live* in which he records the longevity of three cockatoos who had lived 80, 81, and 120 years (*Ibis* 41.1 [1899]: 19–42). There is also a reference to these birds in Arthur Prestwick, "After Four Years of It," *Aviculture Magazine,* 5th ser., 48 (1943): 160–63.

3. The Eleanor Cockatoo is often known as the Medium Sulphur-crested Cockatoo because of its smaller size compared to the other Sulphur-crested Cockatoos, but it is bigger than any of the Yellow-crested Cockatoos (*Cacatua sulphurea*).

4. Despite considerable controversy, poisons used under special license are still employed to destroy various animals, and are still minimally used to control avian invasion of crops. The poison commonly used is Compound 1080 Poison (sodium monofluoroacetate), a poison that is naturally found in forty Australian native plants. This particular poison is used because birds have a high tolerance to it, whereas various other life forms do not, and additionally, the compound when mixed with water is a color that does not attract species whose harm is to be avoided. For additional information on this product and its usage contact the Department of Primary Industries, Parks, Waters, and Environment, GPO, Box 44, Hobart, Tasmania, Australia 7001 (re: AgDex 685, Number 14, Issn 8759-2).

Chapter 5

1. Beauty of Birds, "Blue-eyed Cockatoos," http://beautyofbirds.com/blueeyedcockatoo.html.

2. What is required to keep the Blue-eyed Cockatoo physically and emotionally healthy while in captivity is not completely understood, and it is therefore generally believed that the species probably lives longer in the wild than in captivity.

3. Planet of Birds, http://www.planetofbirds.com/psittaciformes-cacatuidae-blue-eyedcockatoo-cacatua-oph.

4. It is this color of the periophthalmic ring that gives the species its name, the Blue-eyed Cockatoo. Its eyes are not blue, however; the irises are rather brownish-black.

5. Various students of ornithology have commented on the Blue-eyed Cockatoo's similarity to the sulphur-crested group (see Forshaw 1977, p. 131, for example), and for a while it was considered a form of the sulphur-crested species.

6. The Blue-eyed Cockatoo is the only cockatoo species in eastern New Guinea.

7. Emphasis added.

8. Further information on the breeding program can be obtained from Mary Ellen LePage, (408) 997-3131, 15466 Los Gatos Blvd., Suite 105–198, Los Gatos, CA, 95032. Mail@birds2pet.

Chapter 6

1. Initially, the Slender-billed Cockatoo was considered the nominate race of two subspecies: the eastern Slender-billed Cockatoo (*Cacatua tenuirostris*) and the western version of the nominate race, the Western Long-billed Cockatoo (*Cacatua pastinator*). But there were some minor but important differences between the two: the *C. pastinator* was larger, had less color on the breast, including feathers in the nape region, and its beak was shorter. Yet despite the fact that the two subspecies were isolated at opposite ends of the island continent, there were sufficient similarities between the two subspecies to lead early field workers and ornithologists to conclude they were one species. Others differed in opinion. Because the *C. pastinator* closely resembled the Little Corella (*Ducorps Sanguinea*), some authorities such as Caley in 1973 even considered the *C. pastinator* as a race belonging to the *Ducorps Sangininea*. It was only recently that the *C. pastinator* was concluded to be a distinct race. It should be noted that the relationship between the Slender-billed Cockatoo and the Western Long-billed Cockatoo has provided ammunition for considerable disagreement.

2. The actual incubation period requires clarification. The San Diego Zoo reported that the incubation period was 29 days (Lint 1959), while the Adelaide Zoo, which reported its first successful breeding of the species, cited "approximately 24 days" (Lendon). All current literature cites the Adelaide Zoo's 24-day period as the actual incubation time required for hatching (e.g., Info Barrel; North West Bird Club; Birds in Back Yards; Zilva 2012; Bird Care 2012).

Chapter 7

1. The *Cacatua Pastinator Derbyi* was recently shown to be the senior name for the subspecies formerly known as *C.P. Butleri*, which had been named in honor of a Western Australian legend, naturalist W.H. (Harry) Butler (see J. Ford, Emu 85 (1887): 172–

176.). The species is still referred to by some as Butler's Cockatoo, or *C.P. Butlerii*.

2. World Parrot Trust, "Western Corella (*Cacatua pastinator*)," 2012, http://www.parrots.org/indexphp/encyclopedia/wildstatus/western_corella/.

3. Endangered. Schedule 1—Western Australian Wildlife Conservation Act.

4. Vulnerable, under Federal Environmental Protection and Biodiversity Conservation Act.

5. Ron Johnstone, Department of Terrestial Vertebrates, Western Australian Museum, Perth, 2011.

6. The species was placed on a protected list with fines of up to $10,000 levied on anyone convicted of poisoning or shooting the cockatoos. Additionally, zoos and aviculturalists were encouraged to breed the species in captivity to prevent it from becoming extinct. On Nov. 12, 2012, after 72 years, the government of Western Australia announced that the species was no longer in immediate danger of extinction.

Chapter 8

1. ICUN Red List, 2012, http://icunredlist.org/details106001408/0.

2. This observation may be based on aviculturalists' experience with the species in aviaries; the Ducorp's Corella is known to be aggressive to other birds within the aviary confines, including peers (Malyasia Bird Forum 2012).

3. For a delightful, well written piece on a companion Ducorp's Corella named Milo, owned by Tracy Muth, see http://www.angelfire.com/ak4/birds/dcmilo.html. Besides telling Ms. Muth he loves her, he kisses her with beak and sounds, likes to play catch, loves to wrestle with her, loves to be held, and has approximately forty words in his vocabulary.

Chapter 9

1. World Parrot Trust, "Goffin's Cockatoo (*Cacatua goffini*), 2012, http://parrots.org/index.php/encyclopedia/wildestatus/goffins-cockatoo.

Chapter 11

1. When the cockatoo was common throughout its entire distribution, Rand and Rabor wrote, "The irregularities in the pattern of geographical (size) permit no sub-species to be recognized," although it was recognized that variations in size were found between populations.

2. www.birdboutique.com/umcoc.html.

3. The Katala Foundation is a nonprofit, non-governmental organization founded to support wildlife programs, particularly to protect and preserve the critically endangered Red-vented Cockatoo. The foundation works in close collaboration with various European zoos and organizations to establish conservation programs, in addition to collaborating with Philippine groups and government agencies.

4. The cockatoo is protected by the Wildlife Conservation and Protection Act of the Philippines or Republic Act 9147. The Katala Foundation notes, "Vio-lations will lead to severe penalties and several years imprisonment."

Chapter 12

1. Government of Australia, http://www.galahs.galahs.com.au/content/php/article 048.php.

2. During the 1905 Royal Australian Ornithological Union's campout on Kangeroo Island, Mathews did not report one Galah. According to local residents the first birds were seen in 1929 and by 1950 were "firmly entrenched."

3. Boehm (1959) chronicled the pace of population expansion in the Mount Mary Plains region. The first Galah was reported seen in 1918. In 1923, a flock of five birds were present, and within a few years, flocks of twenty individuals were common. By 1938, in twenty years, flocks of up to 200 birds were occasionally encountered.

4. The problem of finding a suitable nesting site must involve considerable frustration for disappointed pairs, and acts of desperation are not at all unusual. Macgillivray (in Mathews 1916) observed a pair that had located a deep hollow, usually a preferred type of nesting site, but one that was so deep that the pair "was found to have essayed the impossible task of filling a hollow tree from the butt upwards and had put in over two feet of leaves before giving it up."

Chapter 13

1. It was originally believed that the species was endemic and distributed throughout Victoria. Mathews in 1913, for example, had included the full state as being part of the species' range. But even in Mathews' day, the Leadbeater was immensely popular, and it is highly probable that the occasional individuals sighted from time to time were escapees, or individuals deliberately released. It is found naturally, however, in Victoria's northern border region adjacent to South Australia.

Chapter 14

1. http://www.parrotlink.com.Home.ParrotProfiles.Cockatoos.

2. WWF, Government of Australia GPO 528, Sydney, NSW Australia.

3. The Marquess of Tavistock for years had an extensive aviary collection containing a considerable diversity of species. He was an accomplished aviculturalist, a field naturalist, and a prolific writer on diverse avian topics. His contributions based on his experiences are still invaluable almost a century later.

Chapter 15

1. S. Murphy, S. Legge, and R. Heinsohn, "The Breeding Biology of the Palm Cockatoo (*Probosciger aterrimus*): A Case Study of a Slow Life History, *Journal of Zoology* 261: 327–329.

2. Government of Australia, http://www.environ

ment.gov.au/biodiversity/threatened/publications/
action/birds2000/pubs/palm-cockatoo.pdf.

3. After studying the species' dusting behavior for numerous years, Dr. E.D. D'Ombrain (1933) wrote, "The usual gland over the end of the spine has a tuff of down feathers.... This is full of powder secreted by the gland. To use the powder, the bird throws the head completely back, at the same time elevating the end of the spine to meet the back of the head. The latter is then rubbed into the tuff and enough powder is obtained to dust over the whole of the feathers, including the under feathers."

4. For another interesting account of how the Palm Cockatoo manipulates the smallest of seeds, see D.T. Holyoak, "Adaptive Significance of Bill Shape in the Palm Cockatoo," *Aviculture Magazine* 70 (1972): 99–100.

5. It is possible that Eastman and Hunt's error stems from a reading of Dr. D'Ombrain's notes (1933) regarding his pet Palm Cockatoo, Tom. Dr. D'Ombrain wrote that the bird laid "usually two for a clutch, although it has been stated that only one is the clutch." Since Dr. D'Ombrain (in his description of nest construction that immediately preceded the above quotation) seems to have drawn heavily from the McLelland account (in Macgillivray,1914), it is quite probable that Dr. D'Ombrain either misread the summations of McLelland's field notes, or failed to recollect the details correctly. Whatever the case, what happened then is purely speculative at this point. It is clear, however, that Eastman and Hunt are totally in error and were quite remiss in not reviewing all the literature. As a matter of fact, there is only one published account of a two-egg clutch, that being at the San Diego Zoo in the United States in 1948; both eggs were infertile (Preswick 1948).

6. At the time of this writing (summer 2012), a search of the Internet identified six or seven advertisements of Palm Cockatoos for sale in the United States and Canada. The oldest cockatoo offered for sale was seventeen years old. The age of the others were undisclosed. Prices were $17,000 to $20,000 per bird. In researching the Internet under Palm Cockatoo (*Probisciger aterrimus*), a number of specialized breeders were also identified advertising the species—but either as "sold out" or suggesting that their Palm Cockatoos were currently brooding, and that young fledged Palm Cockatoos would be available in the near future.

7. The Palm Cockatoo was originally assumed to be related to the Macaw, and thus was called the Arara Cockatoo.

8. "Old Tom" is a misnomer, for after the bird had been in the D'Ombrain family for several years—all the while everyone assuming Tom was a cock—it began laying eggs. The name "Old Tom," however, remained the same.

Chapter 16

1. Dr. Bob's All Creatures Pet Health Site, http://www.petdoc.ws.

2. WWF, Government of Australia, GPO 528, Sydney, New South Wales, Australia.

3. The two-month span between laying and hatching is an obvious error either in the record keeping or in the editing of the final copy of the reporting publication. Sir Edward Hallstrom, who himself successfully bred the species in later years, reported that the incubation period was 29 days, which he personally knew was accurate because he had artificially incubated the egg (Proceedings, 10th Annual Ornithological Congress, 1950).

4. This writer once owned a delightful, engaging Blue-Fronted Amazon (*Amazona aestiva*) named Pow-Pow for over twenty years. He was a television star on several occasions. Pow-Pow had an amazing repertoire of slightly more than 300 words and phrases. Every time he would utter something we thought was new, a list attached to the kitchen fridge door was checked, and if it was new, the word was added to the list. Pow-Pow acquired his vocabulary by mimicking everyday household conversations and television programs—some of the TV expressions were embarrassing, given the modern, spicy dialogue expressed by some movie characters.

5. At the time when we had Pow-Pow as a pet, a parrot that had been on television several times, we were living in a small town in Ontario, Canada. One day the bird became listless and stopped eating. Had there been a local veterinarian I would have immediately solicited his medical advice. But the nearest city with an avian veterinary specialist was in Toronto, four driving hours distant. The following afternoon I left Pow-Pow with the specialist, who called later that evening to inform us that Pow-Pow had expired, cause unknown. A good rule of thumb regarding a bird's health is that if it eats nothing one day, be concerned: if it eats nothing the following day, be distressed enough to seek professional assistance, immediately.

Chapter 17

1. Although three subspecies have been more or less accepted as types of Black Glossy Cockatoo, there is some disagreement concerning this classification based on Forshaw and Cooper's argument that the differences between subspecies are minimal at best, the size being a point of contention disagreed with by others.

2. Government of Australia, http://www.glossyblack.org.au/glossy-fact-sheet.html.

3. In North America, there were sport shootings similar to the Australian cockatoo slaughters, in that in a very short span of a few years over sixty million buffalo were slaughtered, almost invariably simply for sport shooting. Hunters such as the notorious Buffalo Bill killed hundreds per day, day after day, and became famous for it. But unlike Australia, there was never much public resistance to the continued slaughter of the buffalo, as there was to the organized sport of shooting captive cockatoos.

4. Hallstrom was elated to report that one Glossy female actually laid a clutch of two eggs that measured 32.0–36.0 mm (1.3"–1.4") in length and 25.0–28.2 mm (1"–1.1") in diameter. He described the eggs as

fairly smooth and lustreless. It is unclear whether the eggs hatched and, if so, whether the nestlings fledged.

Chapter 18

1. http://www.parrotlink.com.home.parrotprofiles.cockatoos.
2. http://www.birdlife.org/datazone/speciesfactsheet/php?id=1392.

Chapter 19

1. Bird Care, "White-tailed Black Cockatoo," http://www.birdcare.com.au/white_tailed_black_cockatoo/htm.

Chapter 20

1. On YouTube (http://www.youtube.com/), using the search term "Yellow-tailed Black Cockatoos as pets," there are a host of videos taken of the cockatoo in urban settings, from front yards to decorative garden bushes, in a variety of urban and suburban communities: the number of postings strongly suggests that the species is far more common in heavily populated areas than many naturalists or ornithologists believe is the case. (There were no videos, however, showing yellow-tailed black cockatoos as pet companions.)
2. The mean average age of the nesting trees preferred by the cockatoo is 221 years, the age accounting for its height and diameter. As forestry policies favor harvesting the largest trees, the number of suitable nesting sites is reduced. Current silvicultural proposals for a rotation time for harvesting trees is 80–150 years, which is insufficient time for trees to acquire the desirable height and size preferred by breeding pairs (Nelson and Morris 1994).
3. The reasons for relegating one nestling to an almost certain death are not well understood. However, it is clear that the evolutionary process enhances the probability that there will be at least one surviving nestling per nest, for should the first egg fail to hatch, or should that first nestling perish, the second nestling's survival will prove the nesting successful.

Chapter 21

1. The Cockatiel was not considered a member of the cockatoo family, and was consequently misclassified as belonging to the Broad-tailed Parakeets, among other misclassifications, despite the fact that the form had some obvious cockatoo similarities: the crest as a communication device, for example. For a variety of reasons, it was excluded as a member of the *Familia Cacatuidae* in most taxonomical system classifications, despite contrary professional opinions by noted ornithologists such as Salvadori (1891), Lendon (1951), Forshaw (1969), Holyoak (1972), and Courtney (1974) (see Courtney 1974). In 1984 the species' status was finally settled once and for all: a molecular study of the bird's protein allozymes proved that the Cockatiel had a much closer relationship to cockatoos than to other parrot species (Adams, et al., 1984), and that its mitochondrial 12SrRNA sequence demonstrated that the species was distinctly related to the dark cockatoos (Brown et al. 1999).

Additionally, it should be noted, the Cockatiel is related to all other cockatoos because it not only has an erectile crest, but has powder down, a gall bladder, and various color combinations rarely found outside the Cockatoo family. It should be noted that despite this biological evidence, there is still some opposition to the Cockatiel's inclusion in the cockatoo family.
2. There have been numerous references in the literature concerning the species near Adelaide. For example, Ashby (in Mathews 1916) wrote of a small flock observed over the city in 1900, and a flock of some thirty or so individuals in the nearby hills during 1906 or 1907. Similarly, Captain White (in Mathews 1916) wrote, "This was a numerous bird in the late summer on the Adelaide plains.... They are seldom, if ever, seen here now [1916]."

In fact, the Adelaide area was always part of the species' migratory route in the past. Captain White attributed the decline in numbers to their capture by bird catchers; this may have been the case a century ago, but what was basically unknown by field observers in Adelaide and elsewhere at the time and until recently was that the species was nomadic in nature.
3. There is ample biological avicultural literature regarding hybridization available for breeders.
4. See *Aviculture* (1943, pp. 18 and 42; 1944, pp. 139 and 187; and 1945, pp. 285 and 342). See also *Aviculture Magazine* (1931, p. 30; 1954, p. 35; and 1900, p. 3).
5. See, for example, Hamilton Scott in *Aviculture Magazine* 8 (1930): 224; or John Bauer, *Aviculture* 1937, p. 67, and 1940, p. 93.

Bibliography

Introduction

Alderton, David. 2002. "Parrots." *The Guardian* (Manchester, UK) April 6.

Cameron, Matt. 2007. *Cockatoos*. Collingwood, Australia: CSIRO.

McMillan, R.J. 1997. "Land of Parrots: An Historical Sketch." Parrot Society. http://www.parrot society.org.au/articles/art_032.htm.

Penelope, E. 2012. *The Library of History of Diodorus Siculus*. Chicago: University of Chicago Press.

Chapter 1

Alderton, David. 2003. *The Ultimate Encyclopaedia of Caged and Aviary Birds*. London: Hermes House.

Arndt, T., and T. Pittman. 2003. "White Cockatoos." Lexicon of Parrots. Bretten, Germany: Arndt.

Avian Companions. 2012. "Umbrella Cockatoo." http://www.aviancompanions.com/umbrella. htm.

Beauty of Birds. 2012. "Umbrella Cockatoos aka White Cockatoos, Umbrella Cockatoos." http: //www. beautyofbirds.com/umbrellacockatoos. html.

Birdlife International. 2001. *Threatened Birds of Asia: The Bird Life International Red Data Book*. Cambridge, UK: Birdlife International.

_____. 2012. "Bird Life Fact Sheet: White Cockatoo (*Cacatua Alba*)." http://www.birdlife.org/ datazone/speciesfactsheet.php?id=1402.

Clubb, Susan. 2012. "Umbrella Cockatoo." http:// www.susanclubb.com/pdfs/umbrcock.pdf.

Forshaw, Joseph M. 1977. *Parrots of the World*. Neptune, NJ: TFH.

Greene, W.T. 1979. *Parrots in Captivity*. Originally published in three volumes between 1884 and 1887. Neptune, NJ: TFH.

Guinn, D.S. 1970. "Umbrella Crested Cockatoos." *Aviculture*, pp. 3–9.

Highall, Carol. 2012. "Dr. Bob's All Creatures Pet Health Site." http:www.petdoc.com.

Indonesia Parrot Protection for Life. 2006. "Kakatua Putih—Cacatua Alba—White Cockatoo." http: //indonesiaparrotprotection.wordpress.com/ parrot-centre/parrot-information/kakatua.

IUCN Red List. 2006. "Cacatua Alba." http:// www.iucnredlist.org/details/22684789/0.2012.

Juniper, T., and M. Parr. 1998. *Parrots: A Guide to the Parrots of the World*. East Sussex, UK: Pica.

Lane, E. 2004. "Cacatua Alba White Cockatoo." Animal Diversity Web. http://animaldiversity. ummz.umich.edu/site/accounts/information/ Cacatua_alba.html. Accessed July 29, 2012.

Lantermann, W., S. Lantermann, and M. Vriends. 2000. *Cockatoos: A Complete Pet Owner's Manual*. Hong Kong: Barron's.

Mulawka, Edward J. 1981. *Taming and Training Parrots*. Neptune, NJ: TFH.

Plath, Karl, and Malcolm Davis. 1971. *This Is the Parrot*. Neptune, NJ: TFH.

Prestwick, Arthur. 1951. *Records of Parrots Bred in Captivity*. Vol. 2: *Cockatoos and McCaws*. London, UK: Self-published.

Risdon, S.D. 1968. "The Breeding of a Young Umbrella Cockatoo." *Aviculture Magazine* 74: 15–16.

Schneider, Paul E. 1960. "Breeding of the Umbrella or Great White Crested Cockatoo." *Aviculture Magazine* 66: 208.

World Parrot Trust. 2012. "White Crested Cockatoo." http://www.parrots.or/index.php/encyclo pedia/pofile/white_crested_cockatoo/.

Chapter 2

Avian Companions. 2012. "Moluccan Cockatoos." http://www.aviancompanions.com/moluccan. htm.

Avicultural Bulletin. 1974. September, p. 144.

Beauty of Birds. 2011. "Moluccan or Salmon-crested Cockatoos." http://www. beautyofbirds. com/moluccancockatoos.html.

Bird Care. 2012. "Salmon-crested Cockatoo." http: //www.birdcare.com.au/salmon_crested_cocka too.htm.

Greene, W.T. 1979. *Parrots in Captivity*. Originally published in three volumes between 1884 and 1887. Neptune, NJ: TFH.

International Association of Avian Trainers and Educators. 2012. "Moluccan Cockatoos (*Cacatua moluccensis*)." http://www.iaate.org/companion-parrots/171-moluccan-cockatoo-fact-sheet.

IUCN Red List. 2012. "*Cacatua Moluccensis*." http://www.iucnredlist.org/details/22684784/0.

Jones, Major V. Dilwyn. 1961. "News and Views." *Aviculture Magazine* 67: 152.

Kinnaird, M.F., T.G. O'Brien, F.R. Lambert, and D. Purmiasa. 2003. "Density and Distribution of the Endemic Seram Cockatoo *Cacatua moluccensis* in Relation to Land Use Patterns." *Biological Conservation* 109: 227–235.

Lint, Kenton C. 1951. "Breeding of the Rose Breasted Cockatoo (*Cacatua moluccensis*)." *Aviculture* 57: 223–24.

O'Connor, Neil. 1972. "Breeding of the Moluccan Cockatoo." *Aviculture Magazine* 78: 4–7.

Schonwetter, M. 1964. *Handbuch der Oologie*. Berlin: Akademie-Verlag.

Stott, Ken. 1951. "Parrots in the Zoological Gardens of San Diego." *Aviculture* 57: 68–71.

Streseman, E. 1952. "On the Birds Collected by Pierre Poivre in Canton, Manila, India, and Madagascar (1751–56)." *Ibis* 94.3: 511.

World Parrot Trust. 2012. "Moluccan Cockatoo I (*Cacatua moluccensis*)." http://www.parrots.org/index.php/encyclopedia/wildstatus/moluccan_cockatoo.

Wright, Vance. 1948. "Hand-feeding Parrot-like Birds." *Aviculture* 18: 35–36.

Chapter 3

Agista, D., and D. Rubyanto. 2001. "Telaahj awal status: Penyeybaran dan Populasi Kakatua-kecil jambul-kuning (Cacatua sulphurea parvula) di Taman Nasional Komodo, Nusa Tenggara Timur." PHKA/Birdlife International—Indonesia programme. Bangor, Laporan No. M17.

Agista, D., Sumardin, A. Hamid, F.M. Malo, S. Alam, Harjun, and C. Mamengko. 2001. "Telaah awal status, penyebaran dan populasi Kakatua-kecil jambul-kuning, (*Cacatua sulphurea parvula*) di Taman Nasional Rawa Aopa Watumohai, Sulawesi Tenggara dan Pulau Pasoso, Salawesi Tengah." PHKA/BirdLife Inter-national-Indonesia Programme. Bogar. Laporan No. 16.

AnAge: The Animal Aging and Longevity Data Base. 2012. "*Cacatua sulphurea*." http://www.geomicshttp://www.genomics.senescence.info/species/entry.php?species=Cacatua_sulphurea.

Animal World. 2012. "Lesser Sulphur Crested Cockatoo." http://www.animal-world.com/encyclo/birds/cockatoos/lessersulphur.php.

Arndt-Verlag. 2012. "*Cacatua-sulphurea* (Gmelin, 1788)." http://www.arndt-verlag.com/project/projekt/parsi.cgi?Desc=E063.htm&Pic=063_1.JPG.

Behrens, S. 1995. "Ein Hilferuf fur den Gelbwangenkakadu, *Cacatua sulphurea*." *Papaggeien* 9: 280–85.

Bird Life International. 2012. "Bird Life Fact Sheet: Yellow-crested Cockatoo (*Cacatua Sulphurea*)." http://www.birdlife.org/datazone/speciesfactsheet.php?id=1398.

Butchart, S.H.M., T.M. Brooks, C.W.N. Davies, G. Dharmaputra, G.C.L. Dutson, J.C. Lowwen, and A. Sahu. 1996. "The Conservation Status of Forest Birds on Flores and Sumbawa, Indonesia." *Bird Conservation International* 6.4: 335–70.

Collar, N.J., M.J. Crosby, and A.J. Stattersfield. 1994. *Birds to Watch 2: The World List of Threatened Birds*. BirdLife Conservation Series 4. Cambridge, UK: BirdLife International.

Convention on International Trade in Endangered Species of Wild Fauna and Flora (CITES). 1994. "Consideration of Proposals for Amendment of Appendices I and II." http://www.cites.org/common.cop/13/raw_props/KE-Lion.pdf.

_____. 2004. Thirteenth Meeting of the Conferences of the Parties. Bangkok, Thailand, October 3–14.

Forshaw, Joseph M. 1977. *Parrots of the World*. Neptune, NJ: TFH.

Greene, W.T. 1979. *Parrots in Captivity*. (Originally published in three volumes between 1884 and 1887.) Neptune, NJ: TFH.

Hong Kong Magazine. 2005. February 18, pp. 6–7.

Imansyah, M.J., D.G. Angorro, N. Yangpatra, A. Hidayat, and Y.J. Benu. 2005. "Sebaran karakteristik pohon sarang Katatua (*Cacatua sulphurea parvula*) di pulau Komodo, Taman Nasional Komodo." *Laporan* 4: pp 5 -8.

Indonesian Parrot Project. 2012. "Project Abbotti—Saving the World's Rarest Cockatoo." http://indonesian-parrot-project.org/project_abbotti.html.

Inskipp, T., and H. Corrigan. 1992. "Review of Significant Trade In Animal Species included in CITES Appendix II." WCMC/IUCN. http://www.cites.org/eng/cop/08/doc/E-30.pdf.

Innskipp, T., S. Broad, and R. Luxmoore. 1988. "Significant Trade in Wildlife: A Review of selected species in CITES Appendix II, 3: Birds." Cambridge, UK: International Union for Conservation of Nature and Natural Resources and Secretariat of the Convention of the International trade in Endangered Species of Wild Fauna and Flora.

IUCN Red List. 2012. "*Cacatua Sulphurea*." http://www.iucnredlist.org/details/106001398/0.

Johnstone, R.E., and P. Jepson. 1996. "The Roti Island, Nusa Tanggara, Indonesia." *Western Australian Naturalist* 21: 23–35.

Jones, M.J., M.D. Linsay, and S.J. Marsden. 1995. "Population Sizes, Status and Habitat Associations of the Restricted Range Species of Sumba, Indonesia." *Bird Conservation International* 5 (1): 21–52.

Kendell, S. Brian. 1955. "Breeding the Citrin-Crested Cockatoo." *Aviculture Magazine* 61: 226–29.

_____. 1956. "Breeding the Timor Cockatoo." *Aviculture Magazine* 62: 6–9.

_____. 1960. "My Cockatoos in 1959." *Aviculture Magazine* 66: 13–17.

Mackinnon, J., and K. Phillips. 1993. *A Field Guide to the Birds of Borneo, Sumatra, Java and Bali.* Oxford: Oxford University Press.

Mayre, E. 1937. "Birds Collected During the Whitney South Sea Expedition. XXXVI. Notes on New Guinea Birds." *American Museum Novitates* 947: 1–11.

McPeek, R. 1976. "Citrin Crested Cockatoos." *Aviculture Bulletin*, March, pp. 31–33.

Mulawka, Edward J. 1979. "Responsible Aviculturalism." *Bird World*, June–July, pp. 27–28.

_____. 1982. "Taming and Training Parrots." Neptune, NJ: TFH.

Nandika, D. 2006. "Recent Observations of the Critically Endangered Sulphurea Subspecies of Yellow-Crested Cockatoo." *Psittascene* 18: 10–11.

Rensch, B. 1931. "Die Vogelwelt von Lombok, Sumbawa und Flores." *Mitt. Zoologia, Berlin* 17: 451–637.

Rudkin, Francis H. 1942. "Notes." *Aviculture* 12: 288.

Schonwetter, M. 1964. *Handbuch der Oologie.* Bd.1, Lief 9, Berlin: Akademie—Verlkag.

Smith, Clifford. 1970. "Breeding of the Lesser Sulphur Crested Cockatoo." *Aviculture Magazine* 76: 238–39.

Trainor, C. 2002. "A Preliminary List of Important Bird Areas in East Timor: Interim List of Priority Sites for Biodiversity Conservation in Asia's Newest Country." BirdLife International—Asia Program.

Trainor, C.R. 2007. "Birds of S.E. Tapuala Peninsula, Roti Island, Lesser Sundas, Indonesia." *Forktail* 21.

Van Bemma, A.C.V., and K.H. Voous. 1951. "On the Birds of the Islands of Muna and Buton, S.E., Celebes." *Truebia* 21: 24–104.

Walker, J.S., D.J. Anggoro, and S.J. Marsden. 2005. "Factors Influencing Nest-Site Occupancy and Low Reproductive Output in the Critically Endangered Yellow-crested *Cacatua sulphurea* on Sumba, Indonesia." *Bird Conservation International* 15: 347–59.

World Parrot Trust. 2012. "Yellow-crested Cockatoo." http://www.parrots.org/index.php/encyclopedia/profile/yellow_crested_cockatoo/.

Wright, Vance. 1948. "Hand Feeding Parrot Like Birds." *Aviculture* 18: 35–36.

Chapter 4

Baldwin, H. 1975. "Birds of Inverell, N.S.W." *Emu* 75: 113–20.

Batey, Isaac. 1907. "On Fifteen Thousand Acres: Its Bird Life Sixty Years Ago, Part 1." *Emu* 7: 1–17.

Beauty of Birds. 2012. "Eleanora Cockatoo." http://www.beautyofbirds.com/eleanoracockatoos.html.

_____. 2012. "Sulphur Crested Cockatoos." http://www.beautyofbirds.com/sulphurcrestedcockatoos.html.

Bedggood, Duke of. 1958. "Parrots and Cockatoos of the Mooroonpa District, Victoria." *Emu* 58: 72.

Bennet, J.C. 1935. "Correspondence—Birds of a Tasmanian Garden." *Aviculture Magazine*, 4th ser., 13: 239–40.

Bird Care. 2012. "Sulphur Crested Cockatoo." http://www.birdcare.com.au/sulphur_crested_cockatoo.htm.

Bird Facts. 2012. "Sulphur-crested Cockatoo." http://www.weirdfacts.com/animalfacts/3241-birdfacts-html.

Cayley, Neville L. 1973. As extensively revised by Alan Lendon. *Australian Parrots in Field and Aviary.* Brisbane, Queensland: Angus and Robertson.

Department of Primary Industries, Parks, Water, and Environment. 2012. " About the Department of Primary Industries, Parks, Water and Environment (DPIPWE).." GPO Box 44, Hobart, Tasmania, Australia 7001. (Re: AgDex 685, #14, ISSN8759–2).

Diamond, Jared M. 1972. *Avifauna of the Eastern Highlands of New Guinea.* Cambridge: Nuttall Ornithological Club.

Forshaw, Joseph M. 1977. *Parrots of the World.* Neptune, NJ: TFH.

Frith, H.J., ed. 1969. *Birds in the Australian High Country.* Melbourne: A.H. and A.W. Reid.

Gurney, E. 1899. "On the Comparative Ages of Which Birds Live." *Ibis* 41: 19–42.

Hill, J.A. 1916. "Wary Cockatoos. (Stray Feathers)." *Emu* 66: 56.

IAATE. 2012. "Sulphur Crested Cockatoo." http://www.iaate.org/companion-parrots/201-sulphur-crested-cockatoo-fact-sheet.

Jones, J. 1951. "The Hattah Lakes Camp-out." *Emu* 52: 225–254.

MacGillivray, W. 1914. "Notes on Some North Queensland Birds." *Emu* 13: 132–86.

Mathews, G.M. 1916. *The Birds of Australia*. Vol. 4. London, UK: Witherby.

Mosey, H. 1956. "Birds Observed on a Visit to New Guinea June to August 1950." *Emu* 56: 357–66.

Oiseaux. 2012. "Sulfur Crested Cockatoo." http:// www, oiseaux-birds.com/card-sulphur-crested-cockatoo.html.

Patel, R., B. Nirvdoa, John M.R. Nelson, R. Micah, Irena Schultz, and Charles Schultz. 2008. 'Investigating the Human Specificity of Synchronization to Music." In *Proceedings of the 10th International Conference on Music Perception and Cognition*. Aug. 25–29, 2008. Sapporo, Japan: Hokkaido University.

Prestwick, Arthur. 1943. "After Four Years of It." *Aviculture Magazine*, 5th ser., 48: 160–63.

Rand, A.L. 1942. "Results of the Archbold Expeditions #43. Birds of the 1938–1939 New Guinea Expedition." *Bulletin of the American Museum of Natural History* 79: 425–516.

Rand, A.L., and E.T. Gilliard. 1968. *Handbook of New Guinea Birds*. Garden City, New Jersey: Natural History Press.

Ripley, S.D. 1964. "A Systematic and Ecological Study of Birds of New Guinea." *Bulletin of the Peabody Museum of Natural History* 19: 1–85.

Roberts, P.E. 1957. "Notes on the Birds of the Cumberland Islands." *Emu* 57: 303–10.

Rowley, Ian. 1997. "Family *Cacatuidae* (Cockatoos)." In *Handbook of the Birds of the World*, ed. del Hoyo Josep; Elliot Andrew, and Sargatal Jordoi. Volume 4, *Sandgrouse to Cuckoos*. Barcelona: Lynx Edicions.

Tavistock, Marquess of, and J. Delacour. 1926. "Cockatoos." *Avicultural Magazine*, 4th ser., 4.4: 148–55.

Tubb, J.A. 1945. "Field Notes on Some New Guinea Birds." *Emu* 44: 249–373.

Tumblr. 2012. "Blue-eyed Cockatoo." http://www. tumblr.com/tagged*blue-eyedcockatoo*.

White, Capt. H.L. 1913. "White Cockatoos—Stray Feathers." *Emu* 8: 101.

Chapter 5

Avian Companions. 2012. "Blue-eyed Cockatoos." http://www.aviancompanions.com/BlueEyed Cockatoo.htm.

Avicultural Magazine. 1966. "News and Views." 72: 90.

Beauty of Birds. 2012. "Blue-eyed Cockatoos." http://beautyofbirds.com/blueeyedcockatoo. html.

Bird Life International. 2012. "Bird Life Fact Sheet: Blue-eyed Cockatoo (*Cacatua Ophthalmica*)." http://www.birdlife.org/datazone/speciesfact sheet/php?id=30025.

Birdchannel. 2012. "Blue-eyed Cockatoo." http:// www.com/bird-species/blue-eyed-cockatoo. aspx.

Blomerley, Keith. 2012. "Blue-eyed Cockatoo." http://www.planetofbirds.com/psittaciformes-cacatuidae-blue-eyed-cockatoo-cacatua-oph thalmica.

Cameron, M. 2007. *Cockatoos*. Collingwood, Victoria, Australia: CSIRO Publishing.

Dutson, G. 2011. *Birds of Melanasia: Bismarcks, Solomons, Vanuatu, New Caledonia*. London: Christopher Helms.

Forshaw, Joseph M. 2012. "New Britain's rare & Beautiful Blue-eyed Cockatoo." Bird Talk Magazine. http://asopa.typepad.com/asopa_people/ 2012/07/new-britains-rare-beautiful-blue-eyed-cockatoo.html.

Forshaw, Joseph M. 1977. *Parrots of the World*. Neptune, NJ: TFH.

Gilliard, E.T., and M. LeCroy. 1967. "Results of the 1958–1959 Gilliary New Britain Expedition. 4. Annotated list of the birds of the Whiteman Mountains, New Britain." *Bulletin of the American Museum of Natural History* 135: 173–216.

Griffiths, A.V. 1965. "Breeding the Blue-Eyed Cockatoo." *Avicultural Magazine* 71: 109–11.

Juniper, T., and M. Parr. 1998. *Parrots: A Guide to Parrots of the World*. Sussex, UK: Pica.

LaPage, Mary Ellen. Telephone (408) 977-3131. 15466 Los Gatos Blvd, Suite 105–198, Los Gatos, CA, 95032.

Layard, E.L.C. 1880. "Notes on a Collecting Trip in the New Hebrides, the Solomon Islands, New Britain and the Duke of York Islands." *Ibis* 22.3: 290–309.

Lendon, A.H. 1951. *Australian Birds Kept in Captivity*. London: Avicultural Society.

Marsden, S.J., J.D. Pilgrim, and R. Wilkinson. 2001. "Status, Abundance, and Habitual Use of Blue-eyed Cockatoo Cacatua ophthalmica on New Britain, Papua New Guinea." *Bird Conservation International* 11: 151–60.

Orenstein, R.I. 1976. "Birds of the Plesyumi Area, Central New Guinea." *Condor* 78: 370–74.

Parrot Link. 2012. "Blue-eyed Cockatoo." http:// www.parrotlink.com/cms//index.php?page= blue-eyed-cockatoo—-new.

Planet of Birds. 2012. "Blue-eyed Cockatoos." http://www.planetofbirds.com/psittaciformes-cacatuidae-blue-eyed-cockatoo-cacatua-ophthalmica.

Rutgers, A. 1970. *Birds of New Guinea*. New York: St. Martins.

The Web Site of Everything. 2010. "Blue-eyed Cockatoo." http://thewebsiteofeverything.com /animals/birds/Psittaciformes/Psittacidae/ Cacatua-ophthalmica.

Wilkinson, R. 1999. *Blue-eyed Cockatoo Cacatua ophthalmica: European Studbook*. 2nd ESB ed. Chester: North England Zoological Society.

Wilkinson, R., M. Pilgrim, A. Woolham, P.I. Morris, A. Morris and B. West. 2000. "Husbandry and Breeding of Blue-eyed Cockatoos at Chester Zoo 1996–1998." *International Zoo Yearbook* 37: 116–25.

World Parrot Trust. 2012. "Blue-eyed Cockatoo (*Cacatua ophthalmica*)." http://www.parrots. org/index.php/encyclopedia/profile/blue_ eyed_cockatoo/.

Chapter 6

Avian Companions. 2012. "Western Long Billed Corella—*Cacatua pastinator*." http://www. aviancompanions.com/SlenderBilledCockatoo. htm.

Aviculture Magazine. 1966. "News and Views." 72: 140.

Binns, Gordon. 1953. "Birds of Terrang, Southwestern Australia." *Emu* 53: 211–21.

Bird Care. 2012. "Western Long Billed Corella." http://www.birdcare.com.au/long_billed_ corella.htm.

Bird Life International. 2012. "Bird Life Fact Sheet: Long-billed Cockatoo *Cacatua Tenuirostris*)." http://www.birdlife.org/datazone/speciesfact sheet.php?id=1407.

Birds in Back Yards. 2012. "Long Billed Corella." http://www.birdsinbackyards.net/finder/dis play.cfm?id=101.

Forshaw, Joseph M. 1977. *Parrots of the World*. Neptune, NJ: TFH.

Government of Australia. 2012. "Western Long-billed Cockatoo." http://museum.wa.gov.au/ explore/online-exhibitions/cockatoo-care/ western-long-billed-corella.

Greene, W.T. 1979. *Parrots in Captivity*. Originally published in three volumes between 1884 and 1887. Neptune, NJ: TFH.

IUCN Red List. 2012. "*Cacatua Tenuirostris*." http://www.iucnredlist.org/apps/redlist/ details/106001407/0.

Info Barrel Lifestyle. 2012. "Long-Billed Cockatoo—Characteristics." http//www.infobarrel. com/long-billed_Corella_-_Characteristics.

Lendon, A. 1950. "Notes." *Australian Aviculture* 56: 99.

_____. 1970. "The Breeding of the Corella (Long-billed or Slender-billed Cockatoo)." *Avicultural Magazine* 76: 236–38.

Lint, Kenton C. 1959. "Breeding of the Slender-billed Cockatoo." *Aviculture Magazine* 65: 107–09.

Mathews, G.M. 1914. "A List of the Birds of Melville Island, Northern Territory, Australia." *Ibis* 56: 91–132.

_____. 1916. *The Birds of Australia*. Vol. 4. London: Witherby.

North West Bird Club. 2012. "Slender (Long) Billed Corella." http://www.northwestbirdclub tasmania.org.au/Long_billed_Corella.html.

Pizzey, Graham, and Frank Knight. 1997. *Field Guide to the Birds of Australia*. Sydney, Australia:

Prestwick, Arthur. 1954. *Records of Parrots Bred in Captivity (Additions)*. London, UK: Published by the author.

Slater, P. 1970. *A Field Guide to Australian Birds*. Melbourne, Australia: Rigby.

Souef, D. Le. 1903. "Descriptions of Birds' Eggs from the Port Darwin District, Northern Australia. Part II." *Emu* 2: 139–59.

Zilva, Ralph de. 2012. "Long Billed Corella at Cedar Creek, Queensland, Australia." http:// www.redbubble.com/people/ralphanthony.

Chapter 7

Aviculture Magazine. 1966. "News and Views." 72: 140.

Bird Care. 2012. "Western Long Billed Corella." http://www.birdcare.com.au/long_billed_corel la.htm.

Bird Life International. 2012. "Bird Life Fact Sheet: Western Corella (*Cacatua Pastinator*)." http:// www.birdlife.org/datazone/speciesfactsheet. php?id=1406.

Carter, T. 1912. "Notes on *Licmetis pastinator*. (Western Long-billed Cockatoo)." *Ibis* 9 (6): 223–35.

_____. 1916. "On Some West Australian Birds Collected between the North-West, Cape and Albany (950 Miles Apart)." In *The Birds of Australia*, ed. G.M. Mathews. Vol. 4. London: Witherby.

_____. 1924. "Birds on the Broome Hill District." *Emu* 23.4: 306–318.

Chapman, T., and B. Cale. 2006. "Draft Muir's Corella (*Cacatua pastinator pastinator*) Recovery Plan 2006–2115." Species and Communities Branch, Department of Conservation and Land Management, Perth, Australia.

Department of Environment and Conservation. Government of Western Australia. 2007. "Fauna Note No, 4. Muir's Corella." https://www.dec. wa.gov.au/index2.php?option=com_docman& task=doc_view&gid=1121&Itemid=99999999

_____. 2007. "Fauna Note No.19, Butler's Cockatoo." Government of Western Australia. https://www.dec.wa.gov.au/component/option,com_docman/Itemid,2123/gid,1135/task,doc_details/19_butlers_corella.pdf.

_____. 2012. "Muir's Corella No Longer a Threatened Species." Government of Western Australia. http://dec.wa.gov.au/news/media-statements/dec/item/23705-muir-s-corella-no-longer-a-threatened-species.html.

Department of the Environment. Australian Government. 2012. "*Cacatua Pastinator Pastinator—* Muir's Corella (Southern), Western Long-billed Corella (Southern)." Species Profile and Threats Database, Department of the Environment, Canberra, Australia. http://www.environment.gov.au/cgi-bin/sprat/public/publicspecies.pl?taxon_id=25981.

Feral.org. 2012. "Breeding Ecology of the Western Long-billed Corella, *Cacatua pastinator pastinator*." http://www.feral.org.au/breeding-ecology-of-the-western-long-billed-corella-cacatua-pastinator-pastinator/.

Ford, Julian E. 1957. "Additional Notes on the Bird Life of Leonare, Western Australia." *Emu* 57: 23.

Forshaw, Joseph M. 1977. *Parrots of the World*. Neptune, NJ: TFH.

Garnett, S.T., and G.M. Crowley. 2000. *The Action Plan for Australian Birds 2000*. Canberra, Australia: Environment Australia.

Greene, W.T. 1979. *Parrots in Captivity*. Originally published in three volumes between 1884 and 1887. Neptune, NJ: TFH.

Higgins, P.J. (ed.) 1999. *Handbook of Australian, New Zealand, and Antarctic Birds*. Vol. 4, *Parrots to Dollarbird*. Melbourne: Oxford University Press.

International Species Information System (ISCS). 2006. "Species Holdings." http://www.isis.org.

IUCN Red List. 2012. "*Cacatua pastinator*." http://www.iucnredlist.org/details/106001406/0.

Johnstone, R.E., and G.M. Storr. 1998. *Handbook of Western Australian Birds*. Vol. 1, *Non-passerines (Emu to Dollarbird)*. Perth, Western Australia: West Australian Museum.

Johnstone, Ron. 2011. "Information Sheet: Western Long-billed Corella: Muir's Corella *Cacatua pastinator pastinator* and Butler's Corella *Cacatua pastinator butleri*." Department of Terrestrial Vertebrates, Western Australian Museum, February.

Lendon, A. 1970. "The Breeding of the Corella (Long-billed or Slender Billed Cockatoo)." *Aviculture Magazine* 76: 236–38.

Lint, Kenton C. 1959. "Breeding of the Slender Billed Cockatoo." *Aviculture Magazine* 65: 107–09.

Massam, M., and J.L. Long. 1992. "Long Billed Corellas Have an Uncertain Status in the South-west of Western Australia." *Western Australian Naturalist* 39: 30–34.

Masters, J.B., and A.L. Milhinch. 1974. "Birds of the Shire of Northam, About 100km East of Perth WA." *Emu* 74 (4): 228–44.

Mulawka, Edward J. 1981. "Taming and Training Parrots." Neptune, NJ: TFH.

North, A.J. 1912. "Nests and Eggs of Birds Found Breeding in Australia and Tasmania." In *Australian Museum Special Catalogue* 3:1. Sydney: Australian Museum.

Prestwick, Arthur. 1954. *Records of Parrots Bred in Captivity (Additions)*. London, UK: Published by author.

Schodde, R., and I.J. Mason. 1997. "Aves (Columbidae to Coracidea)." In *Zoological Catalogue of Australia* 37. 2., ed. W.E.K. Houston and A. Wells. Melbourne, Australia: CSIRO.

Serventy, D.L., and H.M. Whittell. 1962. *Birds of Western Australia*. Perth, Australia: Patterson Brokenshaw.

Smith, G.T., and L.A. Moore. 1991. "Breeding Ecology of the Western Billed Corella *Cacatua pastinator pastinator*." *Wildlife Research* 18: 91–110.

Storr, G.M. 1991. "Birds of the South-west Division of Western Australia, Records of the Western Australian Museum." *Emu*, Suppl. 35.

World Parrot Trust. 2012. "Western Corella (*Cacatua pastinator*)." http://www.parrots.org/index.php/encyclopedia/profile/western_corella/.

Chapter 8

Alderton, David. 2003. *The Ultimate Encyclopedia of Caged and Aviary Birds*. London: Hermes House.

Cain, A.J., and C.J. Gailbraith. 1956. "Field Notes on the Birds of the Eastern Solomon Islands." *Bulletin of the British Museum of Natural History* 98: 100–34.

Forshaw, Joseph M. 1977. *Parrots of the World*. Neptune, NJ: TFH.

IUCN Red List. 2012. "Cacatua ducorpsii." http://www.iucnredlist.org/details/106001408/0/print.

Layard, E.L.C. 1880. "Notes on a Collecting Trip to the New Hebrides, the Solomon Islands, New Britain, and the Duke of York Islands." *Ibis* 22.3: 290–309.

Malaysia Bird Forum. 2012. "Ducorp's Cockatoo." http://ducorps-cockatoo.birdforum.com.my/.

Mayre, E. 1945. *Birds of the Southwest Pacific*. New York: MacMillan.

Mulawka, Edward J. 1981. *Taming and Training Parrots*. New Jersey: TFH.

Muth, Tracy. 2012. "Make Your Bird a Star: Milo."

http://www.angelfire.com/ak4/birds/dcmilo. html.

Sea World. 2012. "Ducorp's Cockatoo." http://www.seaworld.org/animal-info/animal-bytes/animalia/eumetazoa/coelomates/deuterostomes/chordata/craniata/aves/psittaciformes/ducorps-cockatoo.htm.

World Parrot Trust. 2012. "Ducorp's Cockatoo." http://www.parrots.org/index.php/encyclopedia/profile/ducorps_corella.

Chapter 9

Alderton, D. 1982. *Parrots, Lories, and Cockatoos.* Surrey, UK: Saigas.

Beauty of Birds. 2012. "Goffin's Cockatoo or Tanimbar Cockatoo." http://beautyofbirds.com/goffinscocktoo.html.

Bird Care. 2012. "Goffin's Cockatoo." http://birdcare.com.au/goffin%_cockatoo.htm.

Bird Life International. 2012. "Bird Life Fact Sheet: Tanimbar Cockatoo (*Cacatua Goffiniana*)." http://www.birdlife.org/datazone/speciesfactsheet.php?id-1404.

Forshaw, Joseph M. 1977. *Parrots of the World.* Neptune, NJ: TFH.

Goffin's Cockatoo. 2012. "Goffin Cockatoo Behavior and Training." http://www.goffinscockatoo.com/goffin-cockatoos-behavior-training.html.

Greene, W.T. 1979. *Parrots in Captivity.* Originally published in three volumes between 1884 and 1887. Neptune, NJ: TFH.

Hartert, E. 1901. "On the Birds of the Key and South-east Islands of the Ceram-Laut." *Novitates Zoologicae* 8: 1–20.

IUCN Red List. 2012. "*Cacatua Goffiniana*." http://www.iucnredlist.org/details/22684800/0.

Juniper, Tony, and Mike Parr. 1998. *Guide to Parrots of the World.* New Haven, CT: Yale University Press.

Low, R. 1985. *Endangered Parrots.* UK: Blandford.

Mulawka, Edward J. 1981. *Taming and Training Parrots.* Neptune, NJ: TFH.

O'Connor, Neil. 1997. "Breeding Goffin's Cockatoo." *Aviculture*: 83.

Parrot Link. 2012. "Goffin's Cockatoo." http://www.parrotlink.com/cms/index.php?page-goffins.

Roselaar, C.S., and J.P. Michels. 2004. "Systematic Notes on Asian Birds. 48. Nomenclatural Chaos Untangled, Resulting in the Naming of the Formerly Undescribed Cacatua Species from the Tanimbar Islands, Indonesia (Psittaformes: Cacatuidae)." *Zoologische Verhandeliongen* 350: 183–96.

Roselaar, C.S., and T.G. Prins. 2000. "List of Types of Specimens of Birds in the Zoological Museum of the University of Amsterdam (ZMA), Including data described by ZMA staff but without types in ZMA." *Beaufortia* 50: 95–126.

Schulte, E.G.B. 1960. "Breeding of the Umbrella or Great White Crested Cockatoo." *Aviculture Magazine* 66: 208.

World Parrot Trust. 2012. "Goffin's Cockatoo (*Cacatua goffini*)." http://www.parrots.org/index.php/encyclopedia/wildstatus/goffin-cockatoo.

Chapter 10

Bird Care. 2012. "Little Corella." http://www.birdcare.com.au/little_corella.htm.

Blaauw, F.E. 1927. "On the Breeding of the Bare-eyed Cockatoo of Australia." *Ibis* 69.2: 425–26.

Carter, Thomas. 1904. "Birds Occurring in the Region of the North West Cape." *Emu* 3: 171–77.

Cayley, Neville, L. 1973. As extensively revised by Alan Lendon. *Australian Parrots in Field and Aviary.* Brisbane, Australia: Angust and Robertson.

Crawford, D.H. 1972. "Birds of the Darwin Area with Some Records from Other Parts of Northern Territory." *Emu* 72: 131–46.

Forshaw, Joseph M. 1977. *Parrots of the World.* Neptune, NJ: TFH.

Goodfellow, Walter. 1935. "A Collection on Melvin Island." *Aviculture Magazine*, 4th ser., 13: 316–24.

Hill, J.A. 1916. "Wary Cockatoos (Stray Feathers)." *Emu* 66: 56.

Hougerwerf, F.A. 1964. "On Birds New for New Guinea or with a Larger Range than Previously Known." *British Ornithologists Club* 84: 70–77.

Kilgour, J.A. 1904. "A Trip to the River Ord." *Emu* 4: 37–43.

MacGillivray, W. 1914. "Notes on Some North Queensland Birds." *Emu* 131: 133–86.

_____. 1916. "The Region of the Barrier Range, Part 1." *Emu* 10: 16–34.

Mathews, G.M. 1916. *The Birds of Australia.* Vol. 4. London: Witherby.

Mdahlem. 2012. "Little Corella." http://www.mdahlem.net/birds/12ltcorel.php.

North, A.J. 1911. "The Birds of Coolabah and Brewaina, New South Wales North-west." *Australian Museum Special Catalogue* 1:3. Sydney: Australian Museum.

Parr, Mike, and Tony Juniper. 2010. *Parrots: A Guide to Parrots of the World.* Sydney, Australia: A. and C. Black.

Pizzey, Graham, and Frank Knight. 1997. *Field Guide to the Birds of Australia.* Sydney, Australia:

White, S.A. 1913. "Field Ornithology in South Australia." *Emu* 13: 16–32.

Whitlock, F.L. 1910. "On the East Murchison." *Emu* 9: 181–219.

World Parrot Trust. 2012. "Little Corella." http://

www.parrots.org/index.php/encyclopedia/pro
file/little_corella/.

Chapter 11

Bird Life International. 2012. "Bird Life Fact Sheet: Philippine Cockatoo (*Cacatua haematuropygia*)." http://www.birdlife.org/datazone/species factsheet.php?id=1403.

Boussekey, Marc. 1995. "Conservation of the Red-vented Cockatoo." *Psittacine Magazine* 7.4 (no. 25): 7.

Collar, N.J., N. Mallari, and B.R. Tabaranza. 1999. *Threatened Birds of the Philippines*. Manila, Philippines: Haribon Foundation.

Grant, Oglivie W.R. 1896a. "On the Birds of the Philippines—Part VII. The Highlands of Mindora." *Ibis* 38.4: 457–77.

_____. 1896b. "On the Birds of the Philippines—Part VIII. The Highlands of Negros." *Ibis* 38.4: 525–65.

_____. 1896c "On the Birds of the Philippines—Part IX. The Islands of Samar and Leite." *Ibis* 39.2: 209–52.

Harrison, C.J.O., and D.T. Holyoak. 1970. "Apparently Undescribed Parrot Eggs in the Collection of the British Museum (Natural History)." *British Ornithologists Club* 90: 42–46.

Katala Foundation, Inc. 2012. "Learn about the Philippine Cockatoo." http://www.philippinec ockatoo.org/philippine%20cockatoo.htm.

Lambert, F.R. 1994. "The Status of the Philippine Cockatoo *Cacatua haematuropygia* in Palawan and the Sulu Islands, Philippines." Gland Switzerland: Species Survival Commission.

Low, Rosemary. 2012. "Consistent Success with the Red-Vented Cockatoo." http://www.parrots.org /pdfs/all_about_parrots/reference_library/con servation/Consistent%20Success%20with%20 the%20Red-vented%20Cockatoo.pdf.

Lowe, W.P. 1916. "Some Birds of Palawan." *Ibis* 58.4: 607–23.

Palawan Council for Sustainable Development. 2012. "Philippine Cockatoo." http://www.pcsd. ph/photo/fauna/philippinecockatoo.htm.

PBworks. 2008. "Philippine Cockatoo." http://ec op.pbworks.com/w/page/18520758/Philip pine%20Cockatoo.

Philippine Clearing House Mechanism for Biodiversity. 2012. "Philippine Cockatoo Conservation Program." http://www.chm.ph/index.php? option=com_content&view=article&id=297% 3Aphilippine-cockatoo-conservation-program &catid=87&Itemid=90.

Txtmania.com. 2012. "Philippine Cockatoo (*Cacatua haematurapygia*)." http://www.Txtmania. com/articles/cockatoo.php.

Porter N.S. 1953. "The Birds of Calicoan, Philippine Islands." *Wilson Bulletin* 65: 152–270.

Rabor, D.S. 1977. *Philippine Birds and Animals*. Quezon City, Philippines: University of Philippine Press.

Rand, A.L., and D.S. Rabor. 1960. "Birds of the Philippine Islands: Siquijor, Mt. Malindang, Bohol, and Samar." *Fieldiana: Zoology* 35: 223–441.

Sharpe, Bowdler. 1884. "In a Collection of Birds Made in South Palawan by Mr. E. Lampiere." *Ibis*: 316–22.

Walden, A.V., and E.L. Layard. 1872. "On Birds Recently Observed or Obtained in the Island of Negros, Philippines." *Ibis*: 93–107.

Whitehead, John. 1890. "Notes on the Birds of Palawan." *Ibis*: 38–61.

Widmann, Peter, and Lacerna Widmann. 2008. "The Cockatoo and the Community: Ten Years of Philippine Cockatoo Conservation Programme." *BirdingAsia* 1: 23–29.

World Parrot Trust. 2012. "Red-vented Cockatoo (*Cacatua haematuropgia*)." http://www.parrots. org/index.php/encyclopedia/captivestatus/red_ vented_corella.

Chapter 12

Alderton, David. 2003. *The Ultimate Encyclopedia of Caged and Aviary Birds*. London: Hermes House.

Alexander, W.B.B. 1916. "Birds of the North and North West Australia." In *The Birds of Australia*, vol. 4, ed. G.M. Mathews. London: Witherby.

Allen, G.H. 1950. "Birds as a Biotic Factor in the Environment of Pastures, with Particular Reference to Galahs (*Cacatua roseicapilla*)." *Journal of Australian Institute of Agricultural Science* 16 (1): 18–25.

Austin, O.L. 1916. "The Resident Birds of Guadeloupe." In *The Birds of Australia*, vol. 4, ed. G.M. Mathews. London: Witherby.

Aviculture. 1944. "Secretary's Page." 14: 214–15.

_____. 1966. "News and Views." 72: 140.

Bernsey, F.L. 1906. "Birds of the Richmond District, North Queensland." *Emu* 6: 211–21.

Boehm, Edward F. 1959. "Parrots and Cockatoos of the Mount Mary Plains, South Australia." *Emu* 59: 83–87.

Boosey, Edward. 1950. "Breeding Results at the Kenston Foreign Bird Farm." *Aviculture Magazine* 56: 213, 218.

British Naturalist. 1913. "Notes.": 156, 204, 232.

Clendinem, D.L.J. 1941/42. "Correspondence." *Victorian Naturalist*: 7.

Cockatoo Heaven. 2012. "Galah Cockatoos." htt p://www.Birdsnways.com/cockatoo/galah.htm.

Cosgrave, R. 1912. "Notes." *Aviculture* 4: 269.

Department of Primary Industries, Victoria, Australia. 2011. "Department of Sustainability and Environment Information Note: Reducing Cockatoo Damage to Crops" http://www.land manager.org.au/link/dse-information-note-redu cing-cockatoo-damage-crops

Dickson, D.J. 1951. "The First Fifty Years of the Royal Australian Ornithologists Union." *Emu* 51: 185–284.

Emu. "Notes." 1909. 9: 36.

Forshaw, Joseph M. 2006. *Parrots of the World: An Identification Guide.* Illustrated by Frank Knight. New Jersey: Princeton University Press.

Galahs Australia. 2005. "The Australian Galah." http://galah.galahs.com.au/content/php/arti cle024.php.

_____. 2005. "Health." http://galah.galahs.com. au/content/php/article048.php.

Goodwin, Derek. 1974. In *Birds of the Harold Hall Australian Expeditions, 1962–1970.* Ed., B.B. Hall. London. British Museum of Natural History.

Greene, W.T. 1979. *Parrots in Captivity.* Originally published in three volumes between 1884 and 1887. Neptune, NJ: TFH.

Jackson, William. 1919. "Haunts of the Letter-Winged Kite (*Elanus scriptus*)." *Emu* 18: 160–72.

Kendall, H. 1903. "Stray Feathers." *Emu* 3: 56.

Kendall, S. Brian. 1984. "Notes on My Cockatoos in 1963." *Aviculture Magazine* 70: 26, 27.

Lawson, F. 1905. "A Glance at the Birds of the Moira River (Western Australia)." *Emu* 4: 132–37.

Lea, A.M., and J.T. Gray. 1935. "The Food of Australian Birds." *Emu* 27: 275–92.

Lendon, A. 1949. "Notes." *Aviculture Magazine* 55: 31.

_____. 1950. "Australian Parrots in Captivity." *Aviculture Magazine* 56: 76, 161–67.

_____. 1973. "Editor." In *Australian Parrots in Field and Aviary,* ed. Neville L. Cayley. Brisbane, Australia: Angust and Robertson, 1973.

Lord, E.A.R. 1956. "The Birds of the Murphy's Creek District, Southern Queensland." *Emu* 56: 100–26.

MacGivillary, W. 1910. "The Region of the Barrier Reef. Part 1." *Emu* 10: 16–34.

Marshall, R. 2012. "Galah or Rose-breasted Cockatoo Roseate." http://beautyofbirds.com/galah cockatoos.html.

Mathews, G.M. 1916. *The Birds of Australia.* Vol. 4. London: Witherby.

_____. 1920. *The Birds of Australia: Supplement #1.* London: Witherby.

Mayre, E. 1951. "Notes on Some Pigeons and Parrots from Western Australia." *Emu* 51: 137–45.

Mulawka, Edward J. 1983. *Blue Fronted Amazon Parrots.* Neptune, NJ: TFH.

Prestwick, Arthur. 1951. *Records of Parrots Bred in Captivity, Part II: Cockatoos and Macaws.* London: Published by author.

Rudkin, Francis H. 1929. "Nesting of the Rose-breasted Cockatoos." *Aviculture Magazine* 1: 45–46.

Sedgewick, E.H. 1952. "Bird Life at Leonora, Western Australia." *Emu* 59: 285–96.

Sedley, Henry. 1947. "The F.H. Rudkin Jr. Collection." *Aviculture* 17: 27–29.

Serventy, D.L., and H.M. Whittell. 1962. *Birds of Western Australia.* Perth, Australia: Patterson Brokenshaw.

Sharland, M. 1952. "Recent Tasmanian Records." *Emu* 52: 59–62.

Stang, David, 2012. "Species *Cacatua roseicapilla.*" http://zipcodezoo.com/animals/c/cacatua_rose icapilla.

Stone, A.C. 1912. "Birds of Lake Boga, Victoria." *Emu* 12: 112–22.

Tavistock, Marquess of. 1932. "The Rearing of White Breasted Roseate Cockatoos." *Aviculture Magazine* 10: 240–42.

Warham, John. 1957. "Notes on the Roosting Habits of Some Australian Birds." *Emu* 57: 78–81.

_____. 1970. "Galah Cockatoos in the Wild." *Aviculture Magazine,* Sept., pp. 14–19.

Whitlock, L. Lawson. 1909. "Notes on Birds Observed on the Filbarra Goldfield, North Western Australia." *Emu* 8: 173–94.

Chapter 13

Alexander, W.B. 1916. "Birds of the North and North-west of Australia." In *The Birds of Australia,* vol. 4, ed. G.M. Mathews. London: Witherby.

Avian Companions. 2012. "Major Mitchell's Cockatoo." http://www.aviancompanions.com.Major Mitchell'sCockatoo.htm.

Aviculture. 1940. "The Nest Box." 10: 176–77.

Beauty of Birds. 2010. "Leadbeater's or Major Mitchell's Cockatoo aka Pin." http://www. beautyofbirds.com/leadbeaterscockatoos.html.

Bennet, K.B. 1912. *Australian Special Catalogue* 3:1. Sydney: Australian Museum

Bird Care. 2008. "Major Mitchell's Cockatoo." http://www.birdcare.com.au/major_mitchell's_co ckatoo.htm.

Bird Life International. 2012. "Bird Life Fact Sheet: Major Mitchell's Cockatoo (*Cacatua Leadbeateri*)." http://www.birdlife.org/datazone/species factsheet.php?id=1397.

Chandler, L.G. 1913. "Bird Life of Kow Plains." *Emu* 13: 33–45.

_____. 1938. "Camera Notes on Parrots and the Pink Cockatoo." *Emu* 37: 299–300.

Cumming, W.D. 1966. "News and Views." *Aviculture Magazine* 72: 176.

Del Hoyo, J., A. Elliot, and J. Sargatal. 1997. *Handbook of Birds of the World*. Vol. 4, *Sandgrouse to Cuckoos*. Barcelona, Spain: Lynx.

Environmental Protection Agency. New South Wales Government. 2007. "Major Mitchell's Cockatoo (*Cacatua Leadbeateri*)." http://www.environment.nsw.gov.au/savingourspeciesapp/project.aspx?ProfileID=10116.

Ezra, A. 1940. "Leadbeater's Cockatoo." *Aviculture Magazine*, 5th ser., 5: 306–07.

Forshaw, J., and F. Knight. 2010. *Parrots of the World*. NJ: Princeton University Press.

Forshaw, Joseph M. 1977. *Parrots of the World*. Neptune, NJ: TFH.

Grant, W. R. Ogilvie. 1916. In *The Birds of Australia*, vol. 4, ed. G.M. Mathews. London: Witherby.

Greene, W.T. 1979. *Parrots in Captivity*. Originally published in three volumes between 1884 and 1887. Neptune, NJ: TFH.

Hall, B.P., ed. 1974. *Birds of the Harold Expeditions (Results of the Harold Hall Australian Expeditions, #33)*. London: British Museum of Natural History.

Hindwood, K. 1966. *Australian Birds in Color*. Honolulu, Hawaii: East-West Centre.

Jones, J. 1952. "The Hattah Lakes Camp-out, October 1951." *Emu* 52.

Kendall, S. Brian. 1964. "Notes on My Cockatoos in 1963." *Aviculture Magazine* 70: 26–7.

Lendon, A. 1973. "Editor." In *Australian Parrots in Field and Aviary*, ed. Neville L. Cayley. Brisbane, Australia: Angust and Robertson.

Mathews, G.W. 1913. *Australian Avifauna Record* 1, 8. London: Witherby.

Oboiko, Michael. 1941. "Breeding Leadbeater's Cockatoo." *Aviculture Magazine* 11: 16–19.

Parrot Link. 2012. "Leadbeater Cockatoo." http://www.parrotlink.com/cms//index.php?page=leadbeater-cockatoo-new.

Queensland Government. 2012. "Regional Ecosystems." http://www.ecosystem.conservation@epa.qld.gov.au.

Quist, Ben. 1986. "Major Mitchell Cockatoo (*Cacatua leadbeateri*)." *The Avicultural Review* 8.4 (April).

Rowley, I., and G. Chapman. 1991. "The Breeding Biology, Food, Social Organization, Demography and Conservation of the Major Mitchell or Pink Cockatoo, *Cacatua leadbeateri*, on the Margin of the Western Australia Wheat Belt." *Australian Journal of Zoology* 39: 211–61.

Vane, E.N.T. 1951. "Psitticorial." *Aviculture Magazine* 57: 60–62.

White, Captain H.L. 1913. "White Cockatoos—Stray Feathers." *Emu* 13: 101.

Chapter 14

Avian Companions. 2012. "Gang-gang Cockatoo." http://www.aviancompanions.com/GangGangCockatoo.htm.

Barrett, Charles. 1946. *Australian Bird Life*. Melbourne, Australia: Oxford University Press.

Bedford, Duke of. 1952. "Foreign Birds at Liberty." *Aviculture Magazine* 58: 158–69.

Bell, Alan. 1956. *Some Common Australia Birds*. London: Oxford University Press.

Beruldsen, G. 1980. *Field Guide to Nests and Eggs of Australian Birds*. Adelaide, Australia: Rigby.

Berwick Leader News. 2012. "Vulnerable Gang-gang Die in Captivity." Berwick, Victoria, Australia. Jan. 13.

Bird Care. 2005. "Gang-gang Cockatoo." http://www.birdcare.com.au/gang_gang_cockatoo.htm.

Bird Life International. 2012. "Bird Life Fact Sheet: Gang-gang Cockatoo (*Callocephalon Fimbriatum*)." http://www. Birdlife.org/datazone/speciesfactsheet.php?id=1395.

Cayley, Neville, L. 1973. As extensively revised by Alan Lendon. *Australian Parrots in Field and Aviary*. Brisbane, Australia: Angust and Robertson.

Chambers, L.E. 1995. *The Gang-gang Cockatoo in Field and Aviary*. Brunswick East, Victoria, Australia: Victorian Ornithological Research Group.

Donpaulna Aviaries. 2012. "Breeding Gang-gang Cockatoos." http://www.buyabird.com.au/donpaulna/articles/breeding-gang-gang-cockatoos.html.

Forshaw, Joseph M. 1977. *Parrots of the World*. Neptune, NJ: TFH.

Frith, H.J., ed. 1969. *Birds in the Australian High Country*. Melbourne, Australia: A.H. and A.W. Reid.

Gibbons, P., and D. Lindenmayer. 2000. *Tree Hollows and Wildlife Conservation in Australia*. Canberra, Australia: CSIRO.

Government of Australia. 2011. "The Gang-gang Cockatoo." GP0528, Sydney, NSW, Australia.

Greene, W.T. 1979. *Parrots in Captivity*. Originally published in three volumes between 1884 and 1887. Neptune, NJ: TFH.

Hart, Velma. 1973. "The Gang-gang Cockatoo Baby Boy." *Aviculture Bulletin*, Dec., pp. 25–27.

Hedges, George. 1926. "Breeding of the Gang-gang Cockatoo." *Emu* 25: 292–94.

Higgins, P.J. (ed.) 1999. *Handbook of Australian, New Zealand, and Antarctic Birds*. Vol. 4, *Parrots to Dollarbird*. Melbourne: Oxford University Press.

Howe, Frank. 1924. "Nest and Egg of the Gang-gang Cockatoo." *Emu* 24: 67–70.

Lendon, A. 1947. "Aviculture Society in South Australia." *Aviculture Magazine* 53: 104–08.

Mathews, G.M. 1916. *The Birds of Australia.* Vol. IV. London: Witherby.

McGrath, John. 2012. "Gang-gang Cockatoo Notes." http://www,members. westnet/com.au/youerweena/gang%/html.

Mollierocks. 2012. "Pictures of My Gang-gang—Raymond." http://www. Mytoos.com/forum/ub bthreads.php?ubb=showflat&Number=98834.

New South Wales Environment and Heritage. 2011. "Gang-gang Cockatoo Population, Hornsby and Ku-ring-gai Local Government Areas—Endangered Population Listing." February. http://www.environment.nsw.gov.au/determinations/GangGangCockatooNorthSydneyEndPopListing.htm.

New South Wales Scientific Committee. 2008. "Gang-gang Cockatoo (*Callocephalon Fimbriatum*)." http://www.environment.nsw.gov.au/resources/nature/schedules/Ganggang.pdf.

Prestwick, Arthur. 1951. *Records of Parrots Bred in Captivity.* Part 2, *Cockatoos and Macaws.* London: Published by author.

Russel, J.K. 1921. "Stray Feathers." *Emu* 21: 239.

Shields, J., and F. Crome. 1992. *Parrots and Pigeons of Australia.* Sydney, Australia: Angus and Robertson.

Tavistock, Marquess of. 1938. "The Breeding of the Gang-gang Cockatoo." *Aviculture Magazine,* 5th ser., 3: 258–60.

Chapter 15

Barnard, H.G. 1911. "Field Notes from Cape York." *Emu* 11: 17–32.

Beauty of Birds. 2012. "Palm Cockatoos aka Black Palm Cockatoo." http://www. beautyofbirds.com/palmcockatoos.html.

Bird Life International. 2012. "Bird Life Fact Sheet: Palm Cockatoo *Probosciger aterrimus*." http://www.birdlife.org/datazone/speciesfactsheet.php?id=1389.

D'Ombrain, A.F. 1945. "Additional Notes on a Great Black Palm Cockatoo in Captivity." *Emu* 45: 308–11.

D'Ombrain, D.E. 1933. "Notes on the Great Black Palm Cockatoo." *Emu* 33: 114–21.

Diamond, Jared M. 1972. *Avifauna of the Eastern Highlands of New Guinea.* Cambridge, UK: Nuttall Ornithological Club.

Eastman, William R., and Alexander C. Hunt. [1966]. *The Parrots of Australia.* Sydney, Australia: Angus and Robertson.

Forshaw, Joseph M. 1964. "Some Field Observations on the Great Palm Cockatoo." *Emu* 64: 327–31.

_____. 1977. *Parrots of the World.* Neptune, NJ: TFH.

Greene, W.T. 1979. *Parrots in Captivity.* Originally published in three volumes between 1884 and 1887. Neptune, NJ: TFH.

Heinsohn, R., Tanyza Zeriga, Stephen Murphy, Paul Igag, Sarah Legge, and Andrew L. Mack. 2009. "Do Palm Cockatoos (*Probosciger aterrimus*) Have Long Enough Lifespans to Support Their Low Reproductive Success?" *Emu* 109: 183–91.

Holyoak, D.T. 1972. "Adaptive Significance of Bill Shape in the Palm Cockatoo." *Aviculture Magazine* 78: 99–100.

Juniper, T., and M. Parr. 1998. *Parrots: A Guide to the Parrots of the World.* East Sussex, UK: Pica.

Lendon, A. 1950. "Australian Birds in Captivity." *Aviculture Magazine* 56: 127–35.

Lowe, W.P. 1916. "Some Birds of Palawan." *Ibis* 58.4: 607–23.

MacGillivray, George. 1916. In *The Birds of Australia,* vol. 4, ed. G.M. Mathews. London: Witherby.

MacGillivray, W. 1914. "Notes on Some North Queensland Birds." *Emu* 13: 132–86.

Murphy, Stephen, Sarah Legge, and Robert Heinsolm. 2006. "The Breeding of the Palm Cockatoos (*Probisciger aterrimus*): A Case of Slow Life History." *Journal of Zoology* 261: 327–39.

Parrot Tag. 2012. "Palm Cockatoo." http://www.parrottag.org/sources/Flash/pcockatoo.htm.

Prestwick, Arthur. 1954. "Records of Parrots Bred in Captivity. (Additions)." London: Published by the author.

Rand, A.L. 1942a. "Results of the Archbold Expeditions #42. Birds of the 1936–37 New Guinea Expedition." *Bulletin of the American Museum of Natural History* 79: 289–366.

Rand, A.L., and E.T. Gilliard. 1968. *Handbook of New Guinea Birds.* Garden City, New Jersey: Natural History Press.

Ripley, S.D. 1964. "A Systematic and Ecological Study of Birds of New Guinea." *Bulletin of the Peabody Museum of Natural History* 19: 1–85.

Rothschild, W., and S. Hartert. 1901. "Notes on Papuan Birds." *Novitates Zoologicae* 8: 55–88.

Slater, P. 1970. *A Field Guide to Australian Birds.* Melbourne, Australia: Rigby.

Tavistock, Marquess of. 1928. "The Display of the Palm Cockatoo." *Aviculture Magazine,* ser. 4, 6: 291.

That Bird Blog. 2008. "Hand Rearing Palm Cockatoos, Probosciger aterrimus—Part 1." http://blogs.thatpetplace.com/thatbirdblog/2008/04/17/hand-rearing-palm-cockatoos-probosciger-aterrimus-part-1/.

Wood, G.A. 1984. "Tool Use by the Palm Cockatoo

Probosciger aterrimus During Display." *Corella* 8.4 (Dec.): 94–95.

World Association of Zoos and Aquariums. 2012. "Palm Cockatoo." http://www.waza.org/enzoo/visit-the-zoo/parrots/proboscigeraterrimus.

World Parrot Trust. 2012. "Palm Cockatoo (*Probosciger aterrimus*)." http://www.parrots.org/index.php/encyclopedia/profile/palm_cockatoo/.

Chapter 16

Attiwell, A.R. 1960. "Red-tailed Cockatoos in South-east South Australia." *South Australia Ornithologist* 23: 37–38.

Baker, Joe. 2012. "Rare, Unusual, Difficult to Find: Black, Palm Red-tail and Gang-gang Cockatoos, Blue Napes, Hawk Heads." Birds of Paradise Aviaries. http://www.bopahi.com/rare.htm#OBC.

Bell, Alan. 1956. *Some Common Australian Birds*. London: Oxford University Press.

Bird Care. 2008. "Red-tailed Black Cockatoo." http://www.birdcare.com.au/red_tailed_black_cockatoo.htm.

Cochrane, P. 1902. "Notes on Migration and Cockatoos, Cooktown District, North Queensland." *Emu* 8: 47–49.

Courtney, J. 1996. "The Juvenile Food Begging Calls, Food Swallowing Vocalization and Begging Postures in Australian Cockatoos." *Australian Bird Watcher* 16: 236–49.

Crawford, D.H. 1972. "Birds of the Darwin Area with Some Records from Other Parts of the Northern Territory." *Emu* 72: 131–48.

Department of Environment and Conservation. State of Western Australia. 2009. "Red-tailed Black Cockatoo." *Fauna Notes*. June.

Department of the Environment. 2013. "*Calyptorhynchus banksii graptogyne*—Red-tailed Black Cockatoo (south-eastern)." Species Profile and Threats Database, Department of the Environment, Canberra, Australia. http://www.environment.gov.au/cgi-bin/sprat/public/publicspecies.pl?taxon_id=25982.

Ford, J.R. 1965. "New Information on the Distribution of birds of South-western Australia." *The Western Australian Naturalist* 10.1: 7–12.

Forshaw, Joseph M., and William T. Cooper. 2002. *Australian Parrots*. 3rd ed. Robina, Queensland, Australia: Alexander Editions.

Hall, B.P., ed. 1974. *Birds of the Harold Hall Expeditions, 1962–1970*. London: British Museum of Natural History.

Hall, Robert. 1902. "Notes on a Collection of Bird Skins from the Fitzroyi River, Northwestern Australia." *Emu* 2: 49–68.

Hallstrom, Sir Edward. 1959. "Some Breeding Re-

sults in the Hallstrom Collection." *Aviculture Magazine* 65: 80–81.

Harrison, C.J.O., and D.T. Holyoak. 1970. "Apparently Undescribed Parrot Eggs in the Collection of the British Museum (Natural History)." *British Ornithologists Club* 90: 42–46.

Higgins, P.J. (ed.) 1999. *Handbook of Australian, New Zealand, and Antarctic Birds*. Vol. 4, *Parrots to Dollarbird*. Melbourne: Oxford University Press.

International Ornithologists' Union. 1950. *Proceedings of the 10th Annual International Ornithological Congress*. Uppsala, Sweden.

Johnstone, R.E., and G.M. Storr. 1998. *Handbook of Western Australian Birds*. Vol. 1, *Non-passerines (Emu to Dollarbird)*. Perth, Western Australia: West Australian Museum.

Lendon, A. 1950. "Australian Parrots in Captivity." *Aviculture Magazine* 56: 127–35.

Lim, T.K., L. Bowman, and S. Tidemann. 1993. "A Report on the Survey of Winged Vertebrate Pest Damage on Crops in the Northern Territory." *Technical Bulletin* (Northern Territory Dept. of Primary Industry and Fisheries), p. 209.

Lint, Kenton C. 1955. "Breeding of the Red-tailed Cockatoo." *Aviculture Magazine* 61: 86–87.

Parrot Society of Australia. 1997. "Permission to Shoot: Red-tailed Black Cockatoos." Reprinted courtesy of *Cooktown Local News*. June. http://www.parrotsociety.org.au/articles/art_018.htm.

Rural Industries Research and Development Corporation. 1997. *Sustainable Economic of Native Australian Birds and Reptiles—Can Controlled Trade Improve Conservation of Species?* Barton, Australia: The Corporation. On-line summary, http://www.rirdc.gov.au/pubshortreps/sustain.html.

Saunders, D.A. 1974. "Red Tailed Black Cockatoo Breeding Twice a Year in the Southwest of Western Australia." *Emu* 77: 107–10.

Sedgewick, Eric H. 1949. "Bird Movements in the Wheat Belt of Western Australia." *The Western Australian Naturalist* 2.2: 25–33.

Storr, G.M. 1967. *List of Northern Territory Birds*. Special Publications of the Western Australian Museum, No. 4. Perth, Australia: Government Printer.

_____. *Birds of the Northern Territory*. Special Publications of the Western Australian Museum, 7. Perth, Australia: Western Australia Museum.

Tavistock, Marquess of. 1932a. "Correspondence." *Aviculture Magazine* 10: 111.

_____. 1932b. "The Things That Didn't Come Off and New Arrivals." *Aviculture Magazine* 10: 248–56.

_____. 1936. "Breeding Notes for 1936." *Aviculture Magazine*, 5th ser., 6: 258–62.

World Parrot Trust. 2012. "Red-tailed Black Cockatoo." http://www.parrots.org/index.php/encyclopedia/profile/red_tailed_black_cockatoo.

Chapter 17

Avian Companions. 2012. "Glossy Black." http://www.aviancompanions.com/GlossyBlackCockatoo.htm.

Bird Care. 2005. "Glossy Black Cockatoo." http://www.birdcare.com.au/glossy_black_cockatoo.htm.

Cayley, Neville, L. 1973. *Australian Parrots in Field and Captivity*. Revised by Alan Lendon. Brisbane: Angust and Robertson.

Chapman, T.F. 2007. "Foods of the Glossy Black Cockatoo (*Calyptorhynchus lathami*)." *Australian Field Ornithology* 24: 20–36.

Chrome, Francis, and James Shields. 1992. *Parrots and Pigeons of Australia*. Pymble, New South Wales: Angus and Robertson.

Department of the Environment. Australian Government. 2012. "*Calyptorhynchus Lathami Halmaturinus*—Glossy Black Cockatoo (Kangeroo Island), Glossy Black-Cockatoo (South Australian)." http://www.environment.gov.au/cgi-bin/sprat/public/publicspecies.pl?taxon_id=64436.

Forshaw, Joseph M., and William T. Cooper. 2002. *Australian Parrots*. 3rd ed. Robina, Australia: Alexander Editions.

Garnett, S.T., L.P. Pedler, and G.M. Crowley. 1999. "The Breeding Biology of the Glossy Black Cockatoo *Calyptorhynchus lathami* on Kangeroo Island, South Australia." *Emu* 99: 262–79.

Hallstrom, Sir Edward. 1954. "Breeding of Glossy Black Cockatoos." *Aviculture Magazine* 60: 163–64.

_____. 1959. "Some Breeding Results in the Hallstrom Collection." *Aviculture Magazine* 65: 80–81.

Higgins, P.J. (ed.) 1999. *Handbook of Australian, New Zealand, and Antarctic Birds*. Vol. 4, *Parrots to Dollarbird*. Melbourne: Oxford University Press.

Joseph, L. 1982. "The Glossy Black Cockatoo on Kangeroo Island." *Emu* 82: 46–49.

Llewelyn, L.C. 1974. "Records of Red-tailed Black Cockatoos in Southeastern Australia." *Emu* 74: 249–53.

Mathews, G.M. 1916. *The Birds of Australia*. London: Witherby.

Mooney, P.A., and L.P. Pedler. 2005. "Recovery Plans for the South Australian Subspecies of the Glossy Black Cockatoo (*Calyptorhynchus lathami halmataurinus*): 2005–2010." Adelaide, South Australian Department for Environment and Heritage. http://www.environment.gov.au/biodiversity/threatened/publications/recover/c-lathami-halmaturinus/index.html.

New SouthWales Scientific Committee. 2008. "Glossy Black Cockatoo *Calyptorhynchus lathami* (Review of Current Information in NSW)." http://www.environment.nsw.gov.au/resources/nature/schedules/GlossyBlackCockatoo.pdf.

Pedler, L. 2003. "Breeding Season Report, September 2003." Department for Environment and Heritage, Kingscote, South Australia.

Pedler, L., and P.A. Mooney. 2005. "Annual Census Report October 2005." Department for Environment and Heritage, Kingscote, South Australia.

Pepper, J.W. 1996. "The Behavioural Ecology of the Glossy Black Cockatoo (*Captorhynchus lathami*)." Ph.D. Dissertation, University of Michigan, Ann Arbour.

Schodde, R., I.J. Mason, and J.T. Wood. 1993. "Geographical Differentiation in the Glossy Black Cockatoo *Calyptorhynchus lathami* (Temminck) and Its History." *Emu* 93: 156–66.

Taronga Zoo (Australia). 2011. "Australian Wildlife Keepers Welcome Glossy Black Cockatoo Chick." http://taronga.org.au/blog/2011-07-21/australian-wildlife-keepers-welcome-glossy-black-cockatoo-chick.

Wheeler, J.R. 1959. "The R.A.O.U. Campout at Kangeroo Island, South Australia." *Emu* 60: 265–80.

Chapter 18

Bird Care. 2008. "White-Tailed Black Cockatoo." http://www.birdcare.com.au/white_tailed_black_cockatoo/htm.

Bird Life International. 2012. "Bird Life Fact Sheet: Baudin's Black Cockatoo (*Calyptorhynchus baudinii*)." http://www.birdlife.org/datazone/speciesfactsheet.php?id=1390.

Cayley, Neville, L. 1973. As extensively revised by Alan Lendon. *Australian Parrots in Field and Aviary*. Brisbane, Australia: Angust and Robertson.

Chapman, T., and N. Masson. 2005. "Reducing Fruit Damage by Baudin's Cockatoo." Department of Conservation and Land Management Western Australia Fauna Note 1.

Chapman, T.F. 2007. "An Endangered Species That Is Also a Pest: A Case Study of Baudin's Cockatoo *Calyptorhynchus baudinii* and the Pome Fruit Industry in South-west Western Australia." *Journal of the Royal Society of Western Australia* 90: 33–40.

Davis, S.J.J.F. 1970. "The Movements of the White-tailed Cockatoo (*Calyptorhynchus baudinii*) in

South Western Australia." *Western Australia Naturalist* 10: 33–42.

Department of the Environment. Australian Government. 2013. "*Calyptorhynchus baudinii*—Baudin's Black-Cockatoo, Long-billed Black-Cockatoo." http://www.environment.gov.au/cgi-bin/sprat/public/publicspecies.pl?taxon_id=769.

Forshaw, Joseph M. 2006. *Parrots of the World: An Identification Guide*. Illustrated by Frank Knight. New Jersey: Princeton University Press.

Garnett, S.T., ed. 1993. *Threatened and Extinct Birds of Australia. Royal Australian Ornithologists Union Report 82*. 2nd (corrected) ed. Melbourne: Royal Australian Ornithologists Union and Canberra; Australian National Parks and Wildlife Service.

Garrett, S.T., and G.M. Crowey. 2000. *The Action Plan for Australian Birds 2000*. Canberra, Australia: Environment Australia.

Higgins, P.J. (ed.) 1999. *Handbook of Australian, New Zealand, and Antarctic Birds*. Vol. 4, *Parrots to Dollarbird*. Melbourne: Oxford University Press.

Johnstone, R.E., and G.M. Storr. 1998. *Handbook of Western Australian Birds*. Vol. 1, *Non-passerines (Emu to Dollarbird)*. Perth, Australia: West Australian Museum.

Johnstone, Ron. 2010. "Information Sheet: Baudin's Cockatoo *Calyptorhynchus baudinii*." Department of Terrestrial Vertebrates, Western Australian Museum. November.

Mathews, G.W. 1916. *The Birds of Australia*. Vol. 4. London: Witherby.

Mawson, P., and R. Johnstone.2010. "Conservation Status of Parrots and Cockatoos in Australia." *Eclectus* 2: 4–9.

Milligan, A. 1903. "Notes on a Trip to the Sterling Range." *Emu* 3: 9–19.

Oiseaux. 2012. "Long Billed Black Cockatoo." http://www.Oiseaux-birds.com/card-long-billed-black-cockatoo.html. July 28.

Perry, D.H. 1948. "Black Cockatoos and Pine Plantations." *Western Australian Naturalist*: 133–35.

Planet of Birds. 2012. "Long Billed Black Cockatoo (*Calyptorhynchus baudinii*)." http://www.Planetofbirds.com/psittaciformes-cacatuidae-long-billed-black-cockatoo-caly. July 29.

Saunders, D.A. 1974. "Subspeciation in the White-tailed Black Cockatoo, *Calyptorhynchus baudinii* in Western Australia." *Australian Wildlife Research* 1.1: 55–69.

Serventy, D.L., and H.M. Whittell. 1962. *Birds of Western Australia*. Perth, Australia: Patterson Brokenshaw.

World Parrot Trust. 2012. "Baudin's Black Cockatoo." http://www.parrots.or/index.php/encyclopedia/wildstatus/baudins_black_cockatoo.

Chapter 19

Berry, P.F. 2008. "Counts of Carnaby's Cockatoo (*Calyptorhynchus latirostris*) and records of Flock Composition at an Overnight Roosting Site in Metropolitan Perth." *Western Australian Naturalist* 26: 1–11.

Bird Care. 2002. "White-tailed Black Cockatoo." http://www.birdcare.com.au/white_tailed_black_cockatoo.htm.

Bird Life International. 2012. "Bird Life Fact Sheet: Carnaby's Black Cockatoo (*Calyptorynchus Latirostris*)." http://www.birdlife.org/datazone/speciesfactsheet.php?id=1391.

Cale, B. 2002. "Carnaby's Black Cockatoo. (*Calyptorhynchus latirostris*). Recovery Plan 2002–2012." http://www.dec.wa.gov.au/pdf/plants_animals/threatened_species/frps/carnabys_wmp36.pdf.

Department of Conservation and Land Management. Australian Government. 1999. "Captive Breeding Program for Carnaby's Cockatoo (*Calyptorhynchus Latirostris*). 1996–1998." http://www.environment.gov.au/cgi-bin/sprat/public/publicspecies.pl?taxon_id=59523.

———. 2013. "Final DEC for 2012–2013." http://www.dec/wa/gov.au/.

Department of the Environment. Government of Australia. 2012. "*Calyptorhynchus Latirostris*—Carnaby's Black-Cockatoo, Short-billed Black-Cockatoo." http://www.environment.gov.au/cgi-bin/sprat/public/publicspecies.pl?taxon_id=59523.

Department of Environment and Conservation. Government of Western Australia. 2007. "Fauna Note No. 5. Carnaby's Cockatoo." http://archive.agric.wa.gov.au/objtwr/imported_assets/content/pw/vp/bird/5_carnabys_cockatoo.pdf.

Forshaw, Joseph M. 2006. *Parrots of the World: An Identification Guide*. Illustrated by Frank Knight. Princeton, NJ: Princeton University Press.

Garnett, S.T., ed. 1993. *Threatened and Exotic Birds of Australia. Royal Australian Ornithologists Union Report 82*. 2nd (corrected) ed. Melbourne: Royal Australian Ornithology Union; and Canberra: Australian National Parks and Wildlife Service.

Garnett, S.T., and G.M. Crowley. 2000. *The Action Plan for Australian Birds 2000*. Perth Australia: Environment Australia and Birds Australia.

Government of Western Australia. 2008. "Gnangara Sustainability Strategy Draft Situation Statement." Perth, Australia: Department of Water.

Higgins, P.J. (ed.) 1999. *Handbook of Australian, New Zealand, and Antarctic Birds*. Vol. 4, *Parrots to Dollarbird*. Melbourne: Oxford University Press.

Johnstone, R.E., and G.M. Storr. 1998. *Handbook of Western Australian Birds*. Vol. 1, *Non-passerines (Emu to Dollarbird)*. Perth, Australia: West Australian Museum.

Johnstone, R.E., and T. Kirby. 2008. "Distribution, Status, Social Organization, Movements, Organization of Baudin's Cockatoo (*Calyptorhynchus baudinii*) in Southeast Western Australia." *Records of the Western Australian Museum* 25: 107–18.

Juniper, T., and M. Parr. 1998. *Parrots: A Guide to Parrots of the World*. Sussex, UK: Pica.

Mawson, P., and R. Johnstone. 1997. "Conservation Status of Parrots and Cockatoos in Western Australia." *Eclectus* 2: 4–9.

Oiseaux. 2012. "Short Billed Black Cockatoo." http://www.oiseaux-birds.com/card-short-bille d-black-cockatoo.html.

Perry, D.H. 1948. "Black Cockatoos and Pine Plantations." *Western Australian Naturalist* 1: 133–35.

Platt, John R. 2012. "The Carnaby's Cockatoo." *Scientific American*: 2.

Saunders, D.A. 1974. "Subspeciation in the White-tailed Black Cockatoo, *Calyptorhynchus baudinii*, in Western Australia." *Australia Wildlife Research* 1.1: 55–69.

———. 1980. "Food and Movements of the Short-Billed Form of the White-tailed Black-Cockatoo." *Australian Wildlife Research* 7: 257–69.

———. 1982. "The Breeding Behavior of the Short Billed Form of the White-tailed Black Cockatoo *Calyptorhynchus funereus*." *Ibis* 124: 422–55.

———. 1990. "Problems of Survival in an Extensively Cultivated Landscape: The Case of Carnaby's Cockatoo *Calyptorhychus latirostris*." *Biological Conservation* 54: 277–90.

Saunders, D.A., and J.A. Ingram. 1998. "Problems of Survival in an Extensively Cultivated Landscape: The Case of the Carnaby's Cockatoo *Caloyptorhynchus funereous latirostris* in Remnants of Native Vegetation." In *Nature Conservation: The Role of Remnants of Native Vegetation*, ed. D.A. Saunders, G.W. Arnold, A.A. Burbidge, and A.J.M Hopkins, pp. 249–58. Sydney, Australia: Surrey Beatty and Sons, Chipping Norton.

Shah, B. 2006. "Conservation of Carnaby's Black Cockatoo on the Swan Coastal Plain, Western Australia Project Report." Perth, Western Australia: Western Australia Birds.

Valentine, Leonie E., and William Stock. 2008. "Food Resources of Carnaby's Black-Cockatoo (*Calyptorhynchus Latirostris*) in the Gnangara Sustainability Strategy Study Area." Edith Cowan University and Department of Environment and Conservation. Government of Western Australia, Perth, Australia.

World Parrot Trust. 2012. "Carnaby's Black Cockatoo (*Calyptorhynchus latirostris*)." http://www. parrots.org/index.php/encyclopedia/captivesta tus/carnabys-black-cockatoo.

Chapter 20

Barker, R.D., and W.J.M. Vestjens. 1984. *The Food of Australian Birds*. Vol. 1, *Non-passerines*. Melbourne, Australia: Melbourne University Press.

Bird Care. 2012. "Yellow-tailed Black Cockatoo." http://www.birdcare.com.au/yellow_tailed_bla ck_cockatoo.htm.

Cameron, M. 2008. *Cockatoos*. Collingwood, Victoria: CSIRO.

Cayley, Neville, L. 1973. As extensively revised by Alan Lendon. *Australian Parrots in Field and Aviary*. Brisbane, Australia: Angust and Robertson.

Christidis, L., and W.E. Boles. 2008. *Systematics and Taxonomy of Australian Birds*. Collingwood, Austraalia: CSIRO.

Dawson, Jill. 1994. The Yellow-Tailed Black Cockatoo. *Calyptorhynchus funereus funereus* and *Calyptorhynchus funereus xanthanotus*: Report on the Yellow Tailed Black Cockatoo Survey *1983-1988 I*. Nupawading, Victoria: Bird Observers Club of Australia.

Forshaw, Joseph M. 2006. *Parrots of the World: An Identification Guide*. Illustrated by Frank Knight. New Jersey: Princeton University Press.

Hall, Robert. 1910. "The Birds of Eyre Peninsula, South Australia." *Emu* 9: 131.

Higgins, P.J. (ed.) 1999. *Handbook of Australian, New Zealand, and Antarctic Birds*. Vol. 4, *Parrots to Dollarbird*. Melbourne: Oxford University Press.

Lendon, A. 1950. "Australian Parrots in Captivity." *Aviculture Magazine* 56: 127–35.

Littler, F.M. 1910. *A Handbook of the Birds of Tasmania*. Launceston, Tasmania: F.M. Littler.

Marshall, Rob. 2012. "Yellow-tailed Black Cockatoo (*Calyptorhunchus funereous*)." *The Avicultural Review*. The Avicultural Society of New South Wales. http://www.aviculturalsocietynsw. org/_articles/yellow-tail-black1999.htm.

Mathews, G.M. 1916. *The Birds of Australia*. Vol. 4. London: Witherby.

Mcinnes, R.S, P.B. Carne, and P.B. Carne. 1978. "Predation of Cossid Moth Larvae by Yellow-tailed Black Cockatoos Causing Losses in Plantations of Eucalyptus grandis in North Coastal North South Wales." *Australian Wildlife Research* 5.1: 101–21. DOI:10.1071/WR9780101.

Melbourne Parks and Gardens. 2012. "Melbourne

Information." Australian Tourist Information Centres. http://www.melbourneinfocentre.com. au/information/melbourn/things-to-do-andsee /melbourneparks-and gardens.

Nelson, J.L., and B.J. Morris. 1994. "Nesting Requirements of the Yellow-tailed Black Cockatoo, *Calyptorhynchus funereus*, in Eucalyptus Regnans Forest and Implications for Forest Management." *Wildlife Research* 21.3: 267–78.

Saunders, D.A. (1979) "Distribution and Taxonomy of the White-Tailed and Yellow-tailed Black Cockatoo *Calyptorhynchus spp.*" *Emu* 79.4: 215–27.

Slater, P.A. 1970. *Field Guide to Australian Birds*. Melbourne, Australia: Rigby.

Tavistock, Marques of, and J. Delacour. 1926. "Cockatoos." *Aviculture Magazine*, 4th ser. 100.2: 148–55.

Van Weenem, Jason, 2009. "Threatened Species— Yellow Tailed Black Cockatoos Critically Endangered Eyre Peninsula Yellow-Tailed Black Cockatoos." Department for Environment and Heritage. Biodiversity. Department for Environment and Heritage South Australian Government. http:// www.Environment.sa.gov.au/biodiversity.theate ned-species/yellowtailed.html. August.

Chapter 21

Adams, M., P.R. Baverstock, D.A. Saunders, R. Schodde, G.T. Smith, and P.R. Baverstock. (1984) "Biochemical Systematics of the Australian Cockatoos (*Psittaciforme: Cacatudinae*)." *Australian Journal of Zoology* 32.3: 363–77.

Austin, Thoms B. 1907. "Notes on Birds from Talbragar River, N.S.W." *Emu* 7: 37–38.

Aviculture. 1900, p. 3; 1930, p. 224; 1931, p. 30; 1937, p. 67; 1940, p. 93; 1943, pp. 18 and 42; 1944, pp. 139–187; 1945, pp. 285 and 342; 1954, p. 35.

Batey, Isaac. 1907. "On Fifteen Thousand Acres: Its Bird Life Sixty Years Ago. Part 1." *Emu* 7: 1–17.

Bauer, John. 1937. *Aviculture* 37: 67.

Bennet, K.B. 1912. *Australian Special Catalogue* 3:1. Sydney: Australian Museum.

Brown, D.M., and C.A. Toft. 1999. "Molecular Systematics and Biogeography of the Cockatoos (*Psittaformes Cacatuidae*)." *Auk* 116.1: 141–57.

Cayley, Neville, L. 1973. As extensively revised by Alan Lendon. *Australian Parrots in Field and Aviary*. Brisbane, Australia: Angust and Robertson.

Courtney, John. 1974. "Comments on the Taxonomical Position of the Cockatiel." *Emu* 74.2: 97–102.

Crawford, D.H. 1972. "Birds of the Darwin Area with Some Records from Other Parts of the Northern Territory." *Emu* 72: 131–48.

Forshaw, Joseph M. 1977. *Parrots of the World*. Neptune, NJ: TFH.

Frith, H.J., ed. 1969. "Birds in the Australian High Country." Melbourne, Australia: A.H. and A.W. Reid.

Grant, Robert. 1912. *Australian Museum Special Catalogue* 3:1. Sydney: Australian Museum.

Green, W.T. 1979. *Parrots in Captivity*. Originally published in three volumes from 1884 to 1889. Neptune, NJ: TFH.

Holyoak, D.T. 1972. "Short Communication: The relation of *Nymphicus* to the *Cacatuidinea*." *Emu* 72.2: 77–78.

Kavanau, Lee. 1987. *Behavior and Evolution: Lovebirds, Cockatiels, and Budgerigars*. Los Angeles: Science Software Systems.

Lendon, A. 1951. *Australian Birds Kept in Captivity*. London: Avicultural Society.

MacGillivray, W. 1910. "The Region of the Barrier Range, Part 1." *Emu* 10: 16–34.

_____. 1913. "Notes on Some North Queensland Birds." *Emu* 13: 132–86.

Macklin, C.H. 1931. *Aviculture* 9.6: 156–60.

Mathews, G.M. 1916. *The Birds of Australia*. Vol. 4. London: Witherby.

McCaffery, E. 2009. "Cockatiel Cottage." http:// www.cockatielcottage.net. Accessed January 10, 2013.

Pizzey, Graham, and Frank Knight. 1997. *Field Guide to the Birds of Australia*. Sydney, Australia:

Salvadori, T. 1891. *Catalogue of the Psittaci, or Parrots, the Collection of the British Museum: Catalogue of Birds*. Vol. 20. London: [British Museum].

Smith, D. 1976. "Species of Birds in Captivity." *Aviculture Magazine* 82.1 (Jan./March): 25.

Smith, G. 1978. *Encyclopedia of Cockatiels*. New Jersey: TFH.

Spoon, T., and J. Milliam. 2006. "The Importance of Mate Behavioral Compatibility in Parenting and Reproductive Success by Cockatiels, *Nymphicus hollandicus*." *Animal Physiology* 71: 315–26.

Index